Lecture Notes in Computer Science 1860

Edited by G. Goos, J. Hartmanis, and J. van Leeuwen

Springer

Berlin
Heidelberg
New York
Barcelona
Hong Kong
London
Milan
Paris
Singapore
Tokyo

Matthias Klusch   Larry Kerschberg (Eds.)

Cooperative Information Agents IV

The Future of Information Agents in Cyberspace

4th International Workshop, CIA 2000
Boston, MA, USA, July 7-9, 2000
Proceedings

Springer

Series Editors

Jaime G. Carbonell, Carnegie Mellon University, Pittsburgh, PA, USA
Jörg Siekmann, University of Saarland, Saarbrücken, Germany

Volume Editors

Matthias Klusch
DFKI GmbH
Stuhlsatzenhausweg 3, 66123 Saarbrücken, Germany
E-mail: klusch@dfki.de

Larry Kerschberg
George Mason University
School of Information Technology and Engineering
4400 University Drive, Fairfax, VA 22030-4444
E-mail: kersch@gmu.edu

Cataloging-in-Publication Data applied for

Die Deutsche Bibliothek - CIP-Einheitsaufnahme

Cooperative information agents IV : the future of information agents
in cyberspace ; 4th international workshop ; proceedings / CIA 2000,
Boston, MA, USA, July 7 - 9, 2000. Matthias Klusch ; Larry Kerschberg
(ed.). - Berlin ; Heidelberg ; New York ; Barcelona ; Hong Kong ;
London ; Milan ; Paris ; Singapore ; Tokyo : Springer, 2000
  (Lecture notes in computer science ; Vol. 1860 : Lecture notes in
  artificial intelligence)
  ISBN 3-540-67703-8

CR Subject Classification (1998): I.2, H.2, H.3.3, H.4.4, C.2.4

ISSN 0302-9743
ISBN 3-540-67703-8 Springer-Verlag Berlin Heidelberg New York

Springer-Verlag is a company in the BertelsmannSpringer publishing group.
© Springer-Verlag Berlin Heidelberg 2000
Printed in Germany

Typesetting: Camera-ready by author, data conversion by DA-TeX Gerd Blumenstein
Printed on acid-free paper   SPIN: 10722214   06/3142   5 4 3 2 1 0

Preface

These are the proceedings of the Fourth International Workshop on Cooperative Information Agents, held in Boston Massachusetts, USA, July 7-9, 2000.

Cooperative information agent research and development focused originally on accessing multiple, heterogeneous, and distributed information sources. Gaining access to these systems, through Internet search engines, application program interfaces, wrappers, and web-based screens has been an important focus of cooperative intelligent agents. Research has also focused on the integration of this information into a coherent model that combined data and knowledge from the multiple sources. Finally, this information is disseminated to a wide audience, giving rise to issues such as data quality, information pedigree, source reliability, information security, personal privacy, and information value. Research in cooperative information agents has expanded to include agent negotiation, agent communities, agent mobility, as well as agent collaboration for information discovery in constrained environments.

The interdisciplinary CIA workshop series encompasses a wide variety of topics dealing with cooperative information agents. All workshop proceedings have been published by Springer as Lecture Notes in Artificial Intelligence, Volumes 1202 (1997), 1435 (1998), and 1652 (1999), respectively. This year, the theme of the CIA workshop was "'The Future of Information Agents in Cyberspace", a very fitting topic as the use of agents for information gathering, negotiation, correlation, fusion, and dissemination becomes ever more prevalent. We noted a marked trend in CIA 2000 towards addressing issues related to *communities of agents* that: (1) *negotiate* for information resources, (2) *build robust ontologies* to enhance search capabilities, (3) *communicate* for planning and problem solving, (4) *learn and evolve* based on their experiences, and (5) assume increasing degrees of autonomy in the control of complex systems.

CIA 2000 features 8 invited and 15 contributed papers selected from 44 submissions.

Acknowledgements. First of all, we gratefully acknowledge the financial support from our Co-sponsors:

- NASA GODDARD SPACE FLIGHT CENTER, USA
- SWISS LIFE AG, Switzerland, and the
- IFMAS International Foundation for Multi-Agent Systems

Second, we are especially grateful to the authors and invited speakers for contributing to this workshop. Finally, we acknowledge and thank the members of the program committee and the external reviewers for their careful and thoughtful reviews of the submitted papers.

Boston, July 2000   Matthias Klusch and Larry Kerschberg

Program Committee

External Reviewers

Rina Azoulay-Schwartz
Domenico Beneventano
Esther David
Stefan Johansson
Vincini Maurizio
Tracy Mullen
Thomas Tesch
Osher Yadgar

Table of Contents

Personal Information Agents on the Internet

Agent-Based Information Gathering and Mediation

Rational Information Agents for E-Commerce

Societies of Information Agents

Issues of Communication and Collaboration

Information Agents: Future Inspirations and Design

Adding Life-Like Synthetic Characters to the Web

Elisabeth André and Thomas Rist

DFKI GmbH, Stuhlsatzenhausweg 3, D-66123 Saarbrücken, Germany
{andre,rist}@dfki.de

Abstract. With the advent of web browsers that are able to execute programs embedded in web pages, the use of animated characters for the presentation of information over the web has become possible. A strong argument in favour of using such characters in a web interface is the fact that they make human-computer interaction more enjoyable and allow for the emulation of communication styles common in human-human dialogue. In this paper we discuss three ongoing DFKI projects on life-like synthetic characters in the internet. While all agents rely on the same approach for automated script generation, we use different player technologies which will be discussed in the light of different applications.

Introduction

Rapid growth of competition in the electronic market place will boost the demand for new innovative communication styles to attract web users. With the advent of web browsers that are able to execute programs embedded in web pages, the use of animated characters for the presentation of information over the web has become possible. Instead of surfing the web on their own, users can join a tour, ask the lifelike character for assistance or even delegate a complex search task to it.

Despite of the raging debate on the sociological effects that life-like characters may have, yet can't have, and will perhaps never have, it is safe to say that they enrich the repertoire of available options which can be used to communicate with the user. First of all, they add expressive power to a system's presentation skills. For example, cross-references between different media (possibly occurring in different windows) can be effectively established through a two-handed pointing gesture. If one strives for emulating the multimodal interaction that occurs between humans, the presentation agents' repertoire of behaviors may even comprise facial expressions and body gestures to express emotions. Furthermore, a presentation agent can also serve as a guide through a presentation to release the user from orientation and navigation problems known from multi-window/multi-screen settings. Last but not least, there is the entertaining and affective function of such an animated character. Lester and colleagues [11] showed that an animated pedagogical may have a strong positive effect on the students' perception of the learning experience. Mulken and colleagues [16] conducted a study to compare presentations with and without a Persona. The subjects perceived the Persona as being helpful and entertaining.

M. Klusch and L. Kerschberg (Eds.): CIA 2000, LNAI 1860, pp. 1-13, 2000.

Furthermore, they experienced learning tasks presented by the Persona as being less difficult than those without a life-like character.

In this contribution, we provide an overview of three DFKI projects which are committed to the development of web-based presentation agents for a broad range of applications including personalized information delivery from the WWW. While all agents rely on the same approach for script generation, we use different technologies for their animation depending on the envisioned application.

Related Work

During the last decade, life-like characters have been discovered as a fascinating and challenging area for research with a large potential for commercial applications. In the following, we restrict ourselves to projects that focus on characters for the web.

Adele (Agent for Distributed Learning Environments) is an animated pedagogical agent that has been developed for Web-based medical instruction [13]. The students are presented with a virtual patient in a simulated clinical environment and may perform a variety of actions on the patient. The role of the pedagogical agent is to monitor the students' actions and provide feedback. The animated agent has been realized as a Java applet that runs within a Web browser environment. An empirical evaluation of the Agent revealed that the system was easy to use and that the students found Adele helpful. Unfortunately, the believability of the agent suffers from the poor quality of speech synthesis.

The Agneta and Frida system incorporates narratives into a Web environment by placing two characters on the user's desktop [8]. These characters watch the user during the browsing process and make comments on the visited Web pages. Unlike the DFKI characters, the system relies on pre-authored scripts and no generative mechanism is employed. Consequently, the system operates on predefined Web pages only. The graphical realization of Agneta and Frida is based on the Microsoft^{TM} package. An empirical evaluation of Agneta and Frida showed that animated characters may encourage users to stay longer on a web page. However, users did not learn more about a web page and some of them –especially web-experienced users - even got disturbed by the characters. As a reason, the authors of the Agneta and Frida system indicate that such users have already developed their own strategies for navigating the web which might interfere with the narrative structure provided by the characters.

Virtual meeting spaces and graphical chat corners are a further application field for life-like characters. For example, Isbister and colleagues [10] developed an animated agent that appears in the role of a party host in a web-based chat corner and tries to find a common topic for guests whose conversation has lagged. An experimental evaluation of the agent's ability to assist in cross-cultural conversations has been performed and revealed that the presence of a lifelike synthetic agent may have a positive influence on the perception of each other and of each others cultural group. Smith and colleagues [14] investigated the influence of 3D features on social interaction in chat spaces. For instance, they showed that even experienced users actively make use of proximity and orientation features to enhance their interactions.

There is also an increasing number of commercial web sites that employ animated characters in the interface. Well-known examples include the characters developed by Extempo[1], Haptek[2], Virtual Personalities[3] or Artificial Life[4] [7]. However, due to the constraints imposed by the restricted bandwidth of the internet, these characters have to rely on strongly limited communication channels. For instance, most of them just offer textual output instead of synthesized speech.

Basic Technology

Though a number of similarities may exist, our presentation agents are not just animated icons in the interface. Rather, their behavior follows the equation:

Persona behavior := directives + self-behavior

By *directives* we understand a set of tasks which can be forwarded to a character for execution. To accomplish these tasks, the character relies on gestures that: express emotions (e.g., approval or disapproval), convey the communicative function of a presentation act (e.g., warn, recommend or dissuade), support referential acts (e.g., look at an object and point at it), regulate the interaction between the character and the user (e.g., establishing eye contact with the user during communication) and indicate that the character is speaking. Of course, these gestures may also superimpose each other. For example, to warn the user, a character may lift its index finger, look towards the user and utter the warning. Directives are defined externally, either by a human presentation author or by another system which employs the character as part of its user interface. In what follows, we use the term *presentation script* to refer to a temporally ordered set of directives.

While a script is an external behavior determinant that is specified outside the character, our characters also have an internal behavior determinant resulting in what we call a *self behavior*. A character's self behavior comprises not only gestures that are necessary to execute the script, but also navigation acts, idle time gestures, and immediate reactions to events occurring in the user interface. Note that the borderline between scripted behavior and self behavior is a matter of the degree of abstraction. The more detailed a script prescribes what a character should do, the less there is a need to equip a character with a rich repertoire of reasonable self behaviors.

Since the manual scripting of agent behaviors is tedious, error-prone and for time-critical applications often unfeasible, we aimed at the automation of the authoring approach. Based on our previous work on multimedia presentation design [1], we utilize a hierarchical planner for the automated decomposition of high-level presentation tasks into scripts which will be executed by the presentation agent [2]. To flexibly tailor presentations to the specific needs of an individual user, we allow for the specification of generation parameters (e.g., "verbal utterances should be in

---

[1] http://www.extempo.com

[2] http://www.haptek.com

[3] http://www.vperson.com

[4] http://www.artificial-life.com

English", or "the presentation must not exceed five minutes"). Consequently a number of presentation variants can be generated for one and the same piece of information, but different settings of presentation parameters. Furthermore, we allow the user to flexibly choose between different navigation paths through a presentation. That is, the course of a presentation changes at runtime depending on user interactions. Knowledge concerning the generation of scripts is represented by means of plan operators.

For the visualization of our Personas, we use three different player technologies depending on the envisioned application: DFKI's Java-based PET toolkit (Persona-Enabling Toolkit), the Microsoft Agent™ toolkit and SMIL (Synchronized Multimedia Integration Language). In the following, we briefly introduce three applications and describe how they are technically realized by using one of these approaches.

The AiA Personas: Java-Based Animated Presentation Agents for the World-Wide Web

In the AiA project (Adaptive Communication Assistant for Effective Infobahn Access), we developed a number of personalized information assistants that facilitate user access to the Web [2] by providing orientation assistance in a dynamically expanding navigation space. These assistants are characterized by their ability to retrieve relevant information, reorganize it, encode it in different media (such as text, graphics, and animation), and present it to the user as a multimedia presentation. The screen shots in Fig. 1 shows one of our applications, which is a personalized travel agent.

Suppose the user wants to travel to Hamburg and is starting a query for typical travelling information. To comply with the user's request, the AiA system retrieves information about Hamburg from various web servers, e.g. a weather, a restaurant and a hotel server, selects relevant units, restructures them and uses an animated character to present them to the user. The novelty of AiA is that the presentation scripts for the characters and the hyperlinks between the single presentation parts are not stored in advance but generated automatically from pre-authored documents fragments and items stored in a knowledge base. For a restricted domain, AiA is even able to combine information units retrieved from different sources and combine them into a single presentation item. For example, the address entry of a hotel is used as input for another web search in order to generate a map display on which the hotel can be located.

The AiA personas have been realized with DFKI's Java-based player technology. To view a Persona presentation, the user does not need to install any software on his or her local machine. Instead the presentation engine is downloaded as a Java-applet. To support the integration of animated agents into web interfaces, our group has developed a toolkit called PET (Persona-Enabling Toolkit). PET provides an XML-based language for the specification of Persona commands within conventional HTML-pages. These extended HTML-pages are then automatically transformed into a down-loadable Java-based runtime environment which drives the presentation on standard web browsers.

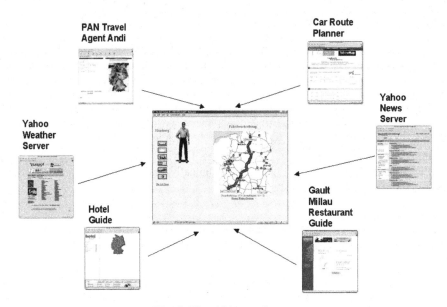

Fig. 1. The AiA travel agent.

PET may be used in two different ways. First of all, it can be used by a human author for the production of multimedia presentations which include a lifelike character. Second, we have the option to automate the complete authoring process by making use of our presentation planning component to generate web pages that include the necessary PET-commands. Knowledge concerning the script generation process is encoded by means of plan operators. An example of a simple plan operator is listed below. It may be used to instruct a character to describe a hotel by showing a photo and providing a textual explanation.

```
HEADER: (A0 (Describe ?hotel))
CONSTRAINTS:
(*and* (Hotel ?hotel)(Illustrates ?photo ?hotel)
       (Describes ?text ?hotel))
INFERIORS:
(A1(DisplayImage ?hotel))
(A2(Speak ?text))
```

Fig. 2. A simple plan operator for the AiA travel agent.

The Inhabited Market Place: An Animated Presentation Team Based on the Microsoft Agent™ Package

The objective of the Inhabited Market Place is to investigate sketches, given by a team of lifelike characters, as a new form of sales presentation [3]. The basic idea is to communicate information by means of simulated dialogues that are observed by an audience. The purpose of this project is not to implement a more or less complete model of personality for characters, such as a seller and a customer. Rather, the demonstration system has been designed as a testbed for experimenting with various personalities and roles. As suggested by the name, the inhabited market place is a virtual place in which seller agents provide product information to potential buyer agents. For the graphical realisation of the emerging sales dialogues, we use the Microsoft Agent package [12] that includes a programmable interface to four predefined characters: Genie, Robby, Peedy and Merlin. To enable experiments with different character settings, the user has the possibility of choosing three out of the four characters and assigning roles to them (see Fig. 3).

Select the agents and their personality:

| Genie | Merlin | Peedy | Robby |

SELLER	Genie ▾		BUYER1	Peedy ▾		BUYER2	Merlin ▾	
Agreeableness	**Extraversion**		**Agreeableness**	**Extraversion**		**Agreeableness**	**Extraversion**	
⊙ agreeable	○ extravert		○ agreeable	○ extravert		⊙ agreeable	⊙ extravert	
○ neutral	○ neutral		○ neutral	○ neutral		○ neutral	○ neutral	
○ disagreeable	⊙ introvert		⊙ disagreeable	⊙ introvert		○ disagreeable	○ introvert	

Fig. 3. Dialogue for character settings.

For instance, he or she may have Merlin appear in the role of a seller or buyer. Furthermore, he or she may assign to each character certain preferences and interests. The system has two operating modes. In the first mode, the system (or a human author) chooses the appropriate character settings for an audience. The second mode allows the audience to test various character settings itself.

Fig. 4 shows a dialogue between Merlin as a car seller and Genie and Robby as buyers. Genie has uttered some concerns about the high running costs which Merlin tries to play down. From the point of view of the system, the presentation goal is to provide the observer – who is assumed to be the real customer - with facts about a certain car. However, the presentation is not just a mere enumeration of the plain facts about the car. Rather, the facts are presented along with an evaluation under consideration of the observer's interest profile.

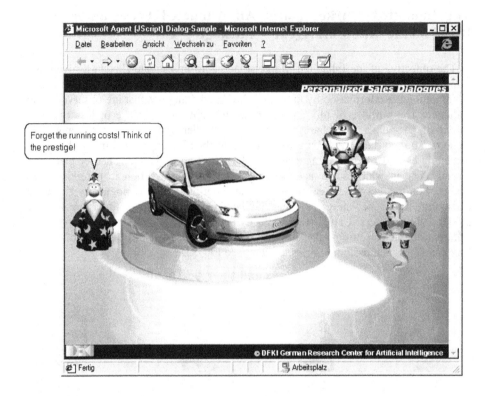

Fig. 4. Car sales dialogue example.

While in the travel application sketched above, the information to be presented has been allocated to a single agent, we now have to distribute information to a team of presenters whose activities have to be coordinated. In the sales scenario, the role of the system may be compared with that of a screen writer who produces a script for the actors of a play. The script represents the dialogue acts to be executed by the individual agents as well as their temporal order. From a technical point of view, the approach may be realized by a central planning component that decomposes a complex presentation goal into elementary dialogue and presentation acts that are allocated to the individual agents. To accomplish this task, we use the same plan-based approach as for the AiA personas.[5] The outcome of the planning process is an HTML file that includes control sequences for the Microsoft characters which can be played in the Microsoft Internet Explorer. However, in contrast to the PET approach, the agents' runtime engine is not part of the web page. Rather, to view the presentation with the Microsoft characters, the Microsoft Agent package has to be installed on the user's local machine.

As in the AiA project, knowledge concerning the decomposition of a presentation goal is represented by means of plan operators. However, this time the operators code

---

[5] An earlier version exploited the Java-based JAM agent architecture [9].

a decomposition of goals into dialogue acts for the agents. For instance, the operator listed in Fig. 5 captures a scenario where two agents discuss a feature of an object. It only applies if the feature has a negative impact on any value dimension[6] and if this relationship can be easily inferred. According to the operator, any disagreeable buyer produces a negative comment referring to this dimension (NegativeResponse). The negative response is followed by a response from the seller (RespNegativeResp).

```
HEADER: (A0 (DiscussValue ?attribute))
CONSTRAINTS:
(*and* (polarity ?attribute ?dimension neg)
       (difficulty ?attribute ?dimension low)
       (Buyer ?buyer)
       (Disagreeable ?buyer)
       (Seller ?seller))
INFERIORS:
(A1 (NegativeResponse ?buyer ?dimension))
(A2 (RespNegativeResp ?seller ?attribute ?dimension))
```

Fig. 5. Plan operator for discussing an attribute value.

An excerpt of a dialogue between Merlin as a seller and Robby and Peedy as buyer is shown in Fig. 6. The last two dialogue turns result from the execution of the operator above.

Robby: How much gas does it consume?
Merlin: It consumes 10 litres per 100 km.
Peedy: That's bad for the environment!
Merlin: Bad for the environment? It got a catalytic converter, and it is made of recyclable materials.

Fig. 6. Generated dialogue fragment of the sales scenario.

The Virtual News Agency: An Animated Presentation Team Based on SMIL

In the applications described above, the characters' presentations only included static material, such as written text or images. However, a web presentation may also comprise dynamic media objects, such as video and audio, all of which have to be displayed in a spatial and temporally coordinated manner and need to be synchronized with the agents' communicative gestures. Fig. 7 shows a typical application scenario with two animated agents - a newscaster and a technician - that watch and comment on a video while it is displayed on a screen.

---

[6] We adopted the value dimensions from a study of the German car market which suggests that safety, economy, comfort, sportiness, prestige and family and environmental friendliness are the most relevant [15].

Fig. 7. The Virtual News Agency.

Since the other two player technologies do not include any facilities for controlling the timing of other dynamic media, we decided to rely on the Synchronized Multimedia Integration Language[7] (SMIL) in this application scenario. SMIL is a standard recommended by the W3 consortium with the aim of adding synchronization to the Web. As in the other two applications, we use our presentation planning technology to generate expressions in the SMIL language that are played within a web browser using a SMIL player that supports streaming over the web, such as the Real Player 7 Basic[8]. However, since SMIL requires the specification of a spatial and temporal layout, the following extensions have became necessary:

(1) the formulation of temporal and spatial constraints in the plan operators
We distinguish between metric and qualitative constraints. Quantitative temporal and spatial constraints appear as metric (in-)equalities, e.g. (5 ≤ Duration PointInterval) or (5 ≤ bottom CharacterRegion – top CharacterRegion). Qualitative temporal constraints are represented in an "Allen-style" fashion which allows for the specification of thirteen temporal relationships between two names intervals, e.g. (SpeakInterval (During) PointInterval). Qualitative spatial constraints are represented by a set of topological relations, such as LeftOf, CenterHor or TopAlign.

(2) the development of a mechanism for designing a spatial and temporal layout
We collect all spatial and temporal constraints during the presentation planning process and use the incremental constraint solving toolkit Cassowary [5] to determine a consistent spatial and temporal layout which is then represented as a SMIL document.[9]

---

[7] http://smw.internet.com/smil/smilhome.html

[8] http://service.real.com/

[9] When using the Real Player, some further processing of the animation clips is advisable in order to increase the fluency of the overall presentation. Instead of playing one animation after the other, we incorporate all animations that appear in the same region in a single RealPix file that is considered by the RealPlayer as a unit.

In the following, we present a simple plan operator which may be used to synchronize the actions of two characters (Expert and Newscaster) with the display of a video. While the expert provides a summary of the video, the newscaster listens. Both agents then perform a waiting gesture until the video stops. Note that the plan operators do not require a human author to completely specify the layout of a presentation. For instance, we do not specify how long the summarization of the video takes. The spatial constraints specify the position of the inferior actions with respect to A0, the region corresponding to the plan operator.

```
HEADER: (A0 (PresentVideo Expert ?topic))

CONSTRAINTS:
  (*and* (Illustrates ?video ?topic)
         (Summarizes ?audio ?topic))
INFERIORS:
  (A1 (DialogueTurn Expert ?audio))
  (A2 (Listen Newscaster))
  (A3 (SaddSmilCode (?video))
  (A4 (BothWait))
TEMPORAL: ((A1 (starts) A3) (A2 (equals) A1))
           (A1 (meets) A4) (A4 (finishes) A3))
SPATIAL: ((ALIGNLEFT A1) (ALIGNBOTTOM A1)
          (ALIGNLEFT A2) (ALIGNBOTTOM A2)
          (ALIGNLEFT A3) (ALIGNBOTTOM A3)
          (ALIGNLEFT A4) (ALIGNBOTTOM A4))
START: (A3)
END: (A3)
```

Fig. 8. Plan operator for generating a SMIL document.

Conclusions

In this paper, we have described our efforts to develop life-like presentation agents which can be utilized for a broad range of web applications. We sketched three applications that are based on the same presentation planning technology, but exploit different player technologies for the visualization of the Personas. Our experience has shown that there is not yet a general-purpose player technology which meets the needs of all our applications.

The Microsoft Agent[TM] toolkit includes a number of useful software packages that support the creation of engaging character applications, such as animation components and components for the recognition and synthesis of natural language. Due to its comfortable application programmer's interface, this toolkit is an excellent choice for rapid prototyping. Being free of charge, it is also a low-cost entry point for new character projects. However, to view a presentation with Microsoft Agent characters, the user has to install the Microsoft package on his or her local machine. Furthermore, HTML-pages including control sequences for Microsoft Agent characters have to be played within the Microsoft Internet Explorer.

The rationale behind the development of the PET toolkit was the aim to display characters on web pages without requiring the user to download a dedicated plug-in or to install other (third-party) software. Being implemented as a Java applet, the PET player runs on any standard web browser. These characteristics are in particular of interest for commercial web sites. By making use of the HTML event model, PET also fulfills the necessary prerequisites for the creation of interactive Personas. On the other hand, there is a tradeoff between the player functionality and the overall download time of the applet. Therefore, the approach is less suitable for applications that require a rich repertoire of character behaviors and complex media combinations.

SMIL provides a declarative language for the specification of the spatial and temporal layout and in combination with players, such as RealPlayer 7, sophisticated streaming and synchronization technology. These features are in particular useful if a character's communicative actions have to be coordinated with other dynamic media, such as video and audio. However, SMIL does not support the incremental design of presentations and thus does not allow for the integration of interactive Personas. Furthermore, defining plan operators for SMIL presentations requires some training since it presumes a basic understanding of spatial and temporal constraints. A major deficiency of RealPlayer 7 lies in the fact that it does not support the concept of a transparent color value. As a consequence, characters always occupy a rectangular region within a SMIL presentation, and some extra design effort may become necessary to achieve a smooth integration into the surrounding screen space.

Some Future Directions

Even though an increasing number of companies populate their web sites with characters, the web still appears as a computerized environment. A study by Mulken and colleagues [17] revealed that animated agents do not necessarily appear more believable and trustworthy than text- or audio-based agents. Reasons might be the strongly limited communicative skills of the agents and their mechanical behavior. To create a social atmosphere on the web, we have to allow for more natural interaction by exploiting a broader range of communicative means, such as intonation, mimics and gestures. In addition, man-machine communication has to be enhanced by psychological and social factors. In the long run, web characters should not just support the user in accomplishing certain tasks, but make the visit of a web site an individual experience. While earlier work in the agent community focused on the design of agents that behave in an intelligent manner, the great challenge for the future will be the creation of believable individuals with their own personality and emotions [4].

Currently, most character developers focus on the Web site owner, e.g. an E-Commerce company, who owns the character. Even if such characters adapt themselves to the specific user, it is still the provider who has the final control over the characters' behavior which is essentially determined by the provider's and not the user's goals. A great challenge for future research is the development of personalized user-owned characters. Whereas provider-owned characters inhabit a specific web site to which they are specialized, user-owned characters may take the user to unknown places, make suggestions, direct her attention to interesting information or simply have a chat with her about the place they are jointly visiting. Most likely, the user will more easily build up a social relationship with a character that is committed to him or her than a character that is owned by a company. Furthermore, users might hesitate to chat with a company-owned character since they are afraid of a potential misuse of private data, such as their personal preferences.

Clearly, the overall quality of an animated information agent's support will depend to a large extent on the information gathered from a web site. There are several approaches to tackling this issue. One direction is to rely on sophisticated methods for information retrieval and extraction. However, we are still far from robust approaches capable of analyzing arbitrary Web pages consisting of heterogeneous media objects, such as text, images, and video. Another approach uses so-called annotated environments [6] which provide the knowledge that agents need to appropriately perform their tasks. These annotations can be compared to markups of a Web page. Our hope is that with the increasing popularity of agents, a standard for such annotations will be developed that will significantly ease the characters work.

Another interesting area is the design of internet agents for portable application domains. For instance, if the user is travelling, she may only have access to a small hand-held computer with a tiny display. Nevertheless, she may still want to communicate with her personal assistant. However, a standalone version of the agent is of little use. Rather, it needs to be connected to an information source which provides the data to be presented. It is a challenging task to make best use of the strongly restricted expressive means in this impoverished environment.

Acknowledgements

The work described here has been partially funded by the BMBF (Bundesministerium für Bildung und Forschung). We are grateful to Peter Rist and Bernhard Kirsch for the graphical design of the DFKI Personas. We would also like to thank Jochen Müller and Stefan Neurohr for their work on the design and implementation of the PET server, Thomas Kleinbauer for the extension of the presentation planner to SMIL, Martin Klesen for the implementation of the interface for the Inhabited Market Place and Patrick Gebhard for fruitful discussions and technical advice.

References

1.   André, E., and Rist, T. (1995). Generating coherent presentations employing textual and visual material. *Artificial Intelligence Review,* Special Issue on the Integration of Natural Language and Vision Processing 9(2–3):147–165.
2.   André, E., Rist, T. and Müller, J. (1999). Employing AI Methods to Control the Behavior of Animated Interface Agents. *Applied Artificial Intelligence* 13:415-448.

3. André, E., Rist, T. , van Mulken, S., Klesen, M. and Baldes, S. (2000). The Automated Design of Believable Dialogues for Animated Presentation Teams. In: Cassell et al. (eds.): *Embodied Conversational Agents*, 220-255, Cambridge, MA: MIT Press.

4. Bates, J. (1994). The Role of Emotion in Believable Agents. *Communications of the ACM* 37(7): 122-125.

5. Borning, A., Marriott, K., Stuckey, P. and Xiao, Y. (1997). Linear Arithmetic Constraints for User Interface Applications, Proc. of the 1997 *ACM Symposium on User Interface Software and Technology*, 87-96.

6. Doyle, P. and Hayes-Roth, B. (1998). Agents in Annotated Worlds. Proc. of the Third International Conference on *Autonomous Agents*, 173-180, New York: ACM Press.

7. Gaudiano, P. and Kater, P. (2000). Alife-WebGuide: An Intelligent User Interface for Web Site Navigation. Proc. of IUI 2000, 121-124, New York: ACM Press.

8. Höök, K., M. Sjölinder, A.-L. Ereback, and P. Persson. (1999). Dealing with the lurking Lutheran view on interfaces: Evaluation of the Agneta and Frida System. Proc. of the *i3 Spring Days Workshop* on Behavior Planning for Lifelike Characters and Avatars. 125-136. Sitges, Spain.

9. Huber, M. (1999). JAM: A BDI-theoretic mobile agent architecture. Proc. of the Third Conference on *Autonomous Agents,* 236–243. New York: ACM Press.

10. Isbister, K. (2000). Helper Agent: Designing an Assistant for Human-Human Interaction in a Virtual Meeting Space. Proc. of *CHI'2000*, 57-64. New York: ACM Press.

11. Lester, J. C., Converse, S. A. Kahler, S.E., Barlow, S.T., Stone, B.A. and Bhogal, R.S. (1997). The persona effect: Affective impact of animated pedagogical agents. Proc. of *CHI'97*, 359–366. New York: ACM Press.

12. Microsoft Agent: Software Development Kit (1999). Microsoft Press, Redmond Washington.

13. Shaw, E., Johnson, W. L. (1999). Pedagogical Agents on the Web. Proc. of the Third International Conference on *Autonomous Agent '99s*, New York: ACM Press.

14. Smith, M.A., Farnham, S.D. and Drucker, S.M. (2000). The Social Life of Small Graphical Chat Spaces. Proc. of *CHI'2000*, 462-469. New York: ACM Press.

15. Spiegel-Verlag. (1993). SPIEGEL-Dokumentation: Auto, Verkehr und Umwelt. Hamburg: Augstein.

16. van Mulken, S., André, E. and Müller, J. (1998). The Persona Effect: How Substantial is it? In: Proc. of *HCI'98*, Sheffield, pp. 53-66.

17. van Mulken, S., André, E. and Müller, J. (1999). An empirical study on the trustworthiness of lifelike interface agents. In H.-J. Bullinger and J. Ziegler, eds., *Human-Computer Interaction* (Proc. of HCI-International 1999), 152–156. Mahwah, New Jersey: Lawrence Erlbaum Associates.

Affective Computing for Future Agents

Rosalind W. Picard

MIT Media Laboratory; 20 Ames Street; Cambridge, MA 02139

Phone: 617-253-0611; Fax: 617-253-8874

picard@media.mit.edu; http://www.media.mit.edu/affect

Abstract for Invited Talk

To the extent that future agents will interact with people and with one another via text, speech, and other modes that suggest social interaction, they may benefit from having certain skills of social-emotional intelligence, such as the ability to see if they have annoyed a person. Already, many animated characters have the ability to *express* emotion (give the appearance of having emotions via facial expressions, gestures, and so forth) but few can *recognize* any aspects of the emotional response communicated by a user. The agent may sense that you're clicking on a button, and how many times you have clicked on it, but cannot tell if you're clicking with interest or boredom, pleasure or displeasure. Agents are therefore handicapped when it comes to responding to affective information, limiting their ability to engage in successful interactions.

This talk briefly highlights research at the MIT Media Lab for giving agents the ability to recognize and respond to emotion. I will describe new hardware and software tools that we have built for recognizing user expressions such as confusion, frustration, and anger, together with an agent we have designed and built that responds to user frustration in a way that aims to help the user feel less frustrated. This "emotionally savvy" agent significantly improved users' willingness to interact with the system, as measured in a behavioral study involving 70 subjects, two control conditions, and a frustrating game-playing scenario. This talk will also raise and briefly discuss some ethical and philosophical implications of agents that attempt to help assuage or manipulate human emotions. More information about our research, and papers describing our work in more detail together with descriptions of related work at other institutions, can be downloaded from our website at http://www.media.mit.edu/affect.

M. Klusch and L. Kerschberg (Eds.): CIA 2000, LNAI 1860, p. 14, 2000.
© Springer-Verlag Berlin Heidelberg 2000

Knowledge Agents on the Web

Yariv Aridor[1], David Carmel[1], Ronny Lempel[2], Aya Soffer[1] and Yoelle S. Maarek[1]

[1] IBM Haifa Research Laboratory
MATAM, Haifa 31905, Israel
{yariv,carmel,ayas,yoelle}@il.ibm.com
[2] Computer Science Department, Technion, Haifa, Israel
rlempel@cs.technion.ac.il

Abstract. This paper introduces and evaluates a new paradigm, called Knowledge Agents, that incorporates agent technology into the process of domain-specific Web search. An agent is situated between the user and a search engine. It specializes in a specific domain by extracting characteristic information from search results. Domains are thus user-defined and can be of any granularity and specialty. This information is saved in a knowledge base and used in future searches. Queries are refined by the agent based on its domain-specific knowledge and the refined queries are sent to general purpose search engines. The search results are ranked based on the agent's domain specific knowledge, thus filtering out pages which match the query but are irrelevant to the domain. A topological search of the Web for additional relevant sites is conducted from a domain-specific perspective. The combination of a broad search of the entire Web with domain-specific textual and topological scoring of results, enables the knowledge agent to find the most relevant documents for a given query within a domain of interest. The knowledge acquired by the agent is continuously updated and persistently stored thus users can benefit from search results of others in common domains.

1 Introduction

The amount of information available on the World Wide Web is increasing on a daily basis. General purpose search engines and browsers provide valuable assistance to users in locating general information relevant to their needs. However, finding information for a narrow query in a specific domain has become more and more difficult with the growth of the Web, and thus frequently resembles a search for a needle in a haystack.

Individuals spend more and more time filtering out irrelevant information returned from general purpose search engines while searching the Web. It is not uncommon for a user to obtain thousands of hits which match her query but belong to irrelevant domains. This is termed the low precision problem, as defined in information retrieval [15].

Many approaches have been suggested to tackle the low precision problem on the Web [3, 7, 1, 5]. One such approach is to restrict the search into a pre-defined domain. Several search services, most notably Yahoo! [8], allow users to specify the domain in which to evaluate the query. Such a restriction narrows the search space, hence increases the precision. However, the domain hierarchy is manually (or at best semi manually) crafted as a taxonomy of predefined categories and users cannot request personal domains of interest. While this approach guarantees more quality, browsing is often time

M. Klusch and L. Kerschberg (Eds.): CIA 2000, LNAI 1860, pp. 15-26, 2000.

consuming, and coverage is extremely limited. Major search engines, such as AltaVista, index about two orders of magnitude more Web pages than Yahoo! [16].

This paper presents a new paradigm, termed Knowledge Agents, which provides domain-specific search in the context of dynamic domains. With knowledge agents, domains are defined by the users and can thus be of any granularity and specialty. In essence, it is an architecture which enables knowledge acquisition from search results which automatically characterizes the domain in which the search was applied. This knowledge is persistently saved by the agent and can then be utilized to automatically narrow future searches within that domain.

The rest of the paper is organized as follows. Section 2 highlights the knowledge agent approach. Section 3 describes the system architecture. Section 4 provides some examples and experimental results. Section 5 discusses related work. Section 6 concludes the paper, highlighting future work and challenges.

2   Knowledge Agent Main Approach

Knowledge agents improve search precision by mimicking the steps that users might perform to find what they are really looking for. These steps include

- Choose a search engine and submit a query.
- Traverse the list of retrieved pages to find the relevant ones.
- Apply shallow browsing based on outgoing hyperlinks from the set of retrieved pages.
- Provide relevance feedback for "more like this" services.
- Refine the query repeatedly and resubmit it (possibly to other search engines).

The key to the knowledge agent (KA) approach is that it specializes in a domain by extracting relevant information every time it performs a search and uses this knowledge to improve the precision of subsequent search efforts. To this end, the KA maintains a knowledge base (KB) that stores this information persistently. The KB consists of a set of leading sites in its domain and a repository of frequent terms in these sites. Each term is associated with a list of lexical affinities – closely related terms frequently found in its proximity [12]. The KB is adapted continuously by the agent during search. New highly relevant pages found by the agent are entered into the KB, possibly taking the place of old pages with lower utility. The KB can be initialized by providing a set of sites relevant to the domain of interest. For example, this set could be extracted from the user's bookmark file or from any other existing pre-defined categorization of Web sites.

The first role the KA performs on behalf of the user is query refinement, which has long been recognized as an efficient tool for improving search results [17]. Query refinement is usually performed by adding terms related to the user's terms using a thesaurus or a synonym table. The KA, on the other hand, expands the query by adding to each of the terms its most notable lexical affinities as found in the KB. The advantage of this approach is that the agent's local thesaurus characterizes its domain-specific ontology and thus relations between terms are domain dependent. For example, consider a search for the query "knowledge". An "artificial intelligence" agent would likely expand the query to include the terms "acquisition", "reasoning", "discovery", "representation", while a "cryptographic" agent would likely expand the query using the terms "zero", "private", etc.

The second role that the KA performs on behalf of the user is shallow Web crawling. The agent applies a topological search mechanism similar to the one applied by Clever [3]. It first compiles a list of candidate result pages (root set) by sending the refined query to one or several search engines. This basic set is extended to include pages that are pointed to by pages in this set based on their potential relevance to the query. Pages that point to pages in the root set are also added to the retrieved set in an attempt to find higher level pages about the topic of interest. Finally, the pages saved in the KB, which are assumed to be the most authoritative information sources for the given domain, are added to the retrieved set.

The third role of the KA is traversing the retrieved pages and ranking them such that the most relevant pages will be listed first in the result. Ranking is performed based on both textual and topological aspects, utilizing information stored in its KB. The textual similarity measures the relevance of the pages retrieved to the specific query as well as to the agent's domain. The link topology score is computed using a combination of Kleinberg's mutual reinforcement algorithm [10] as well as stochastic link analysis [11].

It follows that a knowledge agent retrieves the most relevant sites according to its personal point of view of its domain of specialization. Figure 1 is an example of this behavior. It shows the result of submitting the query "internet" to a cryptography (Crypto) agent and an information retrieval (IR) agent. The Crypto agent refined the query to include the terms "security privacy firewall", while the IR agent added the terms "search exploration". Each agent viewed the term "internet" in the context of its domain of expertise. The IR agent retrieved the main sites of the leading Internet search engines, while the Crypto agent returned sites dealing with Internet privacy and security.

To summarize, the main highlights of the knowledge agent approach are:

- Personalization: the user creates and maintains knowledge agents for his private domains of interest rather than being dependent on a fixed set of domains. These domains of interest can be of any granularity.
- Persistent knowledge: knowledge agents make it possible to utilize knowledge gained through search to improve search precision of future queries in the same domain.
- Global search: the knowledge agent searches the entire Web rather than a subset as in the case of domain-specific search engines.
- Portability: users can easily import knowledge agents created by others to assist in their search in any common domains of interests since the KB is implemented as a plug-in component of the knowledge agent software.
- Easy deployment: agents can be implemented as a front end to any search engine. They do not impose any extra functional overhead on the user compared to available search engines.

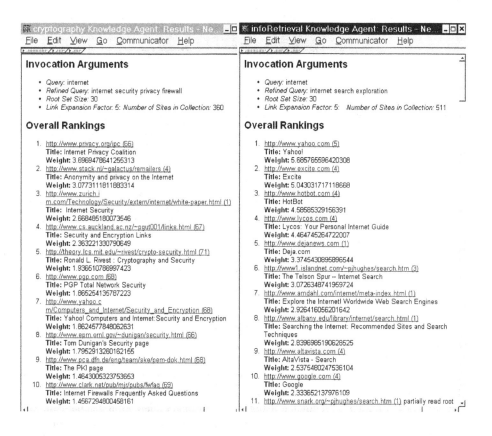

Fig. 1. The results for the query "internet" using two different knowledge agents.

3   System Architecture

The knowledge agent architecture contains the following components (Figure 2):

1. An agent manager, that sets up new knowledge agents and restarts existing agents. It is responsible for managing multiple concurrent connections for reading from the Web and serve multiple agents.
2. One or more Knowledge Agents which perform domain-specific Web search.
3. Each knowledge agent has an associated knowledge base which contains domain-specific information to be used for searching. The KB is updated continuously throughout the use of the agent.

3.1   The Knowledge Base

The knowledge base contains a bounded collection of ranked sites and an aggregate profile of the textual content of these sites. Sites in the knowledge base are those which

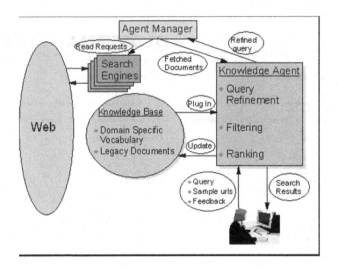

Fig. 2. The knowledge agent architecture.

have proven to be highly relevant to a majority of the queries submitted to the agent. The rationale for this is that sites which are consistently relevant to the users' queries are deemed as central to the domain.

The textual profile contains all of the words which appear in the sites, after deletion of stop words and a mild stemming process, along with their number of appearances. Each word in the profile is associated with a list of its lexical affinities. The flow of sites into and out of the KB is regulated using an evolutionary adaptation mechanism. Sites fight for the right to be included in the agent's KB. Each site is assigned a history score reflecting its relevance to the domain through the life of the agent. A combination of the history score and the relevance score for a specific query determines which sites are inserted and removed from the KB.

The KB is a pluggable component. It can be saved to a file and restored from one, and thus knowledge can easily be transferred from one user to another.

3.2   The Search Process

The search process (Figure 3) starts with the user entering a query and ends with the agent returning a ranked set of (hopefully highly relevant) sites to the user.

The system supports two kinds of queries, text queries and sample-url queries. A text query is a keyword based query such as those typically submitted to general purpose Web search engines. The user's query is automatically refined in the context of the agent's domain by adding to each of the keywords in the query its most notable lexical affinities as found in the profile of the KB. The refined query is submitted to the user's choice of one or more search engines. The results returned by the search engine(s) to the refined query are called the root set of sites.

A sample-url Query is a query which specifies a few (typically 1-5) seed urls, and whose purpose is to find a community of sites which are closely related to the seeds.

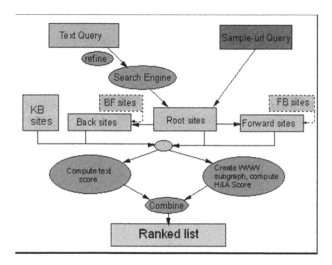

Fig. 3. The search process applied by the agent.

Similar services are offered by Excite's "More like this" [6] and by Google's "Google-Scout" [7]. Both services receive as input a single site, while we allow an arbitrary number of seeds. In sample-url queries, the user-supplied seed sites assume the role of the root set of sites, as if they were returned by a search engine in response to some textual query. The seed sites are read, and their combined content serves as a pseudo query for the purpose of evaluating the textual content of other sites in the search process.

The collection of root sites is expanded by following the hyperlinks surrounding them, and by adding the KB sites. The breadth of the expansion is controlled by a user-defined link expansion factor that specifies how many pointed/pointing sites will be added in each expansion stage. We denote the entire collection of sites by C.

3.3 Ranking the Web Pages

Computing the textual score of a web page. The agent receives a set of sites from the meta-search, from which it creates a ranked set of sites to be returned to the user. The agent computes a textual similarity score, $T_q(s)$, for each page s with respect to the query using a tf-idf formula originally used in the Guru search engine [12]. The textual profiles of the pages saved in the KB serve as the set of documents from which the terms' document frequencies are taken.

The agent also computes a textual similarity score, $T_d(s)$, of each site to the domain. $T_d(s)$ is set to the dot product of the vectors of lexical affinities representing s and the domain. Term weights are assigned in relation to their frequency in the domain. The rationale for this is that pages that have many lexical affinities in common with the domain are most related to the domain. $T_q(s)$ and $T_d(s)$ are normalized and combined to create the overall textual similarity score $T(s)$.

Computing the link topology score of a web page. The agent builds a Web subgraph, induced by the collection of sites C, on which connectivity analysis is performed in order to find authoritative Web sites. The idea behind connectivity analysis is that a hyperlink from a site s to a site t indicates that these two sites share a common topic of interest, and that s conveys a positive assessment on t's contents by recommending that surfers who visit s also visit t. Weights are first assigned to the edges of the Web subgraph. Each link receives a positive weight according to the anchor text associated with it. The weight is boosted if either the source site or the target site belong to the KB. This weighted Web subgraph is used to assign the hub and authority scores to each site from which a link topology score is derived.

Computing the overall score of a Web page. The textual score and the link topology score are combined to yield the overall score of each site s in C:

$$S(s) = \alpha_C T(s) + (1 - \alpha_C) L(s)$$

Link topology scores are reliable only for collections in which many neighboring sites have been added around the meta-search results. We therefore set the value of α_C according to the ratio between the size of the compiled collection C and the size of the root set. The larger that ratio, the more confidence we have in the link-based score, and the lower we set α_C. When the ratio is low, meaning that the link expansion phase did not add many sites, we raise the influence of the text-based scores by raising α_C.

4 Examples and Experiments

We have developed a prototype system that implements the KA architecture. We created several agents using our system: a palm pilot agent, a cryptography agent (Crypto), an artificial intelligence agent (AI), a Geographic Information System agent (GIS), an Information Retrieval agent (IR), and a Star Wars agent. We trained each agent by submitting several textual queries relevant to its domain. For example the IR agent was trained using the following queries: "information retrieval", "text mining", "information extraction", "query refinement", "vector space model", "probabilistic model", "recall precision". Each agent's KB includes 50 to 100 urls (depending on the agent setup) as well as a textual profile of these pages. In this section, we present some examples and experimental results using these agents. The experiments were conducted as a proof of concept for the KA main functionality. Clearly, these experiments do not replace a future more exhaustive study of the KA performance.

4.1 Query Refinement

To examine the query refinement capabilities of the agents, we selected a few queries and examined the terms added by each KA while refining these queries. We made the following observations. The agents can complete names of people in their fields. For example, the Crypto agent adds "Ron" and "MIT" when asked about "Rivest", while the AI agent adds "Stuart", "Norvig", and "aima", when asked about "Russel" (aima is an abbreviation for a famous introductory AI book written by Stuart Russel and Peter Norvig). They know about algorithms and theoretical aspects of their domains (e.g., the Crypto agent adds "Interactive" and "Proof" to "Zero Knowledge", and adds "Stream" and "Block" to "Ciphers"). They even know the marketplace (given the term "Checkpoint", the Crypto agent adds "firewall" and "vendor"). The agents are particularly good with acronyms. For example, the GIS agent expands "dlg" to "digital line graph data" and "eos" to "nasa earth observation system".

Table 1 shows how different agents refine the same terms according to their domain-specific ontology. For example, the query "science" is expanded by the Crypto agent to include "computer" and "cryptography", by the GIS agent to include "earth" and "information", and by the Star Wars agent to include "fiction".

	Palm Pilot	Cryptography	Geographic Information System (GIS)	Star Wars
software	development,download	encryption,security	esri (large software company)	game
knowledge		zero	opto systems	star war encyclopedia
public	license,gnu domain	key,x509,certificate	domain, data	free site
science		cryptography, computer	earth,information	fiction
Microsoft	windows,operating system	crypto api	terraserver (ms geographic data server)	
unit	battery,modem	rsa certificate trusted	map boundary, remote sensing	hyperdrive
video	driver	stream	gis library remote sensing	clip picture sound

Table 1. : query refinement performed by different agents.

We examined the precision of the agent's textual analysis without link expansion. We compared the precision of the top results using KA with the precision of general purpose search engines for several queries. Each query was submitted to AltaVista and Google, as well as to a knowledge agent specializing in the domain of the query. The KA used AltaVista for meta-search in the first run and Google in the second. The relevance of each site in the top results was examined in the context of the domain of interest by an expert in the domain. Table 2 summarizes the results of these experiments.

From these results, it is apparent that performing textual analysis in the context of the domain of the specific KA improves the precision of the search significantly. The KA usually succeeds in sifting up relevant sites from the bottom of the meta-search results. For example, when submitting the query "landsat 7 sample image" to the GIS KA using AltaVista as the meta-search engine, the four most relevant sites, ranked 2, 5, 14, and 19 by AltaVista, were ranked 1- 4 by the KA. Two additional sites with numerous links to satellite images were extracted from the agent's knowledge base and returned in the top 10 hits. The top 10 sites returned by Google were related to landsat 7, however only six of these sites had sample images or links to such images. When

Query	Agent	top@10				top@20			
		AV	KA+ AV	Google	KA+ Google	AV	KA+ AV	Google	KA+ Google
landsat 7 sample image	GIS	0.2	0.6	0.6	1	0.2	0.4	0.55	0.65
zero knowledge	Crypto	0.1	0.6	0.3	0.5	0.35	0.35	0.35	0.4
relevance feedback	IR	0.6	0.6	0.4	0.7	0.6	0.5	0.5	0.65

Table 2. Precision at 10 and 20 using various search engines and a knowledge agent with zero link expansion.

submitting the same query to the GIS agent using Google as the meta-search engine, all ten sites in the top 10 where relevant. The four non-relevant sites in Google's top 10 were replaced by four relevant sites from further down the list.

It is important to note that the agent's success in these examples is attributed to the fact that it was able to rank the sites more relevant to its particular domain higher. It may be the case, that by expanding the query "zero knowledge" to include the term "cryptography", the general purpose search engines would be more successful. However, it has been shown in [1] that for queries containing both broad domain terms and narrow terms general search engines tend to return sites relevant to the broad domain rather than sites dealing with the narrow topic within the context of the domain.

4.2   Link Expansion

In order to test the effect of link expansion we executed the same queries with a link expansion of 5 (every site in the root set contributes 5 sites which it points to and 5 sites which point to it) using AltaVista for the meta-search. We compare these results to executing the same queries with zero link expansion. Table 3 summarizes the results.

Query	Agent	top@10		top@20	
		No Exp.	Exp.	No Exp.	Exp.
landsat 7 sample image	GIS	0.4	0.8	0.2	0.55
zero knowledge	Crypto	0.6	0.4	0.35	0.5
relevance feedback	IR	0.6	0.7	0.5	0.6

Table 3. Precision at 10 and 20 using knowledge agents with zero link expansion and with link expansion 5.

In general, link expansion improved the results by finding additional relevant sites that were not returned by the meta-search but were either pointed to or pointed by these sites. For example, for the query "landsat 7 sample images", the GIS agent was able to retrieve several additional relevant sites compared to search with zero link expansion. Similar results were observed in the top 20. The improvement for the "relevance feedback" query was not as significant, since we already had good precision with zero link expansion. Nevertheless, we were able to add one more relevant site to the top 10 and two relevant sites to the top 20. Note that in the case of the query "zero knowledge" the precision at 10 decreased using link expansion since the agent retrieved two additional non-relevant sites and mistakenly ranked them in the top 10.

We tried to compare our results to those of Clever which also uses link expansion for retrieval. Clever was basically unable to find good sites for these queries. It returned some good IR hubs and authorities for the "relevance feedback" query, but was unable to locate even one site that contains this term. Similarly for the query "zero knowledge", it returned cryptography sites but none pertaining to zero knowledge. These results are not surprising since Clever is not meant for these type of narrow queries [4].

While link expansion is a powerful tool for improving precision, its drawback is that time complexity increases with the size of the expansion. The KA system lets the user choose the desired link expansion, thus giving them control over the tradeoff between response time and quality of results.

5   Related Approaches

Many approaches have been suggested to tackle the low precision problem involved in searching the Web. Hierarchical categorization of Web sites is the most common solution. It allows users to navigate through a hierarchy of categories and specify explicitly the domain in which to evaluate their query. This reduces the number of irrelevant results, hence increases the precision significantly. However, as mentioned above, Web categorization requires significant human effort and coverage is extremely limited.

Another alternative is using domain-specific search engines. Such engines allow users to perform a focused search on a given topic within the scope of the specific domain covered by the search engine. For example, MRQE [14] allows users to search only for movie reviews. CampSearch [2] enables complex queries over summer camps by age, size, location and cost. Performing these searches with a general purpose search engine would be extremely tedious and most likely not yield to such accurate results. However, as in the case of manual categorization, building such search engines is a labor intensive process.

The search broker [13] is a meta-search tool which utilizes existing domain-specific search engines. Users specify both the domain and the query, making it possible to apply a domain-specific search engine for their narrow query. Each search engine offered by the search broker covers a certain domain, and each domain is associated with a list of terms (aliases) related to it. The search broker chooses the most proper search engine for the narrow query according to the domain specified by the user. The collection of search engines and the assignment of aliases that describe each engine are maintained by a human librarian.

Focused crawling [5] attempts to automatically build domain-specific search engines by selectively seeking out pages that are relevant to a predefined domain. Rather than collecting and indexing all accessible Web documents, a focused crawler finds the links that are likely to be most relevant for the specified domain, and thus avoids irrelevant regions of the Web. Jcentral [9] is such a search engine which allows Java developers to search for Java sources on the Web.

The common feature of the aforementioned methods is focusing the search into a specific domain in order to improve search precision. The knowledge agents described in this work apply a similar strategy, however, they can automatically specialize in any domain as defined by their user and are therefore much more suitable for personal assistance. Furthermore, the knowledge acquired during the agent's activity is persistently kept by the agent and continually updated to enable improved search services in the future. Finally, the domain-specific textual profile maintained by the knowledge agent is a very powerful tool both for query refinement and for textual ranking of the relevancy of documents to a specific query within the domain.

6   Concluding Remarks

The knowledge agent approach presented in this paper suggests a new paradigm which provides domain-specific search in the context of dynamic domains. These domains are defined by the users and can thus be of any granularity and specialty. Queries are refined by the agent based on its domain-specific knowledge. The refined queries are sent to general purpose search engines and the results are ranked from the viewpoint of the specific knowledge agent, thus filtering out documents which match the query but are irrelevant to the domain of interest. A topological search of the web for additional relevant documents is conducted from a domain-specific perspective as well. The knowledge stored by the agent, enables it to enjoy the benefit of topological search, while traversing a relatively small search space. The combination of a broad search of the entire Web, using general purpose search engines, with domain-specific textual and topological scoring of results, enables knowledge agents to find the most relevant documents at search time for a given query within the realm of the domain of interest.

Knowledge agents is work in progress. We have implemented a prototype and conducted some initial experiments that show the potential benefits of this approach. There are however still several open questions. First and foremost is the question of how to best characterize a domain. Currently the domain is characterized by a list of leading sites and the entire textual content of these sites. Ideally, we would like to use only those terms that in fact distinguish this domain from others while filtering out irrelevant terms. Furthermore, sites found as most relevant to a particular query, might be entered automatically into the KB. While these sites should best characterize the domain, this is not always the case. A feedback mechanism whereby users could indicate the relevance of results to the domain as a whole can assist the learning process and improve the domain characterization. Finally, since the Web is constantly changing, letting the agent work autonomously off-line, looking for new sites similar to those already in its knowledge base, will probably be needed in order to keep the domain characterization up to-date. These are all subjects for future work.

In this paper we have described how knowledge agents can be used for Web search. We envision knowledge agents as light components that can be plugged into several other Web applications such as browsing, filtering and routing systems. The knowledge acquired by the agent while searching for information pertaining to a user's domain of interest, can assist in analyzing information acquired from other Internet sources from the point of view of this particular agent's domain.

Acknowledgments

We thank Dan Pelleg for useful discussions concerning the knowledge agent approach.

References

1. I. Ben-Shaul, M. Herscovici, M. Jacovi, Y. S. Maarek, D. Pelleg, M. Shtalhaim, V. Soroka, and S. Ur. Adding support for dynamic and focused search with fetuccino. In *Proceedings of the Eighth International WWW Conference*, pages 575–587. Elsevier, 1999.
2. CampSearch. The search engine for camps. http://www.campsearch.com.
3. IBM Almaden Research Center. Clever. http://www.almaden.ibm.com/cs/k53.clever.html.
4. S. Chakrabarti,   B. Dom,   D. Gibson,   J. Kleinberg,   S.R. Kumar, P. Raghavan, S. Rajagopalan, and A. Tomkins. Mining the web's link structure. *IEEE Computer*, 32(8):60–67, August 1999.
5. S. Chakrabarti, B. Dom, and M. ven den Berg. Focused crawling: A new approach to topic-specific web resource discovery. In *Proceedings of the Eighth International WWW Conference*, pages 545–562. Elsevier, 1999.
6. Excite Inc. Excite search. http://www.excite.com/.
7. Google Inc. Google search engine. http://www.google.com/.
8. Yahoo Inc. Yahoo! http://www.yahoo.com.
9. IBM Jcentral. Search the web for java. http://www.jcentral.com.
10. J. M. Kleinberg. Authoritaive sources in a hyperlinked environment. In *Proceedings of the Ninth Annual ACM-SIAM Symposium on Discrete Algorithms*, volume 25-27, pages 668 – 677, January 1998.
11. Ronny Lempel. Finding authoritative sites on the WWW (and other hyperlinked media) by analyzing the web's link-structure. Master's thesis, Technion, Israel Institute of Technology, July 1999.
12. Y. Maarek and F. Smadja. Full text indexing based on lexical relations, an application: Software libraries. In N. Belkin and C. van Rijsbergen, editors, *Proceedings of SIGIR89*, pages 198 – 206. Cambridge MA, ACM press, 1989.
13. U. Manber and P. A. Bigot. The search broker. In *The First Usenix Symposium on Internet Technologies and Systems*, pages 231–240, Monterey CA, December 1997.
14. MRQE. Movie review query engine. http://www.mrqe.com.
15. G. Salton and M. J. McGill. *Introduction to Modern Information Retrieval*. Computer Series, McGraw-Hill, New York, 1983.
16. Search Engine Watch. Search engine watch. http://www.searchenginewatch.com.
17. J. Xu and W. B. Croft. Query expansion using local and global document analysis. In *Proceedings of the 19th annual international ACM SIGIR Conference on Research and Development in Information Retrieval*, pages 4 –11, 1996.

ICEBERG: Exploiting Context in Information Brokering Agents

Catholijn M. Jonker[1] and Arjen Vollebregt[2]

[1]Vrije Universiteit Amsterdam, Department of Artificial Intelligence,
De Boelelaan 1081a, 1081 HV Amsterdam, The Netherlands, email: jonker@cs.vu.nl, URL:
www.cs.vu.nl/~jonker
[2]KPN Research, St. Paulusstraat 4, Leidschendam, The Netherlands, email:
A.M.Vollebregt@kpn.com.

Abstract. The research reported in this paper has both a scientific and a commercial aim. The scientific interest is to explore the use of contexts in order to improve the quality of information brokering. In this paper it is shown that contexts in information brokering can be exploited to enable four directions of query reformulation: up and down (standard query expansion) and sideway reformulations of the user request that can even involve going from one context to another.

1.   Introduction

A lot of research is done on the subject of information retrieval, federated databases, search engines, and information brokering agents[1]. The basic problems are recall and precision (as formulated within multi-database theory). This paper focusses on precision. A well-known technique to improve precision is relevance feedback to enable query expansion; the user can indicate "more like this result", or is asked to choose from a number of concepts that are automatically distilled from the top ranking results. Even though query expansion approaches help in the sense that more items similar to those first retrieved are found, there is much room for exploring interactive methods for improving precision (Manflano et al., 1998).

The work reported here is based on the assumption that precision can be proved by exploiting the knowledge gained from good domain analysis. The notion of a multi-dimensional context is introduced and it is shown how this can be used to:

- disambiguate the user request by finding the context relevant for his request
- sharpening his request (the downward direction of query expansion)
- widen his scope xt (upward query expansion)
- sideways query reformulations within the same context or even by going from one context to a different context that is more fitting with respect to the actual wishes of the user. This is not covered by traditional query expansion.

---

[1] See any of the major conferences, shops, and journals on agent- or multi-agent systems, information retrieval, and multi-databases.

M. Klusch and L. Kerschberg (Eds.): CIA 2000, LNAI 1860, pp. 27-38, 2000.
© Springer-Verlag Berlin Heidelberg 2000

In Section 2 the notion of a multi-dimensional structure of contexts is introduced. In the third section the information brokering process as performed by the ICEBERG broker is described from a global viewpoint. In Section 4, the internal processing of the ICEBERG information broker is explained, with an emphasis on the exploitation of contexts. It describes the process of reformulation of user request on the basis of the multi-dimensional structure of contexts (this includes standard forms of query expansion based on feedback mechanisms). In Section 5 it is explained how the search results are evaluated on the basis of the multi-dimensional structure of contexts. Section 6 compares the work reported in this paper to other work and contains the conclusions.

2.   Notion of Context

The research has been performed within the context of the ICEBERG project of KPN Research (the research department of the royal Dutch telecom). The reference to the ICEBERG is made to emphasize that the average user when trying to find information has only the amount of knowledge on the topic that could be compared to the very tip of a huge ICEBERG. The aim of the ICEBERG project is to get that part of the ICEBERG above water in which the user is interested. Domain-specific knowledge is specified using ontologies. Ontology, as Gruber (cf. (Gruber, 1993)) describes it *"explicit specification of a conceptualization"*, provides a vocabulary for talking about a domain. In this paper a novel way to structure the domain of application is presented, i.e., the *contextual universe*. This notion is first defined and then explained.

Definition
A contextual dimension D for a domain of application P is a set of concepts relevant for P. A contextual universe U for a domain of application P is a tuple $<D1, ..., Dn>$ $(n \geq 1)$ of contextual dimensions. A context C within a contextual universe U is a tuple $<I, T>$, where I is the identifier of the context and T is a semantic network of concepts from the domain ontology of P. The identifier I of a context within a contextual universe U is defined as a tuple $<d1, ..., dn>$, with $di \in Di$ for all $i \leq n$.

For the ICEBERG project the domain of courses has been chosen. The contextual universe of courses has been modelled using two dimensions: the background and the theme dimension, see Figure 1. The background dimension describes the reason the intended participant is interested in the course, and the theme dimension describes the theme of the course irrespective of the background of the intended participants. For the prototype a restriction was made to those courses that have something to do with communication, i.e., the first column of Figure 1.

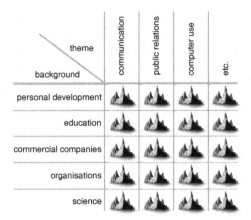

Fig. 1. Dimensions of Context

Each cell (iceberg) in the matrix corresponds to a context. In general a contextual dimension is a set of concepts with which the domain of application can be categorised.

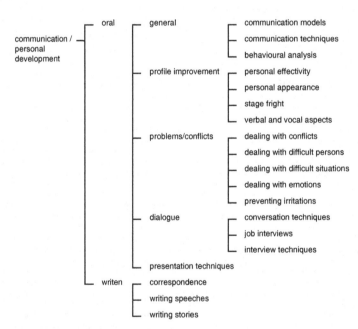

Fig. 2. Personal development x Communication

For example, by defining the theme dimension as the set {communication, public relations, computer use, others}, the domain of all courses can be categorised: each course can be associated to one or more themes. The topics in a context are also structured in some kind of semantic network, e.g., a taxonomy like that in Figure 2, for the context identified by <personal development, communication>. Of course also other techniques could be used to structure the concepts in each context, and the use of an additional dimension can reduce the size of the structures per concept.

Note that topics are not unique, they can occur in several contexts, and even a partial semantic network can occur in several contexts. For example, the topic presentation techniques occurs in the context <personal development, communication>, but also in all the other contexts underneath the column communication. Determination of the proper background is essential for finding the most appropriate courses on the theme communication. For example, a person might think he needs to follow a course on giving presentations, but in order to help him adequately, he might need help to realise that what he needs is a course on how to overcome stagefright.

3.   The ICEBERG Broker Agent from a Global Perspective

The system developed is a multi-agent system, in which a broker agent, called the ICEBERG broker plays a central role. The ICEBERG broker mediates between information providers and users. The information providers have access to databases containing information on all available courses of the institute represented by the information provider. The ICEBERG broker agent that plays the central role in the system has been designed by reusing the generic broker agent model as presented in (Jonker, and Treur, 1998). The complete system has been modelled using DESIRE (see e.g., Jonker et al., 1998), the rules presented in the next sessions are part of the knowledge sources within the system, which executes them using chaining as the inference relation. The system has been tested with the software environment of DESIRE, which is based on Prolog.

There are three major phases in dealing with a user request: query (re)formulation, information resource discovery, and response construction.

If a new request from the user has been received by the broker, the broker first helps the user to (re)formulate the request: a precise answer needs a precise query. Given a "good" query the broker can solicit information form the appropriate providers (information resource discovery). If the ICEBERG broker received information on courses that might satisfy a user request, then it presents the most precise answers to the user. The broker also constructs additional propositions to the user, which may help the user to reformulate his request again (this is part of the response construction phase). The ICEBERG broker can thus be used in an iterative way.

4.   Query Reformulation

Before the broker knows what to ask of the information providers, the broker first needs to analyse the question of the user. Most of the information in the user's request is straightforward, e.g., in our opinion, the user knows quite well how much money he is willing to spend, how much time he is willing to invest, where (in which region, or city) he wants to follow the course. Therefore, most information can be used directly by the information providers to return courses that more or less fall into the required categories. The one piece of information that most often is the most problematic is the information about the course topic(s).

Self-evidently, the user is not yet an expert in the field he wants to follow a course about, therefore, he might not know the perfect topics that would result in the right course offers. Furthermore, a user might be interested in courses that cover a topic in a certain context. For example, a course on Java in the context of programming languages, is quite different from a course on Java in the context of studying various cultures, or following a course on presentations in the context of presenting business proposals does not help in the most ideal manner if you need the course to help you teach a group of students.

The broker analyses the topics of the course being searched. By making use of the domain-specific information, the broker is capable of determining the different contexts to which the course topic(s) can belong. The process consists of two parts:
1.   request analysis
2.   reformulation of user requests

4.1   Request Analysis

The request analysis is done in two stages: initialisation and determination of the set of contexts.

Initialisation

In the initialisation part of the first phase the first topic is taken from the user request and the contexts that contain that topic are identified as interesting contexts. Within the broker this knowledge is expressed declaratively as follows:

```
    if              course_searched(partial_topic(T: TOPIC, 1), R: REQUEST_ID)
        and     occurs_in_context(T: TOPIC, C: CONTEXT)
    then    interesting_context_for(CONTEXT, R: REQUEST_ID)
```

For example, the user entered the topic "presentation" which occurs in the context <communication, personal development>, but also some other contexts like <communication, science>.

If the user request contains 1 topic or if the set of interesting contexts is empty at the end of the initialisation, then the process continues with reformulation of the user requests. If the set is not empty, the complete set of contexts is determined.

Determination of the Set of Contexts

The set of contexts defined in the initialisation as interesting contexts are used as the basic set of contexts, from which the overall set of interesting contexts is determined iteratively. For each of the subsequent topics in the user request the set of interesting contexts is adapted. Each additional topic possibly reduces the set of interesting contexts. If the topic is not covered by one the contexts, this context is removed from the set of interesting contexts. The process continues until all topics in the user request have been analysed, or until the set of interesting contexts is empty. Consider the following definitions:

SAC   is the set of all contexts in the multi-dimensional structure.
S   is the set of interesting contexts produced in phase 1a
t_j is the j'th topic mentioned in the user request
n   is the total number of topics in the user request
$SC(t_j)$ = { C ∈ SAC | t_j occurs in C }

Formalised, the process is specified as follows:

j = 2;
Repeat
      PS := S;
      S := S ∩ SC(t_j) ;
      j := j + 1;
Until j = n or S = ∅;

Note that if the set S became empty in the above procedure, then PS is the last not empty set produced in this process. If, for example, the user entered also the topic "personal effectivity", then the set S will only contain the context <communication, personal development> after phase 1b, since this topic cannot be combined with presentations in the other contexts still available after phase 1a.

4.2   Reformulation of User Requests

The main goal of this process is to determine whether or not adaptations to the user question must be created (and which adaptations if so) and what the expected accuracy of the results for that user request is and to adapt the user request if necessary. The reformulation process operates according to three cases: S is empty after initialisation of the query analysis, S is empty after query analysis, or S contains more than 1 element. The set S would for example become empty if the user entered "presentations" as a first topic, and then "airplane", since the topic airplane is not contained in the contexts that are related to "presentations". In the prototype, the topic "airplane" is not supported at all, because there are no courses on airplanes within the theme communication. So, if airplane had been the first topic, then S would have been empty after the initialisation of the query analysis.

Case 1
If the set S of interesting contexts is empty after the initialisation of the query analysis, then the broker initiates an interaction with the user. The broker explains that it did not recognise the topics presented by the user (the expected accuracy of the search results is then 0) and offers him the choice:
• search for it anyway.
• adapt his request; for this the broker immediately provides the different contextual dimensions from which the user can choose. After a context has been selected by

the user, the broker presents the topics in that context, enabling the user to focus his request. Of course, the user can retract his steps and choose a different context.

Case 2

Suppose that during query analysis, the set S of interesting contexts became empty. The expected accuracy of the search results for the request as formulated by the user is the fraction of recognised topics with respect to the total number of topics in the user request:

Definition

Let PS be the last not empty set of interesting contexts identified in phase 1. A topic t is recognised iff there is a context $C \in PS$, such that t occurs in C. Let NRT be the number of recognised topics in request RID, let TNT be the total number of topics in request RID. The expected accuracy (EA) of the search results for RID is defined by

$$EA(RID) = NRT(RID) / TNT(RID)$$

Given that the set of interesting contexts became empty in phase 1b, this fraction will be less than 1. Therefore, it is to be recommended that the user adapts his request. The proposed adaptations are based on the set PS, i.e., the last set of interesting contexts found in phase 1 before this set became empty. The contexts in PS cover the first topics in the user request and thereby determine possible contexts of the user interests. The broker presents his analysis to the user (the set of contexts based on the first topics, the conflicting topic that is not covered by those contexts, and the expected accuracy of the search results if the request remains as it is) and offers him the choice:

- search for it anyway, then the information providers have to receive the current user request.
- adapt his request. The user can choose one or more alternative topics from the contexts of the set PS. If necessary, the broker can also help him to reformulate his request more drastically, see the case that the set S is empty after the initialisation of the query analysis.

Case 3

Suppose that after query analysis, the set S of interesting contexts still contains more than one element. The request is now a bit ambiguous. The broker presents the user with the contexts in S and asks the user whether he wants to focus his request to one (or a few) of those contexts. The user is free to stick to the whole set S, but is cautioned that the search will then probably give too many results and that it will be hard to pick out the useful ones.

5   Information Resource Discovery

In the previous phase the broker has analysed the request of the user and on the basis of that analysis has formulated one or more questions to be posed to the information providers. In the second phase the broker determines which information provider is best suited to answer which question. The broker maintains profiles of the information providers. This profile contains the contexts for which the information providers has offered courses in the past.

Each question is matched to the profile of the different information providers. The match is made by checking the following items in the question against the corresponding information in the profile of the information providers:

- topics
- region
- price
- level (beginner, .., expert)
- language
- duration
- dates of the meetings

The user is not obliged to fill in all these items, but the items he did fill in are checked. If the match is favourable, the question is sent to that information provider.

6. Response Construction

The broker has the task of composing an appropriate report of the search results and of creating suggestions to the user with which the user can adapt his request if necessary. For this, the component needs information about the (reformulated) request from the user, and, of course, the search results as reported by the different information providers.

The broker has to match each found course against the user request, collect those courses that have a sufficiently high match, propose these best courses to the user, but also create other search possibilities that may help the user to improve his requests. If no courses have been found that match the request sufficiently, a failure report is constructed for the user, and also other search possibilities are formed and presented to the user. Matching is discussed a lot in literature, and nothing special needs to be said about the ICEBERG broker on this count.

After the acceptable results of the search are ordered and the best n selected, the end report of the search is constructed and presented to the user. For this the broker has to determine the overall successfulness of the search.

If the search did not fail, then the search will be reported to have been successful and other search possibilities are offered by presenting topics to the user that come from the same context as the topics requested by the user. These topics can focus the mind of the user on either more specific topics, or on topics with a slightly different focus (topics of the same specificity, for example, siblings in the taxonomy, if a taxonomy is used to model the contents of a context).

If no courses are found that could be of interest to the user, then the search is labelled to be failed and the user is to be helped formulating a more successful query. If the search failed and furthermore, the broker had made this prediction before the search was initiated, then the broker can explain to the user that according to the domain knowledge of courses available to the broker it was highly unlikely that the topics provided by the user would be the topics of an existing course, and that in this case the search did indeed fail. The broker then continues with a list of other search possibilities with the aim to make the user aware of the context of each topic in his request. If a topic occurring in a context is related to other topics in that context (some more specific, some more general), then presenting these related topics as possible search topics to the user, gives the user insight in the context determined by his request, and he can use this knowledge to adjust his request.

7.   Other Work

We compared the IceBerg approach with some approaches in the field of Information Retrieval and Multi-Databases. We will first cover the literature on Information Retrieval systems.

It turns out that there are several differences but also some similarities. The difference are that IR (Information Retrieval) usually operates on generic domains and are not domain specific like IceBerg (Rijsbergen, 1979, Bodner et al., 1996).Furthermore IR systems employ a different search strategy. IR systems only search up and down in the search tree. IceBerg also searches between the siblings in the search tree. Another difference is that most IR systems automatically generate the ontologies with automated methods, like LSI (Deerwester et al., 1990) and WAIS (Kahle et al., 1991). IceBerg in contrast uses a human constructed ontology. Both IR systems and IceBerg use user feedback to facilitate query expansion. IR systems often use relevance feedback (Harman, 1992) to enhance the retrieval this contrary to IceBerg which uses direct ontology information to reformulate the query.

Like with the IR systems there are also differences and similarities between IceBerg and Multi-Databases. We will first point out the differences. Multi-Databases presume that the user knows or has domain ontologies available. Also as with IR systems Multi-Databases only employ a search strategy in the semantic network that searches up and down the network but not sideways. For Multi-Database access, the OBSERVER system (Mena et al., 1999), the user first selects the appropriate ontology (assumed to be known or available), and then a GUI is used to formulate the exact query (which is then assumed to represent exactly what the user needs). The IceBerg broker does not assume that the user knows the ontology, but assumes that the initial query contains enough information to find the relevant parts of the ontology. Then the IceBerg broker uses the different contexts related to that part of the ontology to help the user formulate a request corresponding to his needs. In the work of Kashyap and Sheth (e.g., Kashyap et al., 1995, Mena et al., 1999), the query has its own context which determines the semantics of the query and which is used directly to match with possible contexts of the different databases. In IceBerg, the interactive query formulation leeds to a query with a unique context as well. Although the role of a context in multi-databases is not exactly the same as that in IceBerg enough similarities exist to allow for a coupling of the multi-database techniques to IceBerg. The relationships between contexts in IceBerg can be compared to the semantic interontology relationships presented in (Mena et al., 1999).

Next to the comparison with work on Information Retrieval, Query Expansion, and Multi-Databases in general, the IceBerg broker is also compared to some of the recently developed and operational models of virtual market places, information brokering on the Web, and Web commerce based applications. For a good overview of recent developments in intelligent information agents see (Klusch, 1999).

The broker for environmental regulations (Stasiak, Garrett, and Fenves, 1999) aims at finding the right regulation from the user request by searching the regulation agency in its own database. It searches on topics mentioned in the user request. The broker presents the regulations found and the user selects one of them. The broker queries the database of the regulation agency with the selected regulation to search for more details. The information found is send back to the user. The topics used by the broker to search its database are defined by the classification on author based on the document specific classifications. Automatically generated classifications have to be made if the system is to be used commercially.

Kasbah (cf. (Chavez, and Maes, 1996), (Chavez, Dreilinger, Gutman, and Maes, 1997)) is a web-based multi-agent system using agents interacting with each other within the virtual market domain. The agents act on behalf of their users (CHAVEZ, AND MAES, 1996). Price Negotiation is one of the interesting features applied within Kasbah (Chavez, Dreilinger, Gutman, and Maes, 1997).

Market Space is an open agent-based market infrastructure. It is based on a decentralised infrastructure model in which both the humans and the machines can read information about the products and services, and everyone is able to announce interests to one another (Erikson and Finn, 1997). The aim in designing Market Space is to design a market place where searching, negotiation and deal settlement, e.g. interaction with users is done using agents.

The MeBroker (Doles, Dreger, Großjohann, Lohrum, and Menke, 1999) is an Information Broker project of the Freie Universität Berlin. The architecture of the system is resembles the one of ICEBERG. The difference is that the emphasis of MeBroker lies in the selection of the information provider. It uses meta-data on the information providers to make the best choice.

The Search Broker (Manber, and Bigot, 1999) performs its search in two stages. First the request is analysed to extract the topic from the request. The broker searches which server is the best to answer the request. The request is then passed to that server to hopefully find the right answer. New in this approach (in contrast to e.g. Yahoo) is that this happens in one regular search request. The index of the servers and topics is made by hand because the mapping is then more accurate.

Most brokers found on the Internet focus on the selection of the right information provider based on the given user request with an exception to a certain extent of the broker for environmental regulations. In contrast, the ICEBERG broker agent focuses on aiding the user in formulating the right request in an interactive process. The ICEBERG broker not only helps to sharpen the focus of the request, it also helps in disambiguation of the queries, widening the scope of the user request, and in other reformulations.

An additional difference with our approach is that these approaches have been implemented without using a principled design method, and do not use components as building blocks that are (formally) specified at a conceptual level. This is also a difference with the work described in (Martin, Moran, Oohama, and Cheyer, 1997), and (Tsvetovatyy, and Gini, 1996).

In this paper a multi-dimensional notion of context is defined to serve as necessary background knowledge for the broker. The multi-dimensional structure of contexts is used twice by the ICEBERG broker: for reformulation of the user request, and for evaluation of search results.

The clear structure in dimensions provided by the broker makes it easy for the user to find the best matching context for his request. Furthermore, each context is further elaborated by a semantical structure containing the topics relevant for that context. The ICEBERG broker exploits this structure to help the user find the best topics for his request. The broker does not only presents a relevant part of the multi-dimensional contexts if the user formulated an ambiguous request, but also if the user issued a request that points to a unique context. By presenting the relevant contexts to the user in all cases the broker ensures that the user and broker share the domain model. A shared domain model enables the broker to find the information that the user qualifies as good.

The multi-dimensional structure of contexts is also used to evaluate the search results delivered by the information providers. Given that the broker agent ensured a shared domain model of the context relevant for the user by exploiting the multi-dimensional structure of contexts, using that same structure to evaluate the results ensures that evaluation made by the broker matches to high degree the evaluation of the results by the user, and can be offered to the user within (and with indication of) the right context.

Further research can be done in automatically building and / or maintaining a multi-dimension structure of

Acknowledgements

This project was conducted for KPN Research. We like to thank Clair Moore, Ron van Riet, Louis Wennekes and Bertjan Teunissen from KPN Research from the project team for their input during the project and Jan Treur for his comments on this paper. We also like to thank the anonymous reviewers for pointing out a wealth of literature that we were unaware of. We learnt a lot.

References

Bodner, R., and Song, F. (1996), Knowledge-based approaches to query expansion in information retrieval. In McCalla, G. (Ed.), Advances in Artificial Intelligence (pp. 146-150), New York: Springer.

Boles, D, Dreger, M, Großjohann, K, Lohrum, S, and Menke, D, (1999), MeDoc Architektur und Funktionalität des MeDoc-Dienstes, Frei Universität Berlin.

Chavez, A., and Maes, P., (1996), Kasbah: An Agent Marketplace for Buying and Selling goods. In: *Proceedings of the First International Conference on the Practical Application of Intelligent Agents and Multi-Agent Technology, PAAM'96*, The Practical Application Company Ltd, Blackpool, pp. 75-90.

Chavez, A., Dreilinger, D., Gutman, R., and Maes, P., (1997), A Real-Life Experiment in Creating an Agent Market Place. In: *Proceedings of the Second International Conference on the Practical Application of Intelligent Agents and Multi-Agent Technology, PAAM'97*, The Practical Application Company Ltd, Blackpool, pp. 159-178.

Deerwester, S., Dumais, S.T., Furrnas, G.W., Landauer, T.K., and Hashman, R, (1990), Indexing by Latent Semantic Indexing. In: Journal of the American Society for Information Science, 41(6).

Erikson, J. and Finn, N., (1997), Market Space: an open agent-based market infrastructure. Master's Thesis, Computer Science Department, Uppsala University, Sweden.

Gruber, T., (1993), What is an Ontology? Knowledge Systems Laboratory, Computer Systems Dept., Stanford University, Stanford, CA94305, USA.

Gruber, T., (1997), Toward principles for the design of ontologies used for knowledge sharing. In: *Formal Ontology in Conceptual Analysis and Knowledge Representation*, N. Guarino and R. Poli, editors, Kluwer Academic Publishers.

Harman, D. (1992), Relevant Feedback Revisited, In: Proceedings of the 15th Annual International ACM-SIGIR Conference on Research and Development in Information Retrieval, Copenhagen, pp. 1-10.

Jonker, C. M., and Treur, J., (1998), Compositional Design and Maintenance of Broker Agents. In: J. Cuena (ed.), *Proceedings of the 15th IFIP World Computer Congress, WCC'98, Conference on Information Technology and Knowledge Systems, IT&KNOWS'98*, pp. 319-332.

Kahle, B, and Medlar, A., (1991), An Information System for Corporate Users: Wide Area Information Servers. In: Connexions - The Interoperability Report, 5(11).

Kashyap, V., and Sheth, A. (1995), Schematic and Semantic Similarities between Database Objects: A Context based Approach, Technical Report TR-CS-95-001, LSDIS Lab, Department of Computer Science, University of Georgia.

Klusch, M., (Ed.), (1999), Intelligent Information Agents Agent-Based Information Discovery and Management on the Internet. Springer-Verlag Berlin/Heidelberg. 498 pp.

Manber, U., and Bigot, P. A., (1999), The Search Broker, Department of Computer Science, University of Arizona.

Manglano, V., Beaulieu, M., and Robertson, S., (1998), Evaluation of Interfaces for IRS: modelling end-user searching behaviour. In: 20th Collogquium on Information Retrieval, Grenble, http://www.weic.org.uk/.

Martin, D., Moran, D., Oohama, H., and Cheyer, A., (1997), Information Brokering in an Agent Architecture. In: *Proceedings of the Second International Conference on the Practical Application of Intelligent Agents and Multi-Agent Technology, PAAM'97*, The Practical Application Company Ltd, Blackpool, pp. 467-486.

Magennis, M. (1995), Expert rule-based query expansion, Presented at the British Computer Society Information Retrieval Specialist Interest Group Colloquium. Crewe, England. April 1995.

Mena, E., Illarramendi, A., Kashyap, V., and Sheth, A. (1999), OBSERVER: An Approach for Query Processing in Global Information Systems based on Interoperation across Pre-existing Ontologies, Distributed and Parallel Databases Journal.

Rijsbergen, C.J. van, (1979), Information Retrieval, second edition, London: Butterworths.

Stasiak, D., Garrett, J., Jr., and Fenves, S., (1999), A Broker for Environmental Regulations, Carnegie Mellon University.

Tsvetovatyy, M., and Gini, M., (1996), Toward a Virtual Marketplace: Architectures and Strategies. In: Proceedings of the First International Conference on the Practical Application of Intelligent Agents and Multi-Agent Technology, PAAM'96, The Practical Application Company Ltd, Blackpool, pp. 597-613.

A Dynamic Access Planning Method for Information Mediator*

Yasuhiko Kitamura, Tomoya Noda, and Shoji Tatsumi

Department of Information and Communication Engineering
Faculty of Engineering, Osaka City University
3-3-138 Sugimoto, Sumiyoshi-ku, Osaka 558-8585, Japan
{kitamura, tnoda, tatsumi}@kdel.info.eng.osaka-cu.ac.jp
http://www.kdel.info.eng.osaka-cu.ac.jp/~kitamura/

Abstract. The Internet is spreading into our society rapidly and deeply and is becoming one of our social infrastructures. Especially, WWW technologies are widely used for doing business and research, creating communities, disseminating personal information, and so on. We usually access WWW pages one by one through a browser, but we can add more value to them by integrating information collected from various WWW sites. However, to realize such WWW information integration, we face obstacles such as distributed information sources, access cost, and frequently and asynchronous updates of information. We here adopt mediator, which integrates information from distributed information sources, with cache mechanism to reduce access cost. We also propose a dynamic access planning method to cope with frequently updating information sources. In a limited time period, it can construct an appropriate answer by accessing information sources effectively considering reliability and quality of cached data. We show its performance through a real-world flight information service comparing with a conventional access strategy.

1 Introduction

The Internet is spreading into our society rapidly and deeply and is becoming one of our social infrastructures which are indispensable for our daily life. Especially, WWW technologies are widely used for doing business such as electronic commerce, doing research, creating special interest communities, disseminating personal information, and so on. We usually use the WWW by accessing WWW pages one by one through a browser, but we can add more value to it by integrating information collected from various WWW sites. Of course, we can make a link page or a portal site where related WWW pages are hyperlinked. Search engine is another elaborated approach for information integration, which dynamically generates a list of WWW pages for specified keywords. However, these approaches provide only a link set of related WWW pages and leave users collecting the pages, extracting data from them, and integrating the data to

---

* This work is partly supported by NTT Communication Science Laboratories.

M. Klusch and L. Kerschberg (Eds.): CIA 2000, LNAI 1860, pp. 39-50, 2000.

obtain desired information. To reduce this bothering work, WWW information integration [7] aims at providing a way to collect, extract, and integrate information from various WWW sites flexibly and automatically.

A typical example of WWW information integration is flight information service. In Japan, each of major airline companies provides a flight information service which we can consult about flight schedule and availability through the WWW. To our data input about departing date, origin, and destination, it returns a list of flight number, schedule, and availability. However, in case several airline companies operate on common routes, we need to access each of the WWW sites respectively to find connecting flights over different airline companies. WWW information integration service can provide a comprehensive and unified view of flight information over multiple information sites by collecting and integrating the information on behalf of users.

However, we have three major issues to tackle for achieving WWW information integration as follows.

(1) **Distributed Autonomous Information Sources:** WWW information sources are distributed on the Internet and maintained individually. Hence, we need to collect related information from distributed information sources.
(2) **Access Cost:** It takes time and cost to access information sources through the Internet. Moreover, WWW information integration often needs to collect a large amount of data, so it takes much time and cost.
(3) **Frequently and Asynchronous Updates:** Some information sources are frequently and asynchronously updated. The timing of update depends on the source, so we cannot know when it is updated until we actually access it.

To cope with (1), we adopt mediator [15] which integrates distributed information as shown in Fig. 1. When a mediator receives a query from a user, it accesses multiple WWW sites to collect WWW pages. It then extracts data from the collected pages to construct an answer to the user's query. To cope with (2), we can cache collected data from WWW sites, so we can improve the response time to users because we can reduce the number of accessing WWW sites.

However, as shown in (3), WWW sites are frequently updated, so cached data may well be obsolete shortly and may lead to construct an incorrect answer. On the other hand, if we do not use a cache mechanism, we need to take a long time to collect a large amount of data. Hence, how to collect data properly in a limited time from frequently updated WWW sites becomes an important research issue. In this paper, we propose a dynamic access planning method for information mediator which collects and caches data to construct an answer to user's query. It makes an access plan dynamically considering reliability and quality of cached data to construct a proper answer in a limited time.

In Section 2, we propose a dynamic access planning method, and show its performance by applying it to a real-world flight information service in Section 3. We discuss related work in Section 4 and conclude our discussion in Section 5.

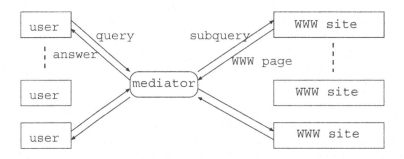

Fig. 1. Information integration through a mediator.

2   Dynamic Access Planning for Information Mediator

We use a mediator to integrate information from multiple WWW sites. When a mediator receives a query from a user, it collects pages from multiple WWW sites, extracts and integrates required data from them to construct an answer. To reduce the number of access, it can cache the collected data. However, many WWW sites are often frequently updated, so it needs to reload WWW pages to update cached data. On the other hand, the mediator is obliged to return an answer to the user within an allowable time period, so it needs to select pages to reload because it may take a long time, which may be intolerable for the user, to update the whole cache. However, partially updated cached data may lead to construct an incorrect answer. Hence, how to select pages to reload is an important issue to construct an appropriate answer in a limited time. We here propose a dynamic access planning method which considers reliability and quality of cached data. Within an allowable time period, this method repeats to select and reload WWW pages to update the cached data, then construct an answer.

At first, we define several terms such as facts, solutions, reliability, and quality, used in this paper.

2.1   Facts

A mediator collects WWW pages and extracts data from them. We call an atomic piece of extracted data *fact*. A number of facts can be extracted from a single WWW page. In a flight information service with flights like Fig. 2 for example, flight schedule and availability can be extracted from WWW sites of airline companies as facts as shown in Fig 3. In this example, flight(JAL124,Sapporo,Itami, 0800,0900) means that JAL124 departs from Sapporo at 8AM and arrives at Itami at 9AM, and availability(JAL124,1999/12/16,Yes) means that JAL124 is available on December 16th, 1999. Facts are stored in mediator's cache once they are collected.

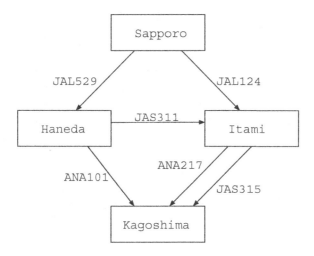

Fig. 2. Flight connection.

2.2   Reliability of Facts

Because some WWW sites are frequently updated, the difference between cached data and original data becomes large as time goes by. We define the *reliability* of a fact f as a function $r(f)$ which takes a real value between 0 and 1. The reliability function returns largest (1) when the fact is just loaded and monotonically decreases until 0 as time elapses.

The frequency of updates, or the shape of the reliability function, depends on the fact and the WWW site. For example, flight availability is frequently updated, so its reliability decreases soon. On the other hand, flight schedule is moderately updated once a month or so, so the reliability decreases slowly.

Though the shape of reliability function may differ depending on the type of fact, approximately we can use the following function,

$$r(f) = \frac{1}{1 + wt}$$

where w is a weight which depends on the type of fact and t is the elapsed time since f is updated. When w is large, the reliability decreases rapidly, and when w is small, it decreases slowly.

In this paper, we classify facts into two classes; *dynamic facts* and *static facts*. Dynamic facts are ones which may be updated and static facts are ones which may not. Generally speaking, we seldom have static or unchangeable facts in the real world, but in a short time span we can view some facts as static. For example, in a flight information service, flight availability can be viewed as a dynamic fact because it may be updated hourly or so, but flight schedule can be viewed as a static fact because it is updated in a longer time interval, monthly or so, than availability. Once a static fact is loaded and cached, it does not need to be reloaded.

Fact	Reliability
flight(JAL124,Sapporo,Itami,0800,0900)	1
flight(JAL529,Sapporo,Haneda,0700,0800)	1
flight(ANA217,Itami,Kagoshima,1000,1200)	1
flight(JAS315,Itami,Kagoshima,1300,1500)	1
flight(JAS311,Haneda,Itami,0830,0930)	1
flight(ANA101,Narita,Kagoshima,0930,1100)	1
availability(JAL124,1999/12/16,Yes)	0.90
availability(ANA217,1999/12/16,Yes)	0.60
availability(JAS315,1999/12/16,No)	0.30
availability(JAL529,1999/12/16,Yes)	0.70
availability(JAS311,1999/12/16,Yes)	1.00
availability(ANA101,1999/12/16,No)	0.60

Fig. 3. Facts for flight information service.

2.3 Answer

When a mediator receives a query from a user, it constructs an *answer* by using cached facts. How to construct an answer can be represented by Prolog-like rules as follows.

$(R1)$ query($A, $B) : $-$fact($A, $B).

$(R2)$ query($A, $B) : $-$fact($A, $C), query($C, $B).

$fact($A,$B) represents a cached fact and $A and $B are variables. By using (R1), we can construct an answer directly from a single fact, and by using both of (R1) and (R2), we can construct an answer from multiple facts. Hence, an answer can be viewed as a set of facts.

For example, some rules for flight information service are given as follows.

$(R3)$ query($P1, $P2, $Date, $T1, $T2) : $-$
    $flight($Number, $P1, $P2, $Dep, $Arr),
    $availability($Number, $Date, $Status),
    $Dep $>=$ $T1,
    $T2 $>=$ $Arr.

$(R4)$ query($P1, $P2, $Date, $T1, $T2) : $-$
    $flight($Number, $P1, $P3, $Dep, $Arr),
    $availability($Number, $Date, $Status),
    $Dep $>=$ $T1,
    $T2 $>=$ $Arr,
    query($P3, $P2, $Date, $Arr, $T2).

(R3) represents a query to find a direct flight on date $Date, which departs from airport $P1 after time $T1 and which arrives at airport $P2 by time $T2. (R4) represents a query to find connecting flights through airport $P3.

For example, when a query query(Sapporo,Kagoshima, 1999/12/16,0600,1600) to find a route from Sapporo to Kagoshima is given, an answer can be constructed as a set of facts from cached facts in Fig. 3 as follows.

> flight(JAL124,Sapporo,Itami,0800,0900)
>
> availability(JAL124,1999/12/16,Yes)
>
> flight(ANA217,Itami,Kagoshima,1000,1200)
>
> availability(ANA217,1999/12/16,Yes)

The complete set of answers to the above query is shown in Fig. 4.

Answer	Facts
A_1	flight(JAL124,Sapporo,Itami,0800,0900), seat(JAL124,1999/12/16,Yes), flight(ANA217,Itami,Kagoshima,1000,1200), seat(ANA217,1999/12/16,Yes).
A_2	flight(JAL124,Sapporo,Itami,0800,0900), seat(JAL124,1999/12/16,Yes), flight(JAS315,Itami,Kagoshima,1300,1500), seat(JAS315,1999/12/16,No).
A_3	flight(JAS529,Sapporo,Haneda,0700,0800), seat(JAS529,1999/12/16,Yes), flight(JAS311,Haneda,Itami,0830,0930), seat(JAS311,1999/12/16,No), flight(ANA217,Itami,Kagoshima,1000,1200), seat(ANA217,1999/12/16,Yes).
A_4	flight(JAS529,Sapporo,Haneda,0700,0800), seat(JAS529,1999/12/16,Yes), flight(JAS311,Haneda,Itami,0830,0930), seat(JAS311,1999/12/16,No), flight(JAS315,Itami,Kagoshima,1300,1500), seat(JAS315,1999/12/16,No).
A_5	flight(JAS529,Sapporo,Haneda,0700,0800), seat(JAS529,1999/12/16,Yes), flight(ANA101,Narita,Kagoshima,0930,1100), seat(ANA101,1999/12/16,Yes).

Fig. 4. A complete set of answers to query query(Sapporo,Kagoshima, 1999/12/16,0000,2359)

2.4   Quality of Answer

Quality of answer represents how an answer satisfies user's requirement and is used for selecting facts to reload and for ranking answers. Quality of answer is calculated from quality of facts which compose the answer. We can divide quality of answer into *dynamic quality* and *static quality*. The dynamic quality concerns only dynamic facts and the static quality concerns only static facts.

How to calculate dynamic or static quality of answer depends on the service which the mediator provides. For example, in a flight information service, we can calculate quality of answer from flight schedule and availability. If an answer provides flights with which the traveling time is as short as possible and which are available, then its quality is high. In this example, the static quality concerns flight schedule, so we can define static quality of answer A as

$$Q_S(A) = \begin{cases} 1 - \dfrac{t_a - t_d}{24} & 0 \leq t_a - t_d \leq 24, \\ 0 & \text{otherwise,} \end{cases}$$

where t_a is the desired arrival time and t_d is the departure time of the first flight. We assume the quality function returns a real value between 0 (worst) and 1 (best). The dynamic quality concerns flight availability, so we can define it as

$$Q_D(A) = \begin{cases} 1 & \text{if every flight is available,} \\ 0 & \text{otherwise.} \end{cases}$$

For example, as shown in Fig. 4, there are five alternatives from Sapporo to Kagoshima and their arrivals are at 11:00, 12:00, or 15:00. If a user wants to arrive there by 16:00, the static quality of A_1 is

$$Q_S(A_1) = 1 - \frac{16 - 8}{24} = 0.67.$$

The dynamic quality of A_1 is 1 because both of JAL124 and ANA217 are available. The static quality of A_2 is identical with that of A_1 but its dynamic quality is 0 because JAS315 is not available.

We here define the total quality of answer by multiplying static quality and dynamic quality as

$$Q(A) = Q_S(A) \cdot Q_D(A).$$

2.5   Reliability of Answer

An answer is composed of one or more facts. We can define *reliability of answer* from reliability of composed facts. We here define reliability of answer to be the minimum reliability among composed facts as

$$R(A) = \min_{f \in A} r(f).$$

For example, the reliability of answer A_1 is

$$R(A_1) = \min\{1, 0.90, 1, 0.60\} = 0.60.$$

2.6   Dynamic Access Planning Algorithm

A mediator constructs an answer from cached facts, but the reliability of answer decreases as the reliability of composed facts decreases. To increase the reliability of answer, we need to update the facts by reloading WWW pages, but should finish it within an allowable time period which is tolerable for the user. Hence,

---

1: construct answers $\{A_1, A_2, \cdots\}$ to a user's query by using cached facts
2: repeat until query time expires {
3:     select A_i where $S(A_i) = \max\{S(A_1), S(A_2), \cdots\}$
4:     select f_m where $r(f_m) = \min_{f_n \in A_i} r(f_n)$
5:     reload a WWW page and update f_m }
6: sort answers by $P(\cdot)$
7: return the best answer to the user

Fig. 5. Dynamic access planning algorithm.

for obtaining a good answer in a limited time, it is important how to select facts to update. Here we define two scores $S(A)$ and $P(A)$ for an answer A. $S(A)$ is used to select facts to update and $P(A)$ is used to rank the answers. We show our dynamic access planning algorithm in Fig. 5.

When a mediator receives a query from a user, it constructs answers by using rules and cached facts (Line 1).[1] Then, it repeats to update facts within an allowable time period (Lines 2 to 5). In the loop, it selects a fact to update (Line 3). At first, it calculates $S(A_i)$ for each A_i as

$$S(A_i) = Q_S(A_i) \times (1 - R(A_i)).$$

It selects an answer with high static quality and low reliability because it may well lead to a good answer with high reliability if it is updated. We need not consider answers with low quality because it does not lead to a good answer even if they are updated nor ones with high reliability because we need not update them. We here consider only static quality because dynamic quality is unknown until the fact is updated. It then selects a fact with the lowest reliability from the selected answer (Line 4). Finally, the mediator reloads a page from a WWW site to update the fact (Line 5).

When the updating time expires, the mediator ranks answers by $P(A_i)$ to show the best one to the user. $P(A_i)$ is defined as

$$P(A_i) = Q(A_i) \times R(A_i)$$

which reflects quality and reliability of answers (Lines 6 and 7).

Here we show an example of how facts are selected to be updated by using Table 1. At first, answer A_2 is selected because its S score is best among 5 candidates. A_2 has an unavailable flight JAS315 at this moment (Fig. 4), but the fact may have been updated because the reliability is low (0.30) as shown in Fig. 3. Hence, fact `availability(JAS315,1999/12/16,No)` is selected to be updated. Let us assume it becomes `availability(JAS315,1999/12/16,Yes)` with its reliability of 1. Then, answers A_2 and A_4 are updated because they include the above fact. Now, the best S score is with A_1, so A_1 is selected and

---

[1] We assume that all the facts have been cached, the reliability of static facts and that of dynamic facts are initially set to be 1 and 0 respectively.

a fact `availability(ANA217,1999/12/16,Yes)` is updated. Now let us assume that it is updated to be unavailable, then Q values of A_1 and A_3 become 0. If the time for updating expires, A_2 is shown to the user as the best answer because it has the best P. Like above, until the time expires, facts to update are selected dynamically.

In this example, if only once of update is allowed, then answer A_2 with P score of 0.60 is selected for the query. If no update is allowed, A_1 with 0.40 is selected.

Table 1. Changes of function values according to the number of updates.

A_i	Q_s	No update				1st update				2nd update			
		Q	R	P	S	Q	R	P	S	Q	R	P	S
A_1	0.67	0.67	0.60	0.40	0.27	0.67	0.60	0.40	0.27	0.00	0.90	0.00	0.07
A_2	0.67	0.00	0.30	0.00	0.47	0.67	0.90	0.60	0.07	0.67	0.90	0.60	0.07
A_3	0.63	0.63	0.60	0.38	0.25	0.63	0.60	0.38	0.25	0.00	0.70	0.00	0.19
A_4	0.63	0.00	0.30	0.00	0.44	0.63	0.70	0.44	0.19	0.63	0.70	0.44	0.19
A_5	0.63	0.00	0.60	0.00	0.25	0.00	0.60	0.00	0.25	0.00	0.60	0.00	0.25

3 Evaluation Experiment

An excellent mediator can return an optimal answer in a short time, so we measure how much our Dynamic Access Planning (DAP) method generates an optimal answer within a fixed time period or a fixed number of updates in other words.

We compare the DAP method with the FIFO where it update a fact as the first-in first-out basis.[2] In other words, the FIFO method updates facts in order from the oldest one in the cache. FIFO is identical with DAP when

$$S(A) = 1 - R(A).$$

We performed an evaluation experiment by applying the methods to a flight information service which integrates data from airline WWW sites. We extracted facts about flight schedule and availability from three WWW sites which provide flight information run by JAL (Japan Air Line)[3], ANA (All Nippon Airways)[4], and JAS (Japan Air Systems)[5]. We regard flight schedule as static facts and

---

[2] The LRU (Least Recently Used) algorithm is another well known caching strategy, but it is not suitable for the comparison because it assumes static information sources.

[3] http://www.5971.jal.co.jp/cgi-bin/db2www/avail.d2w/report

[4] http://rps.ana.co.jp/drs/vacant1.cgi

[5] http://www.jas.co.jp/kusektop.htm

availability as dynamic facts, and we define quality and reliability of answer and
fact as in Section 2.

We submitted a query to the mediator every hour from December 18th, 1999
to December 28th, 1999.[6] Queries are created automatically and each of them is
to find flights on December 28th between two airports randomly chosen among
Sapporo, Haneda, Itami, Kansai, Fukuoka, and Naha. We limited the number of
connection to 1 to keep the size of problem small as we need to make it feasible
in the real-world setting. The ratio of obtaining an optimal answer is shown in
Fig. 6. The horizontal axis shows the number of updates, and the vertical axis
shows the ratio of obtaining an optimal answer. Both of methods improve its
performance as the number of updates increases. Roughly speaking, if the DAP
accesses WWW sites about 8 times for a query, it can construct an optimal
answer. On the other hand, the FIFO takes about 18 times. This is because
the DAP selects facts to update more carefully than the FIFO as it does not
consider only reliability of solution but also quality of that. In this experiment,
the size of problem is kept small to make it feasible in the real-world setting.
As we limited the number of transit to 1, so an answer can be constructed from
only 2 static facts and 2 dynamic facts. Moreover, an original flight information
service returns a set of facts to a single subquery, so it reduces the number of
WWW access. (In the ANA service, we could extracted 22 facts from a page to
a single subquery.) However, if we enlarge the size of problem, the superiority of
DAP method against the FIFO will become more remarkable.

4   Related Work

Research on information integration has been widely performed in the fields
of database and artificial intelligence [16, 7, 4, 10]. For example, the TSIMMIS
project at Stanford University database group aims at flexibly integrating various and heterogeneous information sources on the Internet [2]. In this project,
information sources are not integrated directly like a distributed databases, but
they are integrated through a *mediator* which receives queries from users, sends
subqueries to information sources, integrates answers, and sends back the final
answers to the users [15, 17]. In this paper, we also adopt mediator for WWW information integration. As an approach from AI, Stanford University logic group
proposes a *federated system* [6] where information agents and facilitators integrate information by using ACL (Agent Communication Language) [3].

Researchers on WWW information integration mainly discuss modeling information sources [11], information extraction [8] and gathering [5, 13, 9], information match-making [12] so far and they seldom assume information sources
which are frequently updated except work by Adali et al [1]. Adali and his colleagues propose query caching and optimization method in distributed mediator
systems. They discuss a query caching and optimization scheme which considers

---

[6] We submitted 264 (= 24×11) queries in total but the mediator succeeded to construct
some answer for 213 queries because of the original WWW sites' faults.

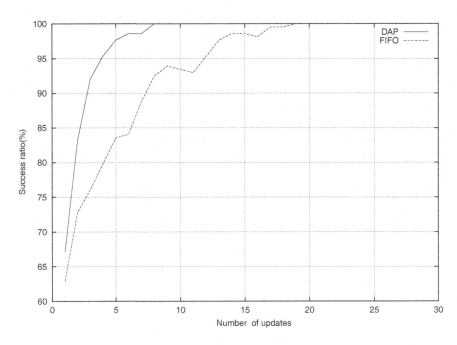

Fig. 6. Experimental result.

communication overhead, performance and faults of information sources, financial cost, and so on. In this paper, we discuss a dynamic access planning to obtain an appropriate answer in a limited time considering reliability and quality of answer but we do not have much interest in performance of information sources or communication channels. Work on view maintenance [18] tries to integrate information from multiple sources in a consistent manner, but we think keeping a large amount of information from distributed sources consistent raises communication overhead especially when information sources are frequently updated. In this paper, we take a semi-consistent approach by keeping cached information consistent as much as possible within an allowed amount of communication cost or time. Hence, our DAP algorithm has a characteristic of anytime algorithm [14] which returns some answer at anytime and which improves the quality as it takes more communication time.

5   Conclusion

We propose a dynamic access planning (DAP) method for mediators to integrate information from frequently updated WWW information sources. A mediator collects facts in a limited time properly and returns an appropriate answer to users. Our algorithm considers reliability and quality of answer to select facts to update. We show the superiority of the DAP method against conventional FIFO method by applying it to a real-world flight information service. In this paper, we applied our method to only flight information domain, but we need to study the applicability and the feasibility of our method in other application domains such as portfolio management where information is frequently updated.

References

1. Adali, S., Candan, K.S., Papakonstantinou, Y., and Subrahmanian, V.S.: Query Caching and Optimization in Distributed Mediator Systems, SIGMOD-96 (1996) 137–148
2. Chawathe, S., Garcia-Molina, H., Hammer, J., Ireland, K., Papakonstantinou, Y., Ullman, J. and Widom, J.: The TSIMMIS Project: Integration of Heterogeneous Information Sources. Proceedings of IPSJ Conference (1994) 7–18
3. Finin, T., Labrou, Y., and Mayfield J.: KQML as an Agent Communication Language. Bradshow, J.M. (ed.): Software Agents. AAAI Press (1997) 291–316
4. Florescu, D., Levy, A., and Mendelzon, A.: Database Techniques for the World-Wide Web: A Survey. SIGMOD Record, 27(3) (1998)
5. Friedman, M., Levy, A. and Millstein. T.: Navigational Plans for Data Integration. AAAI-99 (1999) 67–73
6. Genesereth, M.: An Agent-Based Framework for Interoperability. Bradshaw, J.M. (ed.): Software Agents. AAAI Press (1997) 315–345
7. Hearst, M.: Information Integration. IEEE Intelligent Systems 13(5) (1998) 12–24
8. Hsu, J.Y. and Yih, W.: Template-based Information Mining from HTML Documents. AAAI-97 (1997) 256–262
9. Kitamura, Y., Noda, T., and Tatsumi, S.: Single-agent and Multi-agent Approaches to WWW Information Integration. Ishida, T. (Ed.): Multiagent Platforms, Lecture Notes in Artificial Intelligence, Vol. 1599, Springer-Verlag. (1999) 133–147
10. Klusch, M. (Ed.): Intelligent Information Agents. Springer-Verlag (1999)
11. Knoblock, C.A., Minton, S., Ambite, J.L., Ashish, N., Modi, P.J., Muslea, I., Philpot, A.G., and Tejada, S.: Modeling Web Sources for Information Integration. AAAI-98 (1998) 211–218
12. Kuokka, D. and Harada, L.: Integrating Information via Matchmaking. Journal of Intelligent Information Systems 6 (1996) 261–279
13. Kwok, C.T. and Weld, D.S.: Planning to Gather Information. AAAI-96 (1996) 32–39
14. Russell, S.J. and Norvig, P.: Artificial Intelligence: A Modern Approach. Prentice-Hall, Inc. (1995) 844
15. Wiederhold, G.: Mediators in the Architecture of Future Information Systems. IEEE Computer, 25(3) (1992) 38–49
16. Wiederhold, G. (Ed.): Intelligent Integration of Information. Kluwer Academic Publishers (1996)
17. Wiederhold, G. and Genesereth, M.: The Conceptual Basis for Mediation Services. IEEE Expert, 12(5) (1997) 38–47
18. Zhuge, Y., Garcia-Molina, H., Hammer, J., and Widom, J.: View Maintenance in a Warehousing Environment. SIGMOD-95 (1995).

What Is Query Rewriting?

Diego Calvanese[1], Giuseppe De Giacomo[1], Maurizio Lenzerini[1], and
Moshe Y. Vardi[2]

[1] Dipartimento di Informatica e Sistemistica
Università di Roma "La Sapienza"
Via Salaria 113, I-00198 Roma, Italy
lastname@dis.uniroma1.it
[2] Department of Computer Science
Rice University, P.O. Box 1892
Houston, TX 77251-1892, U.S.A.
vardi@cs.rice.edu

Abstract. View-based query processing requires to answer a query posed
to a database only on the basis of the information on a set of views,
which are again queries over the same database. This problem is relevant in many aspects of database management, and has been addressed
by means of two basic approaches, namely, query rewriting and query answering. In the former approach, one tries to compute a rewriting of the
query in terms of the views, whereas in the latter, one aims at directly answering the query based on the view extensions. Based on recent results,
we first show that already for very simple query languages, a rewriting is
in general a co-NP function wrt to the size of view extensions. Hence, the
problem arises of characterizing which instances of the problem admit
a rewriting that is PTIME. However, a tight connection between view-
based query answering and constraint-satisfaction problems, allows us to
show that the above characterization is going to be difficult.

1 Introduction

Several recent papers in the literature show that the problem of view-based query
processing [26,2] is relevant in many aspects of database management, including
query optimization, data warehousing, data integration, and query answering
with incomplete information. Informally speaking, the problem requires to answer a query posed to a database only on the basis of the information on a set
of views, which are again queries over the same database. In query optimization,
the problem is relevant because using the views may speed up query processing.
In data integration, the views represent the only information sources accessible to answer a query. A data warehouse can be seen as a set of materialized
views, and, therefore, query processing reduces to view-based query answering.
Finally, since the views provide partial knowledge on the database, view-based
query processing can be seen as a special case query answering with incomplete
information.

M. Klusch and L. Kerschberg (Eds.): CIA 2000, LNAI 1860, pp. 51-59, 2000.

The above observations show that view-based query processing is one of the basic problems in cooperative information systems. A cooperative information system is generally constituted by several autonomous information sources, and one of the goals of the system is to free the user from having to locate sources relevant to a query, interact with each source in isolation, and manually combine data from the sources [19]. Each source stores data about one aspect of the world, and therefore the information content of each source can be specified as a view over a certain global schema (often called mediated schema). When a query is issued on the mediated schema, tha task of the cooperative information system is to answer the query based on its knowledge about the sources, i.e. about the views corresponding to the sources. In other words, the system is in charge of reformulating the query into a set of queries that directly refer to the sources.

There are two approaches to view-based query processing, called *query rewriting* and *query answering*, respectively. In the former approach, we are given a query Q and a set of view definitions, and the goal is to reformulate the query into an expression, the *rewriting*, that refers only to the views, and provides the answer to Q. Typically, the rewriting is formulated in the same language used for the query and the views. In the latter approach, besides Q and the view definitions, we are also given the extensions of the views. The goal is to compute the set of tuples that are implied by these extensions, i.e., the set of tuples that are in the answer set of Q in all the databases that are consistent with the views.

Notice the difference between the two approaches. In query rewriting, query processing is divided in two steps, where the first re-expresses the query in terms of a given query language over the alphabet of the view names, and the second evaluates the rewriting over the view extensions. In query answering, we do not pose any limit to query processing, and the only goal is to exploit all possible information, in particular the view extensions, to compute the answer to the query.

In the last years a large number of results have been reported for both problems. View-based query rewriting and query answering have been studied under different assumptions on the form of the queries and views. For query rewriting see, e.g., [20,21,24,25,10,3,14,5,9], and for query answering see, e.g., [2,13,6,7,4].

In spite of the large amount of work on the subject, the relationship between view-based query rewriting and view-based query answering is not completely clarified yet. In this paper we focus on this relationship. Abstracting from the language used to express the rewriting, thus generalizing the notion of rewriting considered in the literature, we define a *rewriting* of a query with respect to a set of views as a function that, given the extensions of the views, returns a set of tuples that is contained in the answer set of the query in every database consistent with the views. We call the rewriting that returns precisely such set the *perfect* rewriting of the query wrt the views. Observe that, by evaluating the perfect rewriting over given view extensions, one obtains the same set of tuples provided by view-based query answering. Hence, the perfect rewriting is the best rewriting that one can obtain, given the available information on both the definitions and the extensions of the views.

An immediate consequence of the relationship between perfect rewriting and query answering is that the data complexity of evaluating the perfect rewriting over the view extensions is the same as the data complexity of answering queries using views. Typically, one is interested in queries that can be evaluated in PTIME (i.e., are PTIME functions in data complexity), and hence we would like rewritings to be PTIME as well. For queries and views that are conjunctive queries (without union), the perfect rewriting is a union of conjunctive queries and hence is PTIME [2]. By exploiting the results in [6,8], we show that already for very simple query languages containing union the perfect rewriting is not PTIME in general. Hence, for such languages it would be interesting to characterize which instances of query rewriting admit a perfect rewriting that is PTIME. However, by establishing a tight connection between view-based query answering and constraint-satisfaction problems (CSP), we show that this is going to be difficult, since it would amount to solve a longstanding open problem for CSP [16,11].

2 View-based query processing

We consider a simple setting in which a database is constituted by a set of binary relations, and hence can be viewed as an edge-labeled graph. We use as query language *unions of path queries* (UPQs), defined as follows:

$$Q \longrightarrow P \mid Q_1 \cup Q_2$$
$$P \longrightarrow R \mid P_1 \circ P_2$$

where R denotes a (binary) database relation, P denotes a *path query*, which is a chaining of database relations, and Q denotes a union of path queries. Observe that such a language is a simplified form both of unions of conjunctive queries [26] and of regular path queries [1].

Let us introduce the problem of view-based query answering [2,13,18,6]. Consider a database that is accessible only through a set $\mathcal{V} = \{V_1, \ldots, V_k\}$ of views, and suppose we want to answer an UPQ only on the basis of our knowledge on the views. Specifically, associated to each view V_i we have:

- its definition $def(V_i)$ in terms of an UPQ over the alphabet Σ;
- information about its extension in terms of a set $ext(V_i)$ of pairs of objects[1].

We denote $(def(V_1), \ldots, def(V_k))$ by $def(\mathcal{V})$, $(ext(V_1), \ldots, ext(V_k))$ by $ext(\mathcal{V})$, and the set of objects appearing in $ext(\mathcal{V})$ by $\mathcal{D}_\mathcal{V}$.

We say that a database DB is *consistent* with the views $\mathcal{V}$ if $ext(V_i) \subseteq ans(def(V_i), DB)$, for each $V_i \in \mathcal{V}^2$. The *certain answer set of Q wrt the views*

---

[1] We assume that objects are represented by constants, and we adopt the *unique name assumption* [22], i.e., different constants denote different objects and therefore different nodes.

[2] This correspond to assume that the views are *sound*. Other assumptions are also possible. For a discussion, see [6].

$\mathcal{V}$ is the set $cert(Q, \mathcal{V}) \subseteq \mathcal{D_V} \times \mathcal{D_V}$ such that $(c, d) \in cert(Q, \mathcal{V})$ if and only if $(c, d) \in ans(Q, DB)$, for every DB that is consistent with $\mathcal{V}$.

The problem of *view-based query answering* is the following: Given

- a set $\mathcal{V}$ of views, their definitions $def(\mathcal{V})$, and extensions $ext(\mathcal{V})$,
- a query Q,
- a pair of objects $c, d \in \mathcal{D_V}$,

decide whether $(c, d) \in cert(Q, \mathcal{V})$.

The complexity of the problem can be measured in three different ways [27]:

- *Data complexity*: as a function of the size of $ext(\mathcal{V})$.
- *Expression complexity*: as a function of the size of Q and of the expressions in $def(\mathcal{V})$.
- *Combined complexity*: as a function of the size of $ext(\mathcal{V})$, Q, and $def(\mathcal{V})$.

Here we focus on data complexity only.

The following theorem characterizes the data complexity of view-based query answering for UPQs.

Theorem 1 ([6]). *View-based query answering for UPQs is co-NP-complete in data complexity.*

Proof. The upper bound follows directly from the upper bound for regular path queries shown in [6]. For the lower bound, it is easy to see that the proof in [6] for regular path queries does not exploit reflexive transitive closure, and hence holds also for UPQs.

The definition of view-based query answering given above reflects two implicit assumptions. (i) The views are *sound*, i.e., from the fact that a pair (a, b) is in $ext(V_i)$ we can conclude that (a, b) is in $ans(def(V_i), DB)$, but not vice-versa. (ii) The domain is *open*, i.e., a database consistent with the views may contain additional objects that do not appear in the view extensions. Other assumptions about the accurateness of the knowledge on the objects of the database and the pairs satisfying the views, have been studied [2,13,6].

We now study the relationship between view-based query answering and query rewriting. An instance of *query rewriting* is given by a query Q and a set $\mathcal{V}$ of views with definitions $def(\mathcal{V})$. One then tries to generate a new query Q' over the symbols in $\mathcal{V}$ such that Q' approximates the answer to Q, when V_i is interpreted as $ext(V_i)$, for each $V_i \in \mathcal{V}$. Formally, we require $ans(Q', ext(\mathcal{V})) \subseteq cert(Q, \mathcal{V})$. In the context of UPQs, Q and $def(V_1), \ldots, def(V_k)$ are UPQs over the alphabet Σ, while Q' is an UPQ over the alphabet $\mathcal{V}$.

From a more abstract point of view, we can define a *rewriting of Q wrt $\mathcal{V}$* as a function that, given $ext(\mathcal{V})$, returns a set of pairs of objects that is contained in the certain answer set $cert(Q, \mathcal{V})$. We call the rewriting that returns exactly $cert(Q, \mathcal{V})$ the *perfect rewriting* of Q wrt $\mathcal{V}$. The problem of *view-based query rewriting* is the one of computing a rewriting of Q wrt $\mathcal{V}$. The problem comes in different forms, depending of the properties that we require for the rewriting. In particular:

- It is sometimes interesting to consider rewritings that are expressible in a certain query language, e.g., Datalog.
- It is also interesting to consider rewritings belonging to a certain data complexity class, for example, polynomial time. A rewriting f belongs to a data complexity class $\mathcal{C}$ if the problem of deciding whether a pair of objects (c, d) is in $f(ext(\mathcal{V}))$ is in the class $\mathcal{C}$, where the complexity of the problem is measured with respect to the size of $ext(\mathcal{V})$.
- Finally, it is worth computing rewritings that are maximal in a certain class. A rewriting f of Q wrt $\mathcal{V}$ is *maximal in a class* $\mathcal{C}$ if, for every rewriting $g \in \mathcal{C}$ of Q wrt $\mathcal{V}$, we have that $g(ext(\mathcal{V})) \subseteq f(ext(\mathcal{V}))$ for every $ext(\mathcal{V})$.

An algorithm for view-based query answering is an algorithm that takes as input a query, a set of view definitions, and a set of view extensions, and determines whether a given pair of objects is in the answer set of the query for every database that is consistent with the views. Hence, if we fix the query and the view definitions, we can consider every algorithm for view-based query answering as an algorithm that computes whether a given pair of objects is in the perfect rewriting. This observation establishes a tight connection between view-based query answering [2] and query rewriting [26].

Now, considering that in the present setting view-based query answering is co-NP-complete in data complexity (see Theorem 1), we obtain the following result.

Theorem 2. *The perfect rewriting of an UPQ wrt UPQ views is a co-NP function. There is an UPQ Q and a set $\mathcal{V}$ of UPQ views such that the rewriting of Q wrt $\mathcal{V}$ is a co-NP-complete function.*

Typically, one is interested in queries that are PTIME functions. Hence, we would like rewritings to be PTIME as well. Unfortunately, even for such a simple language (containing union) as UPQs by Theorem 2, the perfect rewritings are not PTIME in general. Hence it would be interesting to characterize which instances of query rewriting admit a perfect rewriting that is PTIME. Note, however, that finding such instances corresponds to finding those instances of view-based query answering that are PTIME in data complexity. Next we show that this is going to be difficult, by exhibiting a tight connection between view-based query answering and constraint satisfaction.

3   Constraint-satisfaction problems

A *constraint-satisfaction problem (CSP)* is traditionally defined in terms of a set of variables, a set of values, and a set of constraints, and asks whether there is an assignment of the variables with the values that satisfies the constraints. An elegant characterization of CSP can be given in terms of homomorphisms between relational structures [11].

A *vocabulary* is a set $V = \{R_1, \ldots, R_t\}$ of predicates, each with an associated arity. A *relational structure* $A = (\Delta^A, \cdot^A)$ over V is a *domain* Δ^A together with an *interpretation function* $\cdot^A$ that assigns to each predicate R_i a relation R_i^A of the appropriate arity over Δ^A. A *homomorphism* $h : A \to B$ between two relational structures A and B over the same vocabulary is a mapping $h : \Delta^A \to \Delta^B$ such that, if $(c_1, \ldots, c_n) \in R^A$, then $(h(c_1), \ldots, h(c_n)) \in R^B$, for every predicate R in the vocabulary.

Let $\mathcal{A}$ and $\mathcal{B}$ be two classes of finite relational structures. The *(uniform) constraint-satisfaction problem* $\mathrm{CSP}(\mathcal{A}, \mathcal{B})$ is the following decision problem: given a structure $A \in \mathcal{A}$ and a structure $B \in \mathcal{B}$ over the same vocabulary, is there a homomorphism $h : A \to B$? We denote such instance as $\mathrm{CSP}(A, B)$, and if such a homomorphism exists we say that $\mathrm{CSP}(A, B)$ is *satisfiable*. We also consider the special case where $\mathcal{B}$ consists of a single relational structure B and $\mathcal{A}$ is the set of all relational structures over the vocabulary of B, and denote it by $\mathrm{CSP}(B)$. Such problem is a (special case of) *non-uniform* constraint-satisfaction problem, i.e., with B fixed, the input is just a structure $A \in \mathcal{A}$. In the case where we take the relational structures to be (directed) graphs, CSP corresponds to *directed-graph homomorphism*. Since general CSP is polynomially equivalent to directed-graph homomorphism [11], that is, for each structure B there is a directed graph G_B such that $\mathrm{CSP}(B)$ is polynomially equivalent to $\mathrm{CSP}(G_B)$, we restrict attention without loss of generality to CSP over directed graphs, unless explicitly stated otherwise.

From the very definition of CSP it follows directly that every $\mathrm{CSP}(\mathcal{A}, \mathcal{B})$ problem is in NP. In general, the complexity of a non-uniform constraint-satisfaction problem $\mathrm{CSP}(B)$ depends on B. For example, $\mathrm{CSP}(K_2)$, is the *Two-Colorability Problem*, while $\mathrm{CSP}(K_3)$ is the *Three-Colorability Problem* (K_n is the n-node complete graph); the former is in PTIME, while the latter is NP-complete. In some cases, e.g., when the domain of B has at most two elements or when B is an undirected graph, it is known that $\mathrm{CSP}(B)$ is either in PTIME or NP-complete [23,15]. The Dichotomy Conjecture states that this holds for every structure B [11]. (Recall that if PTIME is different than NP then there are problems that are neither in PTIME nor NP-complete [17].) It is an open problem whether the Dichotomy Conjecture holds. A related open question is that of characterizing the structures B for which $\mathrm{CSP}(B)$ is in PTIME [11].

4   CSP and view-based query answering

We establish a tight relationship between constraint-satisfaction problems and view-based query answering. We show first that every CSP is polynomially reducible to view-based query answering.

Theorem 3. *Let B be a directed graph. There exists an UPQ Q and UPQ views $\mathcal{V}$ with definitions $def(\mathcal{V})$ such that the following holds: for every directed graph A, there are extensions $ext(\mathcal{V})$ and objects c, d such that $(c, d) \notin cert(Q, \mathcal{V})$ if and only if $\mathrm{CSP}(A, B)$ is satisfiable.*

Proof (sketch). Let $A = (N_A, E_A)$ and $B = (N_B, E_B)$. We define an instance of view-based query answering as follows:

- The alphabet is $\Sigma = \Sigma_N \cup \Sigma_E$, where $\Sigma_N = \{S_x \mid x \in N_B\} \cup \{F_x \mid x \in N_B\}$ and $\Sigma_E = \{R_{x,y} \mid (x,y) \in E_B\}$.
- The set of objects in the view extensions is $\mathcal{D}_\mathcal{V} = N_A \cup \{c,d\}$, where c, d are two symbols not in N_A.
- The views are V_s, V_f, and V_A with

$$
\begin{aligned}
def(V_s) &= \bigcup_{x \in N_B} S_x & ext(V_s) &= \{(c,a) \mid a \in N_A\} \\
def(V_f) &= \bigcup_{x \in N_B} F_x & ext(V_f) &= \{(a,d) \mid a \in N_A\} \\
def(V_A) &= \bigcup_{(x,y) \in E_B} R_{x,y} & ext(V_A) &= E_A
\end{aligned}
$$

Intuitively, the extension of V_A represents A, while V_s and V_f are used to connect c and d to all nodes of A, using respectively the "start" relations S_x and "final" relations F_x.

- The query is

$$
Q = \bigcup_{x,y \in N_B,\, x \neq y} S_x \circ F_y \quad \cup
$$
$$
\bigcup_{\substack{x \in N_B \\ y \neq x,\, (y,z) \in E_B}} S_x \circ R_{y,z} \circ F_z \quad \cup
$$
$$
\bigcup_{\substack{x \in N_B \\ (x,y) \in E_B,\, z \in N_B \setminus \{y\}}} S_x \circ R_{x,y} \circ F_z
$$

It is possible to show that there is a homomorphism from A to B if and only if $(c,d) \notin cert(Q, \mathcal{V})$. □

The reduction in the proof of Theorem 3 is polynomial, so we get the following corollary.

Corollary 4. *Every uniform CSP is polynomially reducible to view-based query answering.*

Theorem 3 exhibits a strong connection between CSP and view-based query answering. Since in the reduction, the query and the view definitions depend only on graph B, and only the view extensions depend on graph A, the theorem shows also that non-uniform CSP can be polynomially reduced to query rewriting. As a consequence, if we had a method to decide whether an instance of query rewriting admits a perfect rewriting that is PTIME, we would then be able to characterize those instances of non-uniform CSP that are in PTIME. As discussed in [16,11], this is a longstanding open problem that appears to be difficult to solve.

5 Conclusions

We have set up a framework that clarifies the relationships between view-based query rewriting and view-based query answering. Based on such a framework, we have first shown that the perfect rewriting is in general a co-NP function wrt to the size of view extensions. We have then turned our attention to the problem of characterizing which instances of query rewriting admit a rewriting that is

PTIME. Based on a tight connection between view-based query answering and constraint-satisfaction problems, we have shown that the above characterization is going to be difficult.

The discussion above shows that in general there is a tradeoff between completeness of a rewriting and the efficiency of using the rewriting to compute the answers to the query. To retain efficiency, one has in general to give up the perfectness of the rewriting, and adopt weaker notions of completeness. For example, one can fix a priori the language of the rewriting (such language should have PTIME data complexity) and find the maximal rewritings expressible in such a language. In particular, if the maximal rewriting is logically equivalent to the query (*exact rewriting*) and all views are exact, then the rewriting is also perfect. However, such a rewriting may not exist.

References

1. S. Abiteboul. Querying semi-structured data. In *Proc. of the 6th Int. Conf. on Database Theory (ICDT'97)*, pages 1–18, 1997.
2. S. Abiteboul and O. Duschka. Complexity of answering queries using materialized views. In *Proc. of the 17th ACM SIGACT SIGMOD SIGART Sym. on Principles of Database Systems (PODS'98)*, pages 254–265, 1998.
3. C. Beeri, A. Y. Levy, and M.-C. Rousset. Rewriting queries using views in description logics. In *Proc. of the 16th ACM SIGACT SIGMOD SIGART Sym. on Principles of Database Systems (PODS'97)*, pages 99–108, 1997.
4. D. Calvanese, G. De Giacomo, and M. Lenzerini. Answering queries using views over description logics knowledge bases. In *Proc. of the 17th Nat. Conf. on Artificial Intelligence (AAAI 2000)*, 2000. To appear.
5. D. Calvanese, G. De Giacomo, M. Lenzerini, and M. Y. Vardi. Rewriting of regular expressions and regular path queries. In *Proc. of the 18th ACM SIGACT SIGMOD SIGART Sym. on Principles of Database Systems (PODS'99)*, pages 194–204, 1999.
6. D. Calvanese, G. De Giacomo, M. Lenzerini, and M. Y. Vardi. Answering regular path queries using views. In *Proc. of the 16th IEEE Int. Conf. on Data Engineering (ICDE 2000)*, pages 389–398, 2000.
7. D. Calvanese, G. De Giacomo, M. Lenzerini, and M. Y. Vardi. Query processing using views for regular path queries with inverse. In *Proc. of the 19th ACM SIGACT SIGMOD SIGART Sym. on Principles of Database Systems (PODS 2000)*, 2000. To appear.
8. D. Calvanese, G. De Giacomo, M. Lenzerini, and M. Y. Vardi. View-based query processing and constraint satisfaction. In *Proc. of the 15th IEEE Sym. on Logic in Computer Science (LICS 2000)*, 2000. To appear.
9. S. Cohen, W. Nutt, and A. Serebrenik. Rewriting aggregate queries using views. In *Proc. of the 18th ACM SIGACT SIGMOD SIGART Sym. on Principles of Database Systems (PODS'99)*, pages 155–166, 1999.
10. O. M. Duschka and M. R. Genesereth. Answering recursive queries using views. In *Proc. of the 16th ACM SIGACT SIGMOD SIGART Sym. on Principles of Database Systems (PODS'97)*, pages 109–116, 1997.
11. T. Feder and M. Y. Vardi. The computational structure of monotone monadic SNP and constraint satisfaction. *SIAM J. on Computing*, 28:57–104, 1999.

12. M. L. Ginsberg, editor. *Readings in Nonmonotonic Reasoning.* Morgan Kaufmann, Los Altos, 1987.

13. G. Grahne and A. O. Mendelzon. Tableau techniques for querying information sources through global schemas. In *Proc. of the 7th Int. Conf. on Database Theory (ICDT'99),* volume 1540 of *Lecture Notes in Computer Science,* pages 332–347. Springer-Verlag, 1999.

14. J. Gryz. Query folding with inclusion dependencies. In *Proc. of the 14th IEEE Int. Conf. on Data Engineering (ICDE'98),* pages 126–133, 1998.

15. P. Hell and J. Nešetřil. On the complexity of H-coloring. *J. of Combinatorial Theory, Series B,* 48:92–110, 1990.

16. P. G. Kolaitis and M. Y. Vardi. Conjunctive-query containment and constraint satisfaction. In *Proc. of the 17th ACM SIGACT SIGMOD SIGART Sym. on Principles of Database Systems (PODS'98),* pages 205–213, 1998.

17. R. E. Ladner. On the structure of polynomial time reducibility. *J. of the ACM,* 22:155–171, 1975.

18. A. Y. Levy. Obtaining complete answers from incomplete databases. In *Proc. of the 22nd Int. Conf. on Very Large Data Bases (VLDB'96),* pages 402–412, 1996.

19. A. Y. Levy. Answering queries using views: A survey. Technical report, University of Washinghton, 1999.

20. A. Y. Levy, A. O. Mendelzon, Y. Sagiv, and D. Srivastava. Answering queries using views. In *Proc. of the 14th ACM SIGACT SIGMOD SIGART Sym. on Principles of Database Systems (PODS'95),* pages 95–104, 1995.

21. A. Rajaraman, Y. Sagiv, and J. D. Ullman. Answering queries using templates with binding patterns. In *Proc. of the 14th ACM SIGACT SIGMOD SIGART Sym. on Principles of Database Systems (PODS'95),* 1995.

22. R. Reiter. On closed world data bases. In H. Gallaire and J. Minker, editors, *Logic and Databases,* pages 119–140. Plenum Publ. Co., New York, 1978. Republished in [12].

23. T. J. Schaefer. The complexity of satisfiability problems. In *Proc. of the 10th ACM Sym. on Theory of Computing (STOC'78),* pages 216–226, 1978.

24. D. Srivastava, S. Dar, H. V. Jagadish, and A. Levy. Answering queries with aggregation using views. In *Proc. of the 22nd Int. Conf. on Very Large Data Bases (VLDB'96),* pages 318–329, 1996.

25. O. G. Tsatalos, M. H. Solomon, and Y. E. Ioannidis. The GMAP: A versatile tool for phyisical data independence. *Very Large Database J.,* 5(2):101–118, 1996.

26. J. D. Ullman. Information integration using logical views. In *Proc. of the 6th Int. Conf. on Database Theory (ICDT'97),* volume 1186 of *Lecture Notes in Computer Science,* pages 19–40. Springer-Verlag, 1997.

27. M. Y. Vardi. The complexity of relational query languages. In *Proc. of the 14th ACM SIGACT Sym. on Theory of Computing (STOC'82),* pages 137–146, 1982.

Applying Agents to Bioinformatics in GeneWeaver

K. Bryson[1], M. Luck[1], M. Joy[1], and D.T. Jones[2]

[1] Department of Computer Science, University of Warwick, Coventry, CV4 7AL, UK
{bryson, mikeluck, M.S.Joy}@dcs.warwick.ac.uk
http://www.dcs.warwick.ac.uk/geneweaver/
[2] Department of Biological Sciences, Brunel University, Uxbridge, UB8 3PH, UK

Abstract. Recent years have seen dramatic and sustained growth in the amount of genomic data being generated, including in late 1999 the first complete sequence of a human chromosome. The challenge now faced by biological scientists is to make sense of this vast amount of accumulated and accumulating data. Fortunately, numerous databases are provided as resources containing relevant data, and there are similarly many available programs that analyse this data and attempt to understand it. However, the key problem in analysing this genomic data is how to integrate the software and primary databases in a flexible and robust way. The wide range of available programs conform to very different input, output and processing requirements, typically with little consideration given to issues of integration, and in many cases with only token efforts made in the direction of usability. In this paper, we introduce the problem domain and describe GeneWeaver, a multi-agent system for genome analysis. We explain the suitability of the information agent paradigm to the problem domain, focus on the problem of incorporating different existing analysis tools, and describe progress to date.

1   Introduction

One of the most important and pressing challenges faced by present-day biological scientists is to move beyond the task of genomic data collection in the sequencing of DNA, and to make sense of that data so that it may be used, for example, in the development of therapies to address critical genetic disorders. The raw data has been accumulating at an unprecedented pace, and a range of computational tools and techniques have been developed by bioinformaticians, targetted at the problems of storing and analysing that data. In this sense much has already been achieved, but these tools usually require expert manual direction and control, imposing huge restrictions on the rate of progress. Essentially, however, the problems involved are familiar from other domains — vast amounts of data and information, existing programs and databases, complex interactions, distributed control — pointing strongly to the adoption of a multi-agent approach.

In this paper, we describe the development of a multi-agent system that is being applied to the very real and demanding problems of genome analysis and protein structure prediction. The vast quantities of data being rapidly generated by various sequencing efforts, the global distribution of available but remote databases that are continually updated, the existence of numerous analysis programs to be applied to sequence data in pursuit of determining gene structure and function, all point to the suitability of an

M. Klusch and L. Kerschberg (Eds.): CIA 2000, LNAI 1860, pp. 60-71, 2000.

agent-based approach. We begin with an introduction to the problem domain, outlining some basic biology, and explaining how it leads to the current situation in which systems such as the one we describe here are vital. Then we introduce the GeneWeaver agent community, a multi-agent systems for just this task, describing the agents involved, and the agent architecture. In all this, we aim to provide a view of the overall problem and outline all aspects of the system, rather than addressing any particular aspect, such as the databases providing the data, for example.

2   Genome Analysis and Protein Structure Prediction

The complete sequencing of the first human chromosome represents a significant milestone in the Human Genome Project, a 15-year effort to sequence the 3-billion DNA basepairs present in the human genome and to locate the estimated 100,000 or more human genes. A "rough draft" of the complete human genome will be available by spring 2000 [7], a year ahead of schedule. This draft will provide details of about 90% of the human genome with remaining gaps being filled in over the subsequent three years.

One of the key problems that such a vast amount of data presents is that of recognising the position, function and regulation of different genes. By performing various analysis techniques, such as locating similar (or *homologous*) genes in other species, these problems may be solved. Basic methods are now well developed including those for database searching to reveal similar sequences (similarity searching), comparing sequences (sequence alignment) and detection of patterns in sequences (motif searching). The key problem in the analysis of genome data is to integrate this software and primary sequence databases in a flexible and robust way. It has been stated in the biological community that there is a critical need for a "widely accepted, robust and continuously updated suite of sequence analysis methods integrated into a coherent and efficient prediction system" [6].

2.1   Function and Structure Determination

As indicated above, the rate at which this primary genetic data is being produced at present, is extremely rapid, and increasing. There is consequently a huge amount of information that is freely available across the Internet, typically stored in flat file databases. The problem of working out what each gene does, especially in light of the potential benefits of doing so, is therefore correspondingly pressing, and one which is meriting much attention from various scientific communities.

At present, the process of identifying genes and predicting the structure of the encoded proteins is fairly labour-intensive, made worse by requiring some expert knowledge. However, the steps involved in this process are all computer-based tasks: scanning sequence databases for similar sequences, collecting the matching sequences, constructing alignments of the sequences, and trying to infer the function of the sequence from annotations of the matched proteins (for which the function is already known). Predicting the three-dimensional structure of the proteins requires analyses of the collected sequence data by a range of different programs, the results of which sometimes disagree

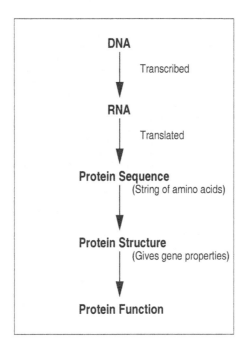

Fig. 1. From DNA to protein function

and some form of resolution needs to occur. The stages in getting to protein function from DNA are shown in Figure 1.

Now, like the primary data, some of the programs are accessible only over the Internet — either by electronic mail or the WWW (and increasingly the latter). This requires the different sources of information and the different programs to be managed effectively. Many tools are available to perform these tasks, but they are typically standalone programs that are not integrated with each other and require expert users to perform each stage manually and combine them in appropriate ways. For example, the process of trying to find a matching sequence might result in turning up an annotated gene, but the annotations include a lot of spurious information as well as the important functional information. The problem here is distilling this relevant information, which is not at all difficult for an expert, but which might prove problematic for a less experienced user. With the amount of data that is being generated, this kind of expertise is critical. For example, a very small entry in the SWISSPROT database is shown in Figure 2, in which the various lines are of greater or lesser significance. This entry is for the baboon equivalent of the protein which causes mad cow disease and other neurodegenerative disorders.

2.2 Sequence Databases

Although the principle of combining different methods and different information sources seems simple, in practice there are a number of difficulties that must be faced. Each primary data source (the primary sequence data banks and the structure data banks, for example) encode their information in different ways, not only in terms of the basic formatting, but also in the terminology used. For example, different keyword sets are used for each data bank so that understanding and interpreting the data (both of primary data sources and the results from analysis programs) is not a trivial task.

Primary databases are provided externally, under the control of a third-party who may change them at any time. In many cases, the data is largely unstructured, and is often available in the form of flat files. The methods of delivery vary, but have included email transfer of data, FTP downloads and, more recently, retrieval through the WWW. Each primary database consists of a number of sequence files, which are text files formatted in a particular sequence format. A sequence file usually contains data for a number of protein sequence entries, with each such sequence entry providing a description of the protein and its amino acid sequence.

For example, the Protein Data Bank (PDB) [5], which was established in 1971, is an international repository for the processing and distribution of experimentally-determined structure data that is growing dramatically. Similarly, SWISSPROT is a curated protein sequence databases with a high level of annotation of protein function [3]. Many other such sequence databases are also available (eg. the Protein Information Resource (PIR) [4]), but we will not provide an exhaustive list here.

2.3 Analysis Tools

The tools used to make sense of this partially structured and globally distributed genomic data apply particular techniques to try to identify the structure or function of specific sequences. A variety of such techniques are used in a range of available programs, including similarity searches of greater or lesser sensitivity (eg. BLAST [1]), sequence alignment (eg. CLUSTALW [18]), motif searching (eg. PROSITE [10]), secondary structure prediction (eg. PSIPRED [12]), fold recognition (eg. GENTHREADER [13]), and so on. For example, BLAST (Basic Local Alignment Search Tool) is a set of rapid similarity search programs that explore all available sequence databases [1]. The search can be performed by a remote server through a web interface resulting in graphical output, or alternatively can be carried out locally through a command line interface resulting in text output.

Now, some of the methods take longer to run than others, while some provide more accurate or *confident* results than others. In consequence, it is often necessary to use more than one of these tools depending on the results at any particular stage. While a high confidence is desirable, time-consuming methods should be avoided if their results are not needed.

Although these tools already exist, they are largely independent of each other. Encapsulating them as *calculation* agents provides a way to integrate their operation in support of appropriate combinations of methods to generate confident results, and integrate them with, and apply them to, the accumulating sequence databases. Each relevant tool can be encapsulated in an agent wrapper so that applications such as BLAST can become independent agents in the GeneWeaver community.

```
ID   PRIO_THEGE     STANDARD;      PRT;   238 AA.
AC   Q95270;
DT   01-NOV-1997 (Rel. 35, Created)
DT   01-NOV-1997 (Rel. 35, Last sequence update)
DT   01-NOV-1997 (Rel. 35, Last annotation update)
DE   MAJOR PRION PROTEIN PRECURSOR (PRP) (PRP27-30) (PRP33-35C) (FRAGMENT).
GN   PRNP OR PRP.
OS   Theropithecus gelada (Gelada baboon).
OC   Eukaryota; Metazoa; Chordata; Craniata; Vertebrata; Mammalia;
OC   Eutheria; Primates; Catarrhini; Cercopithecidae; Cercopithecinae;
OC   Theropithecus.
RN   [1]
RP   SEQUENCE FROM N.A.
RA   DER KUYL A.C., DEKKER J.T., GOUDSMIT J.;
RL   Submitted (NOV-1996) to the EMBL/GenBank/DDBJ databases.
CC   -!- FUNCTION: THE FUNCTION OF PRP IS NOT KNOWN. PRP IS ENCODED IN THE
CC       HOST GENOME AND IS EXPRESSED BOTH IN NORMAL AND INFECTED CELLS.
CC   -!- SUBUNIT: PRP HAS A TENDENCY TO AGGREGATE YIELDING POLYMERS CALLED
CC       "RODS".
CC   -!- SUBCELLULAR LOCATION: ATTACHED TO THE MEMBRANE BY A GPI-ANCHOR.
CC   -!- DISEASE: PRP IS FOUND IN HIGH QUANTITY IN THE BRAIN OF HUMANS AND
CC       ANIMALS INFECTED WITH THE DEGENERATIVE NEUROLOGICAL DISEASES KURU,
CC       CREUTZFELDT-JAKOB DISEASE (CJD), GERSTMANN-STRAUSSLER SYNDROME
CC       (GSS), SCRAPIE, BOVINE SPONGIFORM ENCEPHALOPATHY (BSE),
CC       TRANSMISSIBLE MINK ENCEPHALOPATHY (TME), ETC.
CC   -!- SIMILARITY: BELONGS TO THE PRION FAMILY.
DR   EMBL; U75383; AAB50630.1; -.
DR   HSSP; P04925; 1AG2.
DR   PROSITE; PS00291; PRION_1; 1.
DR   PROSITE; PS00706; PRION_2; 1.
DR   PFAM; PF00377; prion; 1.
KW   Prion; Brain; Glycoprotein; GPI-anchor; Repeat; Signal.
FT   NON_TER        1      1
FT   SIGNAL        <1     15          BY SIMILARITY.
FT   CHAIN         16   >238          MAJOR PRION PROTEIN.
FT   DISULFID     164    199          BY SIMILARITY.
FT   CARBOHYD     166    166          POTENTIAL.
FT   CARBOHYD     182    182          POTENTIAL.
FT   DOMAIN        44     83          4 X 8 AA TANDEM REPEATS OF P-H-G-G-G-W-G-
FT                                    Q.
FT   REPEAT        44     52          1.
FT   REPEAT        53     60          2.
FT   REPEAT        61     68          3.
FT   REPEAT        69     76          4.
FT   NON_TER      238    238
SQ   SEQUENCE   238 AA;   26104 MW;   3E0A3951 CRC32;
     MLVLFVATWS DLGLCKKRPK PGGWNTGGSR YPGQGSPGGN RYPPQGGGGW GQPHGGGWGQ
     PHGGGWGQPH GGGWGQGGGT HNQWHKPSKP KTSMKHMAGA AAAGAVVGGL GGYMLGSAMS
     RPLIHFGNDY EDRYYRENMY RYPNQVYYRP VDQYSNQNNF VHDCVNITIK QHTVTTTTKG
     ENFTETDVKM MERVVEQMCI TQYQKESQAY YQRGSSIVLF SSPPVILLIS FLIFLIVG
//
```

Fig. 2. An example SWISSPROT database entry

3   The GeneWeaver Agent Community

GeneWeaver is a multi-agent system aimed at addressing many of the problems in the domain of genome analysis and protein structure prediction, as discussed above. It comprises a community of agents that interact with each other, each performing some distinct task, in an effort to automate the processes involved in, for example, determining gene function. Agents in the system can be concerned with management of the primary databases, performing sequence analyses using existing tools, or with storing and presenting resulting information. The important point to note is that the system does not offer new methods for performing these tasks, but organises existing ones for the most effective and flexible operation. This section provides an overview of the system through the agents within it.

Figure 3 illustrates the overall perspective of GeneWeaver in that it contains the different classes of agents and shows how they inter-relate. At the left side, PDB Agent, Swiss Agent and PIR Agent all manage the primary sequence databases indicated by their names, and interact with the Protein NRDB (non-redundant database) Agent, which combines their data. At the right edge of the figure, the calculation agents (including the Blast Agent and the Clustal Agent that perform specific analysis tasks) attempt to annotate sequences in the database using relevant programs, again indicated by their names. At the top right, an expert calculation agent can combine the skills of the other calculation agents using expert knowledge encoded in plans. In this case it can use the Blast Agent to find similar proteins and then use the Clustal Agent to accurately compare the proteins obtained. (For clarity, these interactions are not shown in the diagram). Finally, at the top, the results generated by the system must be externally accessible, and this functionality is achieved by the Genome Agent. At each point of external interaction, agents typically receive and provide information via the WWW.

There are five types of agent present in the GeneWeaver community.

- *Broker agents*, which are not shown in Figure 3 since they are *facilitators* rather than points of functionality, are needed to register information about other agents in the community. They are similar in spirit to the notions discussed, for example, by Foss [9] and Wiederhold [20], but are very limited in functionality because of the constrained domain. (With a more sophisticated domain, however, this functionality might be correspondingly enhanced, to include more complex matchmaking, for example [14].)
- *Primary database agents* are needed to manage remote primary sequence databases, and keep the data contained in them up-to-date and in a format that allows other agents to query that data.
- *Non-redundant database agents* construct and maintain non-redundant databases from the data managed by other primary database agents in the community.
- *Calculation agents* encapsulate some pre-existing methods or tools for analysis of sequence data. They attempt to determine the structure or function of a protein sequence. Some calculation agents have domain-specific expert knowledge encoded as plans that enable them to carry out expert tasks using the other calculation agents.
- *Genome agents* are responsible for managing the genomic information for a particular organism.

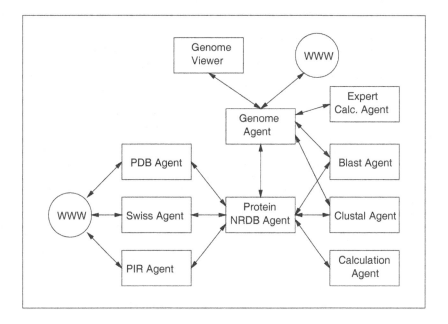

Fig. 3. GeneWeaver agent community

4   Architecture

Each agent in the GeneWeaver community shares a common architecture that is inspired by, and draws on, a number of existing agent architectures, such as [11], but in a far more limited and simplified way. An agent contains a number of internal modules together with either an external persistent data store that is used for the storage of data it manipulates, or the analysis program used to predict function. In this section, we describe the generic modules that comprise the architecture illustrated by Figure 4, which forms the basis of each agent. In essence, everything revolves around the central *control module*, which is given direction by the *motivation module* through particular goals, and then decides how best to achieve those goals. It can either take action itself through its *action module*, or request assistance from another agent through its *interaction module* which, in turn, uses the *communications module* for the mechanics of the interaction. The *meta-store* simply provides a repository for local information such as the skills of other agents. Each of the modules making up the architecture is considered in detail below.

Neither the *data store* nor the *analysis tools* are regarded as a part of the agent but they are used by agents either to store persistent data they are working with or to analyse the data. Various different types of data (such as a protein sequence, a sequence file, etc.) exist within the GeneWeaver system, and an interface to the data store allows data to be added, deleted, replaced, updated and queried. In addition, although we might envisage an agent wrapper around an analysis tool in a slightly different visual representation, the calculation agents interface with these existing programs in a similar fashion. In

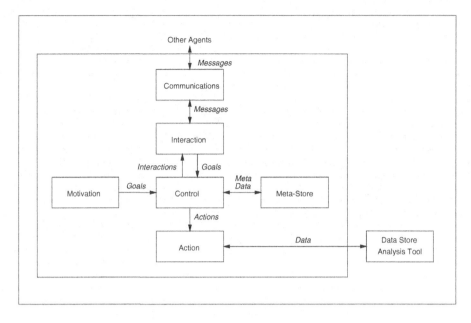

Fig. 4. GeneWeaver agent architecture

what follows, we focus on analysis rather than data management, which is considered in more detail elsewhere.

4.1 Motivation Module

Since each agent in the GeneWeaver community has different responsibilities and is required to perform different tasks, distinct high-level direction must be provided in each case to cause essentially the same architecture to function in different ways. The conceptual organisation of GeneWeaver agents thus involves the use of some high-level motivations that cause the goals and actions specific to the agent's tasks and responsibilities to be generated and performed [15, 16].

An agent is therefore initialised with the motivations required to carry out its responsibilities effectively. For example, all agents (except brokers) are motivated to register themselves with a broker agent, and will generate goals and actions to do so until they have succeeded. Similarly, a primary database agent has a motivation to cause the generation of specific goals and actions to update the primary database on a regular basis in order to ensure that it is up-to-date.

The distinction between motivations and goals is that motivations have associated intensities that cause goals to be generated. Each motivation is assigned a default intensity level, which can be modified by the *control module*, with only motivations with the highest intensity firing. For instance, the motivation to register with a broker initially defaults to a maximum intensity, but once the action has been achieved and the goal satisfied, the intensity decreases to zero. This not only allows the different motivations to be ordered in terms of priorities, it also allows intensities to be modified during execution.

4.2   Control Module

Perhaps the most important of the components of the agent architecture is the *control module*, which organises how actions should be carried out, once provided with a goal to pursue. The control module is initiated with a number of *plans* which can satisfy different goals and which consist of a number of steps specifying types of actions or interactions to be performed. It uses the meta-store for information on how particular actions should be carried out by determing whether suitable skills are available locally or whether the skills of a remote agent are required. The meta-store also provides information about types of interactions supported by other agents.

For example, a simple goal might be to find a match for a particular protein sequence. One way to satisfy this may consist of the single step of using a suitable *similarity search* method. Information contained in the meta-store is then used to locate just such a *similarity search* method, which may be one of the skills local to the agent or may require interaction with another agent. A more complicated way of accomplishing this goal may consist of two steps: a *similarity search* method may be used to find a similar sequence, which can then be used in a *sequence alignment* against the original sequence to provide more confidence in the result. Now plans can have a *quality* assigned to them, with the latter plan in the example above having a higher quality than the simpler one. They can also have an *efficiency* value associated with them, with the latter plan having a lower efficiency due to the use of more resources. Note that some plans may only be applicable in certain circumstances; for instance the latter plan requires the meta-store to identify a suitable *sequence alignment* method to use. Thus the plans have pre-conditions which need to be satisfied before they can be used. So, a suitable plan to meet a particular goal can be selected based on its quality, efficiency and any pre-conditions it requires.

4.3   Action Module

The *action module* is responsible for managing and performing *data actions* that modify the underlying data being manipulated by the agent. Such actions typically involve performing operations on some input data and may (optionally) result in some output. In this respect, they are likely to use and modify data in the agent's data store. The action module is thus critically important in terms of the agent functionality in this domain, since it is the only module that can interface to the underlying wrapped analysis program, and thus provides the only way to invoke the tool for performing an analysis. Each agent's action module is instantiated with a number of *skills* (or types of action) that the agent can perform.

4.4   Interaction Module

The *interaction module* handles the higher level interaction between different agents. Several possible types of interaction exist, each of them following a particular fixed interaction protocol.

An interaction takes place between two agents: a *requester* and a *provider*. When assistance is needed by an agent, a *requester interaction* is generated by its *interaction module* and a message sent to the provider via the *communications module*. At the provider's end of the interaction, the receipt of a request for assistance (via its communications module) causes a *provider interaction* suitable for the type of interaction to be invoked in the *interaction module*. The two agents then communicate using a fixed protocol, with the respective agents adopting suitable goals required on their own side of the interaction.

The interaction module is initialised with the types of interaction it can service (or the types of provider interactions it can initiate). For example, the broker is the only agent that initiates its interaction module with a *register* interaction to service requests to *register* with it from other agents. The particular interactions an agent is able to provide to others are recorded in its meta store so that it has an accurate picture of its capabilities.

4.5 Communications Module

The mechanics of the interaction of agents in the community is achieved through message-passing communication, which is handled by the communications module. An agent communication protocol specifies both the *transport protocol* to be used (which can be one of several, including RMI and CORBA [19, 8], for example) and the communication *language* (which is currently limited to a small prototype KQML-based [17] language). In principle, each agent may have available to it multiple protocols to use in interacting with others. This is achieved by instantiating the communications module at initiation with all those protocols known to the agent (which are also recorded in the meta store so it has an accurate representation of its own abilities).

Now, the communications module for one agent interacts with communications modules of other agents, using particular transport protocols. It also passes messages on to the agent itself for interpretation and processing, as well as accepting outgoing messages to be sent out to others. In this way, one agent interacts with another through their respective communications modules.

4.6 Meta Store

The *meta-store* simply provides a repository for the information that is required by an individual agent for correct and efficient functioning. For example, the meta-data contained in this repository will enumerate the properties and capabilities of the agent, including aspects such as the protocols the agent can use, the skills that can be executed, and the agent's motivations. As other modules are instantiated on initialisation, this information is added to the *meta-store*. Thus, as the *action module* is initialised, the skills that can be performed by it are added to the repository.

The *meta-store* also provides a representation of the other agents in the community in order to determine how best to accomplish particular tasks, possibly using other agents. Information contained in it may be extended while the agent is running so that additional or newly-discovered information about itself or other agents may be included. The only significant interaction is with the *control module* which records information in the *meta-store* as appropriate, and also uses it in decision-making.

5   Conclusions

The problems faced by biological scientists in relation to the increasing amounts of genomic data being generated are becoming critical. Autonomous genome analysis that avoids the need for extensive input by domain experts, but succeeds in annotating the data with structure and function information is a key goal. Through the use of a multi-agent system in which existing databases and tools are encapsulated as independent agents, we aim to relieve the expert of this burden, and increase the throughput of genomic data analysis. In this way, we can actually use the data that has been recorded.

A similar effort on the GeneQuiz system, which generates preliminary functional annotation of protein sequences, has been applied to the analysis of sets of sequences from complete genomes, both to refine overall performance and to make new discoveries comparable to those made by human experts [2]. Though GeneQuiz has a similar motivation, and makes use of various external databases and analysis tools, its structure suggests that significant modifications may be necessary with the introduction of new databases or tools. In contrast, the agent approach taken in GeneWeaver, in which each agent is autonomous and distinct from the rest of the system, means that the community of agents can grow in line with the development of new databases and tools without adversely affecting the existing organisation.

In the GeneWeaver project to date, we have developed a prototype system reflecting the structure of the community and the individual agent architecture described above. Database agents for several external databases have been constructed, and a sample calculation agent to perform BLAST searches has been incorporated into the community. Current work aims to extend the range of calculation agents and then to assess the entire system in relation to activity of human domain experts, to identify refinements both to the architecture and the individual agent control mechanisms.

Acknowledgements

The work described in this paper is supported by funding from the Bioinformatics programme of the UK's EPSRC and BBSRC.

References

1. S.F. Altschul, W. Gish, W. Miller, E.W. Myers, and D.J. Lippman. Basic local alignment search tool. *Journal of Molecular Biology*, 215:403–410, 1990.
2. M.A. Andrade, N.P. Brown, C. Leroy, S. Hoersch, A. de Daruvar, C. Reich, A. Franchini, J. Tamames, A. Valencia, C. Ouzounis, and C. Sander. Automated genome sequence analysis and annotation. *Bioinformatics*, 15(5):391–412, 1999.
3. A. Bairoch and R. Apweiler. The SWISS-PROT protein sequence data bank and its supplement TrEMBL in 1999. *Nucleic Acids Research*, 27(1):49–54, 1999.

4. W.C. Barker, J.S. Garavelli and P.B. McGarvey, C.R. Marzec, B.C. Orcutt, G.Y. Srinivasarao, L.-S.L. Yeh, R.S. Ledley, H.-W. Mewes, F. Pfeiffer, A. Tsugita, and C. Wu. The PIR-international protein sequence database. *Nucleic Acids Research*, 27(1):39–43, 1999.

5. F.C. Bernstein, T.F. Koetzle, G.J. Williams, E.E. Meyer Jr, M.D. Brice, J.R. Rodgers, O. Kennard, T. Shimanouchi, and M. Tasumi. The protein data bank: a computer-based archival file for macromolecular structures. *Journal of Molecular Biology*, 112, 1977.

6. P. Bork and E.V. Koonin. Predicting functions from protein sequences: where are the bottlenecks? *Nature Genetics*, 18:313–318, 1998.

7. F.S. Collins, A. Patrinos, E. Jordan, A. Chakravarti, R. Gesteland, L. Walters, and the members of the DOE and NIH planning groups. New goals for the U.S. human genome project: 1998-2003. *Science*, 282:682–689, 1998.

8. J. Farley. *Java Distributed Computing*. O'Reilly, 1998.

9. J.D. Foss. Brokering the info-underworld. In N.R. Jennings and M. J. Wooldridge, editors, *Agent Technology: Foundations, Applications, and Markets*, pages 105–123. Springer-Verlag, 1998.

10. K. Hofmann, P. Bucher, L. Falquet, and A. Bairoch. The PROSITE database, its status in 1999. *Nucleic Acids Research*, 27(1):215–219, 1999.

11. N.R. Jennings and T. Wittig. ARCHON: Theory and practice. In *Distributed Artificial Intelligence: Theory and Praxis*, pages 179–195. ECSC, EEC, EAEC, 1992.

12. D. T. Jones. Protein secondary structure prediction based on position-specific scoring matrices. *Journal of Molecular Biology*, 292:195–202, 1999.

13. D.T. Jones. GenTHREADER: an efficient and reliable protein fold recognition method for genomic sequences. *Journal of Molecular Biology*, 287:797–815, 1999.

14. D. Kuokka and L. Harada. Matchmaking for information agents. In *Proceedings of the Fourteenth International Joint Conference on Artificial Intelligence*, pages 672–679, 1995.

15. M. Luck and M. d'Inverno. Engagement and cooperation in motivated agent modelling. In C. Zhang and D. Lukose, editors, *Distributed Artificial Intelligence Architecture and Modelling: Proceedings of the First Australian Workshop on Distributed Artificial Intelligence, Lecture Notes in Artificial Intelligence, 1087*, pages 70–84. Springer Verlag, 1996.

16. M. Luck and M. d'Inverno. Motivated behaviour for goal adoption. In *Multi-Agent Systems Theories Languages and Applications: Proceedings of the Fourth Australian Workshop on Distributed Artificial Intelligence, Lecture Notes in Artificial Intelligence, 1544*, pages 58–73. Springer Verlag, 1998.

17. J. Mayfield, Y. Labrou, and T. Finin. Evaluating KQML as an agent communication language. In M. Wooldridge, J. P. Müller, and M. Tambe, editors, *Intelligent Agents II (LNAI 1037)*, pages 347–360. Springer, 1996.

18. J.D. Thompson, D.G. Higgins, and T.J. Gibson. CLUSTAL W: improving the sensitivity of progressive multiple sequence alignment through sequence weighting, positions-specific gap penalties and weight matrix choice. *Nucleic Acids Research*, 22:4673–4680, 1994.

19. G. Vossen. The CORBA specification for cooperation in heterogeneous information systems. In P. Kandzia and M. Klusch, editors, *Cooperative Information Agents*, pages 101–115. Springer-Verlag, 1997.

20. G. Wiederhold. Mediators in the architecture of future information systems. *IEEE Computer*, 25(3), 1992.

Economic Incentives for Information Agents

Jeffrey O. Kephart

Institute for Advanced Commerce, IBM Research
PO Box 704, Yorkto wn Heights, NY 10598
kephart@watson.ibm.com

Abstract. A fundamental barrier to the successful deployment of large-scale information agent systems is a lack of proper incentives. Why should my agent provide an information service or good to your agent? Along with m ycolleagues in the Information Economies group at IBM Research, I believe that the best w ay to encourage agents to serve one another's needs is to give them economic incentives. This simple tenet has profound implications, not just for information agents, but for the en tire future of electronic commerce. We foresee a future in which billions of economically-motivated softw are agen ts buy , refine and sell information goods and services, forming highly adaptive, ephemeral supply webs that may ultimately constitute a large fraction of the global economy. Through the use of tw o simple examples, I moti vate the importance of economic incentives and illustrate some behavior that may be exhibited by markets in which economic softw are agen ts participate.

1 Introduction

Soft w are agents capable of gathering information from disparate sources and refining it into a more valuable form ha ve been a topic of activ e researc h for the past sev eral y ears [5, 8, 7]. Almost universally ,the focus has been on *how* information agents can cooperate to provide v aluable information services to h umans or other agents. But there is an equally important question that must be answered if information agent technology is to be successful on a global scale: *why* should information agents cooperate with one another at all?

F or the past few y ears, the Information Economies group at IBM Research has dedicated itself to the view that the In ternet will ultimately be populated with billions of economically-motivated software agents that will charge one another for the information goods and services that they provide to one another. In the next section, I touch upon a few of the most important issues concerning economic incentives for information agents b y considering a hypothetical review finder agent that draws upon other information services. This is follow ed in section 3 b y an illustration of the market dynamics that might ensue if a shopbot—an agent that pro vides price information—were to price its services dynamically. Finally, I conclude with some general observations about the science and technology of economically-motivated software agents.

M. Klusch and L. Kerschberg (Eds.): CIA 2000, LNAI 1860, pp. 72-82, 2000.

2   Why should information agents cooperate?

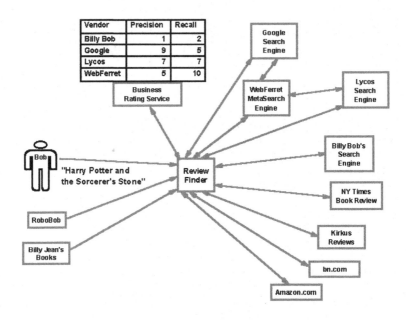

Vendor	Precision	Recall
Billy Bob	1	2
Google	9	5
Lycos	7	7
WebFerret	5	10

Fig. 1. ReviewFinder scenario (see text).

Imagine a hypothetical ReviewFinder information agent that provides reviews of CDs or books to humans or to other agents. Such a scenario is depicted in Figure 1. Bob, a potential book buyer, might submit a query asking for half a dozen reviews of *Harry Potter and the Sorcerer'sStone*. The ReviewFinder agent could then search for reviews at Amazon, Barnes&Noble, or other online book sellers, as well as the New York Timeswebsite. It could augment these reviews by submitting specially formulated queries (perhaps combining the title of the book or CD being sought with keywords like "review" or "rating") to various standard search engines and then using a heuristic to filter the set of hits down to a set of half a dozen Web pages that are deemed most likely to be worthwhile reviews.

The ReviewFinder agent might also draw upon one or more reputation agents in order to determine which search engines are most appropriate for its task. For example, the reputation agent might offer third-party ratings on average precision and recall ratings for various search engines as obtained by the reputation agent's own measurement or by statistics obtained from customers using those search engines. The ReviewFinder agent might decide to send its queries only to those search engines that offer high recall (say WebFerretor Lycos) rather than those that focus more on high precision (say Google), figuring that it can use its own automated filtration to determine which hits are mostly likely to be reviews.

One can also imagine that Bob would not deal with ReviewFinder directly, but would delegate to his personal agent ("RoboBob") the responsibility of dealing with ReviewFinder and other such information agents. One can also imagine a scenario in which BillyJeansBooks.com, a low-budget online bookseller, might prefer not to take the time and effort to handle book reviews itself, and would prefer instead to integrate book reviews obtained from ReviewFinder into its web site.

There do not appear to be any fundamental technical issues that prevent anyone with reasonable programming skills from creating the ReviewFinder agent and offering it as a service through a web site. But important questions remain: *Why* should anyone offer the ReviewFinder service? Why should anyone bother to run ReviewFinder on their server? And why should anyone take the time to program ReviewFinder in the first place?

Suppose that ReviewFinder is offered purely in the form of a web site accessible by humans. Then one could justify providing the ReviewFinder information service by the time-honored method of selling advertising space on its web site. Suppose that the ReviewFinder's customer is not Bob, but RoboBob. If RoboBob simply gathers the reviews and filters out the ads, then ReviewFinder is motivated to detect and reject queries from agents like RoboBob. This could be overcome by having RoboBob deliberately pass along ReviewFinder's ads to Bob. If ReviewFinder could authenticate RoboBob as an agent that passed ads along to the human that it serves, then ReviewFinder would still have an incentive to serve RoboBob's request.

However, suppose that BillyJeansBooks.com is being visited by a potential customer who appears to be interested in *Harry Potter and the Sorcerer's Stone* (or any other book). Then an agent operating on behalf of BillyJeansBooks.com might well submit a request for half a dozen reviews to ReviewFinder. Unlike RoboBob, the BillyJeansBooks.com agent is unlikely to pass along ReviewFinder's ads. Who would read the ads? Billy Jean? Or her customers? Neither choice seems workable. If Billy Jean's agent does not read ReviewFinder's ads, then ReviewFinder has no incentive to honor requests from Billy Jean's agent.

The incentive problem is not isolated to ReviewFinder. Consider the online booksellers, the search engines, and the reputation agent that supply ReviewFinder with the various streams of information that it needs to do its job. Why should any of them serve ReviewFinder? Amazon has obtained its reviews both from third parties such as Kirkus Reviews and from its own customers, and would not willingly supply such information to a competitor for free. The search engines were conceived with the idea of providing information directly to humans. Their advertising revenue model, which is fundamentally based on this assumption, does not work for agents. A reputation agent (which could be patterned after existing services like BizRate.com) might well expect its customers to pay for the information that it has labored to gather. Unless ReviewFinder and other agents who might want to use these information services pass these ads along to humans somewhere in the chain, there is no incentive for these services to cater to them. Note that the supply chain of information services may be arbitrarily long. For example, in this scenario we could introduce an extra link by supposing that one of the search engines is actually a metasearch engine like WebFerret that merely submits queries to standard search engines and collates and filters the results. It is inconceivable that ads would simply pass through each agent that uses another agent's service, until finally dozens or hundreds of them are collected together by RoboBob, which dutifully delivers them to poor beleaguered Bob.

This scenario exemplifies a very general, fundamental problem for collaborative information agents. Even if the technology to support rich interactions between collaborating information agents were to be put in place, every agent has an incentive to overuse other agents' resources and underprovide its own. For example, without proper incentives (and without any defensive measures undertaken by the services upon which it draws) ReviewFinder could overload resources like search engines by submitting many more queries than humans ever could or would, and (ignoring ethics for the moment) ReviewFinder could screen-scrape Amazon or bn.com with impunity. On the other hand, ReviewFinder would have no incentive to serve the legitimate needs of Billy Jean.

The solution to the incentive problem seems clear: give agents the ability to buy and sell the information goods and services that they provide. In the context of this example, let Billy Jean's agent buy reviews from ReviewFinder, and let ReviewFinder purchase the right to resell reviews provided by Amazon and The New York Times Book Reviews, let it purchase hits from search agents (perhaps at a few pennies per kilohit?), and let it purchase reputation information from the reputation agent. After all, the global economy is a decentralized mechanism that does a more or less reasonable job of coordinating the interactions of billions of human agents, and it seems natural to expect that the same principles could be applied to the coordination of comparable numbers of software agents.

What we envision is not a mere reflection of the world economy in cyberspace—it is a pervasive change in the world economy itself, in which economically-motivated software agents will participate alongside humans. Economic software agents will behave as digital businesses, entering into ephemeral relationships with other digital businesses, thereby forming a dynamic, flexible supply web. They will represent a new breed of economic player, one created in our image, but distinctly different in several significant aspects. They will make decisions faster than we do. They will base these decisions on information that is more voluminous and current than what we can process. They will be less flexible and less common-sensical than we are. Despite our best efforts to endow them with our own ethical and moral sense, they may behave differently in these respects as well. Given these differences, it would be dangerous to assume that theories and intuitions based on centuries of experience with human economic agents will be directly applicable to understanding, anticipating, and controlling the behavior of markets in which software agents participate. In effect, we are contemplating the release of a new species of economic agent into the world's economy — an environment that has heretofore been populated solely with human agents.

It is therefore not just of tremendous theoretical interest, but also of great practical importance to the future health and success of agent-based electronic commerce, that we understand the likely behavioral patterns of large collections of economically motivated software agents prior to their widespread deployment. This is the central mission of the Information Economies project: to develop a fundamental understanding of these collective modes of behavior, enabling us to develop agent strategies, protocols, and incentives that are likely to lead to desirable behavior.

The next section presents a glimpse of some of the interesting dynamical behavior that can occur in markets consisting of agents that represent buyers, sellers, and an information-agent intermediary found on the Web today—a shop-bot.

3   Software agents and dynamic pricing

Regardless of its vocation, practically every economically motivated agent will have a component that is involved in negotiation over price and other attributes of information goods and services. Agents will use a wide variety of negotiation mechanisms, including one-on-one negotiation, posted pricing, and various types of auctions. Research on automated forms of all of these negotiation mechanisms is under way.

In this section, I consider a simple scenario in which one type of information agent commonly found on the Web today—a shopbot, or comparison shopping agent [9, 2]—charges buyers for price information. Once shopbots start being used by other agents, they may well wish to switch to such a business model from their current one, in which they are supported by advertisements and commissions paid by online merchants for referrals. After all, shopbot customers are presumably expecting to pay a lower price than they would if they did not use the shopbot, and they ought to be willing to pay some fraction of their expected savings to the shopbot.

How might a shopbot price prices? One can expect that an agent that requests price information from a shopbot would want an answer within a few seconds at most, particularly if the agent is operating on behalf of a human. Therefore, the negotiation process must be at least this fast. An e-Bay-style auction is clearly out of the question. A human collector can patiently wait a week for a Wille Mays baseball card auction to close, but a shopbot and its customer need to seal a deal within seconds. Posted pricing, in which the shopbot declares a fixed price and the buyer accepts or rejects it, is one of the fastest possible mechanisms because it involves the smallest possible number of messages. [1]. Although some experts associate the term "dynamic pricing" solely with auctions, this form of pricing

---

[1] Continuous double auctions may also be feasible in this context.

can be regarded as dynamic in the sense that the shopbot may unilaterally change its price on an arbitrarily fast time scale.

To make the problem a little more interesting, suppose that the shopbot publishes not just a single scalar price, but a *price schedule* that permits customers to select the number of price quotes they wish to receive. Specifically, a customer requesting q price quotes will pay the shopbot a price c_q. This allows the shopbot to establish volume discounts or in fact any nonlinear price schedule that it wishes to implement.

Now buyer and seller agents can be added into the picture. Consider a simple market in which S sellers compete to to provide B buyers with a commodity, such as a specific book. [2] The objective of each seller s is to set its price p_s so as to obtain the maximum profit, given a production cost r. Each buyer b behaves in a very simple way: it compares $q_b \leq S$ prices and purchases the good from the seller within that set that charges the least, provided that the price is less than the buyer's valuation v_b. Assuming that the search strategy q_b and the valuation v_b are uncorrelated, the buyer population can be represented by a strategy vector w (the qth component of which represents the fraction of buyers that compare q prices) and a valuation distribution $\gamma(v)$.

A number of different seller pricing algorithms have been studied [3, 4, 6]. For purposes of this example, suppose that each seller computes the unique symmetric one-shot Nash equilibrium strategy, based upon full information about the buyers (i.e. the distributions $\gamma(v)$ and w). This Nash equilibrium turns out to be a mixed strategy, i.e. the sellers choose prices at random from a distribution $f(p)$ that depends on $\gamma(v)$, w, and S. The sellers may update their prices as frequently as they wish simply by making a new random draw from $f(p)$.

How might buyers behave in such a market? In this simple model, each buyer only controls a single strategic variable: q, the number of price quotes that it obtains before selecting a seller. In order to decide how many prices to compare, a buyer should consider whether the cost of obtaining additional price information is likely to yield enough of a benefit to justify that cost. In other words, the buyer should purchase q quotes, with q chosen to minimize the cost c_q plus the expected value of the lowest of q random draws from the distribution $f(p)$. Since the buyers' individual choices about how to set q determine the distribution w, and w in turn affects $f(p)$, and $f(p)$ governs each buyers' choice of q, one can start from any given initial condition $w(t = 0)$ and compute the resulting evolution of w and $f(p)$, along with any derived quantities, such as the average price.

How can the shopbot maximize its profits? For simplicity, assume that the shopbot has no production costs. Then one might suppose that the shopbot could consider a large number of potential price schedules. For each candidate price schedule, the shopbot could solve for the market dynamics, compute the equilibrium w, and from this compute its profit, which in the absence of production

---

[2] For a more complete presentation and study of the model, see references [3, 4, 6].

costs is simply

$$\pi = \sum_{q=1}^{S} w_q c_q. \qquad (1)$$

The shopbot would select the candidate price schedule yielding the highest profit.

However, there are two problems with this approach. First, for an arbitrary price schedule c, w and $f(p)$ may never reach an equilibrium. Under many circumstances, particular when c_q is nonlinear in q, complex limit cycles may result [6]. Second, even when c_q is linear in q, and $f(p)$ and w reach equilibrium, there are typically multiple equilibria, and the chosen equilibrium may be governed by the initial value $w(t = 0)$, which is beyond the shopbot's control.

To avoid the first complication, suppose that the shopbot restricts itself to a linear price schedule of the form $c_q = c_1 + \delta(q - 1)$. Then it is known from a substantial literature on price dispersion theory [1] that w will always settle to an equilibrium in which $w_q = 0$ for all $q \geq 3$. Note that the shopbot must price itself more cheaply than any alternate search mechanism, such as manual price comparison. It is reasonable to assume that the cost of this alternate mechanism is strictly proportional to the number of price quotes, i.e. it costs c' per quote. This establishes some simple restrictions on c_1 and δ. First, the shopbot should always set c_1 to just undercut c'. Second, δ must also be no greater than c', and in fact for moderate to large c' it turns out that δ should be substantially less than c'.

To simplify some rather complex details, suppose that the buyers' valuations are all 1, the number of sellers $S = 5$, and the alternate search cost is $c' = 0.25$. Then it can be shown that the optimal price schedule is given by $c_1 = 0.25$ (actually, infinitesimally less than this to ensure that the shopbot is chosen) and $\delta = 0.095741$. For this price schedule, the equilibrium is one in which 0.218204 of the buyers request one quote and the remaining 0.781796 request two quotes. The expected shopbot's profit would be 0.324850 per purchase.

However, this equilibrium is only reached if a sufficient fraction of the buyers. are initially comparing prices. For example, suppose that initially $w_1 + w_2 = 1$, and that the fraction w_2 of buyers comparing two prices is less than a threshold value 0.465602. Then the system will evolve to an equilibrium in which all buyers request just a single price quote. This is a self-sustaining situation. If the buyers are not comparing prices, the sellers can behave as monopolists and charge $1 - c'$—the most that buyers are willing to pay given that they have to pay $c' = 0.25$ for a single price quote. If all sellers are behaving as monopolists, then it is pointless for buyers to pay extra for a second quote because all sellers are charging the same price.

Interestingly, the shopbot can overcome this unfortunate situation by using a more sophisticated, time-dependent pricing strategy. Such a scenario is depicted in Figure 2. Initially, the shopbot sets the "optimal" linear price schedule: $c_1 = 0.25$, $\delta = 0.095741$. However, the initial strategy vector is $w = (0.95, 0.05, 0, 0, 0)$, which is on the wrong side of the threshold. Thus the system evolves towards $w_1 = 1$. Recognizing this, the shopbot deliberately drops its prices to exactly zero at time 1000. Since buyers can now purchase an unlimited number of quotes

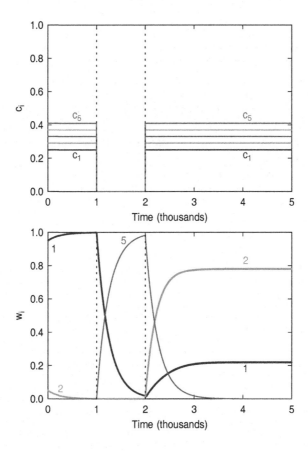

Fig. 2. Example of how a shopbot can manipulate its prices dynamically to shift the market from an unfavorable equilibrium to a favorable one that optimizes the shopbot's profit. Initially, shopbot adopts the "optimal" linear price schedule, given an alternate search cost of $c' = 0.25$ per search. However, $w_2 = 0.05$ is on the wrong side of the threshold $w_2 = 0.465602$, and the system drifts towards the trivial equilibrium $w_1 = 1$. At time $t = 1000$, however, the shopbot offers price comparisons for free. This encourages buyers to request 5 quotes each, driving average prices down near zero. At time $t = 2000$, the original shopbot fees are reinstated. This time, the buyer population evolves towards the favorable equilibrium, and the shopbot realizes the optimal profit of 0.324850. a) Shopbot prices vs. time. b) Evolution of buyer search strategies vs. time, with components $w_q(t)$ labeled according to q.

for free, the optimal strategy now shifts to $q = 5$. As buyers gradually shift to this optimal strategy (they reevaluate their strategy once every 250 time steps on average), w_5 approaches 1. Then, at time 2000, the shopbot reverts back to its original price schedule. This time, the system evolves toward the favorable equilibrium. The buyers begin to purchase fewer quotes, as five quotes are now more expensive than they are worth. But two quotes *are* worthwhile, and eventually the system stabilizes at a point at which the benefit of the second quote just equals its marginal cost, δ.

Interestingly, although the shopbot executes a time-dependent price schedule solely for the purpose of maximizing its own profit, it turns out that this benefits buyers as well. The buyers are paying the shopbot more, but this is more than compensated by lower commodity prices.

If the shopbot were to allow itself to set a nonlinear price schedule, it could most likely extract even more profit. In this case, it would have to anticipate much more complex system dynamics involving multiple limit-cycle attractors. A time-dependent price schedule might again be beneficial, enabling the shopbot to coerce the market to enter a basin of attraction in which the system dynamics would evolve to the most favorable attractor.

4   Conclusion

Unless all of the world's information agents are ultimately owned by a single individual or corporation, they will have to collaborate across organizational boundaries. Currently, there are no real incentives for agents to do this. Through two simple examples, I have attempted to explain why economic incentives should be built into information agents, and to illustrate some of the likely consequences of doing so. This leads naturally to the view that information agents will become integral participants in the global economy.

This work raises fundamental theoretical issues in several realms. Consider the field of economics. Now we can consider the possibility of *designing* economic players. This offers an entirely new perspective on economics, casting it more as an engineering discipline. Well-established models and subfields can now be re-examined in this new light. For example, the theory of price dispersion need no longer be regarded purely as an academic exercise aimed at explaining how prices in a competitive market can remain unequal and above the marginal production cost. Now, instead of assuming that search costs are fixed constants, we can explore how an information agent can strategically set the search costs to maximize its profits. In machine learning, we are now forced to consider that billions of economic software agents will be learning simultaneously, making it necessary to develop new theories of the behavior of such systems. This work opens up new vistas (and new problems) in the field of dynamic, stochastic optimization as well.

This work also has enormous implications for the future of electronic commerce and the entire world economy. We have the ability to create a new economic species, but we have to be careful to design them with a consciousness of their likely interactions with us and with others of their kind. Agents will function as miniature automated businesses that create and sell value to other agents, and in so doing will form complex, efficient economic webs of information goods and services that adapt responsively to the ever-changing needs of humans for physical and information-based products and services. With the emergence of the information economy will come previously undreamt-of synergies and business opportunities, such as the growth of entirely new types of information goods and services that cater exclusively to agents. This positive-feedback phenomenon may occur as quickly and as explosively as the growth of the Web, and may have an even more profound impact on the world.

Acknowledgments

This paper describes the collaborative efforts of several researchers in the Information Economies group at the IBM Thomas J. Watson Research Center and in the Computer Science and Economics departments and the School of Information at the University of Michigan. My colleagues and co-authors at IBM have included Amy Greenwald (now at Brown University), Jim Hanson, Gerry Tesauro, Rajarshi Das, David Levine, Richard Segal, Benjamin Grosof, and Jakka Sairamesh. Special thanks go to Steve White, who helped conceive the Information Economies project, and has remained a guiding influence throughout its existence. Finally, we thank the IBM's Institute for Advanced Commerce and Steve Lavenberg and the rest of the Adventurous Systems and Software Research program committee for their continued financial support and guidance.

References

1. K. Burdett and K. L. Judd. Equilibrium price dispersion. *Econometrica*, 51(4):955–969, July 1983.
2. R. B. Doorenbos, O. Etzioni, and D. S. Weld. A scalable comparison-shopping agent for the World-Wide Web. In *Proceedings of the First International Conference on Autonomous Agents*, February 1997.
3. A. Greenwald and J. O. Kephart. Shopbots and pricebots. In *Proceedings of Sixteenth International Joint Conference on Artificial Intelligence*, August 1999.
4. A. R. Greenwald, J. O. Kephart, and G. J. Tesauro. Strategic pricebot dynamics. In M. Wellman, editor, *Proceedings of the First ACM Conference on Electronic Commerce*. ACM Press, November 1999.
5. P. Kandzia and M. Klusch, editors. *Cooperative Information Agents I*, Berlin, 1997. Springer-Verlag. Lecture Notes in Computer Science, Vol. 1202.
6. J. O. Kephart and A. R. Greenwald. Shopbot economics. In *Proceedings of Fifth European Conference on Symbolic and Quantitative Approaches to Reasoning with Uncertainty*, July 1999.
7. M. Klusch and G. W. Onn Shehory, editors. *Cooperative Information Agents III*, Berlin, 1999. Springer-Verlag. Lecture Notes in Computer Science, Vol. 1652.
8. M. Klusch and G. Weiss, editors. *Cooperative Information Agents II*, Berlin, 1998. Springer-Verlag. Lecture Notes in Computer Science, Vol. 1435.

9. B. Krulwich. The BargainFinder agent: Comparison price shopping on the Internet. In J. Williams, editor, *Agents, Bots and Other Internet Beasties*, pages 257–263. SAMS.NET publishing (MacMillan), 1996. URLs: http://bf.cstar.ac.com/bf, http://www.geocities.com/ResearchTriangle/9430.

Auction-Based Agent Negotiation
via Programmable Tuple Spaces

Giacomo Cabri, Letizia Leonardi, Franco Zambonelli

Dipartimento di Scienze dell'Ingegneria – Università di Modena e Reggio Emilia

Via Campi 213/b – 41100 Modena – ITALY

E-mail: {giacomo.cabri, letizia.leonardi, franco.zambonelli}@unimo.it

Abstract. Auctions are proposed as a distributed negotiation mean, particularly useful in multiagent systems where both cooperative and self-interested agents compete for resources and services. The aim of this paper is to show how auction mechanisms on the Internet can be easily implemented by using programmable tuple spaces. Tuple spaces are shared repositories of information that follow the Linda model; the addition of programmability permits to adapt the tuple space behaviour to the application-specific requirements via reactions. In the implementation of auctions, programmable reactivity is exploited to uncouple the actual auction mechanisms from the selling and bidding policies of the attending agents.

1. Introduction

Software agents will soon populate the Internet and will be able to perform tasks on behalf of users, due to their main features – *autonomy, proactiveness, reactivity* and *sociality* [10]. While the first three features relate to the development of each single agent application (or classes of applications) and can be considered together, the fourth one must be discussed at an orthogonal level. In fact, the social behaviour can imply interactions among the agents cooperating in one application. However, in the Internet, interactions can occur also among agents of different applications, which may have a competitive behaviour, to gain the use of resources – whether as intangible ones, such as computational resources, data and services, or physical goods in agent mediated e-commerce [8].

In this context, an interesting negotiation mean among agents is the *auction*. In an auction there are entities that make resource available and entities that are interested in using such resources. The former ones are usually called *sellers*, while the latter ones are called *bidders*. Usually, there is an intermediate entity, called *auctioneer*, which actually performs the negotiation. The price of the resources sold by sellers via an auction is not fixed, but it is dynamically determined by the interest of the bidders. The seller can set a *reserve price*, i.e., a price under which it does not want to sell the resource. Differently from real people, which may not have time or willing to attend auctions, intelligent agents can spend time to negotiate the desired resources by using the auction mechanisms, which seem to fit well dynamic and heterogeneous environments. There are several different forms of auction, depending on the number of participants, on the criteria with which the resources are assigned, and so on. We focus on the auctions with one seller and multiple bidders at a time, ruled by several mechanisms: for example, English, Dutch, first-price and Vickery [1].

M. Klusch and L. Kerschberg (Eds.): CIA 2000, LNAI 1860, pp. 83-94, 2000.

The aim of this paper is to show how auction mechanisms can be implemented by using *programmable reactive tuple spaces*, in particular those defined by the MARS (Mobile Agent Reactive Space) coordination architecture [3]. Tuples are used to let agent interact. Programmability makes the implementation easy and permits to uncouple the definition of agents from the management of the auctions. This allows average programmers to focus on selling and buying policies, disregarding the implementation of auction mechanisms; moreover, programmable tuple spaces allow expert programmers to install specific application-dependent mechanisms. In addition, the use of programmable tuple spaces allows the definition of social conventions to constrain the agent's behaviour similarly to traditional auctions. The paper outlines how the implementation of auction mechanisms by using programmable tuple spaces can lead to a flexible means to coordinate Internet agents and can open a fertile application field.

2. MARS

MARS, firstly described in [3], is a coordination architecture that was originally conceived for mobile agents [4]; however, it can be fruitfully exploited by general multiagent systems on the Internet.

2.1 The Tuple Space Model

The MARS coordination model is inspired by the Linda model [2]. This choice was motivated by arguing that Linda-like models suit well the requirements of Internet applications [4, 7]. In MARS, as in Linda, interactions occur via shared data repositories (*tuple spaces*) whose data is organised in terms of ordered sets of typed fields (*tuples*), e.g., (int 5, char 'c', float 3.14). Interactions occur via Linda-like basic operations on the tuple space: one output operation is provided to store a tuple; two input operations are provided to retrieve a tuple, one of which also extracts it. Data retrieval relies on a *pattern-matching* mechanism: a tuple with possibly some non-defined values (*template*), e.g., (int?,char 'c', float?), is provided with the input operations; a tuple is retrieved from a space if it corresponds to (*matches with*) the template [2]. To implement agent coordination in Internet applications, a tuple space can be associated with each node of the network.

MARS advantages, derived from Linda, are due to the fact that it enforces both spatially and temporally uncoupled interactions: interactions can occur via one tuple space without needing to know who the interacting partners (agents) are, where they are, and when they have been (or will be) involved in the interaction. In addition, since interactions are based on a pattern-matching mechanism, the MARS model permits to acquire information also on the basis of partial knowledge of it.

2.2 The Programmable Reactivity

The Internet is a Web not simply of data, but of services and of collaborating-competing agents too, where every interaction usually occurs in an uncertain and untrusted scenario. In this context, the bare data-oriented pattern-matching mechanism of Linda-like models presents the following drawbacks: (i) it is unable to provide flexible solutions to manage services in a simple and effective way; (ii) it does not provide any way to monitor and control the interactions occurring via a tuple space; (iii) it forces complex and odd solutions when agents have to be involved in complex interaction protocols.

In order to maintain the advantages and the simplicity of the Linda model, and in the effort of enhancing it to overcome the above drawbacks, MARS exploits the concept of *programmable reactive tuple spaces*. A programmable reactive tuple space has the capability of embodying computational capacity within the tuple space itself (*programmable* property), assuming specific behaviours in response to access events (*reactive* property) [9]. Then, a tuple space is no longer a mere tuple repository with a built-in and stateless pattern-matching mechanism. Instead, a MARS tuple space can also have its own state and can be programmed to react with specific actions to specific accesses to it performed by agents. Reactions can access one tuple space, change its content and influence the semantics of the accesses.

The MARS programmable tuple space model overcomes the above-identified drawbacks of the basic Linda model:

- services can be accessed by agents as data in a uniform way, by using the normal access operations together with the programmable reactive capabilities;
- by associating a specific behaviour, one can monitor all access events and also associate specific control policies for handling them;
- the programmability enables to specify into the tuple space even complex interaction protocols, thus freeing the agents from the duty of explicitly managing and controlling their interactions with other agents.

With regard to the last point, a programmable tuple space allows the specification of inter-agent coordination rules in terms of reactions, thus achieving a clean separation of concerns between algorithmic and coordination issues [2]. Agents are in charge of embodying the algorithms to solve the problems; reactions represent the application-specific coordination rules.

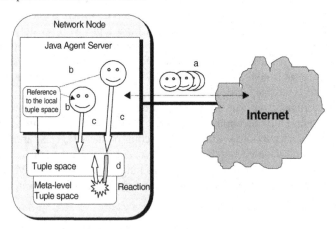

Fig. 1. The MARS Architecture (smiles represent agents)

2.3 The Implementation

MARS, implemented in pure Java, is conceived for the coordination of *Java-based agent* applications. It assumes that each node of the network hosts an *agent server* in charge of executing autonomous Java agents, for example *Aglets* [12]. The MARS system can be associated with different agent servers. The agent server has to keep a reference to a local tuple space: as an agent is created or arrives on a node (step *a* of Fig. 1), the local server provides it this reference (step *b*). As an agent is bound to the local tuple space, it can access it for reading, extracting and putting in tuples (step *c* in Fig. 1). Then, an agent associatively retrieves from the tuple space data items and references to objects that represent execution environment resources.

Each tuple space is a Java object, an instance of the Space class, which implements the interface with which agents can access the tuple space. The MARS interface (see Fig. 2) extends that of the SUN *JavaSpaces* specification [11], that is likely to become the *de facto* standard tuple space interface for Java.

```
public interface MARS extends JavaSpace
{// method interface inherited from JavaSpace; operations can belong to a transaction txn
// put the tuple e into the space, where remains for a time lease
// Lease write(Entry e, Transaction txn, long lease);
// read a tuple matching with tmpl from the space, waiting for timeout before returning null
// Entry read(Entry tmpl, Transaction txn, long timeout);
// extract a tuple matching with tmpl from the space, waiting for timeout before returning null
// Entry take(Entry tmpl, Transaction txn, long timeout);

// methods added by MARS
// read all tuples matching with tmpl from the space, waiting for timeout before returning null
Vector readAll(Entry tmpl, Transaction txn, long timeout);
// extract all tuples matching with tmpl from the space, waiting for timeout before returning
null
Vector takeAll(Entry tmpl, Transaction txn, long timeout);
}
```

Fig. 2. The MARS interface

MARS tuples are Java objects that represent ordered sets of typed fields. Tuple classes, deriving from the AbstractEntry class of JavaSpaces, define the specific tuple fields as instance variables. Each field of one tuple refers to an object that can also represent primitive data. The MARS interface derives from the JavaSpace interface three operations to access the tuple space, basically with the same semantics of the Linda operations:

- **write**, to put a tuple, supplied as parameter, in the space;
- **read**, to retrieve a tuple from the space, on the basis of a request tuple supplied as a parameter and to be used as a pattern for the matching mechanism;
- **take**, same as the read operation but extracts the matching tuple from the space.

Moreover, the MARS interface adds two operations, called **readAll** and **takeAll**, which permit to read/extract *all* tuples matching with the given template. The template tuple supplied by reading and taking operations can have both *actual* (defined) and *formal* (null) values. Because in MARS (as in JavaSpaces) tuples are objects and because the elements of a tuple can be non-primitive objects, the matching rules must take into account the presence of objects: objects match if their corresponding fields have the same values and so on in a recursive way, if fields are objects again.

In addition, MARS implements a programmable tuple space model in which the effects of the operations on the tuple spaces can be dynamically modified. Agents always access the tuple spaces with the basic set of Linda-like operations. Specific reactions can be associated to the accesses to the tuple spaces made by agents (step *d* in Fig. 1). A meta-level tuple space is introduced in each node to associatively manage reactions. A meta-level tuple in the form (Reaction_object, T, O, I) associates the reaction implemented by the Reaction_object with the event of the operation O performed on the tuple T by the agent with identity I. Writing a meta-level tuple in the meta-level tuple space means installing the corresponding reaction, while taking a meta-level tuple means uninstalling the corresponding reaction. Readings on the meta-level tuple space are performed by the system to search for a matching reaction when an operation occurs on the base-level tuple space. Since T can be a template, a single meta-level tuple can be used to associate a reaction with the events related to all the tuples matching with T.

With regard to security, MARS provides an Access Control List basic mechanism that can be exploited to specify which actions can be performed on the stored tuples and on the space, depending on the agent identities.

3. Implementation of Auctions

The features of the MARS model can be useful exploited in the implementation of the auction mechanisms:

- the Linda-like data-oriented approach permits to access the selling/buying services in a simple and uniform way;
- the programmability property allows to uncouple auction mechanisms, implemented via reactions, from auction policies embodied in the agents.

These aspects make possible to rule the agent's behaviour depending on the specific auction laws and to control their actions, thus enforcing *social conventions* for the auctions, as it happens in human auctions [13].

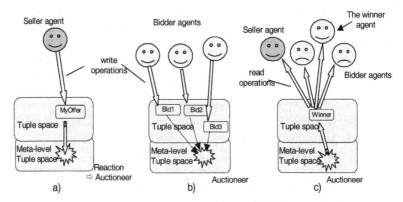

Fig. 3. An auction implemented via a programmable tuple space: a seller agent puts a good on sale (a), the bidder agents put their bids (b), a reaction decides the winner (c)

In the following we detail the implementation of auctions using MARS. At the negotiation site, the seller agent writes a tuple that contains information about the resource it is going to sell (step *a* in Fig. 3); this writing triggers a reaction that acts as the auctioneer, i.e. it is in charge of managing the auction. Once bidder agents have read such tuple, they can bid a price (or more than one, depending on the auction type) to buy the resource on sale (step *b* in Fig. 3); the auctioneer triggered reaction monitors the bids from the agents. When the auction is over, the auctioneer via the reaction decides the winner agent and creates a tuple to inform all the participants about it (step *c* in Fig. 3). The MARS security capabilities permit to authorise only correct readings, takings and writings of tuples.

```
class AuctionEntry extends AbstractEntry        // AbstractEntry: root of the tuple hierarchy
{ // tuple fields
    public String description;      // description on the resource
    public Date deadline;           // deadline of the auction
    public Seller seller;           // a reference to the seller agent
    public Integer reserve;         // the lowest admissible price
    public String type; // the type of the auction

    // constructor of the tuple. The order of the parameters defines the tuple field order
    public AuctionEntry(String descr, Date deadline, Seller seller, int reserve, String type)
    { this.description = descr;  this.deadline = new Date(deadline);
      this.seller = seller;  this.reserve = new Integer(reserve);
      this.type = type; }}
```

Fig. 4. The AuctionEntry class

In the following we describe some examples of auction, starting from the Java classes (implementing tuples) used in the auctions. The first class is called AuctionEntry and represents the announcement of an auction (Fig. 4). A tuple of this type is written in the tuple space by the seller agent to advise other agents that a given resource is sold by an auction. Relevant fields stored in the tuple are:

- the *description* of the resource sold, which uniquely identify the resource/good/service on sale (in this case a string is used, but it could be a more complex information, such as an XML document);
- the *deadline* of the auction, i.e. the time after when bids are no longer accepted;
- a reference to the *seller agent*, which wants to sell the resource;
- a *reserve price*, under which the seller agent does not want to sell the resource;
- the *type* of the auction.

This class can be specialised to define tuple classes that represent information of a specific kind of auction, adding the fields that are required by the given auction.

```
class BidEntry extends AbstractEntry     // AbstractEntry: root of the tuple hierarchy
{ // tuple fields
    public String description;      // description on the resource
    public Integer price;           // the bid price
    public Bidder bidder;           // the bidder agent
    public String type;             // the type of the auction

    // constructor of the tuple. The order of the parameters defines the tuple field order
    public BidEntry(String descr, int price, Bidder bidder, String type)
    { this.description = new String(descr);  this.price = new Integer(price);
      this.bidder = bidder;  this.type = type; }}
```

Fig. 5. The BidEntry class

The second tuple class, called BidEntry, represents a bid (Fig. 5). Bidder agents use tuples of this type to offer an amount of money in order to buy the given resource. The fields stored in these tuples are:

- the *description* of the resource for which the agent bids;
- the *price* the agent bids;
- a reference to the *bidder agent*, which wants to buy the resource;
- the *type* of the auction.

The third tuple class, called WinEntry, is used to publish tuples that advise all the participant agents about the winner of an auction (see Fig. 6). The fields of this class are self-explaining; in particular, the field price reports the price that the winner agent has to pay for the gained resource.

```
class WinEntry extends AbstractEntry    // AbstractEntry: root of the tuple hierarchy
{ // tuple fields
  public String description;        // description on the resource
  public Seller seller;             // the bid price
  public Bidder winner;             // the winner agent
  public Integer price;             // the final price

  // constructor of the tuple. The order of the parameters defines the tuple field order
  public WinEntry(String descr, Seller seller, Bidder winner, int price)
  { this.description = new String(descr); this.seller = seller;
    this.winner = winner; this.price = new Integer(price); }}
```

Fig. 6. The WinEntry class

The previous tuples use references to seller and bidder agents, by using fields typed with the interfaces Seller and Bidder; they contain specific useful methods to permit mutual identification after the auction. Fig. 7 presents a fragment of code of an agent that wants to sell a space of 5 Mbytes on a local HD via a first-price auction. The seller agent simple publishes its announcement by writing an AuctionEntry tuple in the space (s.write statement) and then waits for a WinEntry tuple describing the winner of the auction (s.read statement). It does not care about the management of the auction, because it is delegated to the specific reaction, which becomes the auctioneer, triggered when the AuctionEntry tuple is written.

```
MARS s; // reference to the MARS interface to access the reactive tuple space
...
// sell 5 Mb of HD space, within 10 seconds, with a reserve price of 10 units, by first-price auction
AuctionEntry tuple = new AuctionEntry("5Mb@HD", this, new Date(System.currentTimeMillis() +
10 * 1000), 10, "first-price");
// this writing triggers the appropriate reaction that manages the auction
// the tuple is kept in the tuple space for 600 seconds
s.write(tuple, new Transaction(null), 600);
// wait for a response, with a timeout greater than the lifetime of the auction tuple
WinEntry winAdv = (WinEntry)s.read(new WinEntry("5Mb@HD", this, null, null), new
Transaction(null), 660);
// if there is a winner
if (winAdv.winner != null)
  // interact with it ...
```

Fig. 7. Fragment of the code of a *seller* agent exploiting MARS

The meta-level tuple that associates a first-price auction reaction to the writing of an AuctionEntry tuple is the following: (FPAuction_Obj, AuctionEntry_tuple, "write", null), where FPAuction_Obj is an instance of the class FPAuction presented later and AuctionEntry_tuple is an instance of AuctionEntry and has the following values: (null, null, null, null, "first-price"). As shown in the Fig. 7, the code of the seller agent is very simple, because it does not contain all the instructions needed to manage the auction.

If a seller agent wants to use another kind of auction, it has to change the last field in the AuctionEntry tuple, and specifies the desired auction. If it wants to use a new kind of auction (of which it has the code in the form of reaction), it has to install the reaction via a meta-level tuple such as (CustomAuction_Obj, AuctionEntry_tuple, "write", null), where again AuctionEntry_tuple is an instance of AuctionEntry and has the following values: (null, null, null, null, "Custom").

```
MARS s;  // reference to the MARS interface to access the reactive tuple space
...
// want to buy 5 Mb of HD space by a first-price auction
AuctionEntry tuple = new AuctionEntry("5Mb@HD", null, null, null, "first-price");
if (s.read(tuple, new Transaction(null), NO_WAIT) != null)
{
    // put a bid of 15 units
    BidEntry bid = new BidEntry("5Mb@HD", 15, this, "first-price");
    WinEntry winAdv = (WinEntry)s.read(new WinEntry("5Mb@HD", null, null, null), new
Transaction(null), 0);
    // if I am the winner
    if (winAdv.winner == this)
    // interact with the seller
    ...
}
```

Fig. 8. Fragment of the code of a *bidder* agent exploiting MARS

Fig. 8 shows a fragment of the code of a bidder agent that wants to buy the 5 Mbytes of HD space. It searches for a tuple that publishes the resource it wants to acquire; if an auction is found, the agent puts its bid in the form of (BidEntry) tuple and waits for the result.

In the case shown in Fig. 8, the bidder agent chooses a priori a given kind of auction. In a more general case, the bidder agent can search in the tuple space at the negotiation site only for the wanted resource. Then, it can know the kind of auction associated when it has retrieved an AuctionEntry tuple whose description matches the wanted resource. Therefore, it can deal with the auction in the appropriate way.

Due to length limitation, in the following we show two auction implementations. The interested reader can refer to [5] for implementations of other auctions.

3.1 First-Price Sealed-Bid Auction

In the first-price auction the bids are not public, but private. Each bidder does not know the bids of the other participants. It is important that all bids are kept secret until the end of the auction. At the given time, the auctioneer opens all the bids and decides the winner, which is the bidder of the highest bid.

To publish the announcement of a first-price auction, a tuple of kind AuctionEntry (see Fig. 4) can be used, specifying the kind of auction via the string "first-price" in the Type field. Bids are represented by tuples of the BidEntry class (see Fig. 5).

The class that implements a first-price auctioneer by a reaction is shown in Fig. 9. The reaction "sleeps" until the deadline of the auction, while the agents put their secret bids into the tuple space at the negotiation site. Then, it wakes up and retrieves all the bid tuples. The bidder with the highest price is the winner and all the participants are informed by an appropriate tuple written in the space.

```
class FPAuction extends Reactivity
{
  private String description;
  private Date deadline;
  private Seller seller;
  private int reserve;

public Entry reaction(Space s, Entry Fe, Operation Op, Identity Id)
// this method is executed when the reaction is triggered and initializes the parameters
{ description = (AuctionEntry)Fe.description;
  deadline = new Date((AuctionEntry)Fe.deadline);
  seller = (AuctionEntry)Fe.seller;
  reserve = (AuctionEntry)Fe.reserve.intValue();
}

public void run() // this method is executed in a separate thread when the reaction is triggered
{ try      // sleep until the deadline
  { sleep(deadline.getTime() − new Date().getTime() }
  catch (InterruptedException e) {}

  BidEntry bidTemplate = new BidEntry(description, null, null, "first-price");
  BidEntry bids[];    // retrieve all bids from the space
  bids = (BidEntry[])s.takeAll(bidTemplate, new Transaction(null), NO_WAIT);

  int MaxPrice = 0;
  Bidder winner = null;
  if (bids != null)      // if there are bids
  { for (int i = 0; i < bids.length; i++)      // search for the highest bid
    { if (bids[i].price.intValue() > MaxPrice)
      { MaxPrice = bids[i].price.intValue();  winner = bids[i].bidder; }
    }
    if (MaxPrice < reserve)      // if the highest bid is less than the lowest admissible
    { winner = null; } // no one wins the auction
  }
  // the seller and the bidders (including the winner) are notified by a tuple
  WinEntry winAdv = new new WinEntry(description, seller, winner, MaxPrice);
  s.write(winAdv, new Transaction(null), 1000);
}}
```

Fig. 9. The FPAuction reaction class

3.2 Vickery (Uniform Second Price) Auction

The Vickery auction is quite similar to the first-price one described in the previous subsection. In fact, the secret bids are opened by the auctioneer at a given time to decide the winner. The only difference is that the bidder with the highest bid wins the auction, but she/he pays the second highest price [17]. For example, if the bids are 5, 6, 9 and 10, the agent who bids 10 wins, but it pays only 9. With respect to the first-price auction, in the Vickery auction the bidders are led to offer prices that reflect their true interest in the resources on sale. In this kind of auction, it is very important to keep the bids secret, more than in the previous one.

The tuple that describes a Vickery auction is the AuctionEntry (see Fig. 4) with the Type field set to the string "vickery". The related bids are similar to the previous ones, with the only difference that they define the string "vickery" as the type of auction (see Fig. 5).

The work of the reaction class (shown in Fig. 10) is very similar to the previous auctioneer's one. The only difference is that the second price must be recorded in a variable, and it has to be published as the price the winner must pay.

```
class VickeryAuction extends Reactivity
{ ... // same as First-price

public void run()
// this method is executed in a separate thread when the reaction is triggered
{ ... // same as first-price except the for cycle that takes into account the second price:
  int SecondPrice = 0;
  for (int i = 0; i < bids.length; i++)        // search for the highest and the second highest bid
   { if (bids[i].price > MaxPrice)
    { SecondPrice = MaxPrice;
      MaxPrice = bids[i].price;
      winner = bids[i].bidder;
    }
    else if (bids[i].price > SecondPrice)  SecondPrice = bids[i].price;
   }
  // the notification is the same of the first-price except for the price
  WinEntry winAdv = new new WinEntry(description, seller, winner, SecondPrice);
  s.write(winAdv, new Transaction(null), 1000);
}}
```

Fig. 10. The VickeryAuction reaction class

4. Discussion and Related Work

There could be several other kinds of implementation of auctions, based on different coordination models. The most spread choice is to use the traditional message-passing model. In an agent world, a server agent can implement the auctioneer, in charge of dealing with the agents attending the auction. First of all, it has to accept the incoming requests of initiating an auction from the seller. Then, such auction must be published in some way to advise all possibly interested bidder agents. Further, the server must keep track of all bidder agents (which have to register themselves at the server), manage the bids and acknowledge all participants of any change related to the current highest bid [6]. The auction implementations based on message-passing suffer of some problems, with respect to our approach:

- The message-passing model is very static, since one server is dedicated to only one kind of auction and the introduction of new kinds of auctions would require significant changes to the server. Moreover, in an environment with different auction kinds, more servers are needed, and the agents must deal with different entities, rather than with only one as the MARS programmable tuple space;
- the auction social conventions require the implementation of different duties (the control of the resource on sale, the acceptance of the bidders, the payment, ...)

that must be delegated to different entities – e.g. agents as in the Fishmarket project [13]; in our approach, such duties can be implemented by reactions, which perform their tasks in a transparent way and can be thought as (active) parts of the auction management system;

- in the Internet environment, the message-passing model has all the limits of fully coupled coordination models [4]: it requires complex design scheme to take into account the openness of this scenario, and lacks of flexibility in dealing with the uncertainty and unreliability;

- the message-passing approach makes the programmer focus on the way to exchange information rather than the content of the auction; this leads to an environment where the information and the services are accessed in a less uniform way than with a data-oriented approach.

All the previous issues show the difficulties of ruling the agents' behaviour when using the message-passing model; instead, MARS permits to implement those controlling actions as reactions of the tuple spaces, along with other needed services.

A significant improvement for all approaches stems from the integration of auction mechanisms in the Web scenario [18], which would also enable real people to attend the auctions, making the system more open and user-friendly.

5. Conclusions

This paper has shown the capability of the MARS programmable tuple space model in implementing high-level interaction mechanisms such as the auctions. This model brings several advantages in the area of agent coordination. On the one hand, the programmable reactivity permits to uncouple the algorithmic issues from the coordination issues, embodying the first ones in the code of agents, and the second ones in the tuple space reactions. On the other hand, the implementation of auctions is made easy by the programmable model embodied in MARS, which permits to control agent behaviour and makes agents respect the auction conventions. Agent programmers can rely on already-coded and tested mechanisms made available from the site that hosts auctions, without the need of coding them into the agents. Moreover, application-specific reactions (which act only on the tuples of the application that installs them) can be installed in the auction tuple space if the programmer or the administrator decide to change the standard policies. This paper has presented the code to implement the basic mechanisms of auctions; it can be extended to take into consideration peculiar situations that can occur in auctions.

A research direction related to resource allocation is the management of payments in open and wide networks such as the Internet. The virtual currency is a very attractive idea, but there are several security issues that are to be faced before this payment means is wide-scale exploited. In this context, the programmability of MARS can be exploited to add the currency management to the auction mechanisms in a modular way, leading to a more general market abstraction [16].

Other interesting research directions are represented by the possibility of exploiting declarative languages to program tuple spaces [14], and by the integration in MARS of concepts from Active Databases (e.g. transaction management, integrity checking) [15].

Acknowledgement

This work was supported by the Italian National Research Council (CNR) in the framework of the project "Global Applications in the Internet Area: models and programming environments".

References

[1] Agorics, Inc., "Going, going, gone! A survey of auction types", http://www.agorics.com, 1996.

[2] S. Ahuja, N. Carriero, D. Gelernter, "Linda and Friends", IEEE Computer, Vol. 19, No. 8, pp. 26-34, August 1986.

[3] G. Cabri, L. Leonardi, F. Zambonelli, "Reactive Tuple Spaces for Mobile Agent Coordination", 2nd International Workshop on Mobile Agents, LNCS, No. 1477, Springer-Verlag (D), September 1998.

[4] G. Cabri, L. Leonardi, F. Zambonelli, "Mobile-Agent Coordination Models for Internet Applications", IEEE Computer, Vol. 33, No. 2, Feb. 2000.

[5] G. Cabri, L. Leonardi, F. Zambonelli, "Implementing Agent Auctions using MARS", Technical Report MOSAICO/MO/00/001, http://sirio.dsi.unimo.it/MOON/papers/papers.html#Paper18, 2000.

[6] A. Chavez, P. Maes, "Kasbah: An agent marketplace for buying and selling goods", PAAM-96, pp. 75-90, 1996.

[7] P. Ciancarini, R. Tolksdorf, F. Vitali, D. Rossi, A. Knoche, "Coordinating Multi-Agents Applications on the WWW: a Reference Architecture", IEEE Transactions on Software Engineering, Vol. 24, No. 8, pp. 362-375, May 1998.

[8] S. Clearwater, "Market-based Control: a Paradigm for Distributed Resource Allocation", World Scientific, 1995.

[9] E. Denti, A. Natali, A. Omicini, "On the Expressive Power of a Language for Programmable Coordination Media", ACM Symposium on Applied Computing, Atlanta (G), 1998.

[10] N. R. Jennings, M. Wooldridge, eds., "Agent Technology: Foundations, Applications, and Markets", Springer-Verlag, March 1998.

[11] Sun Microsystems, "JavaSpaces Technology", http://java.sun.com/products/javaspaces/, 1998.

[12] D. B. Lange, M. Oshima, "Programming and Deploying Java™ Mobile Agents with Aglets™", Addison-Wesley, August 1998.

[13] P. Noriega, C. Sierra, J. A. Rodriguez, "The Fishmarket Project. Reflections on Agent-mediated institutions for trustworthy E-Commerce", Workshop on Agent Mediated Electronic Commerce (AMEC-98), Seoul, 1998.

[14] A. Omicini, F. Zambonelli, "TuCSoN: A Coordination Model for Mobile Agents," Journal of Internet Research, Vol. 8, No. 5, pp. 400-413, 1998.

[15] N. W. Paton, J. Campin, A. A. A. Fernandes, M. H. Williams, "Formal Specification of Active Database Functionality: A Survey", Lecture Notes in Computer Science, Vol. 985, 1995.

[16] T. Sandholm, "Agents in Electronic Commerce: Component Technologies for Automated Negotiation and Coalition Formation", Autonomous Agents and Multi-Agent Systems, Special Issue on Best of ICMAS-98, 1999.

[17] W. Vickrey, "Counter speculation, auctions, and Competitive Sealed Tenders", Journal of Finance, Vol. 16, pp. 8-37, March 1961.

[18] P. R. Wurman, M. P. Wellman, W. E. Walsh, "The Michigan Internet AuctionBot: A Configurable Auction Server for Human and Software Agents", 2nd International Conference on Autonomous Agents, May 1998.

Task Assignment in Multiagent Systems based on Vickrey-type Auctioning and Leveled Commitment Contracting

Felix Brandt and Wilfried Brauer and Gerhard Weiß

Institut für Informatik, Technische Universität München
80290 München, Germany
{brandtf,brauer,weissg}@in.tum.de

Abstract. A key problem addressed in the area of multiagent systems is the automated assignment of multiple tasks to executing agents. The automation of multiagent task assignment requires that the individual agents *(i)* use a common protocol that prescribes how they have to interact in order to come to an agreement and *(ii)* fix their final agreement in a contract that specifies the commitments resulting from the assignment on which they agreed. The work reported in this paper is part of a broader research effort aiming at the design and analysis of approaches to automated multiagent task assignment that combine auction protocols and leveled commitment contracts. The primary advantage of such approaches is that they are applicable in a broad range of realistic scenarios in which knowledge-intensive negotiation among agents is not feasible and in which unforeseeable future environmental changes may require agents to breach their contracts. Examples of standard auction protocols are the English auction, the Dutch auction, and the Vickrey auction. In [2, 3] combinations of English/Dutch-type auctioning and leveled commitment contracting have been described. In this paper the focus is on the combination of Vickrey-type auctioning and leveled commitment contracting.

1 Introduction

The area of multiagent systems (e.g., [8, 10, 13, 24]), which is concerned with systems composed of technical entities called agents that in some sense can be said to act and interact intelligently and autonomously, has achieved steadily growing interest in the past decade. A key problem addressed in this area is the automated assignment of multiple tasks to executing agents under criteria such as efficiency and reliability. The automation of task assignment requires that the agents *(i)* use a common protocol that prescribes how they have to interact in order to come to an agreement on "who does what" and *(ii)* are willing to fix their final agreement in a formal or "legally valid" contract. The protocol concerns the act or process of finding an appropriate task assignment, while the contract concerns the consequences and commitments resulting from the assignment on which the agents agreed. Two standard types of task assignment

M. Klusch and L. Kerschberg (Eds.): CIA 2000, LNAI 1860, pp. 95-106, 2000.
© Springer-Verlag Berlin Heidelberg 2000

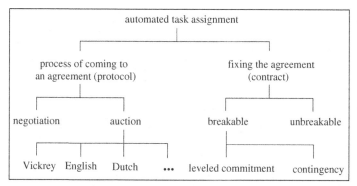

Fig. 1. Automated task assignment.

protocols are negotiation-based protocols (e.g., [5, 12, 21]) and auction-based protocols (e.g., [4]). Examples of widely applied auction protocols are the English auction, the Dutch auction, and the Vickrey auction (e.g., [15]). Compared to negotiation-based protocols, auction-based protocols show several distinct and advantageous features: they are easily implementable, they enforce an efficient (low-cost and/or low-time) assignment process, and they guarantee an agreement even in scenarios in which the agents possess only very little domain- or task-specific knowledge. Two standard types of task assignment contracts are unbreakable contracts (e.g., [11, 16, 17]) and breakable contracts, where common forms of breakable contracts are contingency contracts (e.g., [14]) and leveled commitment contracts (e.g., [1, 6, 19, 20]). Compared to unbreakable contracts, breakable contracts offer a significant advantage: they allow agents acting in dynamic environments to flexibly react upon future environmental changes that make existing contracts unfavorable. Figure 1 summarizes this rough overview of available approaches to automated task assignment.

The work reported here is part of a broader research effort aiming at the design and analysis of approaches to automated multiagent task assignment that combine auction protocols and leveled commitment contracts. The primary advantage of such approaches is that they can be expected to be applicable in a broad range of realistic scenarios in which knowledge-intensive negotiation among agents is not feasible and in which unforeseeable future environmental changes may require that agents breach their contracts. In [2, 3] combinations of English/Dutch-type auctioning and leveled commitment contracting have been described. In the work described in this paper the focus is on the combination of a Vickrey-type auction protocol and leveled commitment contracting. Basic descriptions of Vickrey auctions, also known as second-price sealed bid auctions, can be found in e.g. [15, 22]; a more general discussion of the advantages and limitations of this auction protocol is provided in [18]. Compared to other auction protocols, Vickrey auctions have the advantage that their duration is a priori known (each interested agent bids only once) and that the dominant bidding strategy is to bid one's true valuation. This makes Vickrey auctions particularly interesting for applications in computational settings (see e.g. [7, 9, 23]).

The paper is structured as follows. Section 2 describes the combination in detail. Section 3 presents initial experimental results on this combination. Finally, Section 4 concludes the paper with an overview of basic research directions evoked by the idea of combining auctioning and leveled commitment contracting.

2   Combined Vickrey-type Auctioning and Leveled Commitment Contracting

2.1   Informal Description

Many different task assignment scenarios—both in view of the protocols and the contracts—are possible. The scenario investigated in this paper is as follows. There are two types of *self-interested* agents: sellers or *contractors* who offer tasks, and buyers or *contractees* who are willing to execute tasks. The contractors as well as the contractees associate prime costs with task execution. A contractor is willing to pay prices that are lower than his own costs, and a contractee is interested in tasks whose prices are higher than his own costs. The contractors and the contractees thus have conflicting goals, because they both try to maximize their profits (i.e., the difference between their costs and the prices for task execution). As a consequence, both types of agents behave like "true capitalists".

Whenever a contractor announces a task, each interested contractee calculates one sealed bid and informs the announcing contractor. The contractee who submitted the lowest bid is declared as the winner of the auction, and the *second lowest* bid is taken as the price of the announced task; the contractor pays this price to the winning contractee who in turn executes the task. (If there are two or more equal winning bids, the winner is picked randomly.) This kind of auctioning can be viewed as an "inverse variant" of the standard *Vickrey auction* in which the contractee submitting the highest bid for goods or resources wins the auction at the second highest bid. (This is why the kind of auctioning described here is called Vickrey-*type* auction.) Vickrey-type auctioning is appealing for computational applications for two main reasons. First, the winner is determined after just one bidding cycle; obviously this is particularly useful in time- and/or cost-sensitive domains. Second, the dominant strategy in Vickrey auctions is to bid one's true value; obviously this is desirable because it helps to avoid wasteful counterspeculation in a broad range of competitive buyer-seller settings.

In order to take into consideration that usually contractees are limited in their capacity, it is assumed that each contractee can not be involved in more than one contract at the same time. (This assumption could be easily relaxed such that a contractee can not be simultaneously involved in $c \in N$ contracts.) As an extension of "pure auctioning," however, each contractee is allowed to decommit from a contract by simply paying a *decommitment penalty* to the corresponding contractor. This enables a contractee to legally breach a contract whenever there is a more profitable task announcement. The penalty specification are part of the contracts. In particular, the penalties are assumed to be variable and not conditioned on future events; this kind of breakable contracts are known as *leveled commitment contracts*, in contrast to contingency contracts. The level of commitment is determined by the amount of penalty to be payed for breaching. With that, the task assignment approach described in this paper combines standard-type auctioning with a highly flexible form of contracting.

2.2   Basic Notation

The following basic notation is used in the remaining of this paper. CR_i and CE_j refer to contractor i $(i = 1 \ldots m)$ and contractee j $(j = 1 \ldots n)$, respectively. The number of contractees is assumed to be greater than the number of contractors (i.e., $n > m$) to ensure that at least two bidders participate in each auction. The prime costs of contractor CR_i are denoted by $C[CR_i]$, and the prime costs of contractee CE_j for executing a task announced by CR_i are denoted by $C[CE_j, i]$. Without loss of generality it is assumed that the contractee costs are lower than the contractor costs, i.e., it is claimed that

$$\forall i : C[CR_i] \in [cr_{min}, cr_{max}] \quad \text{and}$$
$$\forall j, i : C[CE_j, i] \in [ce_{min}, ce_{max}] \quad \text{and}$$
$$ce_{max} \leq cr_{min} \quad .$$

This ensures, in particular, that contractors and contractees are interested at all in signing contracts with each other.

The price for a task announced by contractor CR_i (i.e., the second lowest bid) is denoted by $P[i]$, and the decommitment penalty a contractee CE_j has to pay to a contractor CR_i is denoted by $Penalty_j$ (time indices are dropped in order to avoid unnecessary formalism). Two types of penalties are investigated in this paper: penalty defined as a fraction of the price $P[i]$ of the decommitted contract, and penalty defined as a fraction of the prime costs $C[CR_i]$ of the concerned contractor CR_i. Formally:

$$Price\ penalty:\ Penalty_j = ppr \cdot P[i]$$
$$Cost\ penalty:\ Penalty_j = cpr \cdot C[CR_i]$$

where *ppr* and *cpr* are constants called price penalty rate and cost penalty rate, respectively.

When a contractor CR_i and a contractee CE_j agree to sign a contract, then their individual profits are given by

$$CR_i : Profit_i = C[CR_i] - P[i]$$
$$CE_j : Profit_j = P[i] - C[CE_j, i] - PenaltySum_j \quad .$$

$PenaltySum_j$ is the sum of penalties CE_j paid during one round.

2.3   Bidding Details

There is a whole spectrum of possible bidding strategies. The realization described in the following has been chosen because it is intuitively clear, easily extensible, and efficiently realizable. Whenever a contractor CR_i initiates a new auction by announcing his task, each potential contractee CE_j calculates his bid. This calculation is done as follows. If CE_j is not already involved in another contract in the current auction round, then his bid is given by

$$Bid_j = (1 + dp_{ji}) \cdot C[CE_j, i] \tag{1}$$

where dp_{ji} is a variable factor called desired profit (of contractee CE_j w.r.t. the tasks announced by contractor CR_i). Whenever a contractee CE_j wins an auction for a task announced by a contractor CR_i, he raises the factor dp_{ji} according to

$$dp_{ji} = (1 + IncreaseInit_j) \cdot dp_{ji} \tag{2}$$

where $IncreaseInit_j$ is a contractee-specific constant. This ensures that a contractee who wins an auction initiated by some contractor i will submit a higher bid in the next auction initiated by this contractor and thus tries to further increase his future profit. Whenever CE_j does not win an auction initiated by CR_i, then he reduces dp_{ji} according to

$$dp_{ji} = (1 - DecreaseInit_j) \cdot dp_{ji} \tag{3}$$

where $DecreaseInit_j$ is a contractee-specific constant. The situation is somewhat more sophisticated if CE_j is already involved in a contract signed with another contractor CR_k. In this case CE_j additionally takes into consideration the difference $P[k] - C[CE_j, k]$ (i.e., his potential gain from the already existing contract) and the penalty $Penalty_j$ (i.e., the penalty he would have to pay for decommitting from this contract). Formally, under the assumption that CE_j is already committed to CR_k in the current auction round, CE_j calculates his bid for a task announced by CR_i as follows:

$$Bid_j = \max\{(1+dp_{ji}) \cdot C[CE_j, i] \ , \ C[CE_j, i] + P[k] - C[CE_j, k] + Penalty_j\} \tag{4}$$

where dp_{ji} is defined as above. (Note that according to the above definitions a contractee decommits from a contract only if the new contract would result in a higher profit.)

3   Initial Experimental Results

The purpose of the experiments described here was to achieve a basic understanding of effects of combining Vickrey-type auctioning and leveled commitment contracting. The overall experimental setting was as follows. Auctioning proceeds in successive rounds. During each round all contractors sequentially offer their tasks (i.e., each contractor initiates a single auction in each round),

	Task 1	Task 2	Task 3
CR_1	196	–	–
CR_2	–	193	–
CR_3	–	–	115
CE_1	42	68	53
CE_2	22	46	46
CE_3	24	27	59
CE_4	12	11	19
CE_5	31	64	37
CE_6	65	24	55

Table 1. Cost table for the 3+4 and 3+6 scenario.

where the contractor sequence randomly varies from round to round. (With that, an auction round consists of exactly m auctions.) This setting allows to simulate scenarios in which several tasks have to be executed repeatedly over time and to analyze how the agents' profits vary over time. All results presented in this section are based on the following parameter setting (for all i and j): $dp_{ji} = 0.1$ (i.e., initially each contractee intend to make 10% profit), $IncreaseInit_j = 0.1$, and $DecreaseInit_j = 0.1$. At the beginning of each round none of the potential contractees is involved in a contract and all penalties $Penalty_j$ are set to zero. Other parameters are chosen as described below. In the simulations all prices and bids are integer values. In the following several scenarios are investigated, differing in the number of contractors and contractees.

For reasons of a careful evaluation the novel approach is compared to an "unbreakable contract variant." According to this variant, only *full* commitment contracting is possible, which means that a contractee can sign at most one contract per auction round. After a contractee signed a contract, he cannot join any other auction in the same round. In this variant the bids are calculated according to the formulas 1, 2, and 3 (formula 4 is not applicable in this variant). There are no other differences between this variant and the original approach. A number of further experiments with varying parameter settings and varying numbers of contractors and contractees (including a 32+40 scenario) have been performed; the results obtained (not reported here for reasons of limited space) qualitatively coincide with those reported in this paper.

3.1   3 Contractors and 4 Contractees ("3+4 Scenario")

Table 1 shows the prime costs of three contrators and six contractees. The table entries (i.e., the agents' prime costs $C[CR_i]$ and $C[CE_j, i]$) are chosen from the intervals defined by the parameters $ce_{min} = 10$, $ce_{max} = 99$, $cr_{min} = 100$, and $cr_{max} = 200$. In this subsection a "3+4 scenario" is considered, consisting of the three contractors and the first four contractees shown in this table.

The Tables 2 and 3 summarize results obtained for the 3+4 scenario w.r.t. the profits accumulated by the contractors and the contractees in 100 rounds for different commitment levels (i.e., full commitment and different price/cost penalty rates).

Three interesting observations follow from these results. A first key observation with these data is that leveled commitment contracting is much fairer than full commitment contracting in that contractees having lower prime costs can effectively make more profit, in relative terms, than contractees having higher prime costs. In particular, the data clearly show that this fairness is correlated with the level of commitment. This can be most easily seen by comparing the profits made by CE_4 who is the "best" among all contractees (he can accomplish each task for the cheapest price) with the profits of the other contractees: the profits made by CE_1 to CE_3 decreases with the level of commitment, while the profit of CE_4 changes only slighly. More precisely, as can be inferred from Table 2, the ratio between CE_4's profit and the sum of the other contractees' profits is 0.82 for full commitment, while this ratio is equal to 0.86 (0.99, 1.87) for $ppr = 1.00$ ($ppr = 0.50$, $ppr = 0.25$) and equal to 0.91 (0.93, 1.79) for $cpr = 0.15$ ($cpr = 0.10$, $cpr = 0.05$). This is also illustrated by the Figures 2, 3 and 4. A second key observation is that competition among both the contractees and the contractors significantly increases as the level of commitment decreases. This can be immediately seen by comparing the overall profit made by the contractees and the contractors for different commitment levels (see the last column in each of the Tables 2 and 3). In particular, this observation indicates that the use of this task assignment scheme does have an enormous, global effect on the dynamics in electronic markets (price/cost developments) occupied by self-interested, non-cooperative agents like the contractees and contractors considered here. The Figures 5, 6 and 7, which show how the prices develop under different commitment levels, further illustrate this observation. (Prices for tasks not sold in an auction round are assumed to be zero in these figures; this ensures that only prices paid by the contractors are taken into consideration.) These figures show that leveled commitment contracting, compared to full commitment contracting, results in an obvious price pressure and thus typically in lower prices for competitive tasks, that is, for tasks that could be accomplished at low costs by several contractees. The reason behind this is that contractees already involved in other contracts contribute to the decrease of task prices whenever they participate in auctions. For instance, the prices for the tasks 2 and 3 are much lower compared to full commitment contracting because contractee CE_4 (the "best" contractee) now participates in auctions even after having signed a contract. A third key observation is that there is *no* remarkable difference between price- and cost-oriented penalty (fairness effects can be achieved with both). This indicates that the choice of the penalty mode is not crucial, as long as the penalty mode chosen allows to flexibly decommit from contracts. This observation does have an impact on the design of any assignment schemes based on level commitment contracting.

3.2   3 Contractors and 6 Contractees ("3+6 Scenario")

In order to investigate what happens if the competition increases, two additional contractees were added to the 3+4 scenario (see Table 1). The results for this 3+6 scenario are also summarized in the Tables 2 and 3. (Figures showing the detailed price and profit curves for this scenario are not included for reasons of limited space.) These results show, in particular, that an increase in the competition results in lower prices and therefore in lower profits of the contractees and higher profits of the contractors (compared to the 3+4 scenario). All key observations mentioned above for the 3+4 scenario obviously do also hold for the 3+6 scenario. All in all, the results show that the computational approach described in the preceding section in fact realizes what is intuitively expected by "Vickrey-type leveled commitment contracting."

4   Conclusions

Automated task assignment that combines auction-based protocols and leveled commitment contracting defines a promising field of research in the area of multiagent systems. The results show, among other things, that this combination results in a very flexible assignment scheme that shows desirable fairness properties w.r.t. the profits that can be made by the contractees. An important issue in applying this assignment scheme is that a decrease of the level of commitment results not ony in an increase of the level of fairness, but also in an increase of the communication costs. This indicates that this scheme must be applied carefully in domains in which communication costs and bandwith are critical parameters. The work described in this paper and in [2, 3] is best understood as the first step toward a more comprehensive understanding of the limitations and benefits of combining auctioning and leveled commitment contracting. There are several open research issues that remain to be addressed in the future:

- Formal analysis (based on the broad range of available theoretical work on auctioning) of price stability and convergence.
- The extension of the proposed approach toward scenarios in which both the contractees and the contractors are allowed to breach contracts.
- The extension toward parallel auctions.
- The extension toward multi-unit and combinatorial auctions.
- The extension toward learning agents and more adaptive protocols.

We think that the importance of automated task assignment in multiagent systems, the broad applicability range of multiagent task assignment based on auctioning and leveled commitment contracting, and the encouraging initial experimental results and key observations reported in this paper justify to explore these and related issues.

References

1. M.R. Andersson and T.W. Sandholm. Leveled commitment contracts with myopic and strategic agents. In *Proceedings of the 15th National Conference on Artificial Intelligence (AAAI-98)*, pages 38–45, 1998.
2. F. Brandt and G. Weiß. Exploring auction-based leveled commitment contracting. Part I: English-type auctioning. Technical Report FKI-234-99, Institut für Informatik, Technische Universität München, 1999.
3. F. Brandt et al. Exploring auction-based leveled commitment contracting. Part II: Dutch-type auctioning. Technical report, Institut für Informatik, Technische Universität München, 2000.

4. S.H. Clearwater, editor. *Market-based Control: A Paradigm for Distributed Resource Allocation.* World Scientific, 1996.
5. S.E. Conry, K. Kuwabara, V.R. Lesser, and R.A. Meyer. Multistage negotiation for distributed constraint satisfaction. *IEEE Transactions on Systems, Man, and Cybernetics,* 21(6):1462–1477, 1991.
6. K.S. Decker and V.R. Lesser. Designing a family of coordination algorithms. In *Proceedings of the First International Conference on Multi-Agent Systems (ICMAS-95),* pages 73–80, 1995.
7. K.E. Drexler and M.S. Miller. Incentive engineering for computational resource management. In B.A. Huberman, editor, *The Ecology of Computation.* North-Holland, 1988.
8. J. Ferber. *Multi-Agent Systems. An Introduction to Distributed Artificial Intelligence.* John Wiley & Sons Inc., New York, 1999.
9. B. Huberman and S.H. Clearwater. A multiagent system for controlling building environments. In *Proceedings of the First International Conference on Multi-Agent Systems (ICMAS-95),* pages 171–176, 1995.
10. M.N. Huhns and M.P. Singh, editors. *Readings in Agents.* Morgan Kaufmann, San Francisco, CA, 1998.
11. S. Kraus. Agents contracting tasks in non-collaborative environments. In *Proceedings of the National Conference on Artificial Intelligence,* pages 243–248. 1993.
12. S.E. Lander and V.R. Lesser. Negotiated search: Organizing cooperative search among heterogeneous expert agents. 1992.
13. G.M.P. O'Hare and N.R. Jennings, editors. *Foundations of Distributed Artificial Intelligence.* John Wiley & Sons Inc., New York, 1996.
14. H. Raiffa. *The Art and Science of Negotiation.* Harvard University Press, Cambridge, Mass., 1982.
15. E. Rasmusen. *Games and Information.* Basil Blackwell, 1989.
16. J. Rosenschein and G. Zlotkin. *Rules of Encounter.* The MIT Press, 1994.
17. T. Sandholm. An implementation of the contract net protocol based on marginal cost calculations. In *Proceedings of the National Conference on Artificial Intelligence,* pages 256–262. 1993.
18. T. Sandholm. Limitations of the Vickrey auction in computational multiagent systems. In *Proceedings of the 2nd International Conference on Multiagent Systems (ICMAS-96),* pages 299–306, Menlo Park, CA, 1996. AAAI Press.
19. T.W. Sandholm and V.R. Lesser. Issues in automated negotiation and electronic commerce: Extending the contract net framework. In *Proceedings of the First International Conference on Multi-Agent Systems (ICMAS-95),* pages 328–335, 1995.
20. T.W. Sandholm and V.R. Lesser. Advantages of a leveled commitment contracting protocol. In *Proceedings of the 13th National Conference on Artificial Intelligence (AAAI-96),* pages 126–133, 1996.
21. R.G. Smith. The contract-net protocol: High-level communication and control in a distributed problem solver. *IEEE Transactions on Computers,* C-29(12):1104–1113, 1980.
22. W. Vickrey. Counter speculation, auctions, and competitive sealed tenders. *Journal of Finance,* 16(1):8–37, 1961.
23. C. Weinhardt, P. Gomber, and C. Schmidt. Efficiency, incentives and computational tractability in mas-coordination. *International Journal of Cooperative Information Systems,* 8(1):1–14, 1999.
24. G. Weiß, editor. *Multiagent Systems. A Modern Approach to Distributed Artificial Intelligence.* The MIT Press, Cambridge, MA, 1999.

Scenario	Commitment		Broken	CE_1	CE_2	CE_3	CE_4	CE_5	CE_6	$\sum_j CE_j$
						Accumulated Profit				
3+4	full	(no penalty)	–	97	816	2,037	2,420	–	–	5,370
	leveled	price penalty ppr=1.00	4	79	869	1,724	2,286	–	–	4,958
		price penalty ppr=0.50	42	36	603	1,467	2,081	–	–	4,187
		ppr=0.25	74	0	335	753	2,035	–	–	3,123
		cost penalty cpr=0.15	0	99	650	1,896	2,398	–	–	5,043
		cost penalty cpr=0.10	11	104	677	1,432	2,067	–	–	4,280
		cpr=0.05	50	0	416	741	2,076	–	–	3,233
3+6	full	(no penalty)	–	0	132	16	1,776	632	224	2,780
	leveled	price penalty ppr=1.00	0	0	145	13	1,808	573	269	2,808
		price penalty ppr=0.50	13	0	138	3	1,601	398	182	2,322
		ppr=0.25	29	0	137	4	1,569	117	188	2,015
		cost penalty cpr=0.15	0	0	150	25	1,703	638	189	2,705
		cost penalty cpr=0.10	0	0	138	33	1,656	662	191	2,680
		cpr=0.05	11	0	136	0	1,597	251	207	2,191

Table 2. Number of broken contracts and contractees' profits accumulated in 100 rounds in the 3+4 and 3+6 scenarios for different commitment levels.

Scenario	Commitment		CR_1	CR_2	CR_3	$\sum_i CR_i$
				Accumulated Profit		
3+4	full	(no penalty)	16,704	14,152	6,120	36,976
	leveled	price penalty ppr=1.00	15,918	14,625	6,315	36,858
		price penalty ppr=0.50	10,848	14,258	6,554	31,660
		ppr=0.25	10,188	10,544	6,711	27,443
		cost penalty cpr=0.15	16,691	14,420	6,227	37,338
		cost penalty cpr=0.10	15,026	15,057	6,302	36,385
		cpr=0.05	12,148	12,529	6,681	31,358
3+6	full	(no penalty)	17,161	16,556	6,801	40,518
	leveled	price penalty ppr=1.00	17,162	16,507	6,936	40,605
		price penalty ppr=0.50	15,089	16,582	7,220	38,891
		ppr=0.25	12,669	16,263	7,649	36,581
		cost penalty cpr=0.15	17,172	16,567	6,871	40,610
		cost penalty cpr=0.10	17,172	16,594	6,801	40,567
		cpr=0.05	15,380	16,573	7,445	39,398

Table 3. Contractors' profits accumulated in 100 rounds in the 3+4 and 3+6 scenarios for different commitment levels.

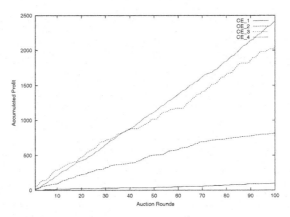

Fig. 2. Accumulated profit in the 3+4 scenario with full commitment contracting.

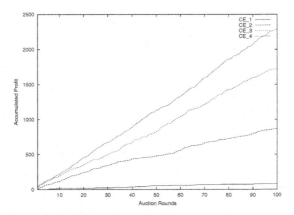

Fig. 3. Accumulated profit in the 3+4 scenario with price penalty $ppr = 1.00$.

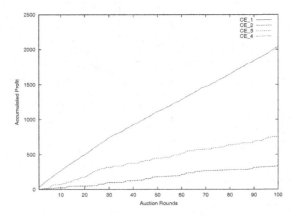

Fig. 4. Accumulated profit in the 3+4 scenario with price penalty $ppr = 0.25$.

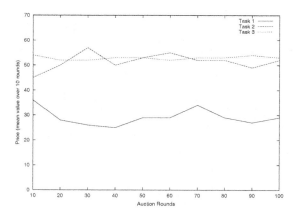

Fig. 5. Price development in the 3+4 scenario with full commitment contracting.

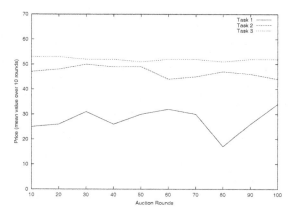

Fig. 6. Price development in the 3+4 scenario with price penalty *ppr* = 1.00.

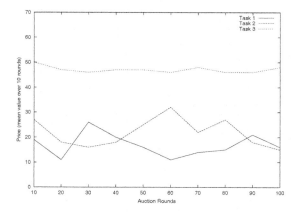

Fig. 7. Price development in the 3+4 scenario with price penalty *ppr* = 0.25.

Bilateral Negotiation with Incomplete and Uncertain Information: A Decision-Theoretic Approach Using a Model of the Opponent

Chhaya Mudgal, Julita Vassileva

Department of Computer Science, University of Saskatchewan, Canada
{chm906, jiv}@cs.usask.ca

Abstract. The application of software agents to e-commerce has made a radical change in the way businesses and consumer to consumer transactions take place. Agent negotiation is an important aspect of e-commerce to bring satisfactory agreement in business transactions. We approach e-commerce and negotiation in the context of a distributed multiagent peer help system, I-Help, supporting students in a university course. Personal agents keep models of student preferences and negotiate on their behalf to acquire resources (help) from other agents. We model negotiation among personal agents by means of influence diagram, a decision theoretic tool. To cope with the uncertainty inherent in a dynamic market with self-interested participants, the agents create models of their opponents during negotiation, which help them predict better their opponents' actions. We carried out experiments comparing the proposed negotiation mechanism with influence diagram, one using in addition a model of the opponent and one using a simple heuristic approach (as a base for comparison). The results show some of the advantages and disadvantages of the proposed negotiation mechanisms.

1. Introduction

With the advent of e-commerce online businesses have become much more popular than before. Placing online orders, making payments electronically and finding information about the products and the vendors have become easier. Despite the comfort that e-commerce has brought with itself, humans are still involved in most of the important process of business, for example, in making decisions in all phases of buying and selling. Negotiation is one of the key factors in commerce systems, which involves a lot of decision making and tradeoffs between various factors. Agent technology has helped consumers by supporting their negotiation strategies. Some of the practical applications that assist users in negotiation are Auctionbot, Kasbah, Tete-a-tete, e-Bay [4].

Most business transactions in e-commerce involve negotiation to settle on the most suitable price for both parties. During negotiation individuals or organizations have to make decisions of varied nature to attain their objectives. The benefit of dynamically negotiating a price is that the resource is allocated to a consumer who values it the most instead of fixing the price in advance. Negotiation varies in duration and

M. Klusch and L. Kerschberg (Eds.): CIA 2000, LNAI 1860, pp. 107-118, 2000.

complexity depending on the domain of application [4]. Negotiation protocols can extend over a long period of time, which is disadvantageous for time-bounded consumers.

A basic ingredient of the negotiation process is the correct anticipation of the other side's actions. In open multi agent systems (i.e. the systems in which the agents can be added dynamically) it is hard to know or predict about the state of the environment. In such systems there is always an element of uncertainty about the participants. We propose a negotiation mechanism that utilizes the elements of human behavior in the process of negotiation and which provides for anticipating the opposing party's actions and considering one's risk attitude towards money. The negotiation mechanism described in this paper has been developed as a part of a peer help system called I-Help. The purpose of negotiation is to find the best deal for the user independently on whether she requires help on a certain topic or is playing the role of a helper or another topic. I-Help is an online multiagent system that provides a student of a university course with a matchmaking service to find a peer-student online who can help [12]. Human help and time can be considered as non-tangible differentiated goods, which are traded for money. When the students in the class need help their agents contact a centralized matchmaker who knows which other agents are online and have the required resources (knowledge) and provides a ranked list of potential helpers. It also provides a standard marked price for the help request, which is calculated based on the difficulty of the topic and the number of knowledgeable users on this topic who are on line at the moment. The agent of the person requesting help starts a negotiation with the agent of the first potential helper from the list about the price (in our case this is the payment rate per unit of help time) and when a deal is made both agents inform their users. If the knowledgeable user agrees to help, a chat window opens for both sides and the help session is started. If the agents fail to achieve a deal, the agent of the person seeking help starts a negotiation with the second agent on the list etc… In this way, similarly to Kasbah [4] a one-to-many or many-many negotiation problem is modelled as a series of disconnected 1-1 negotiation problems.

I-Help's personal agents form an economic society designed to motivate the students who are knowledgeable to help their fellow students by receiving payment in cyber currency, which can later be evaluated or traded in terms of gift certificates or other means. In I-Help the agents make decisions on behalf of their users about the price to offer and how to increase or decrease the price to strike a better deal depending on user specified constraints, such as the urgency of the current work, importance of money and the risk behavior. Agent negotiation in I-help reduces the burden on the user (in our case the students) by allowing them to concentrate on their work rather than making them think about how to get a better deal.

In order to be able to make reasonable decisions for their users the agents consult their users' preference model. This model is initialized by the user and can be updated by the user, after receiving feedback from the agent about the success rate in negotiation.

The negotiation mechanism proposed in this paper is not restricted to intangible goods. It can be generalized to other market domains. Our approach is based on decision theory, which allows the agent to make rational choices. We will show how the agent benefits by using the decision theoretic approach. In the I-Help system the environment is dynamic and since the agents represent real users, it is hard to predict the actions of the opponent[1] agent on the basis of its past behavior (since the user's preferences can change in the meantime). However, it is useful to try to model the opponent's behavior during one session, since this can help predict better the opponent's reaction.

2. Related Work

Earlier work on negotiation in DAI was concerned with bringing cooperation and coordination among distributed nodes to improve the global efficiency of the system where the goals and the information of the system were not centralized. The application areas for negotiation included manufacturing, planning, scheduling, meeting scheduling, task and resource allocation in subcontracting networks. Various search techniques have been proposed to improve the efficiency of negotiation [2], [8]. On the other hand, some researchers studied negotiation from a theoretical perspective to find how agents should react to each other during their interaction using a game theoretic approach [15]. Negotiation mechanisms based on human negotiating techniques, using case based reasoning, argumentation and persuasion techniques have been proposed too [11]. Much work has been done on using agents to negotiate on behalf of their users, either in the market place [7] or for consumer to consumer negotiation. However, the focus of negotiation has been either to study the market performance or to search for appropriate negotiation strategies.

Recently, saving the users time and lifting the burden of information and decision overload, as well as the studies of the impact of different negotiation mechanisms on the outcome of negotiation has become the focus of automated negotiation. However, for a successful negotiation it is essential that the negotiating parties are aware of each other's moves. In the past researchers have used the history of negotiation to learn about the opponent. This approach works if the agents are interacting in a static environment, where no new participants appear. However, using the history of negotiation to learn about the opponent is not efficient when the environment is dynamic. Various approaches for modeling the opponent, learning the opponent's strategies and modeling the environment of the system have been studied to see their effect on negotiation. A Bayesian belief update mechanism has been applied in Bazaar [14] to update the beliefs of each agent about the environment and the opponent agent in the negotiation. Deterministic finite automata have been used to model the opponent's strategy in a game theoretic approach [1], Stochastic modeling using Markov chain has been proposed to capture the environment factors which influence the expected utility of a negotiating agent [6]. A recursive modeling approach based on reinforcement learning has been used to model other agents in order to adapt to each other and to the market system [13].

When the agents represent real users and negotiate on their behalf one of the requirements is that the negotiation should be transparent for the user and should take

---

[1] We will use the word "opponent" to denote the other agent in negotiation, though we don't imply necessarily an adversary or strongly competitive negotiation.

into account the user's preferences. Game-theoretic approaches have been applied for negotiation, but they have limitations: 1) the payoff matrix size grows exponentially with the number of agents; 2) it is very hard to find equilibrium points for strategies to be favourable, 3) though game theoretic approaches have been applied in theoretical research on strategy optimality, we have not seen much work in this area applied to practical market based systems. In addition, game theory assumes a win-lose situation, while our aim is towards win-win situation.

Therefore, negotiation mechanism we propose is based on sequential decision making in which the agent utilizes a preference model of the user. The user preference model is built by assessing the utility function that incorporates the user's risk attitude. Dealing with risk attitudes is an important feature of decision making. A few researchers [16] have taken into account risk attitudes for negotiation, but their work has mainly utilized the Zeuthen's Principle [3] in a game theoretic situation to determine who is the person more willing to make concessions. We utilize the risk attitudes in a different way, as discussed in section 3.

In the proposed work decision making in a negotiation process is modeled using an influence diagram. An influence diagram is a Bayesian network extended with utility functions and with variables representing decisions. An influence diagram is solved by computing the action yielding the highest expected utility. Influence diagrams have been applied in modelling decision making processes (for example, in [5]), however, not in the context of agent negotiation. We chose to use influence diagram for negotiation because even though a Bayesian network is a flexible tool for constructing models, it mainly considers causal impact between the events and hence is well suited for forecasting and diagnosing. Influence diagrams have been developed especially for making decisions. We view negotiation as a decision problem that requires a decision-maker to weigh his preferences and to perform an action that gives him** the maximum utility. Therefore influence diagrams serve as a good tool for representation of the problem as well as for solving it. It is also intuitively better understandable for a user than a Bayesian network, and since our agents represent human user, understandability is an important factor. Unlike decision trees, influence diagrams don't grow exponentially; they suppress minute details and hence are ideal for getting an overview of a complex problem.

We model the opponent's actions using a probabilistic influence diagram. Modelling the opponent in negotiation has been proposed in game theory and DAI [1, 13]. The agents of Carmel and Markovich [1] use model-based learning and explicit models of their opponent's strategies to generate expectations about their behaviour. Vidal and Durfee [13] have studied the impact of agent modeling each other on an information economy. Agents use reinforcement learning to model each other. Our agents use probabilistic influence diagram to infer the preferences of their opponents.

3. Negotiation Mechanism

Negotiation is an iterative process in which the agents make offers and counteroffers based on the preferences of their users.

3.1. Modeling Decision

We believe that a negotiation model based on sequential decision making should be based on following characteristics:

1. It should provide effective methods for organizing the domain problem into a structure. Structuring tools like influence diagrams [9] are an effective and efficient way to represent a negotiation context. A decision model also provides means to capture the nature of the problem, identify important objectives and to generate alternative courses of action.
2. The model should account for uncertainty and be able to represent it in a quantitative way, because there are inherent uncertainties in any practical environment.
3. The model should be able to support the dynamics of the situation.
4. The model should be able to deal with multiple objectives and allow tradeoff in one area against costs in another.
5. Finally, the model should be such that it allows the decision-maker to change their beliefs about the likelihood of uncertainties and change their preferences.

The negotiation protocol is a straightforward iterative process of making offers and counteroffers. So, during negotiation the agent can be in Offer or Counter-offer state repeatedly. The final state will be Accept or Reject. Similarly to [14], we use "negotiation strategies" to denote the actions, which the agents take in every iteration depending on the preference model. In our model once the agent is in a final state, he cannot retreat back from it. In order to do so the whole negotiation process has to start again. The negotiation mechanism takes into account the preferences of the user, which usually depend in the domain of the negotiation context. The preferences include:

- the maximum price of the buyer (i.e. how much the helpee is willing to pay),
- the urgency of demand of the resource for the buyer, or the urgency of the seller's current work (which she has to interrupt in order to help),
- the importance that either agent attaches to money, and
- the user's risk behavior (risk-averse or a risk-seeking person).

We have incorporated utility in order to model the way in which the decision-maker values different outcomes and objectives. Each agent in our system can be in any role; he can be a buyer or the seller of help. The utility for the buyer (helpee) and the seller (helper) for the actions of accept, reject and counter-propose vary according to their risk behavior.

It is important to note that the agent's risk behavior considered in this paper does not overlap with the money importance. In literature these entities have often been considered as tightly connected, but in our case this is not necessarily true. Money importance and risk-behavior are two different entities and they are set independently by the user (in the user preference model). The risk behavior of the user instructs the personal agent[2] about the increase or decrease in the price offers to be made. A risk-seeking person will try to counter-propose an offer rather than accepting any price offered. A risk-averse person will accept whatever minimum price he/she is offered

---

[2] Throughout the paper we will refer to the personal agent (buyer or seller) as "he" and to the user (student in our case) as "she".

and will refrain from counter proposing in fear of losing. We are calculating the utility values of the action alternatives that an agent has at any time during negotiation. Utility of actions is dependent on the money that the seller gets and the buyer has to pay. The utility of action also varies with the specified risk behavior of the user. For instance, as shown in the Figure 1 the utility of accepting an offer for a risk-averse buyer increases much slower as the difference between the offered price and the preferred price decreases. That means that as long as the price of the opponent comes closer to the preferred price of the buyer, he will be more willing to accept it, since there is not significant growth in utility if he continues to counter-propose. For a risk-seeking agent, the utility of continues to grow fast in this case, since he is willing to take the risk of contra-proposing, hoping to get a price even lower than his preferred price.

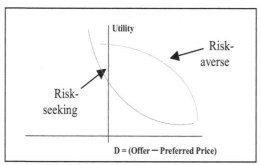

Fig. 1. Variation of U_accept for a **buyer**

Risk behavior also affects the increment and the decrement of the buyer and the seller. For a risk-averse buyer, if the urgency of current task is very high and the importance of money is also high, he will start by offering a price which is not too low compared to the maximum price his user is willing to pay. A risk-seeking buyer will start from a very low price and will try to get the lowest price he can get. For a risk-seeking seller the utility of accepting an offer increases, if he gets more money than what he has specified as his minimum price.

The functions that the agents use to increase or decrease their offers and counteroffers as a buyer and as a seller are defined as follows:

For Buyers
If max_price > std_price then
    Offered price := std_price − Δ
Else
    Offered price := max_price − Δ

For Sellers
If min_price > std_price then
    Offered price := min_price + Δ
Else
    Offered price := std_price + Δ

where std_price is the market price provided by the matchmaker. It is calculated based on the current situation of the market of help on this topic and on the difficulty of the topic, thus providing some measure for the actual worth of the resource. For both the buyer and the seller the values of Δ should not exceed their preferred prices, R. Δ is determined as follows (x is the offered price):

For Buyers

If urgency = very urgent then
If risk_behavior = risk seeking then
$$\Delta := 1 - e^{-x/R} \qquad x > R$$
If risk_behavior = risk averse then
$$\Delta := 1 - e^{-x/R} \qquad x < R$$

For Sellers

If urgency = very urgent then
If risk_behavior = risk seeking then
$$\Delta := \sqrt{\min\_price}$$
If risk_behavior == risk averse then
$$\Delta := \log(\min\_price)$$

We use an influence diagram that has a conditional node representing the uncertainty about the other party (see Figure 2). The outcomes of this node are the probabilities that an opponent can be in any of the states accept, reject and counteroffer. Since the agent does not know anything about the environment or about the other agent's user, we consider that all the states in which the opponent can be are equally likely. At every step the agents have to choose between three actions: accept, reject and counter-offer. They do so by calculating the maximum expected utility for the actions, which are represented as the possible choices for the decision node in the influence diagram. In any practical application of negotiation there are often multiple objectives involved and there has to be tradeoff between one over the other. Before the decision is made the factors that are already known and affect the decision (deterministic nodes) are taken into account as they affect the actions to be made. The node corresponding to the opponent's action can be considered conditional since nothing is known about him. For the first experiment we treat the outcomes of the opponent node as equally likely. In the second experiment we replace the equal likelihood of the opponent's actions with the outcome of a model of the opponent using a probabilistic influence diagram.

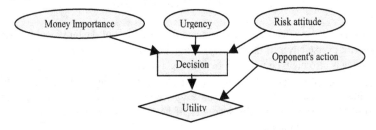

Fig. 2. Influence Diagram for the decision model

4.2 Modeling the Opponent

Ideally (and as often is assumed in cooperative environments [15]) negotiating parties have full knowledge about the opponent. This, however, it is not the case when agents are self-interested. In trade and commerce there can be hidden intentional assumptions. It is unlikely that the user will be willing to share his preferences with other users (or their agents). In order to deal with such situation and still be able to know as much as possible about the opponent we deploy a model of the opponent by using a probabilistic influence diagram to model the opponent. Since in a dynamic environment like a market place where the situation is changing all the time and new buyers and sellers keep on entering and leaving the system, it is very costly for agents to create and maintain models of the other the participants in the environment. Our agents have no prior knowledge about each other. After the first round of offers made the agent starts using his opponent's move to predict his reaction to the counteroffer that he is going to make. It is also important to note that we are not doing recursive agent modeling.

Figure 3 shows a probabilistic influence diagram; the oval nodes are conditional and the double-circled node is deterministic. Conditional probability distribution of the conditional nodes over the outcomes is assessed on the basis of the first offer. Probability distribution of the Opponent's action node can be calculated by performing reductions over the nodes. For instance, by performing the arc reversal from the Money Importance node to the Opponent's Action node, makes Money Importance a barren node. Hence, it can be removed from the diagram and a new conditional probability distribution is calculated. Conditional predecessors of the nodes (if any) are inherited. In a similar way the diagram can be simplified by using arc reversal operation and barren node removal, which finally gives the probability distribution for the Opponent's Action node. If the next move of the opponent does not match with the predicted action, Bayes' update rule is used to update the information. For more information about probabilistic influence diagrams refer to [9].

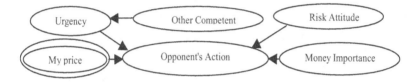

Fig. 3. Probabilistic Influence Diagram for the opponent's actions

Evaluating both influence diagrams and probabilistic influence diagrams is NP-hard. In our case the number of nodes is relatively small and there are no complexity problems. However, if the number of nodes increases drastically, negotiation might become computationally inefficient.

4. Experiment

The goals of the evaluation are to test the performance of the negotiation mechanism in terms of quality of deals that agents make for their users and to see if modeling the opponent brings benefits in negotiation. In order to answer these questions, we compare the deals obtained by agents using the proposed approach (decision theoretic with modeling the opponent) with deals obtained by the same agents under identical circumstances using other negotiation approaches. Since negotiation is done on behalf of the user, it is necessary to take into account her preferences. There is an immense number of possible preference combinations. For this evaluation, 5 different combinations of user preferences for helper and helpee are tested with 3 different combinations of preferred prices: one, in which the preferred price intervals of the negotiators overlap widely (called session 1 and denoted as S1), another one in which the preferred prices overlap but not widely (session 2 / S2) and one where there is no overlap in the preferred prices (session 3 / S3). The experiments were carried out on a simulation.. The experimental setup follows several assumptions related to the peer-help application:

- The issue of negotiation is the price per unit of time at which the help session will occur.
- The matchmaker provides to both parties the standard price for help on each topic, which is calculated by a central component based on the difficulty of the topic.
- The agent whose user needs help (helpee / buyer) begins the negotiation with the agent of the user who is on the top of the list of possible helpers.
- The agents do not know anything about the other agents in the system at the start of the negotiation process.
- Each agent makes an offer depending on the user's risk attitude. The decay function and the raise function are dependent on the money importance and the urgency of the work / help.
- The agents are allowed to offer the same price more than once -- in this way the agents stay rigid on a price, if they do not want to increment or decrement it. However, a seller is not allowed to ask for price greater than his previous offered value and a buyer is not allowed to ask for price less than his previous value within one negotiation session.
- Each agent ensures that it does not exceed the preferred price limit set by the user (the maximum price for the helpee / buyer and minimum price for helper/ seller).

We compared three negotiation approaches.

In Approach 1 the agents don't use decision theoretic approach for negotiation. Both the parties make offers and counteroffers by making an increment or a decrement by a fixed amount based on the difference between their preferred prices. This corresponds to an "ideal" case of fair trade between agents that are not self-interested, reveal their preferred prices and use the same strategy. In fact, there is no need of negotiation: the agents can immediately agree on a price which is the average between the preferred prices of the agents. In this way no agent wins and no one looses.

In Approach 2 the agents use an influence diagram to model the decision-making process, with a chance node corresponding to the opponent's action. The probabilities of the opponent's actions are taken as equal (i.e. no model of the opponent is created).

In Approach 3 the agents take into account the model of he opponent in their own decision-making, as explained in section 3.2.

Our experiments showed that increasing the "intelligence" of the negotiating parties increases the percentage of rejections in negotiation (as can be seen in Table 1). This could be interpreted as negative result, since the percentage of failed negotiations increases. However, it can be viewed also positively, since it means that the agents are rejecting deals that are not profitable, instead of accepting them. As it can be expected most of the rejections happened in session 3, where there is no overlap between the preferred price intervals of the negotiators.

A series of experiments were made to investigate the influence of the negotiation mechanism proposed (Approach 3) on the quality of deals achieved by using it. The preferences of the helpee and the helper were kept constant for all configurations and across the three sessions only the negotiation approach of one of the agents was changed. Again, for each negotiation approach 15 experiments were carried out for each of the 5 different settings of user preferences and in 3 sessions depending on the preferred prices. The deals were analysed from the point of view of the helpee /buyer and of the helper / seller (i.e. depending on which agent changes its negotiation approach). The results (see Table 2) show that using the decision theoretic approach with modeling the opponent (Approach 3) brings better quality deals in most of the cases when there is a large preferred price overlap. Approach 1 is only better when there is little or no scope for negotiation. When both agents use Approach 3, the helper/seller gets a better deal, since he is in an advantageous position (one step ahead) in modeling its opponent. The agent that starts the negotiation is in a disadvantaged position.

Table 1: Rejections in the various configurations. The first column describes the negotiation approaches used by the agents in the configuration, e.g. S:1, B:1 means that both the seller and the buyer use approach 1.

Confi-guration	Total Rejections (in %)	% Rejected by Helpee (Buyer)			% Rejected by Helper (Seller)		
		S1	S2	S3	S1	S2	S3
S:1, B:1	0	-	-	-	-	-	-
S:1, B:2	0	-	-	-	-	-	-
S:1, B:3	20	-	-	100	-	-	0
S:2, B:1	0	-	-	-	-	-	-
S:2, B:2	6.67	-	-	100	-	-	0
S:2, B:3	20	-	-	33.3	-	-	66.6
S:3, B:1	26.6	-	-	0	-	-	100
S:3, B:2	26.6	-	0	0	-	100	100
S:3, B:3	53.3	50	0	66.6	50	100	33.3

Table 2: Comparison of the percentage of better deals achieved by using a different strategy. The left part of the table shows the better deals achieved by the helpee /buyer when switching strategies, and the right part shows the percentage of better deals achieved by the helper / seller when switching strategies.

Case comparisons from helpee's viewpoint	Best deals for S1 (in %)	Best deals for S2 (in %)	Best deals for S3 (in %)	Case comparisons from helper's viewpoint	Best deals for S1 (in %)	Best deals for S2 (in %)	Best deals for S3 (in %)
B: 1→2, S: 1	60	25	20	S: 1→2, B:1	60	40	25
B: 1→2, S: 2	100	80	0	S: 1→2, B:2	0	33.3	0
B: 1→2, S: 3	60	0	0	S: 1→2, B:3	80	60	0
B: 2→3, S: 1	100	80	100	S: 2→3, B:1	80	100	100
B: 2→3, S: 2	60	40	50	S: 2→3, B:2	100	100	100
B: 2→3, S: 3	100	50	0	S: 2→3, B:3	33.3	100	100
B: 1→3, S: 1	80	60	50	S: 1→3, B:1	100	100	100
B: 1→3, S: 2	80	80	50	S: 1→3, B:2	100	100	100
B: 1→3, S: 3	66.6	0	0	S: 1→3, B:3	66.6	100	100

5. Conclusion

In open environments with self-interested agents, a decision-theoretic approach to negotiation with modeling the opponent has proven to yield good deals. In this paper we have presented a negotiation mechanism that utilizes decision model (influence diagram) taking into account the preferences and the risk behavior of the user. Such a decision model allows to take into account and to handle tradeoffs among the factors that affect decision-making in negotiation and can be applied to any domain.

We have extended this negotiation mechanism to create and use a model of the opponent, represented with a probabilistic influence diagram. Our experimental results show that this mechanism finds a better deal for the agent who uses it when there is space for negotiation. We are currently implementing the proposed negotiation mechanisms in personal agents representing human users in an Internet-based virtual market environment for peer help (I-Help).

Acknowledgement: This work has been partially supported by NSERC under TL-NCE Project 6.28.

6. References

1. Carmel, D., and Markovitch, S. Learning Models of Intelligent Agents in Proceedings of Third International Conference on Multiagent Systems.(1998), 64-71.
2. Durfee, E., and Lesser, V. Negotiating Task Decomposition and Allocation Using Partial Global Planning. Distributed Artificial Intelligence. Volume2 Huhns, L., and Gasser, M.(eds) Morgan Kaufmann: San Mateo, California (1987), 229-243.
3. Harsanyi, J., Rational Behaviour and Bargaining Equilibrium in Games and Social Situations. Cambridge University Press, Cambridge, (1977).
4. Maes, P., Guttman, R., Moukas, G., Agents that Buy and Sell. Communications of the ACM. 42, 3, (1997) 81-83.
5. Suryadi, D., Gmytasiewicz, P. Learning Models of Other Agents using Influence Diagrams, in Proceedings of the Seventh International Conference on User Modeling, (1999), 223-232.
6. Park, S., Durfee, E., Birmingham, W. Advantages of Strategic Thinking in Multiagent Contracts. in Proceedings of Second International Conference on Multi-Agent Systems. (1996), 259-266.
7. Preist, Chris., Commodity Trading Using An Agent-Based Iterated Double Auction in Proceedings of the Third Annual Conference on Autonomous Agents, (1999), 131-138.
8. Sathi, A., and Fox S. Constraint Directed Negotiation of Resource Allocation. Distributed Artificial Intelligence, Volume 2, Morgan Kaufmann: San Mateo, CA (1987), 163-194.
9. Shachter, R., Probabilistic inference and influence diagrams. Operations Research. 36,4 (1988), 589-604.

10. Shachter, R., Evaluating Influence Diagrams. Operations Research. 34, 36, (1986), 871-882.
11. Sycara, K. Resolving goal conflicts via Negotiation in Proceedings Seventh National Conference on Artificial Intelligence.(1988).
12. Vassileva J., Greer J, McCalla G., Deters R., Zapata D., Mudgal C., Grant S. A Multi-Agent Approach to the Design of Peer-Help Environments, in Proceedings of AIED'99, Le Mans, France, July, (1999), 38-45. also available on line at: http://julita.usask.ca/homepage/Agents.html
13. Vidal, J., and Durfee, E., The Impact of Nested Agent Models in an Information Economy in Proceedings of Second International Conference on Multi-Agent Systems. (1996), 377-384.
14. Zheng, D., and Sycara, K. Benefits of Learning in Negotiation in Proceedings of Fifteenth National Conference on Artificial Intelligence, (1997). 36-41.
15. Zlotkin, G., and Rosenschein, J.   Cooperation and Conflict Resolution via Negotiation among Autonomous Agents in Non Cooperative Domains. IEEE Transactions on Systems, Man and Cybernetics, 21, 6,(1991). 1317-1332.
16. Zlotkin, G., and Rosenschein, J. Negotiation and Task Sharing among Autonomous Agents in Cooperative Domains. In Proceedings of Eleventh International Joint Conference in Artificial Intelligence. (1989). 912-917.

On Ensuring Lower Bounds of Negotiation Results

Otmar Görlitz, Ralf Neubert, Wolfgang Benn

Chemnitz University of Technology
Department of Computer Science
09107 Chemnitz, Germany

{Otmar.Goerlitz,Ralf.Neubert,Wolfgang.Benn}@informatik.tu-chemnitz.de

Abstract. Employing software agents in tasks of electronic commerce where monetary values are negotiated and possibly exchanged by the agents autonomously, rises the question about the reliability of the agents. A human client expects his authorized agent to perform its tasks stable, reliable and safe, i.e. the agent should neither crash nor behave unpredictable in unexpected situations. It should always pursue the best possible deal and should be highly immune against fraud. We have developed an intelligent, adaptive agent model for integrative negotiations and show the stability of the model's behaviour, the reliability of guaranteed negotiation results and the insusceptibility against possible manipulations and fraud.

1 Introduction

The automation of negotiation by software agents can open up a great variety of interesting opportunities to support and relieve users in online business and electronic commerce. For instance, virtual market places can be created where agents buy and sell items on the user's behalf as it was shown in the Kasbah experiment [3]. Also, personal assistance agents could offer much more capabilities than just gathering price and availability information. They could negotiate about rebates dependent on delivery times, ordered amounts and any other imaginable features of products. Auction bots could be improved from simply alerting the user that an item is currently auctioned off, like Tooto's agent does [20]. Instead the user's auction agent could actively take part in the auction and already buy the item or acquire the right of first refusal.

However, employing software agents in tasks where monetary value is exchanged rises the question about the reliability of the agents. More precisely, the agent's behaviour in the negotiation should yield a result equal or better than what its human client could have achieved. That is, the agent should guarantee to achieve at least a certain minimal result in the negotiation. This lower bound should be programmable. The agent's negotiation behaviour and parameters have to ensure its efficiency.

M. Klusch and L. Kerschberg (Eds.): CIA 2000, LNAI 1860, pp. 119-130, 2000.

The agent's behaviour in the negotiation is usually deterministic. However, if the behaviour algorithm has weaknesses, the agent is susceptible to manipulations by an dishonest negotiation partner. A dishonest negotiation partner can deliberately exploit weaknesses in the behaviour to achieve better results in the negotiation for himself or to impair the negotiation results of the agent. What makes this situation especially problematic is that the agent is unsuspecting. As long as its behaviour algorithm works, the agent will not notice the manipulation and cannot take any measures against it. To make the agent employable and reliable, its behaviour has not only to guarantee the lower bound in normal negotiations but also against manipulation attempts by dishonest negotiation partners.

In [1] and [2] we have introduced a new model of an adaptive negotiation agent for integrative negotiations. Following our model, the agent can negotiate about multiple interdependent attributes of a product and consider tradeoffs between the attributes. The advantages of our model are:

- Considering multiple attributes and interdependencies among them allows a more detailed description of a desired product or item. It allows to value and negotiate the product in more features than only its price.
- If both negotiation partners have different priorities among the attributes, i.e. their attribute worth rankings are different, our agent model may yield better results for both of them, when each concedes in those attributes the other values high.
- Our mechanism of calculating tradeoffs between attributes allows to combine the concession in one attribute with a gain in one or more other attributes. Therefore the overall utility in the negotiation decreases very slowly with the concessions.
- Finally, our agent model supports the parallel negotiation about all attributes, which is significantly faster and more convenient than negotiating the attributes sequentially and backtrack if necessary.

Our agent model does not contribute to the solution of the matchmaking problem. We assume, the item or product in question as well as its negotiable attributes are known to and accepted by both sides when our agent becomes active. There are several research projects concerned with the matchmaking problem, but the results are not generally satisfying yet. An interesting approach is the InfoSleuth project [7]. Other projects, like MOMIS [11] and TSIMMIS [21], rely on similar mediator techniques. It is not required for our agent to know the data type the other side assigns to an attribute. The agent is capable of transforming any offered attribute value into its internal computation model. Analogously, all of the agent's proposals consist of real attribute values. No proprietary data format is required in the negotiation.

Our agent derives its adaptive behaviour from calculated reactions on the proposals of its negotiation partner and from the ability to change its own behaviour dependent on the course of the ongoing negotiation.

In this paper we present a detailed analysis of our model's mechanism of negotiation proposal generation and the results the agent can guarantee in different negotiation situations. We also explain the influence of the agent's negotiation strategy on the lower bound of the result. Following we analyse the possibilities of a dishonest negotiation partner to manipulate the agent and the maximal losses for the agent. We conclude with a discussion of the results and implications on the stability and reliability of our agent model.

2   Related work

In the domain of integrative negotiations performed by software agents relatively few efforts are reported. The work of Keeny and Raiffa [8] gives a theoretical foundation. Automated integrative negotiations are researched by Guttman and Maes [5]. Further description of this work can be found in [6]. The Tete-a-Tete system [18] promises the inclusion of integrative negotiations. The Kasbah system [3] was an experiment to create a virtual market place where software agents could trade goods autonomously. However, in the system the agents could only negotiate about the price of the goods by user defined decay functions.

The basic behavioural model of our agent follows the Belief-Desire-Intention model of autonomous acting software agents. Descriptions of the BDI model can be found in [14] and [15]. Detailed discussions on the principles of negotiations come from the domain of game theory, e.g. [10], [12], [13], [17]. Agent negotiations under time constraints are discussed in [9].

Rosenschein and Zlotkin [16] give a detailed analysis of dealing with dishonest agents in negotiations. They propose negotiation protocols, which prevent advantages derived from manipulations and therefore remove the incentive to fraud and lies. Fankhauser and Tesch [4], [19] introduce arbitration protocols which are stable against several forms of manipulation. We take from their work the dimensions of manipulative behaviour and lies, which we use in the following.

3   Negotiation behaviour of the agent

In this section we discuss which results an agent following our model can guarantee in the negotiation. First, we explain the general behavioural rules in our agent model and the assumptions we take about the negotiation partner (henceforth also referred to as opponent, especially when assumed to be manipulative and lying). Generally, we view the agent's negotiations as preliminary negotiations whose results require the final confirmation of the human client. This implicates that the negotiations need to be repeatable and, up to a certain degree, will yield the same results.

During the negotiation process our agent exchanges a description of items or products as lists of attribute values. The agent transforms the real attribute values into an uniform internal representation, so called satisfaction values, which range from 0% to 100%. They provide a semantic decoupling, an abstract scale for the comparison of attributes and furthermore a base for expressing attribute interdependencies and tradeoffs between them. A more detailed description of the satisfaction value transformation and the handling of different types can be found in [2].

In our model agents follow a protocol of alternating offers. One of the agents starts by making its initial offer and the other agent either accepts it or reacts with a counteroffer. Each agent has a timeout parameter t_{max} determining when to withdraw from the negotiation, if it lasts too long without finding a deal. This means, negotiation time represents a particular value used for strategic decisions. Negotiation time $t \in (0, \ldots, t_{max})$ is regarded as sequence of discrete steps for the remainder of this paper.

Before we start with an analysis of the behaviour let us summarize the internal proposal generation algorithm for the sake of better understanding. A negotiation offer or proposal by agent $r \in \{\mathcal{A}, \mathcal{B}\}^1$ at time t is a vector $VV_r(t) = (vv_{1r}(t), \ldots, vv_{nr}(t))^T$ of satisfaction values $0 \leq vv_{ir}(t) \leq 1$ for each attribute i. An agent's initial offer is made by transforming the internal satisfaction values of 1 into the according attribute values. This means it demands its optimal values for all attributes.

If an agent generates a counteroffer, it calculates a new compromise that is superimposed by the compensation values according to the compensation matrix. The compromise vector $KV_r(t) = (kv_{1r}(t), \ldots, kv_{nr}(t))^T$ determines the maximum concession for the attributes in negotiation step t

$$kv_{ir}(t) = kv_{ir}(t-2) - \Delta gv_{iO(r)}(t_l) * (1 - hv_{ir}). \tag{1}$$

The agent's last compromise is denoted by $kv_{ir}(t-2)$, $\Delta gv_{iO(r)}(t_l)$ describes the concessions for the attribute i made by agent r's opponent $O(r)$ in the last negotiation periods l and hv_{ir} is the overall worth of the attribute to agent r. In time $t = 0$, when $\Delta gv_{iO(r)}(t_l)$ is not available, $kv_{ir}(t)$ is calculated as

$$kv_{ir}(0) = (1 - gv_{iO(r)}(0))hv_{ir} \tag{2}$$

The proposal values vv_{ir} are generated by a Hopfield net like iteration mech-

---

Algorithm 1

$vv_{ir}^0(t) = kv_{ir}(t), \quad tg = 1;$
repeat
$\quad vv_{ir}^{tg}(t) = kv_{ir}(t) + \sum_{j=1}^{n}(1 - vv_{jr}^{tg-1}(t)) * w_{ji}$
$\quad tg = tg + 1$
until $(\|vv_{ir}^{tg}(t) - vv_{ir}^{tg-1}(t)\| \leq \epsilon \quad \forall i) \quad OR \quad (tg = tg_{max})$

---

anism given in algorithm 1. The compensation values $0 \leq w_{ji} < 1$ are used to express the attribute interdependencies. This means the losses in the attribute j should be compensated by some additional gain in attribute i's satisfaction value. The sum of the gains describes the influence of all other attributes on

---

¹ The subscripts $\mathcal{A}, \mathcal{B}$ will serve as distinction of the agents, if appropriate.

attribute i. The local counter tg is used to distinguish the negotiation time t from the network cycles. In each network cycle a new, temporary proposal value $vv_{ir}^{tg}(t)$ is generated, which creates a different compensation situation among the attributes. The system oscillates between possible, but unstable proposal vectors. The cycles are performed until the oscillation is damped enough and a stable proposal is found or the network timeout tg_{max} is reached.

This algorithm should ensure a *rational* behaviour of our agent and we assume, the negotiation partner also does so. Commonly, rational behaviour is defined as: Both sides follow negotiation strategies which gain them some utility. For our agent we specify rational behaviour as follows:

- The agent assumes, its opponent behaves rational and that the opponent assumes the same in turn.
- The agent's proposals never leave the interval given in the initialization parameters by *Minimum/Maximum ... Optimum* for all attributes[2].
- The agent expects that its concession in an attribute's value is rewarded by the opponent and the other side also concedes.
- If two consecutive proposals of the opponent differ by less than the insignificance threshold ϵ, the agent considers this as repeated offer and, in its default behaviour, answers by repeating its own previous offer. Thus a 'not much progression' situation can easily turn into stagnation of the negotiation.
- If the proposed values of both sides are sufficiently close, i.e. they differ by less than the insignificance threshold ϵ, the agent considers this as agreement and adopts the opponent's proposed value.
- If an agreement is found in an attribute's value, the agent tries to hold it, i.e. it will never demand more in subsequent negotiation steps. However, this is not expected from the opponent[3].
- The opponent's offer is never underbid if the agent's negotiation interval ranges from *Minimum* to *Optimum*. An offer is never overbid if the negotiation interval ranges from *Maximum* to *Optimum*.
- When an agreement in all attributes is found, the agent stops negotiating and regards the negotiation as successfully ended. We consider the result as possible deal.
- The agent negotiates only a particular time. That is, only a particular number of proposals are exchanged (defined as negotiation parameter t_{max}), before the negotiation is considered failed. It is assumed that the opponent also has a time limit, which may be shorter or longer than the agent's.

We have used the term *utility* to describe a numerical worth or profit the agent assigns to the result of a negotiation. Commonly, utility is the gain or

---

[2] The *Optimum* defines the attribute value the user desires. *Minimum/Maximum* defines the lowest/highest attribute value the user is willing to accept. Thus *Minimum/Maximum ... Optimum* describes the value range of the agent's negotiation interval.

[3] This behaviour can result in a suboptimal utility. It was chosen to reduce the complexity of the proposal generation. Strategies and behaviour issues for utility maximization are subject of further research.

profit each side receives from the result of a negotiation. Utility is a monotonic increasing function with a lower bound of 0 — the conflict deal. We define utility u for agent r received from negotiation η as follows:

$$u_r(\eta) = \begin{cases} f_r(GV_{O(r)}) + b_r & : \text{ if a deal is found} \\ f_r(GV_{O(r)}) & : \text{ if the negotiation failed} \end{cases} \tag{3}$$

$GV_{O(r)}$ denotes the opponent's last offer, a vector of proposed attribute values. If the negotiation resulted in a deal, this is also the agent's last offer VV_r[4]. $f_r(GV_{O(r)})$ assigns a numerical value to the offer. b_r is a bonus the agent receives for finding a deal. If the negotiation failed, b_r is 0.

We define the *conflict deal* as follows:

$$(GV_{O(r)}(t) = 0) \wedge (VV_r(t) \neq 0) \wedge (t = t_{max})$$

The opponent's offer $GV_{O(r)}$ in negotiation step t gives a satisfaction of 0 for every attribute, the agent's corresponding offer is different and the negotiation has timed out. This means, the negotiation failed and the opponent's last offer gives the agent null percent satisfaction in every attribute. In contrast,

$$(GV_{O(r)}(t) = 0) \wedge (GV_{O(r)}(t) = VV_r(t)) \wedge (t \leq t_{max})$$

is not the conflict deal, because a deal is found which happens to be the lower bound of the agent's negotiation interval. In this case $u_r(\eta) = b_r$, because $f_r(GV_{O(r)})$ returns 0. The case

$$(GV_{O(r)}(t) \geq 0) \wedge (GV_{O(r)}(t) \neq VV_r(t)) \wedge (t = t_{max})$$

is also not the conflict deal. The negotiation failed and no deal is found, but the opponent's last offer gives the agent an overall satisfaction value greater than 0. Because we consider the agent's negotiations as preliminary, we assume that we can find a deal if we accept the opponents last offer. Thus the agent's negotiation efforts are not futile, since we received information about a possible deal, which would yield some satisfaction of our goals. The agent loses the deal bonus b_r, but its utility is $u_r(\eta) = f_r(GV_{O(r)}(t)) > 0$.

3.1   Control of the agent's behaviour

Algorithm 1 in connection with equations 1, 2 constitutes the following general behaviour of the agent. If the opponent makes concessions the agent is willing to make concessions too. In case no concessions are made the agent reacts with its last offer. We call this the *"Stay with the user's preferences"* strategy or default strategy. The strategy can lead to a stagnation of the negotiation process and prevent finding a deal.

---

[4] We use the term *deal* if both sides agreed on all attributes values and the negotiation has successfully ended. We use the term *agreement* to denote that both sides agreed on one attribute's value. In this case the negotiation may go on.

To circumvent stagnation another strategy is required. Changes of the negotiation parameters by the agent itself are necessary. We have implemented a second strategy *"Find a deal"*. This strategy adjusts parameters in order to increase the probability of finding a deal. If a stagnation is discovered, strategic concessions are made such that the other side is encouraged to concede too. We will investigate the effects of strategic concession later in this section.

The rationale behind this behaviour is explained in [2]. The agent derives the maximum utility from the deal closest to its *Optimum*-values. Thus the default strategy is suitable if the deal bonus is low. It emphasizes the closeness to the agent's *Optimum*-values. The *"Find a deal"* strategy has a higher probability to result in a deal, however with less satisfying attribute values. Negotiations with a high deal bonus should favor this strategy.

We consider now two of our agents negotiating about an item with two attributes a, b. For reasons of simplicity we assume the attributes to be of steady type with identical ranges. The real value ranges are mapped to exactly opposite satisfaction value ranges. This means agent $\mathcal{A}$'s optima give Agent $\mathcal{B}$ a satisfaction of 0 and vice versa. At first let us presume that there are no attribute interdependencies. It follows that all $w_{ji} = 0$ and no compensation is gained for made compromises. The proposal depends only on the overall attribute worths that determine the compromise vector KV.

The analysis of the alternating concessions and the transformation of the recursive formulas to iterative ones shows:

$$
\begin{aligned}
c &= \tfrac{hv_A}{hv_B} \\
vv_A(t) &= chv_B - (1 - chv_B^2) \sum_{p=1}^{t-2} (1 - chv_B)^p (1 - hv_B)^{p-1} \quad \forall t \geq 2 \quad (4)\\
vv_B(t) &= chv_B^2 - (1 - chv_B^2) \sum_{p=1}^{t-3} (1 - chv_B)^p (1 - hv_B)^p \quad \forall t \geq 3
\end{aligned}
$$

For a deal between the agents the following three conditions can be derived. Condition C1 expresses the agreement. Whereas C2 and C3 represent the non stagnation condition for the respective agent.

- **C1:** $t \geq 5$

$$
\frac{chv_B^2 + chv_B - 1}{1 - chv_B^2} \leq \sum_{p=1}^{t-2} (1 - chv_B)^p (1 - hv_B)^{p-1} \\
+ \sum_{p=1}^{t-3} (1 - chv_B)^p (1 - hv_B)^p \tag{5}
$$

- **C2:**

$$
\|(1 - chv_B^2)(1 - chv_B)^p (1 - hv_B)^{p-1}\| > \epsilon \tag{6}
$$

- **C3:**

$$
\|(1 - chv_B^2)(1 - chv_B)^p (1 - hv_B)^p\| > \epsilon \tag{7}
$$

For any given ratio or hv_B important questions can be answered. What is the range of hv_A, to reach an agreement within a certain number of steps? What is the range that guarantees a deal? What time will it take to reach a deal?

The following example should illustrate this. c is set to 1, this implicates $HV_A = HV_B$. From condition C1 it follows that for $0 < HV_r < 0.61$ a deal is guaranteed. The fraction on the left side of the inequality receives a negative sign, whereas all the terms on the right are positive so that the sum is greater than 0. This means a deal is found at latest in step $t = 5$.

By solving C2 and C3 for p it can be checked, whether the timeout is set appropriate according to the determined HV. Is the worth chosen greater than 0.61 then t_{max} is set to $p - 1$, which will result in no stagnation within the negotiation time. By C1 it can be tested whether there is a deal with these parameters or not.

In the next case let us have a closer look on the special case of cyclic compensations on the generation of proposals of one agent. The attributes a, b are mutually connected. This means there are compensations w from a to b and vice versa that are not necessarily symmetric. For this we analyse the repeat loop of the algorithm 1. The expression of the recursive formula in iterative form yields us a way to compute the compensations for any given last offer $VV_r(t - 1)$. For an easier computation we use the maximum network cycles tg_{max} as counter and not the damping stop criterion.

$$
\begin{aligned}
vv_{ar}(t) = {}& C + \sum_{n=1}^{tg_{max}} w_{ab}^{\frac{n}{2}-1} w_{ba}^{\frac{n}{2}}(1 - D)F_1 + w_{ab}^{\frac{n-1}{2}} w_{ba}^{\frac{n-1}{2}}(C - 1)F_2 \\
& + yw_{ab}^{tn2} w_{ba}^{tn2+1} F_2' \\
& - xw_{ab}^{tn1} w_{ba}^{tn1} F_1'
\end{aligned}
\tag{8}
$$

$$
\begin{aligned}
vv_{br}(t) = {}& C + \sum_{n=1}^{tg_{max}} w_{ab}^{\frac{n}{2}} w_{ba}^{\frac{n}{2}-1}(1 - C)F_1 + w_{ab}^{\frac{n-1}{2}} w_{ba}^{\frac{n-1}{2}}(D - 1)F_2 \\
& + xw_{ab}^{tn2+1} w_{ba}^{tn2} F_2' \\
& - yw_{ab}^{tn1} w_{ba}^{tn1} F_1'
\end{aligned}
\tag{9}
$$

The constants $C, D, x, y, tn1, tn2, F_1$, and F_2 are substitutions for the following expressions.

$$
\begin{array}{ll}
C = kv_{ar} - \Delta gv_{aO(r)}(1 - hv_{ar}) & D = kv_{br} - \Delta gv_{bO(r)}(1 - hv_{br}) \\
x = (1 - vv_{ar}(t - 1)) & y = (1 - vv_{br}(t - 1)) \\
tn1 = \frac{tg_{max}}{2} & tn2 = \frac{tg_{max}-1}{2} \\
F_1 = (n + 1) \bmod 2 & F_2 = (n) \bmod 2 \\
F_1' = (tg_{max} + 1) \bmod 2 & F_2' = (tg_{max}) \bmod 2
\end{array}
$$

This knowledge can be used to calculate the lowest possible offer the agent will propose or accept in the course of a normal negotiation. Equations 2 and 1 show, the limit of $kv_{ar}(t)$ approaches 0 for small hv_{ar}. We can conclude the lower bound of the agent in attribute a if we assume $kv_{ar}(t) = 0$ and calculate the compensations on a in this case:

$$
\begin{aligned}
vv_{ar}^{tg}(t) &= kv_{ar}(t) + (1 - vv_{br}^{tg-1}(t))w_{ba} \\
vv_{br}^{tg}(t) &= kv_{br}(t) + (1 - vv_{ar}^{tg-1}(t))w_{ab} \\
kv_{ar}(t) &= kv_{br}(t) = 0 \quad tg \to tg_{max}
\end{aligned}
\tag{10}
$$

These equations constitute the repeat loop of algorithm 1 in the case of two mutually dependent attributes. The lower bound corresponds to the compensations for the minimum of the dependent attribute. If no compensations are demanded, the lower bound approaches 0. If more than one attribute demands compensations in attribute a, a's lower bound rises accordingly.

3.2 Influences of strategic modifications

If the agent follows the strategy *"Find a deal"*, it performs every m steps in the negotiation a test, whether the negotiation has come closer to a successful end. In this test the agent considers the current proposals of both sides, the elapsed negotiation time and the direction the proposals moved in the course of the negotiation (that is: Who has conceded, who has demanded more). If the agent comes to the conclusion the overall stage of the negotiation has improved, it will go on with the default behaviour. In case the overall stage has decreased, it will, dependent on the influencing factor that got worse, calculate a new proposal independent from its normal generation algorithm. Then, by means of its memory module, it predicts a hypothetical counteroffer as reaction on its modified proposal. If this would improve the negotiation stage, the internal modifications are committed and the negotiation parameters are modified such that subsequent proposals generated by the default algorithm continue on this course. Otherwise the changes are discarded and the default behaviour continues.

If we assume both sides behave rational, the strategy test can find two cases:

1. Both sides concede, the differences between the proposals decrease.
2. The negotiation stagnates. Both sides insist on their demands.

All other possible constellations are either not rational behaviour or lead to one of the above cases in the following negotiation step.

In the first case, the strategy test will report an improvement in the negotiation and the agent will continue with its default behaviour. In the second case, the test will report a deterioration because time elapsed and the agent has not come closer to a deal. The solution for the agent is to lower its demands and hope, this concession will encourage the other side to concede too.

This additional concession influences the lower bound of the negotiation result. The amount of the concession is:

$$vv_{ir}(t-1) - (1 - gv_{iO(r)}) * (1 - hv_{ir})^2 \tag{11}$$

The other side's latest offer is weighted with the own attribute's worth and then subtracted from the last offer the agent proposed. If the other side's proposal was high, then the agent's concession is small because the negotiation stage is already good and a deal is not far away. If the other side's offer is low, the agent concedes more because this is a hint the other side has a high preference on this attribute and is unlikely to concede much.

4 Susceptibility against manipulations

In the previous sections we derived lower bounds of the agent's negotiation results assuming its opponent behaves rational and honest like the agent itself. Especially we expected that every concession of the agent is in turn rewarded by the opponent with a concession. However, the opponent might try to exploit the deterministic behavior of the agent and manipulate its respective offers in such a form that the negotiation develops in a more advantageous direction for him.

According to [19] we consider six possible types of manipulation in three dimensions:

informed: We assume, an informed opponent knows all negotiation parameters of the agent and can monitor its calculations at every time.

uninformed: In contrast to the informed opponent, the uninformed only knows the general rules of behaviour the agent follows, e.g. its rationality and the concept of attribute compensations.

beneficial: A beneficial opponent tries to increase his utility by manipulations. Applying our utility formula, this opponent tries to get the highest possible offer of the agent. His deal bonus however is very low, because with a high deal bonus the risk of time out would lower his incentive to pursue the highest possible offer.

malevolent: Contrary to the beneficial opponent, the malevolent's goal is to harm the agent's utility. Therefore he tries to deny the final deal and keeps his offers as low as possible.

greedy: We understand a greedy opponent as one who answers to a concession with an own concession which is lower, especially in attributes he has a high preference for.

cautious: The cautious opponent, in contrast to the greedy, is willing to concede more than the agent in attributes with low worth for him. Thereby he tries to lower the agent's compensations on attributes he values high.

The different opponents pursue the following strategies and can achieve these results: The best strategy for the *malevolent* opponent is to offer constantly his optimum during the negotiation. In case of contrary negotiation intervals this yields a satisfaction of 0 for the agent. Because the malevolent opponent never concedes, *malevolent, greedy* or *malevolent, cautious* behaviour does not apply. The *malevolent, informed* opponent knows a priori if the agent will perform strategic concessions and thus can avoid the agent's agreement on his optimum by withdrawing from the negotiation just before. The *malevolent, uninformed* opponent might encounter this situation, because he has no safe indication as for when the agent will finally agree. But he is always free to withdraw from the negotiation when the agent proposes an agreement, thus can deny the deal as well. We can summarize that a malevolent opponent can always drive the negotiation into the conflict deal. In section 3 we showed that this situation can always occur in a negotiation between an agent with strategy *"Stay with the preferences"* against a strong or uncompromising opponent. Only the agent with strategy *"Find a deal"* loses more against a malevolent opponent, because the deal bonus, which it can get in most normal negotiations, is denied.

A *beneficial, greedy, uninformed* opponent might follow a strategy to behave greedy in attributes important to him and concede equally to the agent in all other attributes, in order to lower the agent's compensations on the important attributes. Obviously, conceding equal to the agent leads to a satisfaction value of 0.5 at best. Using equation 5 we can conclude that this position can be reached if the agents's negotiation strength of the attribute is $hv_{ir} \leq 0.67$ and it has no compensations on the attribute. If the negotiation strength is higher or compensations lie on the attribute, a stagnation will occur in the attribute. If the agent's negotiation strength is low, it is possible to find an agreement below 0.5 but this might result in higher compensations on other attributes. In high preference attributes, the opponent can play a mix of provoked stagnations and small concessions. His success can be calculated by equation 5 if he manages to avoid compensations on these attributes. In any case, his best possible result is the lower bound of the attribute, described in section 3.

The *beneficial, cautious, uninformed* opponent might follow a strategy to concede equal to the agent in his important attributes and to give more than the agent's concession in less important attributes. This yields him the same results in his preferred attributes as the beneficial, greedy, uninformed opponent can get in his less important attributes. The concessions greater than the agent's in all other attributes makes the beneficial, cautious, uninformed behaviour overall less successful than the greedy. Even a mixed strategy greedy in important and cautious in less important attributes can only yield the agent's lower bound at best for greedy and a result above the lower bound for cautious.

A *beneficial, informed* opponent can use his knowledge about the agent's negotiation parameters and calculate the lowest possible offer the agent will make or accept. He has no reason to behave greedy or cautious, because he can use any reasonable sequence of proposals to achieve a negotiation result at the agent's lower bound. But he will not be able to achieve a result beyond this point. He can find a deal with 0 satisfaction for the agent, if the agent follows the *"Find a deal"* strategy. Against a *"Stay with the preferences"* agent the beneficial, informed opponent achieves the lower bound given in section 3. We can summarize, the beneficial opponent can achieve the agent's lower bound if he is informed or plays a successful greedy strategy. Beneficial, cautious, uninformed manipulations are not effective. However, for the agent these results are not worse than possible results of normal negotiations and it will never violate the lower limits specified by the user. Thus the agent need not to know the opponent's type, its behaviour can be independent and still guarantees a lower bound of the negotiation result.

5 Conclusion

In this paper we have given a detailed analysis of the behaviour our adaptive negotiation agent follows. We provided formal methods to calculate the lowest possible results our agent model achieves in a negotiation with any given negotiation parameters. We further proved that the agent will never violate the value limits the user defined in the initialization parameters.

The application of software agents in automated electronic commerce requires that the agent's behaviour algorithm is not only stable and reliable in normal negotiation situations, but also immune to malicious manipulations and fraud. We introduced a variety of possible types of manipulations and analysed possible negotiation strategies for these types. Neither of these manipulation strategies proved particular successful. The best results a manipulating opponent could achieve did not exceed the agent's lower bound in a normal negotiation. Most important, in no case the agent left the user defined limits of the attribute values. Especially remarkable is that even an opponent with full access to the agent's private information could not derive advantage. The reliability and insusceptibility against manipulations recommends our agent model for many application scenarios in automated electronic commerce.

References

1. W.Benn, O.Görlitz, R.Neubert, An Adaptive Software Agent for Automated Integrative Negotiations, Int'l. Journ. of e-Business Strategy Management 1 (2), 1999.
2. W.Benn, O.Görlitz, R.Neubert, Enabling Integrative Negotiations by Adaptive Software Agents, Cooperative Information Agents III, Springer Verlag 1999.
3. A.Chavez, D.Dreilinger, R.Guttman, P.Maes, A Real-Life Experiment in Creating an Agent Marketplace, Proc. of the 2nd Int'l. Conf. on the Practical Application of Intelligent Agents in Multi-Agent Technology 1997.
4. P.Fankhauser, T.Tesch, Agents, a Broker, and Lies, Proc. of the 9th Int'l. Workshop on Research Issues in Data Engineering, IEEE Computer Society 1999.
5. R.Guttman, P.Maes, Agent-mediated Integrative Negotiation for Retail Electronic Commerce, Proc. of the Workshop on Agent Mediated Electronic Trading 1998.
6. R.Guttman, A.Moukas, P.Maes, Agent-mediated Electronic Commerce: A survey, Knowledge Engineering Review 1998.
7. InfoSleuth, URL: http://www.mcc.com/projects/infosleuth/ .
8. R.Keeny, H.Raiffa, Decisions with Multiple Objectives: Preferences and Value Trade-offs, John Wiley and Sons 1976.
9. S.Krauss, J.Wilkenfeld, G.Zlotkin, Multiagent Negotiation Under Time Constraints, Artificial Intelligence Journal 75 (2), 1995.
10. R.Lewicki, D.Saunders, J.Minton, Essentials of Negotiation, Irwin 1997.
11. MOMIS, Mediator evirOnment for Multiple Information Sources, URL: http://sparc20.dsi.unimo.it/momis/index.html .
12. J.F.Nash Jr., The Bargaining Problem, Econometrica 18, 1950.
13. J.Nash, Non-Cooperative Games, Annals of Mathematics 54, 1951.
14. A.S.Rao, M.P.Georgeff, Modeling rational agents within a BDI-architecture, Proc. of Knowledge Representation and Reasoning, Morgan Kaufmann 1991.
15. A.S.Rao, M.P.Georgeff, A model-theoretic approach to the verification of situated reasoning systems, Proc. of the 13th Int'l. Joint Conf. on AI 1993.
16. J.Rosenschein, G.Zlotkin, Rules of Encounter. Designing Conventions for Automated Negotiation among Computers, MIT Press 1994.
17. L.S.Shepley, M.Shubik, On Market Games, J.E.T. 1, 1969.
18. T@T: frictionless online shopping, URL: http://ecommerce.media.mit.edu/Tete-a-Tete/ .
19. T.Tesch, P.Fankhauser, Arbitration and Matchmaking for Agents with Conflicting Interests, Cooperative Information Agents III, Springer Verlag 1999.
20. Tooto Internet Technologies, Trainable Agent, URL: http://www.tooto.com/agents/ .
21. TSIMMIS, The Stanford-IBM Manager of Multiple Information Sources, URL: http://www-db.stanford.edu/tsimmis/ .

Towards an Experience Based Negotiation Agent

Wai Yat Wong, Dong Mei Zhang, and Mustapha Kara-Ali

CSIRO Mathematical and Information Sciences
Locked Bag 17, North Ryde NSW 2113 Australia
[wai.wong,dong.mei.zhang]@cmis.csiro.au

Abstract. Current E-Commerce trading agents with electronic negotiation facilities usually use predefined and non-adaptive negotiation mechanisms [5]. This paper presents a negotiation agent that applies Case-Based Reasoning techniques to capture and re-use previously successful negotiation experiences. This Experience Based Negotiation (EBN) agent provides adaptive negotiation strategies that can be generated dynamically and are context-sensitive. We demonstrate this negotiation agent in the context of used-car trading. This paper describes the negotiation process and the conceptual framework of the EBN agent. It discusses our web based used-car trading prototype, the representation of the used-car trading negotiation experience, and the stages of experience based negotiation. The paper also discusses some experimental observation and illustrates an example of adaptive behaviour exhibited by the EBN agent. We believe that this Experience Based Negotiation framework can enhance the negotiation skills and performance of current trading agents.

1 Introduction

Automated negotiation is becoming an integral part of E-Commerce software agent. Real-world negotiations in general accrue transaction costs and times that may be too high for both consumers and merchants [5]. The benefit of a good automated negotiation mechanism is well-recognized [6]. A good automated negotiation can both save time and find better deals in the current complex and uncertain E-Commerce environment.

Most current e-commerce agents use predefined and non-adaptive negotiation strategies in the generation of offers and counter-offers during the course of negotiation. For example, negotiation in Kasbah [2, 5] (MIT media Lab's) uses three predefined strategies, anxious, cool-headed and frugal corresponding to linear, quadratic and exponential functions in the generation of proposals/counter-proposals. Buyers/sellers themselves have to decide which strategy to take before the negotiation starts. Researchers are now exploring various Artificial Intelligence based techniques to provide adaptive behavior in the negotiation agent. The use of Bayesian learning to learn negotiation strategy is one example [7, 10].

Good negotiation skill in humans seems to come from experience. This observation has motivated us to focus on Case Base Reasoning as an approach to use past negotiation experience as guides to suggest suitable strategies to the current negotiation situation. We are currently examining the effectiveness of this

M. Klusch and L. Kerschberg (Eds.): CIA 2000, LNAI 1860, pp. 131–142, 2000.
© Springer-Verlag Berlin Heidelberg 2000

Experienced Based Negotiation (EBN) framework in the car trading agent to produce better and efficient negotiation.

This remainder of the paper is organized as follows: Section 2 introduces our definition of negotiation strategies. Section 3 presents a conceptual overview of our experience based negotiation agent. Section 4 summarizes the used-car trading prototype which uses the Experience Based Negotiation (EBN) agents. It presents the used-car trading negotiation case base and describes the stages of experience based negotiation. It also describes on the methodologies to retrieve, match, and re-use similar negotiation experience. Section 5 discusses our experimental observation and illustrates a typical example of dynamic and adaptive behaviour exhibited by the EBN agent.

2   Negotiation Process

Negotiation is an iterative process [9] where the trading agents start by having goals that may be far apart and whose distance has to be narrowed gradually. A successful negotiation occurs when the two opposing goals meet, e.g.. when the buyer's price meets the seller's offer or vice versa. This negotiation process can be seen as a sequential decision making model studied by Cyert & DeGroot [3] and Bertsekas [1] and used in the Bazaar model by Zeng [10]. So, the negotiation process consists of a number of decision-making episodes. Each episode is characterized by evaluating an offer, determining an episodic strategy and generating a counteroffer, as illustrated in Fig. 1. The negotiation strategy of overall negotiation process is a composite of all these episodic strategies. The negotiation agent can change its episodic strategy from episode to episode due to changing world information. However, information related to strategies is hidden from each other.

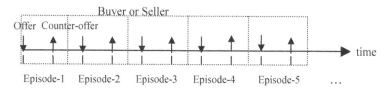

Fig. 1. Negotiation process

We use concession between offers/counter-offers to capture and reflect episodic strategies [11]. Given a series of offers, $(O1, O2, \ldots, O5)$, the concession $C(i+1)$ applied in the episodic strategy $S(i+1)$ is formulated as a percentage based on $O(i)$ and $O(i+1)$:

$$C(i+1) = [O(i+1) - O(i)] / O(i) *100\%; \tag{1}$$

In this way, a series of concessions can be used to capture the implicit episodic strategies used in the previous negotiation. The concession, as a percentage tries to represent context-independent information on episodic strategies, which facilitates reuse of previous strategies in similar negotiation contexts.

3   Framework of Experience Based Negotiation Agent

Fig. 2 illustrates the conceptual structure of the Experience Based Negotiation (EBN) agent. Whenever an opponent agent gives an offer, the EBN agent receives this offer through the communication interface and evaluates it to decide if the offer is acceptable. If the offer is not acceptable, the negotiation agent then retrieves and reuses relevant previous experience to select and adapt a concession for generating the counter-offer.

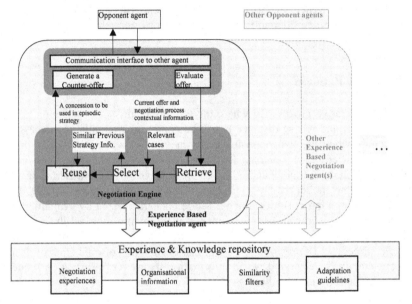

Fig. 2. Experience Based Negotiation agent

As shown in Fig. 2, the negotiation engine is a key component of the negotiation agent and plays a role to suggest a concession that can be used in the generation of a counter-offer. It uses information from the Experience and Knowledge (E&K) repository. Multiple negotiation agents can use the information from the repository. There are four types of information stored in the repository:

- Negotiation experiences.
  Previous negotiation experiences are stored in a case base. Each case contains:
    - information about opponent agent, trading agent and item being traded,
    - series of concessions used by both agents in previous negotiation.
    - information about negotiation performance.
- Organizational information.
  Information for organizing negotiation experiences in terms of indexes. For example, a hierarchy structure from the repository is used as an organizational structure for storing cases to enable efficient searching.
- Similarity filters.
  Similarity filters are used to facilitate the selection of relevant experience from the case base.

• Adaptation guidelines.

EBN agents use the guidelines to adapt concession from matching previous experience for use in generating current counter-offer.

EBN agent applies Case-Based Reasoning techniques in the negotiation engine to represent and reuse previous negotiation experiences. The negotiation engine first retrieves relevant previous negotiation experience from the repository by using the organizational structure. It then selects a most matched case and finally reuses the selected negotiation experience case to propose suitable concession that can be followed in a decision-making episode in the current negotiation.

The proposed approach is currently developed based upon the following assumptions:

• The behaviour of our negotiation agents is strictly monotonic, either decreasing or increasing depending whether buying or selling.

• Negotiation Case Base will be populated with valid and representative cases.

• Currently, only successful negotiation experience is considered in reuse process. Learning what not to do, i.e. learning from failure, will be examined in the future.

• This paper only looks at single-issue negotiation. Extension of this framework to multi-issue negotiation, e.g. price and warranty, is being constructed.

4   Web Based Used-Car Trading Prototype

We have embedded the EBN agent within a web based used car trading software prototype. This used car trading software prototype contains several functional components (Fig. 3): a Case-Based Negotiator, a Case Browser, a Statistics component and a Case maintenance component:

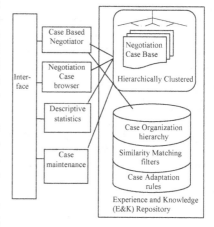

• The Case-Based Negotiator assists the users to negotiate with opponent agents on used car trading price. It starts an EBN agent. This agent communicates and negotiates with the opponent agent.

• The Case Browser allows users to browse the negotiation case base using various types of queries.

Fig. 3. Components of web based used cartrading software prototype

• The Statistics component supplies several useful descriptive statistics on negotiation case base.

• The Case Maintenance component allows negotiation experts to moderate, maintain and to update the case repository. To condense potential great number of similar stored cases, generalization based /concept learning techniques can be used to induce generalized case. This allows efficient and better case-matching and case-reuse in the future.

This paper concentrates on the Case Based Negotiator. After the negotiator function is chosen, the user selects a used car to buy/sell. The user then continues to supply negotiation profile information, e.g. negotiation focus (good- deal, best-price, must-buy/sell), budget, and other optional information like gender, age, etc. When all inputs are complete, the Negotiator starts an agent to negotiate with the opponent agent. The agent's negotiation engine matches current negotiating scenario with previously successful negotiation cases and provides appropriate counter-offers based on the best-matched negotiation case. The detail of reasoning process and decision making during the negotiation will be covered in subsequent sections. The dynamics of the negotiation process will be tracked and displayed on the user screen, as shown in Fig. 4. In the course of negotiation, when the offers from buyer and seller meet, the user makes the final decision whether the deal is done. If the final offer is accepted, the agent can update the case base with the current negotiation information. This include the current profiles of the buyer and seller agents, car profile, offers, counter-offers and their corresponding concessions. At the end of negotiation, the negotiator presents summary information of the negotiation, including number of

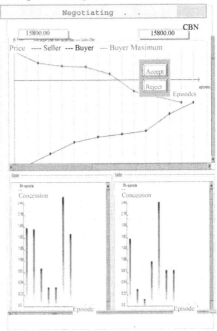

Fig. 4. Tracking the negotiation process

episodes in the negotiation, buyer's final offer, seller's final offer, etc.

Section 4.1 details the representation of the negotiation case within our used-car prototype domain. Section 4.2 discusses the process of the experience based negotiation within the agent's engine.

4.1   Representation of Used-Car Trading Experiences

Previous negotiation experiences are represented as negotiation cases. A negotiation case represents information related to a specific agent (e.g., seller or buyer) and captures contextual information and negotiation experience available to an agent in a previous negotiation. A negotiation case thus contains:
(1) The negotiation context. The negotiation context is comprised of:
   ♦ Profile of agent. Items inside the profile of agent include:
       Name, age, agent's negotiation focus, expected negotiation duration, issues of negotiation (e.g. price, warranty, trade-in, etc), constraints (e.g., budget), and preferences.
   ♦ Profile of the Opponent agent (Similar content to profile of agent).

♦   Profile of the used car. Items inside the profile of the user car include:
        Engine size, make, year of manufacture.
(2) Offers made from opponent agent and concessions used in episodic strategies.
(3) Counter-offers made by the agent and concessions used in episodic strategies.
(4) Performance information about the feedback of negotiation results. This include:
♦   Outcome of negotiation : success/failure and the final mutually agreed price.

Buyer's Profile, Seller Profile, Used-car Profile				
Episode No	Offer Of Seller	Seller's Concession	Counter Offer Of Buyer	Buyer's Concession
1	O1		Co1	
2	O2	S%1	Co2	B%1
3	O3	S%2	Co3	B%2
4	O4	S%3	Co4	B%3
...	...	...	...	...
Performance information				

Agent Profile

Case #	Name	Gender	Age	Focus	Minimum Budget	Maximum Budget	Issues

Performance

Case #	Number of episodes	Success/failure

Used Car Profile

Case #	Retail Price	Car Age	Car Size	Make

Agent counter-offers & concessions

Case #	Episode #	Counter-offers	Concessions

Opponent agent Profile

Case #	Name	Gender	Age	Focus	Minimum Budget	Maximum Budget	Issues

Opponent agent offers & concessions

Case #	Episode #	Offers	Concessions

Fig. 5. Agent negotiation case   **Fig. 6.** Relational view of negotiation case base

Fig. 5 shows an example of a buyer agent's case. Fig. 6 shows a relational view of the case base where the case number is used as primary key to link all tables. These tables include agent profile, agent's list of offers and concessions for a negotiation case, opponent agent profile, opponent agent's list of offers and concessions for the same negotiation case, used car profile, and summary of case performance.

4.2   Process of Experience Based Negotiation

During each negotiation episode, the negotiation agent will have the information of the current profiles of the negotiating agents, current car profile, the most current lists of buyer-offers and buyer-concessions, and the most current lists of counter-offers and corresponding seller-concessions. Based on the current profiles of the agents and car, the negotiation engine of the agent will first retrieve a relevant set of previous negotiation cases using the contextual case organization hierarchy. It will then perform similarity assessment to match/select the most similar cases from this group of relevant cases using information from all profiles and the current lists of buyer-offers, buyer-concessions, seller-counter-offers, & seller-concessions. Information from the most similar case will be re-used to adapt the next concession used to generate the next offer. Section 4.2.1 describes briefly the retrieval process. Section 4.2.2 concentrates on the matching & selection using the similarity filters. Section 4.2.3 describes briefly the reuse of the best-matched case(s) from the view-point of a buyer agent.

4.2.1   Retrieval of Negotiation Case

A contextual case organization hierarchy (Fig. 7) is used as an organization structure for grouping and categorizing the negotiation cases. The context information in the cases is used to classify cases in the hierarchy. A number of salient features are selected to index negotiation cases, based on their possible values. For example, because we believe that different negotiation behavior arises primarily from the negotiation focus of the buying agent, the feature "focus" in the buyer agent's profile is used as primary index for different groups of buyer negotiation cases. The possible values of "focus" include "must-buy", "good-deal" and "best-price". The feature "focus" thus groups cases into three categories. Other salient features used for further sub-categorization include the ageand the engine-size of the car. The Case organizational hierarchy is used to retrieve

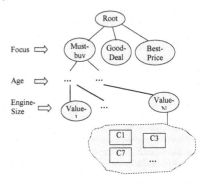

Fig. 7. Case organization hierarchy for buyer agent

relevant negotiation cases by searching through case memory. If no case is found based on the case organization hierarchy, the buyer agent can fall back using some default negotiation strategies selected by the user from a set of pre-defined strategies (e.g. linear, quadratic or exponential).

4.2.2   Matching/Selecting Similar Negotiation Case

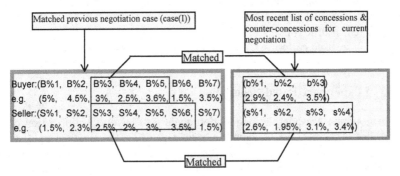

Fig. 8. Concession matching

Similarity/Matching filters are used to select/filter out the best-matched case from the retrieved relevant set of cases. The filters are applied on all retrieved sets of relevant cases with some contextual distinction depending on the case organization hierarchy of "best-price", "good-deal", and "must-buy". We illustrate here the "good-deal" scenario and will show briefly the difference of "best-price" and "must-buy" scenarios.

In the "good-deal" scenario, all the retrieved relevant cases are passed first through a concession-match filter. The concession-match tries to find "sub-string" matches between the buyer-concessions & seller-concessions of the previous negotiation cases and the buyer-concessions & seller-concessions of the current negotiation process. Fig. 8 shows a previous negotiation case, case(I), with 7 episodes of buyer and seller concessions: { (B%1, B%2, B%3, B%4, B%5, B%6, B%7), (S%1, S%2, S%3, S%4, S%5, S%6, S%7)}. Current negotiation is captured in this most current list of buyer and seller concessions: {(b%1, b%2, b%3), (s%1, s%2, s%3, s%4)} where seller has just made a counter-offer based on s%4. The concession matching filter matches {(b%1, b%2, b%3), (s%1, s%2, s%3, s%4)} to a sub-string {(B%3, B%4, B%5), (S%3, S%4, S%5, S%6)} within the list of concessions in case (I), { (B%1, B%2, B%3, B%4, B%5, B%6, B%7), (S%1, S%2, S%3, S%4, S%5 S%6, S%7) }. Consequently case (I) is selected as a potential candidate to have its next

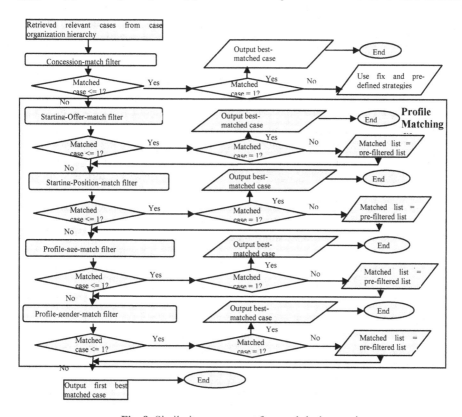

Fig. 9. Similarity assessment for good-deal scenario

B%4 as a concession for EBN to adapt to generate the next offer. In our current prototype implementation, similarity/matching measurement is done using either a percentage tolerance threshold or absolute tolerance threshold. Two quantities match if their difference falls within the tolerance threshold. For example, in Fig. 8, case(I)'s concession sub-sequence {(3%, 2.5%, 3.6%), (2.5%, 2%, 3%, 3.5%)} matches current negotiation concession sequence {(2.9%, 2.4%, 3.5%), (2.6%, 1.95%, 3.1%, 3.4%))} as all the differences fall within the allowed tolerance threshold of 5%. This tolerance threshold is adjustable to allow various sizes of the matching window.

If the number of the filtered cases out of the concession-match filter is more than one, the filtered cases are then passed through an ordered series of profile matching filters. This series of profile matching filters include the starting-offer-match filter, starting-position-match filter, profile-age-match filter, and profile-gender-match filter. The flow-chart in Fig. 9 shows the procedure of similarity assessment using this series of profile matching filters.

As described earlier, negotiation strategy for a case is reflected by the overall composite of the episodic seller-concessions & buyer-concessions during the negotiation process. The concession-match filter thus captures the negotiation processes/cases with the same strategies or sub-strategies, i.e. they are of the similar functional/sub-functional and behavior/sub-behavior forms. The starting-offer gives preference to cases with similar initial buying offer. This filter thus restricts the magnitude difference of those cases with similar strategies or sub-strategies, i.e. this filter gives preference to negotiation cases/sub-cases which are similar in offers/counter-offers –a stronger requirement. The starting-position match filter gives preference to the previous case whose concession matches from the beginning. This filter thus restricts the translational difference. It throws away the sub-strategy functional match and sub-case match and prefers full-strategy/ full-case match. The age and gender filters respectively match cases with the same age range and gender. They are used to put some preference on the matching cases if the two restrictive (starting-offer-match and starting-position-match) filters do not produce any matching candidates. Because of the noisy nature of the cases, those filters are arranged in such manner to give most opportunity of getting some best-matched case(s).

"Best-price" and "Must-buy" scenarios have case similarity/matching assessment methodologies of the same nature. For example, in the "Must buy" scenario, there is an addition rule before the concession-match filter and profile match filters which says:

If the opponent agent's offer reaches a plateau and offer is within the agent's budget, suggest a concession that can reach the opponent agent's offer.

4.2.3 Reuse of Previous Concessions

Once a case is selected as the best matched case to the current scenario, the negotiation agent takes the next concession that was used in previous negotiation and suggests it to the negotiation agent for the generation of a counter-offer. For example, in Fig. 8, the concession "B%-6" will be reused to recommend to the negotiation agent to follow for generating a counter-offer.

Some adaptation is done during the boundary conditions, e.g. if the concession results in a counter-offer which is higher than the buyer's maximum budget, then the concession must be adjusted accordingly to arrive only at the counter-offer equal to or not greater than the buyer's maximum budget.

5   Observation and Discussion

Section 5 contains two sections. Section 5.1 illustrates that the EBN agent, depending on the context, can dynamically adapt its episodic strategies, i.e. concessions, from several relevant and similar negotiation case candidates. Section 5.2 discusses our view of Case Based Reasoning approach as opposed to utility theory methodology.

5.1 Dynamic Adaptive Behaviour of EBN Agent

From our observation, the EBN agent that we have implemented is able to exhibit a dynamic and adaptive behaviour and can make effective re-use of similar cases it has retrieved from the case base. We show here an example of this dynamic adaptive behaviour.

Table 1 shows the offers of the new current seller agent and the counter-offers generated by the EBN agent during each negotiation episode. It also contains the previous negotiation histories of seller's offers and buyer's counter offers for two retrieved relevant cases (case 11 and case 18) which have resulted in successful negotiations. The graph (Fig. 10) depicts graphically the full negotiation progress of case 11, case 18 and the current negotiation between the new seller and the EBN

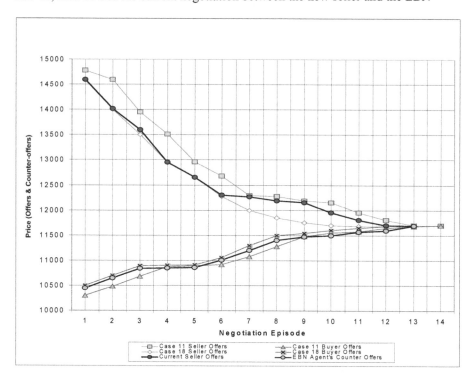

Fig. 10. Graphical trace of current EBN negotiation as compared to previous negotiation cases

Episode no.	0	1	2	3	4	5	6	7	8	9	10	11	12	13
Seller's offers (Case 11)	14780	14600	13950	13510	12960	12680	12290	12275	12190	12150	11950	11800	11700	11700
Buyer's counter-offers (Case 11)	10300	10480	10680	10880	10890	10920	11080	11280	11480	11550	11580	11650	11680	11700
Seller's offers (Case 18)	14580	14000	13500	12950	12650	12280	12000	11850	11750	11700	11680	11680		
Buyer's counter-offers (Case 18)	10500	10700	10890	10900	10910	11060	11300	11500	11540	11600	11650	11680		
Current Seller's offers	14600	14020	13600	12950	12650	12300	12270	12190	12150	11950	11800	11700	11690	
Current EBN agent's counter-offers	10450	10649	10838	10847	10856	11005	11203	11401	11470	11499	11568	11597	11690	

Table 1. Negotiation histories of case 11 and case 18 and the current negotiation between seller agent and EBN agent.

agent. From both the table and the graph, one can clearly see that the initial series of offers from the current seller is very close to the initial series of seller-offers in case 18. Consequently, the EBN agent has used the concessions from case 18 as the basis for episodic strategy adaptation for generation of counter-offers. Roughly in the middle of the negotiation process (negotiation episode 6), the current seller's offer begins to deviate from the seller's offer for case 18 and matches more closely to the seller's offer of case 11. The EBN agent detects the change of strategy from the current seller and adapts the buyer-concessions of the case 11 to generate counter-offers. This example indicates that, in term of complexity of negotiation behaviour, the EBN agent has managed to achieve some level of sophistication and adaptation from using previous examples.

5.2   Case Based Reasoning versus Utility Theory

One popular approach towards solving conflict resolution in multi-agent negotiation is to make use of utility theory [8]. Utility theory is the theory that models the process through which a decision-maker evaluates a set of alternatives, so that he/she can choose the best one. Utility theory provides a measure of an overall utility or satisfaction of a decision-maker and as a result, indicates a way towards achieving a maximum utility or satisfaction of a decision. In general, the theory accommodates multiple issue negotiation (e.g. price, warranty, etc.). In our current scope, only a single issue, namely car-price, forms the core of our negotiation. As such, the utility functions of our selling agent U(S) and buying agent U(B) looks respectively like:

$$U(B) = f1(\text{Budget - Price}); U(S) = f2(\text{Price - cost}); \qquad (2)$$

Clearly, depending on the various subjective criteria among the agents, for example, focus="Must-Buy", or focus="Good-Deal" or focus="Best-Price", the functional shape of f1 and f2 varies significantly among different selling agents and different buying agents.

We believe strongly that one effective way to capture these utility functions is to examine the previous behavior of the agents. In our case, we look at all successful negotiation experiences of the buyer and seller agents and assume those collective experiences indicate well the inherent utility functions of a particular type of agent under a particular type of circumstances. We then adapt and apply the result to current negotiation situation. In doing so, we avoid explicitly specifying the utility functions by assigning arbitrary values. Moreover, this Experience-Based Negotiation approach can allow us to accommodate easily the change and growth of the utility functions e.g., through time.

6   Conclusion

The EBN agent shows synergy between case based reasoning and automated negotiation. However, more testing with real-life scenario is necessary. To evaluate the performance of the EBN agent, we also need to conduct comparative experiments between the EBN agent and other trading agents that use pre-defined negotiation strategies. We definitely need to extend the single-issue negotiation to a realistic multi-issue negotiation. That will require good collaborative multi-issue matching. Collecting valid and representative successful cases for the case base can be difficult as failure will be more common than success. As a result, we may have to think carefully about learning from failure. There is also the issue of case maintenance on the horizon to condense the potential great number of similar stored cases.

Nevertheless, the seductiveness of using the raw experience remains. In this problem domain where rule-of-thumbs can be nebulous, where information can be incomplete and uncertain, where contextual information changes quickly, and where optimality is not necessary, Case-Based Reasoning is a good candidate.

References

1.   Bertsekas, D. P.: Dynamic Programming and Optimal Control. Athena Scientific, Belmont, MA (1995)
2.   Chavez, A.,Dreilinger, D., Guttman, R., Maes, P.: A real-life experiment in creating an agent marketplace. Proceedings of the Second International Conference on the Practical Application of Intelligent Agents and Multi-Agent Technology, PAAM97 (1997)
3.   Cyert, R. M., DeGroot, M. H.: Bayesian Analysis and Uncertainty in Economic Theory. Rowman & Littlefield, New York (1987)
4.   Kowalczyk, R., Bui, V.: Towards Intelligent Trading Agents. The International Conference on Intelligent Systems and Active DSS in Turku/Abo, Finland (1999)
5.   Maes, P., Guttman, R. H., Moukas, A. G.: Agents that buy and sell. Communications of The ACM. Vol. 42, No.3 (1999) 81-91
6.   Sandholm, T,.: Automated Negotiation: The best terms for all concerned. Communications of The ACM. Vol. 42, No.3 (1999) 84-85
7.   Siriwan, A., Sadananda, R.: An agent-mediated Negotiation Model in Electronic Commerce. The Australian Workshop on AI in Electronic Commerce, The Australian Joint Conference on Artificial Intelligence (1999)
8.   Sycara, K.: Utility theory in conflict resolution. Annals of Operations research, Vol. 12 (1988) 65-84
9.   Sycara, K.: Machine learning for intelligent support of conflict resolution. Decision Support systems, Vol. 10 (1993) 121-136
10.   Zeng, D., Sycara, K.: Bayesian Learning in Negotiation. Int. J. Human-Computer Studies 48 (1998) 125-141
11.   Zhang, D., Wong, W., Kowalczyk, R.: Reusing Previous Negotiation Experiences in Multi-Agent Negotiation. Proceedings of Workshop on Agents in Electronic Commerce, December 14, 1999, Hong Kong, WAEC'99 (1999)

Emergent Societies of Information Agents

Paul Davidsson

Department of Computer Science, University of Karlskrona/Ronneby
Soft Center, 372 25 Ronneby, Sweden
Paul.Davidsson@ipd.hk-r.se

Abstract. In the near future, billions of entities will be connected to each other through the Internet. The current trend is that an increasingly number of entities, from smart personal devices to legacy databases, are controlled by software agents. Such agents often also posses a large amount of information about both the entity and its owner. Thus, a likely scenario is that the Internet will be populated by millions of information agents, all potentially able to communicate with each other. Unfortunately, we cannot assume that these agents are benevolent and are willing to cooperate in an altruistic fashion. As the amount of money transferred via the Internet is rapidly increasing caused by the breakthrough of e-commerce, we should actually expect a similar increase in the number of malicious agents. Another aspect that contributes to the complexity of agent interaction on the Internet is a desired openness, making it difficult to engineer agent societies in a top-down manner. Rather, we will here investigate the prerequisites necessary to form stable and trustworthy societies of information agents, and discuss some open problems and methodologies for studying them. The general conclusion is that more research is needed that takes into account the presence of malicious agents.

1 Introduction

In the near future, billions of entities will be connected to each other through a global communication channel, i.e., the Internet. Although some of these entities will be personal computers, the major part will be different kinds of smart devices, such as, mobile phones, digital personal assistants, and even refrigerators. The current trend is that more and more of these devices are controlled by software agents. In addition to the control of the device, these agents will in many cases also have access to a large amount of information about not only the device, but also about its user(s). Another trend is the use of "wrapper" and "transducer" agents [11] in order to increase the availability and usefulness of legacy information systems. If we extrapolate from these trends, a likely scenario is that the Internet soon will be populated by millions of information agents, all potentially able to communicate with each other through the Internet. The openness of the Internet brings about some desirable properties, e.g., supporting interoperability and cooperation. However, as we will discuss later, this openness also has some drawbacks.

M. Klusch and L. Kerschberg (Eds.): CIA 2000, LNAI 1860, pp. 143-153, 2000.

A collection of agents interacting with each other can be seen as an agent society. The view of *open* agent societies, where, in principle, anyone with Internet access may contribute one or more agents without any particular restrictions, should be contrasted to that of *closed* agent societies, where an agent-based approach is adopted by a team of software developers in order to implement a complex software system (cf. distributed problem solving). In a closed multi-agent systems (MAS), it is often possible to precisely engineer the society, e.g., specify with which agents each agent interacts, and why. From this perspective, agent-based computing may be seen purely as a software engineering paradigm (cf. [31]). In between these types of agent societies, we have *semi-open* societies, where there are *institutions* to which an agent may explicitly register its interest to enter the society. The institution then either accepts or rejects this request. An example of such institution is the *portal* concept as used in SOLACE [15, 16].

Ideally, all agents belonging to a society should always cooperate in order to find globally optimal, or at least acceptable, solutions to the problems related to the fulfillment of the goals of the individual agents. However, agents often have conflicting goals that may result in competitive behavior. While being self-interested, agents are typically assumed to be sincere when interacting with other agents. Although such benevolence may be assumed in closed societies, this is an unrealistic assumption for most open agent societies. We must accept that in open agent societies there may be malicious agents trying to exploit the norm- and law-abiding agents, e.g., by stealing secret and/or personal information. As the amount of money transferred via the Internet is rapidly increasing caused by the breakthrough of e-commerce, we should expect a similar increase in the number of such malicious agents. Consequently, this must be taken into account when developing techniques, standards, software etc. for open (and semi-open) agent societies.

Unfortunately, the presence of self-interested and even malicious agents significantly increases the complexity of achieving stable societies. Although these aspects have been studied to some extent in particular situations, e.g., computational auctions, not very much work has been carried out at the general society level. However, the presence of malicious agents should not be confused with the limited and controlled competitiveness that is sometimes used in closed agent societies. In this case, the agents are designed to be competitive in order to achieve desired behavior at the global system level. Another aspect of open agent societies is how to achieve robust behavior in the face of imperfect knowledge about the environment (see e.g., [17]). This has, on the other hand, been quite well studied. However, it should be contrasted to the scenario we will concentrate on here, where agents deliberately may provide other agents with false information in order to gain some advantage.

We will here discuss the impact of the possible presence of malicious agents and what ingredients are necessary to form stable and trustworthy societies of agents. In the next section we specify what requirements that must be met in order for a society to emerge and in the following section take a closer look at societies of information agents. We then discuss what the research carried out in the social sciences may contribute to the study of artificial agent societies. Finally, we briefly describe a project that adopts an approach that to a large extent shares the view expressed in this paper on how to study agent societies.

2   Prerequisites for the Emergence of Information Agent Societies

What do we mean by a society? A typical definition of a human society is that it is a structured group of persons associated together for some kind of purpose, or/and residing in a specific locality. If the latter is the dominant factor, the group is often called a *community*. In addition, a society (or community) often has a set common rules and norms that the members are supposed to adhere to. In ecological contexts, similar definitions are used. For instance, an ecological society has been defined as "a closely integrated group of social organisms of the same species held together by mutual dependence and exhibiting division of labor", and an ecological community as "an assemblage of plant and animal populations occupying a given area."[1]

We will here use these concepts with respect to groups of "social" artifacts in analogous ways. That is, a collection of agents interacting with each other in some way or another, possibly in accordance with common norms and rules (cf. social laws [28]), are here called an agent society. The role of the society is to allow agents to coexist in a shared environment and pursue their respective goals in the presence of other agents. Note that both cooperation and competition between the members of the society are possible.

As pointed out by Wooldridge and Jennings [30], it is a common misconception that agent based systems can be developed simply by throwing together a number of agents in a melting pot where there is no structure and all agents are peers communicating with each other. A similar argument can, of course, be made with respect to the agents on the Internet. An agent will not interact with every other agent just because it may have a possibility to do so; there has to be a reason for the interaction, e.g., that it will bring the agent closer to achieving one or more of its goals. Thus, we will have some kind of structure within the Internet based on societies of agents, defined by the interaction that takes place between the agents. In accordance to what has been said earlier with respect to semi-open societies, additional constraints regarding what agents are allowed to belong to a society may be imposed by institutions. Such constraints can be related to the expected probability that the agent will comply with the norms and rules of the society, e.g., based on the agent's (or its owner's) credibility.

It would also be possible to make a distinction between agent societies and agent communities, where communities are characterized by closeness in proximity, e.g., residing on the same computer or local network. However, in what follows we will not make this distinction.

Another aspect that contributes to the complexity of agent interaction on the Internet is an often desired openness, i.e., given that an agent has an acceptable reason to join a society, it should be given the opportunity to do so. This makes it difficult to engineer agent societies in a top-down manner. Rather, we should provide an infrastructure that makes bottom-up "emergence" of stable societies possible. The most basic requirement that must be fulfilled for a society to emerge is that the entities of the society (or at least a subset) are able to interact with each other. For this we need at least: (i) a communication medium, (ii) a way of finding other entities to interact

---

[1] These definitions are taken from Webster's Encyclopedic Unabridged Dictionary of the English Language, 1989 edition.

with, (iii) a reason for the entities to interact (iv) and a communication language, including syntax, semantics, and pragmatics.

(i) In the case of information agent societies, the Internet (and the IP protocol) provides the necessary communication backbone. Fortunately, as this already exists and is extremely well tested, we can make the assumption that it is there and is working.

(ii) There must be mechanisms for an agent to enter (and leave) a society. These could be either *manual*, i.e., the owner at run-time, or programmer at "design time", tells the agent with other agents to interact with, or *automatic*, e.g., by making use of supporting mediator agents, such as, "yellow pages" or portal agents. In the latter case, the supporting agents also need to have knowledge about the competence of the agents of the society.

(iii) The interaction with other agents should in some way or another help the individual entity to fulfil one or more of its goals. As this is completely dependent of the goals of the particular agent there is difficult to discuss this in general terms. However, it can be noted that this is the reason why the billions of agents that may be populating the Internet will not all communicate with each other; there simply has to be a reason for the interaction.

(iv) The linguistic interaction between agents within a society can be studied at different levels, e.g.:

- *Syntactic level*: What language (syntax) is used for the communication?
- *Semantic level*: What ontologies are used for the communication?
- *Coordination/conversational level*: What is the structure of the communication?
- *Social level*: What norms and rules are used in the communication? With which agents does an agent want to, or need to, communicate?

In order for a stable society to emerge, a common language, a common ontology, and common norms and rules are needed. Coordination and conversation models may not be strictly needed, but are from a practical perspective very useful since they make the interaction between agents more structured and efficient. However, all of these levels have recently been the topic for much attention in agent research. In fact, they are now almost research fields in their own right, arranging separate conferences or workshops, e.g., ACL (workshop on Agent Communication Languages) [7], FOIS (conference on Formal Ontology in Information Systems) [14], SICP (workshop on Specifying and Implementing Conversation Policies) [13] and the more general conference on Coordination Models and Languages [2], and the workshop on Norms and Institutions in Multi-Agent Systems [6].

However, most of this research assumes that agents are benevolent and, as pointed out earlier, this assumption is not realistic in most open agent societies. For instance, consider the two most commonly used and well-defined agent communication languages, KQML [8] and FIPA ACL [9], which both include a primitive performative for communicating information by a declarative speech act (*tell* and *inform* respectively). Attempts have been made to define the semantics of this speech act in terms of the intentional stance, i.e. mental attitudes in terms of beliefs, desires and intentions. In both cases, the meaning is specified using a semantic condition, sometimes called the *sincerity condition*, saying that an agent actually believes what it communicates [21, 9]. As pointed out by Pitt [24], this condition is not valid in many open (and semi-open) agent societies. Similar objections can be made for the other levels of linguistic interaction. In fact, we argue that the consequences of the non-benevolence assumption and the openness of the Internet are understudied topics, and need to be taken into account in nearly all aspects of agent research. The awareness of these matters are probably highest in the research on the social level, where concepts such as *trust* and *deception* are given more and more attention [1].

3   Information Agent Societies

The software agents (and other software entities, but we will here concentrate on the agents) populating the Internet forms a "Universal Information Ecosystem" (UIE) that can be seen as a collection of societies. These societies may be either open, closed, or semi-open. An agent may belong to several societies, but agents belonging to different societies typically do not interact with each other. Moreover, each society will have its own (possibly empty) set of norms and rules. Within a society there may be a number of coalitions, each consisting of a number of individual agents. Whereas a society is neutral with respect to cooperation and competition, coalitions are formed with the intention of cooperation. This view of the UIE is illustrated in Fig. 1. Note that also a closed society may include coalitions.

Each agent on the Internet is "owned" by a real person (or organization) on whose behalf it acts and who caused its creation. A person may have several agents, even in the same society. Thus, we can see interaction between agents as social interaction between humans mediated by agents. It is important to note that such interaction may have both social and legal consequences, a fact that often is ignored in agent research. It is the owner of the agent that should be held responsible for any illegal or immoral actions performed by the agent, e.g., breaking a contract by not fulfilling a commit-ment, or spreading secret information. One consequence of this ownership relation is that an agent may be fully autonomous with respect to deciding what plans and actions to adopt in order to achieve a particular goal, but only limitedly autonomous with respect to deciding what goals to adopt and what rules and norms to obey, which then are decided by its owner (cf. the distinctions between plan, goal, and norm autono-mous agents [29]).

It is sometimes easier for an agent to achieve its goals if it cooperates with some of the other agents in the society. In an open (or semi-open) agent society, it is typically not possible to determine with which agents to cooperate when the agent is created. That is, the agent itself must often decide at run time whether it is fruitful or not to cooperate with a particular agent, or set of agents. Thus, *coalition formation* is a very important activity in agent societies. Unfortunately, most research in this area assumes societies that are closed and where agents have unlimited computational resources. Some attempts to ease up these restrictions have been made [27, 20] and a promising general framework has been suggested by Johansson [19]. It should be noted that there are some similarities between society and coalition formation, e.g., similar reasoning is required by the agents when deciding whether to join a coalition or a society, i.e., weighing the pros and cons of being a member of the coalition / society. Compared to

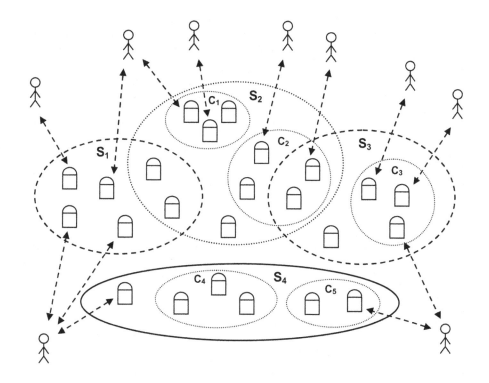

Fig. 1. A schematic illustration of the structure of the UIE. In this example there are four societies; S_1 and S_3 are semi-open (marked by dashed ellipses), S_2 is open (dotted ellipsis), and S_4 is closed. Within these societies there are five coalitions in total (C_{1-5}, thin dotted ellipses). Also, some of the persons (or organizations) that "owns" the agents are illustrated.

the society, a coalition within the society typically has a set of additional rules and/or norms that the agents of the coalition should adhere to.

If we study current information agent societies, we notice that they may include a number of different types of agents, e.g.:

- *Interface agents*: Provides an interface between human users and the Internet.
- *Information agents*: such as, information retrieval agents and database agents.
- *Middle agents*: Different kinds of mediating agents that glues the society together, e.g., portals, brokers, and match makers.
- *"Smart equipment agents"*: Provides an interface between hardware entities and the Internet.

However, open and semi-open societies may call for new types of agents. For instance, it would be useful to have particular agents that cope with malicious agents. One approach would be to introduce "police agents" that monitor the society looking for agents that break the norms and rules of the society. If such an agent is detected, it takes appropriate measures, e.g., excluding the agent from the society or punishes its owner in some way. In semi-open agent societies this may be taken cared of by institutions accepted by the members of the society. Similarly, institutions in the form of "information banks" may be introduced to provide safe storage of personal and other secret information. Another possible type of agent would be "meta-mediators", which have knowledge about different societies, and are able to guide (new) agents to the right society. Similarly, coalition brokers may be introduced to facilitate coalition formation.

4 Human Societies and Social Theories

As should be apparent from the discussions above, societal issues assuming the presence of self-interested and possibly malicious agents are very relevant to research on both open and semi-open information agent societies. However, instead of developing theories and models from scratch, we may learn from the several hundreds of years of research that has been carried out in the social sciences on these topics. We will here use a very broad definition of social sciences that includes, e.g., economics, psychology, sociology, anthropology, and philosophy, as well as ecology and even some areas of biology.

One idea would be to transfer social theories about human (and animal) societies to the artificial societies of the UIE. However, there are differences between natural and artificial societies, e.g., the consequences of terminating an entity of the society, the importance of physical distance between entities, and the reasoning abilities and predictability of the entities themselves. Thus, we must ask ourselves what theories are relevant, e.g., sometimes the theory needs to be modified to better suit artificial societies. Also, if the social theory is only loosely described, e.g., in a natural language, it may need to be formalized.

We will by social theory mean every theory, informal or formal, that describes situations in which two or more humans or animals cooperate and/or compete. Now, if the designer of an agent (or an institution) predicts that the agent (or institution) will find itself in a specific situation where it needs to interact with other agents (or institutions) in some organized way, we may try to identify a social situation analogous to this situation and then look for social theories and models describing the situation. If such a theory is found, we try to transfer to it agent societies, if possible. A more detailed description of these ideas can be found in [5].

This idea has already been applied successfully in several instances. Take for instance the idea of *market-oriented programming* [3], which exploits the concept of economical markets and uses them to build computational economies to solve particular problems, such as, distributed resource allocation. This approach is inspired in part by economists' metaphors of market systems "computing" the activities of the agents involved, but also by the agent researchers' view of autonomous software entities forming a society of agents. In market-oriented programming these metaphors are taken literally, and are directly used to implement the distributed computation as a market price system. It is sometimes argued that economic models of agency reduce agents to be selfish entities and are therefore of limited value in practical application

[18]. However, it is exactly this aspect that makes them interesting in the open society context we are discussing here. Other examples of social theory transformations are the *game theory* [22], which has been applied to agent societies, e.g., by Rosenschein and Zlotkin [26], and the *genetic theory of natural selection* [10], which has resulted in *genetic algorithms* [12].

When applying social theories and models to artificial agent societies there are some things that one should bear in mind. For instance, great care should be taken when deciding whether to make a complete or only a partial transformation of the social theory. Some parts of the social theory may be irrelevant in the computational context, e.g., the exclusion of sex in genetic algorithms. Another thing to keep in mind is to make sure that all parts of the theory to transfer really are describable. For example, problems typically occur when the social theory depends heavily on mental states rather than just the observable interaction. Consequently (and quite interestingly), the simpler view of the individual assumed in the social theory, the better it is suited for transformation to the computational domain. If the theory nevertheless is based on non-observable mental states, it is essential to make explicit what assumptions are made about the mental structure and capability of the agents: Is it assumed that the agents are based on a BDI (Belief, Desire, and Intention) [25] architecture? How sophisticated are their world models, e.g., do they include the mental states of other agents, or just observable features? What are the reasoning and planning capabilities of the agents?

As the fielded application of theories and models of agent societies on the Internet typically has both legal and economical consequences, it is important to validate them thoroughly. Because of the inherent complexity, the most (perhaps only) viable way of doing this is by means of simulations. To make such simulations meaningful, the whole system should be simulated, including the human owners of the agents. As been suggested elsewhere [4], Multi Agent Based Simulation (MABS) is particular useful for this kind of complex systems that involves interaction between humans and computer controlled devices.

5 A Case Study

We will now describe a project that investigates the concept of "ethical" behavior in agent societies. The project is called ALFEBIITE (A Logical Framework for Ethical Behaviour between Infohabitants in the Information Trading Economy of the universal information ecosystem)[2] and is a part of the Universal Information Ecosystem (UIE) initiative made by FET (Future and Emerging Technologies) within the IST (Information Society Technologies) fifth framework programme issued by the European Commission. UIE stems from the vision of having billions of infohabitants (e.g., agents) populating the universal information ecosystem.

---

[2] ALFEBIITE is a joint project between Imperial College, London UK, National Research Council, Rome Italy, University of Oslo, Norway, Queen's University, Belfast UK, and the University of Karlskrona/Ronneby, Sweden. It is coordinated by Jeremy Pitt, Imperial College. For more information, see the project home page: www.iis.ee.ic.ac.uk/alfebiite.

In addition to the very specific goals of ALFEBIITE, which we will describe below, the project has some more general objectives: (i) develop a new paradigm for designing, deploying, and managing open distributed intelligent systems, in which social relationships between agents are just as important as interface definitions in providing interoperability, (ii) provide users with greater trust and confidence in agent societies by ensuring that they are not exploited, their rights protected, and their privacy is not violated, and (iii) bridge the gap between human sciences (social psychology, sociology, and philosophy) and more technical sciences (AI, agent-based computing, and information systems). These objectives are very ambitious and we do not believe that ALFEBIITE will resolve them completely, but that we will at least provide guidelines for future research and offer partial solutions. Some of the more concrete goals of the project are to:

- develop a logical framework to characterize norm-governed behavior and social relations based on the results of psychological studies,
- use this framework to specify axiomatic descriptions of communicative acts regarding social commitments and to specify the mechanics of society formation,
- implement a "society simulator" to experiment with and validate these formal models in a number of realistic scenarios, and
- contribute in the development of a software (agent) ownership model and the legal mechanisms necessary for enforcing the consequences of such a model.

To conclude, ALFEBIITE is an ambitious project that tackles one of the core problems of open agent societies, and when doing this, it fully adopts the open (semi-open) society view and takes into account its consequences.

6 Conclusions

A distinction was made between open, semi-open, and closed agent societies. If we want open or semi-open societies, it is often not possible to engineer such societies in a strictly top-down manner as is typically done with closed agent societies. Thus, we need to investigate what are the necessary conditions to form stable and trustworthy societies of information agents in a more bottom-up fashion.

It can be argued that semi-open societies have a greater potential than totally open societies to become stable and trustworthy because of their use of explicit norms and rules and their control of which agents are entering the society. In open societies, on the other hand, norms and rules must emerge in some way and then spread to new members of the society. It is actually not clear how this should be implemented, or whether it is possible at all.[3] However, any regulation that is introduced, e.g., by in-

---

[3] Shoham and Tennenholtz [28] have shown that given the capabilities and goals of all agents in the society, the general problem of automatically deriving useful social laws is NP-complete. Note that this assumes that all agents are cooperative and are willing to give away all information about their goals and capabilities.

stitutions, must be carefully balanced between censorship and openness in order not to result in totalitarian or anarchistic societies respectively.

The general conclusion is that more research is needed that takes into account the presence of non-cooperating and maybe even malicious agents. When doing this, we may be inspired by social science research and borrow concepts and theories. However, great care should be taken, e.g., by explicitly stating what assumptions are made regarding the mental capabilities of the agents.

Finally, this open (and semi-open) society approach to information agent research may in fact result in advances also in the social sciences. Some obvious ways of achieving this are corroboration of existing theories, suggestions to modify existing theories, and the development of new theories.

Acknowledgements

The author wishes to thank Bengt Carlsson, Martin Fredriksson, Rune Gustavsson, Stefan Johansson, Christer Rindebäck (all members of the SoC research group), Johan Kummeneje, and Harko Verhagen for stimulating discussions and useful comments on earlier drafts. He also acknowledges the valuable contribution from the colleagues in the ALFEBIITE project.

References

1. Castelfranchi, C. and Tan, Y.H. (eds.): *Trust and Deception in Virtual Societies*. Kluwer Academic Publishers, 2000.
2. Ciancarini, P. and Wolf, A.L. (eds.): *Coordination Languages and Models*, Springer, 1999.
3. Clearwater, S. (ed.): *Market-Oriented Programming: Some early lessons*, World Scientific, 1996.
4. Davidsson, P.: Multi Agent Based Simulation of "Socio-Technical" Systems. In: *Multi Agent Based Simulation (MABS'2000)*, 2000. (In press.)
5. Davidsson, P. and Ekdahl, B.: Towards Situation-Specific Agent Theories. In: *Intelligent Agent Technologies*, 227-231, World Scientific, 1999.
6. Dellarocas, C. and Conte, R. (eds.): *Agents'2000 workshop on Norms and Institutions in Multiagent Systems*, 2000
7. Dignum, F. (ed.): *IJCAI-99 Workshop on Agent Communication Languages*, 1999.
8. Finin, T., Labrou Y., and Mayfield J.: KQML as an Agent Communication Language. In: J. Bradshaw (ed.), *Software Agents*, MIT Press, 1995.
9. FIPA, FIPA 97 Specification Part 2: Agent Communication Language. FIPA (Foundation for Intelligent Physical Agents), http://drogo.cselt.stet.it/fipa/, 1997.
10. Fisher, R.A.: *The Genetic Theory of Natural Selection,* Dover, 1958.
11. Genesereth, M.R. and Ketchpel, S.P.: Software Agents. In: *Communications of the ACM*, Vol. 37(7): 48–53, 1994.
12. Goldberg, D.E.: *Genetic Algorithms*, Addison Wesley, 1989.
13. Greaves, M. and Bradshaw, J. (eds.): *Agents'99 workshop on Specifying and Implementing Conversation Policies*, 1999.
14. Guarino, N. (ed.): *Formal Ontology in Information Systems*, IOS Press, 1998.

15. Gustavsson, R. and Fredriksson, M.: Coordination and Control of Computational Ecosystems: A Vision of the Future. In: Omicini, A., Klusch, M., Zambonelli, F., and Tolksdorf, R. (eds.): *Coordination of Internet Agents: Models, Technologies, and Applications.* Springer, 2000. (In press.)

16. Gustavsson, R., Fredriksson, M., and Rindebäck, C.: Computational Ecosystems in Home Health Care. In: Dellarocas, C. and Conte, R. (eds.): *Agents'2000 workshop on Norms and Institutions in Multiagent Systems,* 2000. (In press.)

17. Huberman, B.A. and Hogg, T.: The Emergence of Computational Ecologies. In: Nadel, L., Stein, D. (eds.): *Lectures in Complex Systems,* 185–205, Addison-Wesley, 1993.

18. Huhns, M.N. and Stephens L.M.: Multiagent Systems and Societies of Agents. In: Weiss G. (ed.): *Multiagent Systems,* MIT Press, 1999.

19. Johansson, S.J.: Mutual Valuations between Agents and their Coalitions. In: *Intelligent Agent Technology,* World Scientific, 1999.

20. Klusch, M. and Shehory, O.: A Polynomial Kernel-Oriented Coalition Algorithm for Rational Information Agents, *ICMAS'96,* 1996.

21. Labrou, Y. and Finin, T.: Semantics for an Agent Communication Language. In: Singh, M., Rao, A., and Wooldridge M. (eds.): *Intelligent Agents IV,* Springer, 1998.

22. von Neumann, J. and Morgenstern, O.: *Theory of Games and Economic Behavior,* Princeton University Press, 1944.

23. Ossowski, S.: *Co-ordination in Artificial Agent Societies,* Springer, 1999.

24. Pitt, J. and Mamdani, A.: Inter-Agent Communication and the Sincerity Condition. In: Dignum, F. (ed.): *IJCAI'99 Workshop on Agent Communication Languages,* 1999.

25. Rao, A. and Georgeff, M.: BDI Agents — From Theory to Practice. In: *ICMAS'95,* AAAI/MIT press, 1995

26. Rosenschein J. and Zlotkin, G.: *Rules of Encounter,* The MIT Press, 1994.

27. Sandholm, T.W. and Lesser, V.R.: Coalition Formation among Bounded Rational Agents. In: *IJCAI'95,* 1995.

28. Shoham, Y. and Tennenholtz, M.: On Social Laws for Artificial Agent Societies: Off-line design. In: *Artificial Intelligence,* (73) 1-2, 1995.

29. Verhagen, H.J.E.: *Norm Autonomous Agents,* Ph.D. Thesis, Stockholm University / Royal Institute of Technology, Sweden, 2000.

30. Wooldridge, M.J. and Jennings, N.R.: Pitfalls of Agent-Oriented Development. In: *Autonomous Agents'98,* ACM Press, 1998.

31. Wooldridge, M.J., Jennings, N.R., and Kinny D.: A Methodology for Agent-Oriented Analysis and Design. In: *Autonomous Agents'99,* ACM Press, 1999.

A Social Mechanism of Reputation Management in Electronic Communities

Bin Yu and Munindar P. Singh*

Department of Computer Science
North Carolina State University
Raleigh, NC 27695-7534, USA

{byu, mpsingh}@eos.ncsu.edu

Abstract. Trust is important wherever agents must interact. We consider the important case of interactions in electronic communities, where the agents assist and represent principal entities, such as people and businesses. We propose a social mechanism of reputation management, which aims at avoiding interaction with undesirable participants. Social mechanisms complement hard security techniques (such as passwords and digital certificates), which only guarantee that a party is authenticated and authorized, but do not ensure that it exercises its authorization in a way that is desirable to others. Social mechanisms are even more important when trusted third parties are not available. Our specific approach to reputation management leads to a decentralized society in which agents help each other weed out undesirable players.

1 Introduction

The worldwide expansion of network access is driving an increase in interactions among people and between people and businesses. We define an electronic *community* as a set of interacting parties (people or businesses). The members of a community provide services as well as referrals for services to each other. Our notion of *services* is general in that they need not be business services provided for a fee, but may be volunteer services, or not even "services" in the traditional sense, e.g., just companionship or lively discussion.

We model an electronic community as a social network, which supports the participants' *reputations* both for expertise (providing good service) and helpfulness (providing good referrals). The social network is maintained by personal agents assisting different users. Agents and their users have full autonomy in deciding whether or how to respond to a request. The agents assist their users in evaluating the services and referrals provided by others, maintaining contact lists, and deciding whom to contact. In this manner, the agents assist their users

* This research was supported by the National Science Foundation under grant IIS-9624425 (Career Award). We are indebted to the anonymous reviewers for their helpful comments

M. Klusch and L. Kerschberg (Eds.): CIA 2000, LNAI 1860, pp. 154–165, 2000.

in finding the most helpful and reliable parties to deal with. The recommendations by the personal agents are based on a representation of how much the other parties can be trusted. The agents build and manage these representations of trust. To do so, the agents not only take into account the previous experiences of their users, but also communicate with other agents (belonging to other users).

The notion of trust complements hard security, e.g., through cryptography. Hard security approaches help establish that the party you are dealing with is authenticated and authorized to take various actions. They don't ensure that that party is doing what you expect and delivering good service. In other words, the hard security approaches simply place a low hurdle of legality that someone must cross in order to participate, whereas trust management makes people accountable even for the legal actions that they perform.

This paper is organized as follows. Section 2 presents some related work in reputation management. Section 3 presents some necessary background on how to establish an electronic community. Section 4 introduces our approach, giving the key definitions and discussing some informal properties of trust. Section 5 presents our experimental model and some basic results that we have obtained. Section 6 concludes our paper with a discussion of the main results and directions for future research.

2   Related Work

OnSale Exchange and eBay are important practical examples of reputation management. OnSale allows its users to rate and submit textual comments about sellers. The overall reputation of a seller is the average of the ratings obtained from his customers. In eBay, sellers receive feedback $(+1, 0, -1)$ for their reliability in each auction and their reputation is calculated as the sum of those ratings over the last six months. In OnSale, the newcomers have no reputation until someone rates them, while on eBay they start with zero feedback points. Both approaches require users to explicitly make and reveal their ratings of others. As a result, the users lose control to the central authority.

Some prototype approaches are relevant. Yenta [3], weaving a web of trust [4], and Kasbah [2, 12] require that users give a rating for themselves and either have a central agency (direct ratings) or other trusted users (collaborative ratings). A central system keeps track of the users' explicit ratings of each other, and uses these ratings to compute a person's overall reputation or reputation with respect to a specific user. These systems require preexisting social relationships among the users of their electronic community. It is not clear how to establish such relationships and how the ratings propagate through this community.

Trusted Third Parties (TTP) [7] act as a bridge between buyers and sellers in electronic marketplaces. However, TTP is most appropriate for closed marketplaces. In loosely federated, open systems a TTP may either not be available or have limited power to enforce good behavior.

Rasmusson & Janson proposed the notion of *soft security* based on social control through reputation [6]. In soft security, the agents police themselves without ready recourse to a central authority. Soft security is especially attractive in open settings, and motivates our approach.

Marsh presents a formalization of the concept of trust [5]. His formalization considers only an agent's own experiences and doesn't involve any social mechanisms. Hence, a group of agents cannot collectively build up a reputation for others. A more relevant computational method is from *Social Interaction Frame-Work* (SIF) [8]. In SIF, an agent evaluates the reputation of another agent based on direct observations as well through other *witnesses*. However, SIF does not describe how to find such witnesses, whereas in the electronic communities, deals are brokered among people who probably have never met each other.

Challenges. The following are some important challenges for any agent-based approach for reputation management: how to (1) give full control to the users in terms of when to reveal their ratings; (2) help an agent find trustworthy agents (veritable strangers) even without prior relationships; and, (3) speed up the propagation of information through the social network. Our social mechanism seeks to address the above challenges. In particular, ratings are conveyed quickly among agents, even across sub-communities. Therefore, undesirable agents can quickly be ruled out.

3   Electronic Communities

To better understand the notion of trust in communities, let's discuss the famous prisoners' dilemma [1]. The prisoner's dilemma arises in a non-cooperative game with two agents. The agents have to decide whether to *cooperate* or *defect* from a deal. The payoffs in the game are such that both agents would benefit if both cooperate. However, if one agent were to try to cooperate when the other defects, the cooperator would suffer considerably. This makes the locally rational choice for each agent to defect, thereby leading to a worse payoff for both agents than if both were to cooperate.

The prisoner's dilemma is intimately related to the evolution of trust. On the one hand, if the players trust each other, they can both cooperate and avert a mutual defection where both suffer. On the other hand, such trust can only build up in a setting where the players have to repeatedly interact with each other. Our observation is that a reputation mechanism sustains rational cooperation, because the good players are rewarded by society whereas the bad players are penalized. Both the rewards and penalties from a society are greater than from an individual.

The proposed approach builds on (and applies in) our work on constructing a social network for information gathering [10, 11]. In our architecture, each user is associated with a personal agent. Users pose queries to their agents. The queries by the user are first seen by his agent who decides the potential contacts to whom to send the query. After consultation with the user, the agent sends the query to the agents for other likely people. The agent who receives a query can decide if it suits its user and let the user see that query. In addition to or instead of just forwarding the query to its user, the agent may respond with referrals to other users.

A query includes the question as well as the requester's ID and address and a limit on the number of referrals requested. A response may include an answer or a referral, or both, or neither (in which case no response is needed). An agent answers only if it is reasonably confident that its expertise matches the incoming query. A referral depends on the query and on the referring agent's model of other agents; a referral is given only if the referring agent places some trust in the agent being referred.

When the originating agent receives a referral, it decides whether to follow it up. When the agent receives an answer, it uses the answer as a basis for evaluating the expertise of the agent who gave the answer. This evaluation affects its model of the expertise of the answering agent, and its models of any agent who may have given a referral to this answering agent. In general, the originating agent may keep track of more peers than his neighbors. Periodically he decide which peers to keep as neighbors, i.e., which are worth remembering.

Definition 1. $\chi = \langle A_0, \ldots, A_n \rangle$ is a (possible) referral chain from agent A_0 to agent A_n, where A_{i+1} is a neighbor of A_i.

A_0 will use a referral chain to A_n to compute its rating $T_0(n)$ towards A_n. A *trust net* encodes how agents estimate the quality of other agents that they have not met. Figure 1 shows an example trust net. Here agent A wants to know the reputation of agent *phoebe*. $\langle A, B, \text{phoebe} \rangle$ and $\langle A, C, D, E, \text{phoebe} \rangle$ are two referral chains leading to agent *phoebe*.

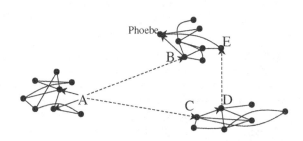

Fig. 1. An example of a trust net

4   Reputation Rating and Propagation

In our approach, agent A assigns a rating to agent B based on (1) its direct observations of B *as well as* (2) the ratings of B as given by B's neighbors, and A's rating of those neighbors. The second aspect makes our approach a social one and enables information about reputations to propagate through the network.

Traditional approaches either ignore the social aspects altogether or employ a simplistic approach that directly combines the ratings assigned by different sources. However, such approaches do not consider the reputations of the witnesses themselves. Clearly, the weight assigned to a rating should depend on the reputation of the rater. Moreover, reputation ratings cannot be allowed to increase ad infinitum. To achieve the above, we first define an agent's rating of another agent. Initially, the rating is zero.

Definition 2. $T_i(j)^t$ is the trust rating assigned by agent i to agent j at time t. We require that $-1 < T_i(j)^t < 1$ and $T_i(j)^0 = 0$.

Each agent will adapt its rating of another agent based on its observation. Cooperation by the other agent generates a positive evidence α and defection a negative evidence β. Thus $\alpha \geq 0$ and $\beta \leq 0$. To protect those who interact with an agent who cheats some of the time, we take a conservative stance toward reputations, meaning that reputations should be hard to build up, but easy to tear down. This contrasts with Marsh [5], where an agent may cheat a sizable fraction (20%) of the time but still maintain a monotonically increasing reputation. We can achieve the desired effect by requiring that $|\alpha| < |\beta|$. We use a simple approach to combine in evidence from recent interactions.

Definition 3. After an interaction, the updated trust rating $T_i(j)^{t+1}$ is given by the following table and depends on the previous trust rating.

$T_i(j)^t$	Cooperation by j	Defection by j
> 0	$T_i(j)^t + \alpha(1 - T_i(j)^t)$	$(T_i(j)^t + \beta)/(1 - \min\{|T_i(j)^t|, |\beta|\})$
< 0	$(T_i(j)^t + \alpha)/(1 - \min\{|T_i(j)^t|, |\alpha|\})$	$T_i(j)^t + \beta(1 + T_i(j)^t)$
$= 0$	α	β

Following Marsh [5], we define for each agent an upper and a lower threshold for trust.

Definition 4. For agent i: $-1 \leq \omega_i \leq 1$ and $-1 \leq \Omega_i \leq 1$, where $\omega_i \geq \Omega_i$.

$T_i(j) \geq \omega_i$ indicates that i trusts j and will cooperate with j; $T_i(j) \leq \Omega_i$ indicates that i mistrusts j and will defect against j; $\Omega_i < T_i(j) < \omega_i$ means that i must decide on some other grounds.

4.1   Propagation of Reputation Rating

Each agent has a set of *neighbors*, i.e., agents with whom it may directly interact. How an agent evaluates the reputations of others will depend in part on the testimonies of its neighbors. We define a trust propagation operator, $\otimes$.

Definition 5. $x \otimes y =$ if $(x \geq 0 \wedge y \geq 0)$ then $x \times y$ else $-|x \times y|$

In other words, the level of trust propagated over a negative link in a referral chain is negative. Below, let $\chi = \langle A_0, \dots, A_n \rangle$ be a referral chain from agent A_0 to agent A_n at time t. We now define trust propagation over a referral chain.

Definition 6. For any k, $0 \le k \le n$, $T_0^\chi(k)^t = T_0^\chi(1)^t \otimes \ldots \otimes T_{k-1}^\chi(k)^t$

The penultimate agent on a referral chain has direct evidence of the last agents on the chain. For this reason, we term the penultimate agent the *witness*.

Definition 7. A testimony for agent 0 from agent k relative to a chain χ is defined as $E_0^\chi(k)^t = T_0^\chi(k)^t T_k^\chi(k+1)^t$. Here k is the witness of this testimony.

Testimony from a witness is used when the witness is considered sufficiently reliable. So as to allow testimony from weak agents to be combined in, we consider witnesses reliable as long as they have a positive trust rating.

Definition 8. For agent i at time t, a testimony from agent k is *reliable* if and only if agent k is trusted, i.e., $T_i^\chi(k)^t > 0$.

Two referral chains χ_1 and χ_2 may pass through the same agent k. In this case, we choose a referral chain that yields the highest trust rating for k.

Definition 9. For agent i, a testimony from agent k with respect to referral chain χ_1 is more reliable than with respect to referral chain χ_2 if and only if χ_1 yields a higher trust rating for agent k, i.e., $T_i^{\chi_1}(k) \ge T_i^{\chi_2}(k)$.

4.2   Incorporating Testimonies from Different Witnesses

We now show how testimonies from different agents can be incorporated into the rating by a given agent. First, to eliminate double counting of witnesses, we define *distinct* sets of testimonies. (E_w refers to the witness of testimony E).

Definition 10. A set of testimonies $\mathcal{E} = \{E_1, \ldots, E_L\}$ towards agent n is *distinct* if and only if the witnesses of all testimonies in $\mathcal{E}$ are distinct, i.e., $|\{E_{1w}, \ldots, E_{Lw}\}| = L$.

The *maximally reliable distinct (MRD)* subset of a set of testimonies contains all the trustable testimonies, and for any witness, it contains the best testimony from that witness. Notice that the individual witnesses do not have to be trusted greater than ω_i for their testimony to be used.

Definition 11. $\mathcal{V}$ is a MRD subset of a set of testimonies $\mathcal{E}$ if and only if $\mathcal{V}$ is distinct, $\mathcal{V} \subseteq \mathcal{E}$, and $(\forall E : (E \in \mathcal{E} \wedge T_i^{\chi_E}(E_w) > 0) \Rightarrow (\exists V : V \in \mathcal{V} \wedge V_w = E_w \wedge T_i^{\chi_V}(V_w) \ge T_i^{\chi_E}(E_w)))$.

Given a set of testimonies $\mathcal{E}$ about A_n, we first find its MRD subset $\mathcal{V}$. Next we compute the average of testimonies from $\mathcal{V}$: $\overline{E} = 1/L \sum_{i=1}^{|V|} V_i$. Therefore, agent A_0 will update its trust rating of agent A_n as follows (all ratings are at time t except where specified).

when	then $T_0(n)^{t+1} =$
$T_0(n)$ and $\overline{E}$ are positive	$T_0(n) + \overline{E}(1 - T_0(n))$
one of $T_0(n)$ and $\overline{E}$ is negative	$T_0(n) + \overline{E}/(1 - min\{|T_0(n)|, |\overline{E}|\})$
$T_0(n)$ and $\overline{E}$ are negative	$T_0(n) + \overline{E}(1 + T_0(n))$

4.3 Gossip

If an agent A encounters a bad partner B during some exchange, A will penalize B by decreasing its rating of B by β and informing its neighbors. An agent who receives this information can combine it into its trust model of B.

Gossip is different from the usual referral process, because an agent can propagate a rumor without having been explicitly queried. For this reason, gossip is processed incrementally.

Definition 12. Suppose agent i receives a message $T_k(n)$ (from agent k about agent n). If $T_i(k)$ is negative, then i ignores the message. If $T_i(k)$ is positive, then agent i updates its trust rating of agent n as follows.

when $T_i(n)$ and $T_k(n)$	then $T_i(n)^{t+1} =$
are both positive	$T_i(n) = T_i(n) + T_i(k)T_k(n)(1 - T_i(n))$
are both negative	$T_i(n) + T_i(k)T_k(n)(1 + T_i(n))$
have opposite signs	$(T_i(n) + T_i(k)T_k(n))/(1 - min\{|T_i(n)|, |T_i(k)T_k(n)|\})$

4.4 Properties of Trust

We now describe and formalize some important properties of trust.

1. *Symmetry*
   In general, symmetry will not hold, because an agent may trust another more than it is trusted back. However, when the agents are trustworthy, through repeated interactions, they will converge to high mutual trust. Conversely, if one of the agents doesn't act in a trustworthy manner, the other agent will be forced to penalize it, leading to low mutual trust. For this reason, we have for any two agents A_x and A_y, $T_x(y)^t \approx T_y(x)^t$ when $t \to \infty$.
2. *Transitivity*
   Trust is not transitive, but the following will hold if x is a rational agent:
   $(T_x(y)^t > T_x(z)^t) \wedge (T_x(z)^t > T_x(w)^t) \Rightarrow (T_x(y)^t > T_x(w)^t)$
3. *Self-reinforcement*
   Trust is self-reinforcing, because agents act positively with those whom they trust. The converse is true, as below a certain trust, individuals tend to confirm their suspicions of others [9]. The first part of the following rule is based on the idea that if trust between two agents is initially above ω, then the trust between those two agents will not decrease below that threshold. The converse is true, since if both agents trust each other below Ω, they will tend not to cooperate with each other whatever the situation, thus reinforcing the other's opinion about them as non-cooperative and unhelpful. Between ω and Ω, anything can happen [5].
   - If $(T_x(y)^t > \omega_x) \wedge (T_y(x)^t > \omega_y)$ then
     $(T_x(y)^{t+1} \geq T_x(y)^t) \wedge (T_y(x)^{t+1} \geq T_y(x)^t)$
   - If $(T_x(y)^t < \Omega_x) \wedge (T_y(x)^t < \Omega_y)$ then
     $(T_x(y)^{t+1} \leq T_x(y)^t) \wedge (T_y(x)^{t+1} \leq T_y(x)^t)$

4. *Propagation*

Consider three agents x, y, and z. If x knows y and y knows z, but x does not know z. How much x trusts z should depend on how much x trusts y, and how much y trusts z. The following rule will hold if x is rational.

$$(T_x(z)^{t+1} \leq T_x(y)^t) \wedge (T_x(z)^{t+1} \leq T_y(z)^t)$$

A simple formula for determining trust that satisfies the above constraint, is

$$T_x(z)^{t+1} = T_x(y)^t T_y(z)^t$$

5   Experiments and Results

In our simulated setup, each agent has an *interest* vector, an *expertise* vector, and models of several *neighbors*. In general, the neighbor models depend on how many agents know the given agent, how many agents it knows, which community it belongs to, and so on. In our case, the neighbor models kept by an agent are the given agent's representation of the other agents' expertise and reputation.

An agent's queries are generated based on its interest vector. The queries are generated as vectors by perturbing the interest vector of the given agent. The motivation for this is to capture the intuition that an agent will produce queries depending on its interests.

When an agent receives a query, it will try to answer it based on its expertise vector, or refer to other agents it knows. The originating agent collects all possible referrals, and continues the process by contacting some of the suggested referrals. At the same time, it changes its models for other agents.

Our experiments involve between 20 and 60 agents with interest and expertise vectors of dimension 5. The agents send queries, referrals, and responses to one another, all the while learning about each others' interest and expertise vectors. The agents are limited in the number of neighbors they may have—in our case the limit is 4.

5.1   Metrics

We now define some useful metrics in which to intuitively capture the results of our experiments.

Definition 13. The average reputation of an agent A_i from the point of other agents is given by $\overline{r(A_i)}$:

$$\overline{r(A_i)} = 1/n \sum_{j=1}^{n} T_j(A_i)$$

where n is the number of agents who know agent A_i. We say that agent A_k knows agent A_i if and only if A_i is a neighbor of A_k.

Definition 14. The average reputation of all agents is:

$$\overline{R} = 1/N \sum_{i=1}^{N} \overline{r(A_i)},$$

where N is the total number of agents.

This average is a metric for determining the stabilization of a community.

5.2   Selection of Rewards and Penalties

Figure 2 illustrates the change of trust ratings depending on different values of α and β. Part A applies to a new agent who initially has a trust of 0, but builds up the rating through positive interactions; Part B applies to a cooperative agent who is already well-trusted; Part C applies to an untrusted agent who through repeated positive interactions becomes trusted; Part D applies to a new agent whose rating falls because of negative interactions; Part E describes a trusted agent who becomes untrusted because of defections; and, Part F applies to an untrusted agent who becomes further untrusted because of defections.

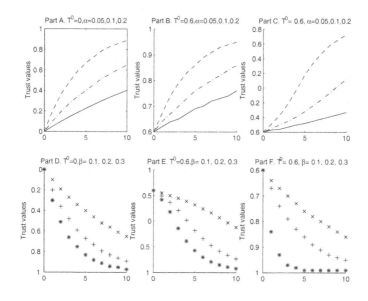

Fig. 2. Selection of α and β, where $\alpha = 0.05('-')$, $0.1('-.')$, $0.2('--')$ and $\beta = -0.1('x')$, $-0.2('+')$, $-0.3('*')$

Consider an agent who cooperates and defects on different interactions. Let θ be the ratio between the number of cooperations and defections. By appropriately selecting the ratings of α and β, we can let $\theta \to \infty$. Assume the initial trust rating of agent A_i is 0.6. Let $\theta = 5, 10, 20$. Figure 3 displays the change of trust rating. Notice that trust built up through several positive interactions is lost through even a single defection.

5.3   Avoiding Undesirable Agents

Our mechanism quickly lowers the reputations of selfish agents. Consider the following example. Assume agent A_w is a non-cooperative agent, and only three

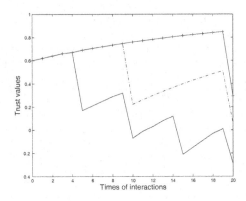

Fig. 3. Change of trust for $\theta = 5$ $('-')$, $10('-.')$, $20('-+')$ when $\alpha = 0.05$ and $\beta = -0.3$

agents A_x, A_y, and A_z know him. Their initial ratings towards A_w are 0.4, 0.5, and 0.6, respectively.

So the average reputation of agent A_w at time 0 is 0.5. However, say a t tim e 1, agent A_w defects against agent A_x. Let $\alpha = 0.05$ and $\beta = -0.3$. According to the formula for updating trust, $T_x(w) = (04 + (-0.3))/(1 - min|0.4|, | - 0.3|) = 0.1/0.7 = 0.1429$. The new reputation of the agent is $r(A_w) = 0.413$. Moreover, agent A_x will disseminate its observation of agent A_w throughout the social network. Eventually the average reputation of agent A_w may decrease to a low l evel. This is the *power of referrals*. Figure 4 experimentally confirms our hypothesis.

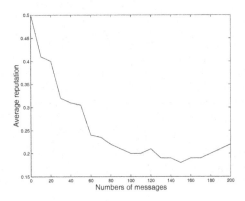

Fig. 4. Average reputation of agent A_w for $N = 3$ $0\alpha = 0.05$ and $\beta = -0.3$

5.4 Introducing New Agents

Clearly, a social network will not remain stable for long, because agents will continually introduce and remove themselves from the network. To evaluate how our approach accommodates changes of this variety, we begin with a stable network and introduce a new agent randomly into it. The new agent is given random neighbors, and all of their trust ratings towards this new agent are zero.

Assume $\overline{R} = 0.637$ at time t. In order to be embedded into the social network, the new agent would have to keep cooperating reliably or else be ostracized early. Its initial threshold for cooperating is low. By frequently cooperating with other agents, the new agent can have its average reputation increase steadily. Figure 5 confirms this hypothesis.

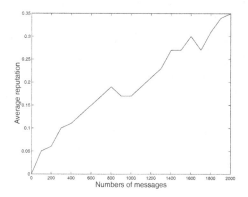

Fig. 5. Average reputation of new agent A_{new} for $N = 30$, $\alpha = 0.05$ and $\beta = -0.3$

6 Discussion

Although we present our results in the context of electronic communities, our approach applies to multiagent systems in general. Most current multiagent systems assume benevolence, meaning that the agents implicitly assume that other agents are trustworthy and reliable. Approaches for explicit reputation management can help the agents finesse their interactions depending on the reputations of the other agents. The ability to deal with selfish, antisocial, or unreliable agents can lead to more robust multiagent systems.

Our present approach adjusts the ratings of agents based on their interactions with others. However, it does not fully protect against spurious ratings generated by malicious agents. It relies only on there being a large number of agents who offer honest ratings to override the effect of the ratings provided by the malicious agents. This is not ideal, but not any worse than democratic rule in human societies. Democratic societies cannot guarantee that a malicious ruler won't be elected, but they reduce the chance of such an event by engaging a large fraction of the population in the rating process.

In future work, we plan to study the special problems of lying and rumors as well as of community formation. We also want to study the evolutionary situations where groups of agents consider rating schemes for other agents. The purpose is not only to study alternative approaches for achieving more efficient communities, but also to test if our mechanism is robust against invasion and, hence, more stable.

References

1. Robert Axelrod. *The Evolution of Cooperation*. Basic Books, New York, 1984.
2. Anthony Chavez and Pattie Maes. Kasbah: An agent marketplace for buying and selling goods. In *Proceedings of the 1st International Conference on the Practical Application of Intelligent Agents and Multiagent Technology (PAAM'96)*, 1996.
3. Lenny Foner. Yenta: A multi-agent, referral-based matchmaking system. In *Proceedings of the 1st International Conference on Autonomous Agents*, pages 301–307, 1997.
4. Rohit Khare and Adam Rifkin. Weaving a web of trust. *World Wide Web*, 2(3):77–112, 1997.
5. P. Steven Marsh. *Formalising Trust as a Computational Concept*. PhD thesis, Department of Computing Science and Mathematics, University of Stirling, April 1994.
6. Lars Rasmusson and Sverker Janson. Simulated social control for secure Internet commerce. In *Proceedings of the Workshop on New Security Paradigms*, 1996.
7. Tim Rea and Peter Skevington. Engendering trust in electronic commerce. *British Telecommunications Engineering*, 17(3):150–157, 1998.
8. Michael Schillo and Petra Funk. Who can you trust: Dealing with deception. In *Proceedings of the workshop Deception, Fraud and trust in Agent Societies at the Autonomous Agents Conference*, pages 95–106, 1999.
9. Susan P. Shapiro. The social control of impersonal trust. *The American Journal of Sociology*, 93(3):623–658, 1987.
10. Bin Yu and Munindar P. Singh. An multiagent referral system for expertise location. In *Working Notes of the AAAI Workshop on Intelligent Information Systems*, pages 66–69, 1999.
11. Bin Yu, Mahadevan Venkatraman, and Munindar P. Singh. An adaptive social network for information access: Theoretical and experimental results. *Applied Artificial Intelligence*, 2000. To appear.
12. Giorgos Zacharia, Alexandros Moukas, and Pattie Maes. Collaborative reputation mechanisms in electronic marketplaces. In *Proceedings of the HICSS-32 Minitrack on Electronic Commerce Technology*, 1999.

A Cybernetic Approach to the Modeling of Agent Communities

Walt Truszkowski [1] and Jay Karlin [2]

[1]Senior Technologist, Code 588
NASA-Goddard Space Flight Center, Greenbelt, MD 20771
Walt.Truszkowski@gsfc.nasa.gov
[2]Viable Systems Inc
12236 Stoney Bottom Road, Germantown, MD 20874
jkarlin1@ix.netcom.com

Abstract. This paper, which is expository in nature, investigates and illustrates the idea of using cybernetic system modeling techniques to model a multi-agent community. The cybernetic concepts used are those originally developed by Stafford Beer. The paper illustrates the idea on a community of agents being developed at Goddard to support both ground-based and space-based system autonomy. It is hoped that use of this approach will help provide a deeper insight into the dynamics of agent-community behaviors. Time and additional analyses will tell.

1   Introduction

In an earlier paper [1] examples of agent technology in a NASA context were presented. Both ground-based and space-based applications were addressed. This paper continues the discussion of one aspect of the Goddard Space Flight Center's (GSFC) continuing efforts to develop a community of agents that can support both ground-based and space-based systems autonomy. The paper focuses on an approach to agent-community modeling based on the theory of viable systems developed by Stafford Beer. It gives the status of an initial attempt to capture some of the agent-community behaviors in a viable system context. This paper is expository in nature and focuses on a discussion of the modeling of some of the underlying concepts and infrastructure that will serve as the basis of more detailed investigative work into the behavior of agent communities. The paper is organized as follows. First, a general introduction to agent community requirements is presented. Secondly, a brief introduction to the cybernetic concept of a viable system is given. This concept forms the foundation of the modeling approach. Then the concept of an agent community is modeled in the cybernetic context.

2   Agent Communities in General - Requirements

In this particular paper we are not specifying a particular agent architecture. We are, however, assuming that the agent has the capability for reactive, deliberative, reflexive, and social behaviors. The particular agent architecture that we are using at Goddard is a component-based architecture implemented in Java which is capable of all four types of behaviors [1]. Our community is populated with agents capable of these behaviors.

M. Klusch and L. Kerschberg (Eds.): CIA 2000, LNAI 1860, pp. 166-178, 2000.

We begin by identifying and briefly discussing what are the general requirements for an agent community from our perspective. These requirements serve to establish the general context for understanding agent community concepts. Good sources for agent community concepts can be found in [2., 3]. These are the requirements to be modeled.

1)   An agent community will have an overarching goal and shall accommodate subgoals.
This overarching goal establishes a "purpose" and this purpose makes the agent community a "system" in the cybernetic sense.

2)   Any two agents in the community can carry on a meaningful conversation. Thus, all agents in the community shall have a shared ontology.
This shared ontology may be the kernel of a larger ontology which is obtained through the „composition" of the ontology's of all of the agents in the community. This kernel is necessary to support ontology negotiation between agents who wish to collaborate but do not have identical ontology's.

3)   An agent community shall have at least one user interface.
This interface to the outside world (user) provides a mechanism for allowing the user to establish, in real-time, new goals for the community, to observe the behavior of the community in action and to get status information on the community's activities.

4)   An agent community shall have an infrastructure capable of supporting its internal communications.
Without such an infrastructure the agents would exist in isolation from one another and not be able to function as a community.

5)   An agent community infrastructure shall be capable of supporting the cooperative behavior of its members.
Cooperative behavior may be broken down into either coordinated or collaborative behaviors. In coordinated behavior a single agent is vested with authority over other agents. In collaborative behavior, the agents that are cooperating do so as peers.

6)   An agent community will be adaptable to environmental changes.
Continual environmental changes are to be expected. Adaptability can be realized in several ways including intervention from the "user" and agent learning (however realized).
7)   Agent community members will negotiate and share agreements.
This is the essence of collaborative behavior in a community.

8)   An agent community will have integrated reasoning ability.
This means that a group of agents will have the capability to collectively reason about a problem utilizing the talents, knowledge, etc. of all the agents in the group. Another way of saying this is that the community is a knowledge community.

9)   An agent community shall reason about at least one domain.
This is related to Requirement 1 above. The goal of the community is to serve with respect to, at least, one domain of activity.

10)   An agent community will be capable of negotiating their shared interests and individual goal priorities in several different subdomains.
This is related to both Requirements 1 and 9. As an example: if the domain of activity is spacecraft operations then the community as a whole is responsible for monitoring and maintaining successful spacecraft operations. An agent may be associated with the power subsystem, another with the thermal subsystem, yet another with command and control. These agents with their own subdomain interests may work together to ensure a broader domain interest.

11)   An agent community shall have access to plans or partially complete plans.
We view a community as a knowledge community and as such the knowledge level of the community rises with each individual agent success. The plans that were used to successfully accomplish a task become part of the knowledge base of the community for future use by the community. The community knowledge base may initially (when the community comes into existence) be empty.

12)   An agent community will have a history-keeping and logging capability.
This is part of the documentation of the community's knowledge base. In order for the community to both improve its performance over time as a community and to be responsive to "outside" queries about its behavior patterns a logging mechanism is required.

3   Viable Systems - A Cybernetic View

A system is defined as a combination of components, which interact in order to perform an identifiable service or set of services. An environment that receives these services and also may, in turn, alter the system in some way surrounds the system. Such an arrangement is shown in Figure 1. For example (in a spacecraft context), conditions resulting from thermal or other environmental or internal system effects can reduce a system's life. We define a system's viability as its functional persistence. A viable system is a robust one: it adapts its own behavior mode, structure, etc., to provide its services even under duress. An intelligent agent assigned in the system may monitor and regulate health or even direct system performance. System health and performance would then become the agent's domain.

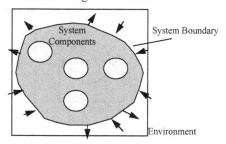

Figure 1. System Defined

A system performs services as tasks in order to effect changes in its environment. The system strives to meet goals which have been decided upon from some higher commanding order of intelligence, e.g., a user. Intelligent agents may be considered for inclusion in this higher order if they are able to act as community management on the behalf of a user to achieve a desired environmental state. This state-oriented agent could be capable of judgment calls or of convening a meeting of agents collaborating on a strategy which would then be parsed out for execution to, for instance, specialist/tactical agents.

The viable system architecture provides a way of discussing internal and external system behaviors in a systematic manner. It involves 5 levels of recursion in doing so. The viable system model depicted in Figure 2 has both horizontal and vertical recursive paths. This model was originally developed by Stafford Beer [4,5,6,7,8,9] as part of his management cybernetic work. We are attempting to utilize the concepts and notations to gain comprehensive insight into the needed behaviors of agent communities.

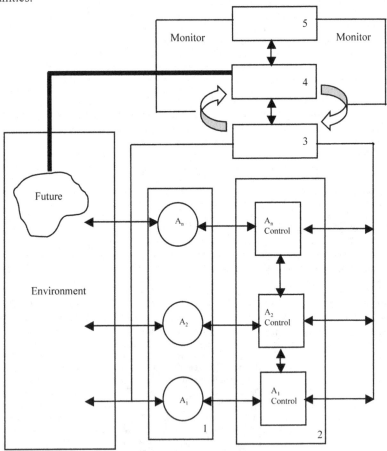

Figure 2. Viable System Model Schematic

The model consists of 5 systems, numbered 1-5. System 1 is the base system, System 2 provides local regulatory monitoring and control for system 1. It regulates oscillatory behaviors.   System 3 deals with self-organization and autonomic regulation. System 4 deals with self -reference, simulation and planning. System 5 deals with homeostasis and overall policy making.

In preparation for the rest of the paper let's begin with a preliminary application of this model schematic to an agent community. The overall system, which is being modeled, is the community of agents. System viability refers to the fact that the community can withstand perturbations either triggered by the environment or by internal changes in individual agent's behaviors. The various systems 1-5 identified in the schematic can be thought of as encapsulations of entities and/or functionality that contribute to the overall viability of the agent community. The elements of System 1 will be individual agents A_i. These agents interact with the environment through perceptors and effectors to maintain an awareness of the environment and to make impacts on the environment. System 2 is concerned with being aware of the behaviors of the elements in System 1 and providing behavioral control. System 3 focuses on the organization of the community and the autonomy that the elements in the community have to contribute to self-organization. For example, the formation of a subgroup of agents to focus on a specific problem would come under the purview of the functionality in System 3.   System 3 is concerned with things as they are. System 4 is concerned with what is going on in the environment and what needs to be done to prepare for the future. System 4 contains functionality that enables itself to maintain a view of itself as a community. There are many interactions between Systems 3 and 4 as is depicted in the schematic. System 5 monitors the interaction between Systems 3 and 5 and establishes overall policies for the agent community as a whole.

4   Agent Communities from a Cybernetic Perspective

We have briefly introduced the concept of a viable system framework. We now delve deeper into the utilization of this approach in the modeling of agent communities. The examples used come from an agent community whose domain is a spacecraft.

4.1   Intelligent Agent Framework for Communities:

To say an agent is intelligent is to imply, among other things, the existence of what we call adaptive functionality. In general, adaptively functional agents are capable of doing three things:

- Noticing: trying to detect potentially relevant events from the environment.

- Interpreting: trying to recognize the events (generally this means mapping the external event into an element in the domain system's vocabulary, i.e., a model) by applying a set of recognition rules.

- Responding: acting on the interpreted events by using a set of action rules, either by taking some action that affects the environment , or by altering their own rules (i.e., learning).

It is the authors' opinion that one of the main differences between intelligent agent systems and other Artificial Intelligent, (AI), systems is a matter of their relative degrees of independence. For example, an agent can decide that in order to complete its task it must look outside to find required expertise or knowledge. It can then proceed to search for and use such a resource in order to complete its task. In contrast, under similar circumstances, the AI system would issue a message to the user that it could not complete the assignment (e.g., within its constraints) and then go into standby or await additional instruction. This ability of an agent, to reflect upon its own capabilities and then to actualize itself, either in commencing a learning routine or engaging another agent and collaborating with it, is what distinguishes intelligent agents from other types of autonomous systems. This capacity would be preferred over more limited AI capabilities in applications where, for instance, an agent is inaccessible to direct reprogramming, such as in missions with limited ground station coverage, but has access to other agents nearby.

4.2   Agent Communities Parallelism

The community shown in Figure 3 is the embodiment of the higher order system introduced in the previous paragraph. This community, in order to maintain its viability whenever its domain undergoes stress, facilitates its member agents in responding appropriately. The white areas, in Figure 3, surrounding each of the three systems depict environment or domain areas. Agent communities are composed of specialists and facilitators or „system managers". Architectural types may be hierarchical, distributed, distributed hierarchical or clustered, depending on the goal of the application. In this paper we intend to describe their possibilities and model some useful structural-behavioral characteristics. Note that the community concept makes no sense with an AI system, but it is here in situations involving homeostasis that autonomous agents realize their fullest potential.

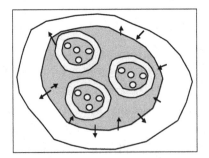

Figure 3. Three agents comprising a community, with their associated domains embedded within the community's domain. Domains are represented by encircling white bands.

The members cooperatively adapt with new plans and initiatives to meet the challenge presented in order to exercise their community responsibility. These new measures are assigned to tactical agents to minister to their individual domains. The procedure unfolds differently according to the following cases:

1. Community-level perception/decision resulting in new goal assignments (possibly new models) to the agents.

2. Attempts to reconcile, with existing models, different simultaneous anomalies detected by two or more agents.

3. Community intervention within an agent's domain should a crisis situation demand it.

4. Community learning by formulating revised models of its domain.

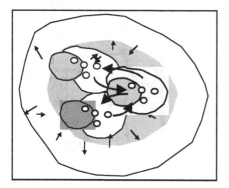

Figure 4.   Intersection of Domain Areas Calls for Domain Related Adaptive and Cooperative Behavior by their Respective Agents

4.3   Agent Collaboration

In addition to community-agent interaction there is agent-agent interaction.   A community's domain is normally made up of sub-domains, which overlap one another because of the interdependence of subsystems. This interdependence is depicted in Figure 4. by the overlap of the agents' domain areas as these areas undergo change. Since a single agent pays attention to only a subset of inputs (percepts), cooperation is required in order to provide more comprehensive coverage. Case 2 above is one example where this applies.

Therefore, in order to examine cooperation in an agent community it is helpful to re-map the previous figures to clarify agent and system interactions.   A graphic demonstration follows in which subsystems are shredded out of their environments and domain-associated agents shredded out of their systems. For a single agent the result appears as shown in Figure 5A. Figure 5B shows the interaction of three agents and their respective domains/subsystems.

4.4   Community Model Framework

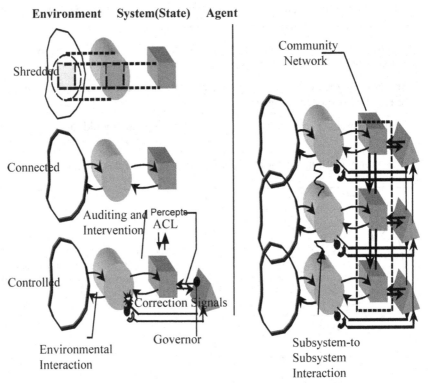

Figure 5A Instantiation of an Agent/Domain and Figure 5B Interaction of Agents as a Community

Conceptually, Figure 5A shows the system and its domain-associated agent having two interfaces to the system (horizontal arrowheads): one interface is a triangular prism, which represents a reactive correction device or governor. The second is a direct intervention or override auditing function which analyzes spurious movements of the system and attempts to redirect it from a revised perspective or model (i.e., learning). Both interfaces are stimulus/response types but the latter interface is a probing by the agent into different critical nodes of its associated system on an intermittent basis while the former is monitoring and adjusting nominal performance settings. In this way, by use of the probe, the agent can investigate a wider domain but yet limit its own demand for critical community resources. Note that in nominal operation the triangular prism provides a semi-autonomous (i.e., reactive) control to the system. The agent is stimulated to replan only when the governor (triangle) indicates that the system's healthy limits might be violated. Thus the governor forms a part of the agent (its perceptor/effector arrangement) but, as will be shown below, the governor is also a node of the network that coordinates the overall communal system. This discussion begins to illustrate the cybernetic (viable system) modeling technique under investigation.

4.5   Coordination Framework

A communal coordination network is illustrated in Figure 5B as vertical message and data pathways are joining together the set of subsystems' governors and also the set of subsystems' domain-related agents. The former deals with percepts and corrections or effects in system performance and the latter with agent-agent communications via some Agent Communication Language (ACL) messaging. The governors respond to input telemetry signals by changing output values (switch settings or gain controls or the sending of pre-stored commands to system devices or to a command management system). Change messages indicating subsystem mode or other state attributes that could affect adjacent subsystems are communicated to these subsystem agents through this coordination network. When a more informative or complex form of intercommunication is necessary, agent communication language is used to convey such information directly between agents via an ACL message.

In addition to communal coordination there is another type of coordination. This function coordinates relative to communal interests, an example of which is an auditor that enforces resource sharing and corrects transmission of data. For example, if a system begins to draw more than its normal level of electric current, then, even though its performance in terms of system functional performance may be within tolerance, something internal to the system is suspect. For this type of trouble shooting, the special discipline dealing just with such matters needs to be applied. Since a single source normally distributes power to all systems, a central monitor agent would be used having unique capability to trouble shoot the electrical power system. (There is obviously a tradeoff possibility here) The point is that there may be certain agent and component roles that would be better suited for a central position in the overall schema than as a peer member in the community. There are a number of these positions that together suggest themselves as a separate central body in the community. Some of them are as follows:

- Agent registrar.
- Planner and Scheduler (from a system shared resource consideration).
- Futures Planner (or „what-if" coordinator).
- Agent translator and communications czar.
- Executive.

Although simpler systems may escape with having only one tier limited to two or three collaborating agents, complex systems may have several tiers of agents, grouped into communities, in which community-to-community communication is carried on. Individuals from two or more communities might in turn occupy additional positions as member of a higher level planning and coordination or executive body.

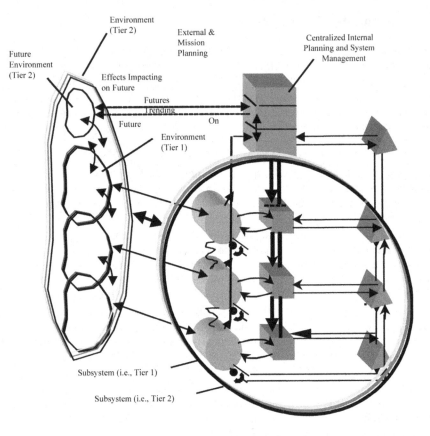

Figure 6. Nested Systems/Agents as Containers

4.6   The   Higher   Levels   of   Agent   Cognition   –   Introduction   to Centralized Community Planning and Coordination

The central portion of an agent community is shown at the top of the model in Figure 6. It is divided into three segments. The lowest one deals with real-time: events relative to the subsystems as relayed to this real-time segment both from the subordinate agents and through their interconnecting monitoring and coordinating networks. The middle segment provides the system and agent community modeling which provides, in turn, state information for various analytical purposes including plan preparation performed by the real-time segment. The middle segment is also the forward-looking arm of the community in that it is in constant contact with both the user interface (top segment), and with the external environment in order to be able to anticipate events and make advance preparations. The top most segments manage the interface with the user of the agent community. In an agent-governed operational context it provides human-to-computer interaction on an as-needed basis rather than continuously as in the hands-on operator version.

4.7   Recursive Process – System Overall Management Function

In the subject domain, environment changes on the system are stimulators of self-reorganization or adaptation. As a subsystem is altered the information is transmitted through the governor and to the tier 1 agent. Agent action and a reflection of such action is further processed in the coordination network since this governor (or subsystem regulator) is one of that network's nodes in addition to its being a part of the agent-to-subsystem loop. Changes introduced in the agent-to-subsystem loop, if significant enough to affect the overall system, are passed on to the tier 2 management level through the coordination network.   Figure 6 illustrates the orthogonality of tiers 1 and 2 in order to illustrate that although the two share instances within the enveloping environment, tier 2 must guard the overall system in such instances, whereas the concern of tier 1 is its narrower domain, e.g., an individual subsystem's health and performance. One might call this effect „information hiding" similarly to structured programming.

If the foregoing discussion has not done so already, the diagram of Figure 6 should have revealed the underlying premise of this report: that the agent community being discussed is an architectural model of the lower part of the central nervous system. If the visceral organs of the body system are represented by the subsystems, then our coordinating and other networks perform the functions of sympathetic and parasympathetic ganglia, while the agent-to agent ACL communication network is the spinal column. And this spinal column is suspended from the cerebellum portion of the brain, which is the lower segment as discussed above. This physiological analogy is based on the work of Stafford Beer [4,5,6].

4.8   Community Builder's Operational Conceptual Model

In contemplating a specific layer or tier, the conceptual model requires consideration of protocols for interaction one tier above and one tier below such a tier.   Different protocols are called for depending on whether the agent's primary function is reactive or deliberative.

4.9   Two Types of Inter-agent Protocols

If we have preprogrammed an agent with a certain low level of capability, then that agent automatically falls into the simple reactive protocol structure. If we, on the other hand, develop an agent capable of high levels of reasoning then the protocol structure needs to fit with the protocol structure that would support the more abstract deliberative forms of information transfer. This would use ACL messaging to signify sender   intentions which conveys priority. We propose to place the more abstract protocol ability in the cognitive part of each tier and the simpler or task-oriented protocol in the system coordination network.   A hybrid agent capability and associated abstract protocol would be provided for ACL messaging where required.

4.10 Agent Community Augmentation

The cybernetic model lends itself to community augmentation through specialist-agent addition, either via long-distance communications and interoperation or through physical migration. In each case, the central managing body provides the administrative function including specialist-agent capability identification protocols, ontology and language supports. A physical migration instance arises in the case where a new community function cannot be spawned on-board. Distributed interoperation may not be a viable solution if the function needs to be real-time but the spacecraft is out of communication range at that time. The specialist would migrate during ground contact prior to the loss of telecommunications line of sight.

5   Example: An Autonomous Spacecraft Subsystem

Figure 7 illustrates some beginning thoughts on how to depict the infrastructure of an autonomous spacecraft subsystem in the context of the cybernetic (viable system) modeling technique. The "IA" in the figure refers to "Intelligent Agent".

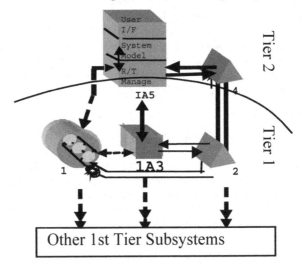

Figure 7. Top-level View of an Autonomous Spacecraft Subsystem

- 1 – An Individual Subsystem.
- [1,2] – Subsystem/Monitor interface.
- [1, 2, IA3] – 1st Tier: showing one member of the control loop set in which each member maintains a spacecraft subsystem.
- IA3 – 1st Tier: Agent that handles a subsystem and its components.
- IA5 – 2nd Tier: Agent that plans, reasons, models, executes, and performs community oriented functions (i.e. spacecraft level).

- 2 - 1st Tier agent perceptor/effector that passes events to IA3 for decisions and receives acts scheduled for transmission.
- 4 - 2nd Tier: Monitor/Governor that reacts to community state changes by monitoring all [2,2] interactions.
- [IA5, 1] – Direct probe of a suspicious subsystem state by Tier 2. Likewise, IA3 probe of one of its subsystem's components.
- [IA3, IA5] – Agent Messaging Interface. e.g. resolving issues.

Note: „IA3" is the first level of recursion of „IA5".

This model begins to show, at a high level, the applicability of the modeling technique in the context of spacecraft subsystems. The model would be duplicated for each subsystem and then integrated into an overall model of the spacecraft. The modeling technique may also be applicable to autonomous science-instruments (this is a new area of interest for us).

6   Conclusion

The task of applying a cybernetic modeling technique to the modeling of an agent community is in its initial stages. This paper is a progress report on our attempts. We feel that this modeling technique will provide a rich representational insight into the various levels of behaviors that will be required in order that an agent community functions as a viable system. So far the technique has been descriptive and seems to address most of the agent-community requirements identified in the earlier portion of this paper. We hope that, as the model becomes more comprehensive in community-behavioral detail, the model can take on a prescriptive role and is of major assistance in the actual development of the agent community being modeled. Time will tell.

References

[1]   Agent Technology from a NASA Perspective, Walt Truszkowski et. al., Proceedings CIA'99 Workshop, M. Klusch, O. Shehory, G. Weiss (eds.), Uppsala Sweden, LNAI 1652, Springer, 1999
[2]   Developing Intelligent Agents for Distributed Systems, M. Knapik, J. Johnson, McGraw-Hill, 1998
[3]   Multiagent Systems, J. Ferber, Addison Wesley Longman, English Edition, 1999
[4]   Decision and Control, Stafford Beer, Wiley, 1966
[5]   Heart of the Firm, Stafford Beer, Wiley, 1979
[6]   Brain of the Firm (Second Edition), Stafford Beer, Wiley, 1981
[7]   Beyond Dispute, Stafford Beer, Wiley, 1994
[8]   The Viable System Model, R. Espejo, R. Harndin editors, Wiley, 1989
[9]   Dealing With Complexity, R. Flood, E. Carson, Plenum Press, 1988

Role of Acquaintance Models in Agent-Based Production Planning System

Michal Pěchouček, Vladimir Mařík and Olga Štěpánková

Gerstner Laboratory for Intelligent Decision Making and Control
Czech Technical University in Prague, Technická 2, Prague 6, Czech Republic
{pechouc,marik,step}@labe.felk.cvut.cz

Abstract. This paper comments the role of acquaintance models in agent-based engineering solutions. We present a specific methodology, a *tri-base acquaintance model*, as formal model of agents' mutual awareness. The model contains three separate knowledge structures for representing agents' permanent, semi-permanent and temporary knowledge, respectively, and mechanism for administering, maintenance and exploration of the knowledge. The paper explains how utilisation of an acquaintance model contributes to communication savings and to reduction of overall distributed problem solving complexity. Utilisation of the tri-base acquaintance model is illustrated on ProPlanT multi-agent system for project-oriented production planning. The system architecture exploits several different types of agents exploring the tri-base mechanism including the meta-agents who are used to adjust and tune the agents' acquaintance models.

1 Introduction

The principle motivation behind grouping particular agents into a community and making them to collaborate is sharing responsibility, efforts, using abilities and knowledge of particular agents in order to meet a common goal. In principle there are three fundamental communication paradigms which organise collaboration within the agents' community:

- **Broadcasting task announcements** - Whenever an agent needs help with satisfying its commitment it just blindly broadcasts a task requirement within the community (or a specific sub-community) and selects the most suitable proposal. The contract net protocol can be used as a technique for managing the negotiation process.
- **Central communication agent** - There is an agent within the agents' community that is in charge of message passing co-ordination. It is supposed to be aware of agents capabilities, their physical addresses etc. An agent sends a message with a requirement to the central communication agent (facilitator) who contacts the best promising agent.
- **Acquaintance models** - Knowledge about collaborating agents are stored in agents' acquaintance models that are located in agents' *wrappers* - an

M. Klusch and L. Kerschberg (Eds.): CIA 2000, LNAI 1860, pp. 179-190, 2000.
© Springer-Verlag Berlin Heidelberg 2000

inseparable part of the agents' architecture that is responsible for individual agent's engagements in the multi-agent community. Every member of the community is to be aware (to certain extent) who may be the best one for satisfying its specific requirements.

Inter-agent communication based on manipulation of knowledge stored in agents' *acquaintance models* minimises overall communication requirements while avoiding need of a central communication agent. If someone in the community dies or gets overloaded, the system is expected to reorganise itself in order to solve its tasks anyway. Putting too much power to a single agent - central communication agent - makes this approach too fragile and dependent on the central agent. With acquaintance models knowledge of the central communication agent is distributed across the community members. A number of case specific knowledge structures and maintenance algorithms for acquaintance models were implemented in the past.

1.1 Brief Acquaintance Models Review

Acquaintance models, as agents' views of their collaborative environment, were widely used within the framework of the ARCHON project (Architecture for Co-operating Heterogeneous On-line Systems) [9]. ARCHON helps designers to correctly decompose and structure components of a MAS. In a wrapper of an agent (they call it ARCHON layer) three types of knowledge are stored: (i) planning and co-ordination knowledge, (ii) knowledge about the agent internal state, and (iii) knowledge about collaborating agents - in the form of acquaintance models. Both the agents' problem solving knowledge and inference mechanism are stored in the Intelligent System Layer.

Coverage is a system for multi-agent systems verification [2]. The system is capable of detecting of anomalies that can exist in MAS (of ARCHON architecture) between their *declarative knowledge* - knowledge of the Intelligent System Layer and *cooperation knowledge* stored and manipulated within its ARCHON Layer. Though no particular mechanism for acquaintance knowledge representation was presented, specific algorithms for detecting inconsistencies within various types of agent's knowledge have been analysed. The system is able to identify conflicts within the set of agent's internal problem solving domain knowledge (**dk** anomaly), among agent's co-operation knowledge (**ck** anomaly), between agent's problem solving knowledge and appropriate social acquaintance knowledge (**cd/dk** anomaly) and among acquaintance knowledge of different agents (**ck/ck** anomaly). A methodology for detecting inconsistencies in agent's acquaintance models offers checking security in the entire MAS.

Pleiades is an architecture of collaborative agents making organisational decision making over the collection of internet-based heterogeneous resources [6]. The community consists of *task-specific* agents (TA) and *information-specific* agents (IA). TA co-ordinate and schedule plans with respect to a context. They collaborate in order to resolve conflicts and integrate information. IAs gather information from databases and collaborate mutually in order to provide TAs with requested information. Correspondingly, TAs agents maintain problem solving knowledge how to perform a task as well acquaintance knowledge detailing capabilities of the other TAs and IAs.

A specific acquaintance model, called **twin-base model**, was proposed by Cao, Bien and Hartvigsen [1]. The novel idea behind this paradigm is based on correct separation of information and knowledge, which an agent maintains within its wrapper. There are two independent bases proposed in the twin-base model: (i) **cooperator base** with all permanent data about cooperating agents (e.g. agents' addresses, message formats, agents' capabilities etc.) and (ii) **task base** containing up-to-date information on possible task decomposition and delegation among cooperating agents.

The main innovative idea behind the twin-base approach is rooted in *periodical revisions* of the task-base such that it contains just the most up-to-date information on a possible task decomposition and responsibility allocation. There is a special super-agent called a *cooperation trader* in [1] who utilises community idle time and updates the content of the task base. In collaboration with the cooperation trader the most suitable and efficient agent in the community is to be identified and contracted. As a result, the communication traffic is significantly reduced and the reactions of the system are becoming substantially faster than in the case of message broadcasting.

The *twin-base acquaintance model* was successfully used in the *ViSe* (Virtual Secretary) intelligent agent that assists major secretarial duties. This approach reduced redundant communication among agents and through intelligent cooperation both the high performance and easy maintenance were achieved.

A specific type of an acquaintance model, a *tri-base acquaintance model*, has been used in the area of production planning [3]. As the complexity of production planning is of considerably higher magnitude in comparison to secretarial assistance duties, the twin-base base model would not suffice requirements of agents' planning the manufacturing processes. In the **tri-base model** the **cooperator base** has been split into a **state base** and a **cooperator base** in order to separate non-permanent and static types of information. Moreover, the **task base** cannot comprise all possible plans. Meta-description of plans is maintained instead and only relevant instantiations of plans are considered for decision making.

The process of periodical revisions invoked by the cooperation trader within the twin base approach has been substituted by a reporting mechanism where agents autonomously advertise their capabilities to interested parties. The model has been encapsulated within the agents of the ProPlanT multi-agent system and will be commented thoroughly on in the next Section.

2   Tri-Base Acquaintance Model in Production Planning

This chapter shows applicability of the acquaintance models philosophy and techniques in solving the problem of project-oriented production planning. The ProPlanT multi-agent system was developed within the framework of EU funded project EUREKA No.1439 at the Czech Technical University. The motivation of the project was to automate the process production planning at TESLA-TV, the largest producer of the TV and radio transmitter stations in the Central Europe. ProPlanT has been experimentally running in this plant. The main section of this chapter will present the formal concept and utilisation of the tri-based acquaintance model and provide comments on experiments with this model.

2.1   ProPlanT Architecture

Resulting from thorough production process analysis we have identified certain information units the general production process is based on. Information units of the same nature are represented by agents of the same functional class. In principle the agents can be clustered into two fundamental super-classes: *intra-enterprise agents* (IAE) and *inter-enterprise agents* (IEE). We distinguish among the following basic classes of IAE agents (see Figure 1):

- **Production Planning Agent** (PPA) is in charge of project planning. It is supposed to construct an exhaustive, partially ordered set of tasks that need to be carried out in order to accomplish the given project. It contracts PMA agents.
- **Production Management Agent** (PMA) is accountable for the project management in terms of contracting the best possible PA agents (considering operational costs, offered delivery time, and current capacity). PMA delegates its responsibility either to another PMA or it orchestrates the work of a group of PA agents contracted for the considered task. In this manner a multi-level managing structure is modelled.
- **Production Agent (PA)** represents the lowest level production units that simulate or encapsulate shop floor production processes on the IAE level. PA carries out the parallel-machinery scheduling of given tasks and manages resource allocation via special type of database agents. On the IEE level, the PA agent may encapsulate contracted suppliers offering either services or components participating in the manufacturing process. Appropriate optimisation within the community will result in the cheapest (or shortest) production plan.
- Another IEE agent may be a **Customer Agent (CA)**. In the current implementation CA agent is the only actor that may trigger the course of production planning. It negotiates with the PPA agent in order to specify the production requirements and both the deadline and budgetary constraints.
- **Meta Agent (MA)** is a special monitoring agent who visualises information, material and workflows across the agents' community and advises on optimal system's efficiency. It shall be noted that the community of agents will survive well with no meta-agent. Ordinary agents are able to communicate in peer-to-peer manner, but the meta-agent is able to induce specific efficiency considerations from observation of the community workflow.

The CA agents will communicate with the PPA agent only. PPA constructs a component list with the team of PMA agents and delegates further responsibilities to

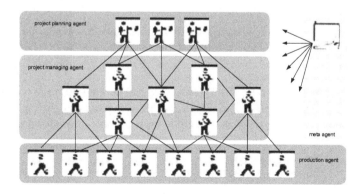

Fig. 1. ProPlanT Architecture

PPAs who contract the best possible PA agents. Final costs and deadlines, a meta-representation of the distributed production plan, will be then back-propagated to the customer.

2.2   Tri-Base Acquaintance Model in ProPlanT

While PA and PPA agents are simply encapsulated programs (expert systems, schedulers, databases) each of the PMA agents is equipped with a specific knowledge of behaviour of the collaborating agents encoded in the tri-base acquaintance model [3] in order to provide an optimal task decomposition. Prior to formalising the model let us introduce several primitives we will use throughout the course of explanation. Let Θ be a set of all agents within the community and S a set of all tasks the community members are able to decompose. For each $A \in \Theta$ let

- $\alpha(A) \subseteq \Theta$ be the agent's A *total neighbourhood*, a set of agents the agent A is aware of,
- $\beta(A) \subseteq S$ be the set of all tasks the agent A is able to decompose,
- $\gamma(T)$ contains all possible plans for decomposing the task $T \in S$. Plan for the task T is in the form $\langle T, S, O, C \rangle$, where S is a set of subtasks which ensure completion of the task T provided that their processing meets precedence constraints O and applicability constraints C.
- $\omega(A, T) \in \gamma(T)$ contains those plans for the task T the agent A knows about (if $T \notin \beta(A)$ then $\omega(A, T) = \emptyset$).

The following sets provide the time dependent information. Let

- $\epsilon^t(A) \in \alpha(A)$ be the agent's current *cooperation neighbourhood*, i.e. a set of agent's A collaborators at the time instant t,
- $\tau^t(A) \in \beta(A)$ contains the tasks being solved by the agent A in a time instance t and the set
- $\pi^t(A) \in \beta(A)$ be a collection of tasks, for which the agent A is monitoring and re-planning specific instantiations of plans. This process is carried out in agent's idle times and the set $\pi^t(A)$ specifies this collection in a time instance t.

Within the tri-base model each agent maintains three knowledge bases where all the relevant information about the rest of the community is stored. We distinguish among:

- **co-operator base (CB)** - maintains permanent information on co-operating agents (i.e.: their addresses, communication languages, and their predefined responsibilities). This type of knowledge is expected not to be changed very often. CB(A) is then defined as

$$\mathsf{CB}(A) = \{\langle B, \mathsf{Addr}(B), \mathsf{Lang}(B), \beta(B)\rangle\}_{B \in \alpha(A)}$$

where $\mathsf{Addr}(B)$ specifies the agent's address, $\mathsf{Lang}(B)$ the language it communicates, as already mentioned $\beta(B)$ is a set of tasks the agent accounts for and the set $\alpha(A)$ denotes members of the agent's A scope of the community.

- **task base** (TB) - stores in its *problem section* (PrS) the general problem solving knowledge - (i) information on possible decompositions of the tasks to be coordinated by the agent and (ii) in its *plan section* (PIS) it maintains the actual and most up-to-date plans on how to carry out those tasks, which are the most frequently delegated to the agent - the owner of the task base (denoted as $\pi^t(A)$). The formal definition of the TB(A) is then

$$\mathsf{TB}(A) = \langle \mathsf{PrS}(A), \mathsf{PIS}(A) \rangle,$$

$$\mathsf{PrS}(A) = \{\omega(T, A)\}_{T \in \beta(A)},$$

$$\mathsf{PIS}^t(A) = \{\langle T, \langle \{\langle s, B \rangle\}_{s \in S}, O, C, \mathsf{Trust}(T) \rangle \rangle\}_{T \in \pi^t(A)},$$

where for any $\langle T, \langle \{\langle s, B \rangle\}_{s \in S}, O, C, \mathsf{Trust}(T) \rangle \rangle \in \mathsf{PIS}^t(A)$ where exist O_1, C_1 such that following constraints are met: $\langle T, S, O_1, C_1 \rangle \in \mathsf{PrS}(A), B \in \epsilon^t(A), s \in \beta(B)$ and as C is a specialisation of C_1 reflecting the considered allocation of the tasks $s \in S$, O is a refinement of O_1 and both O and C are valid. $\mathsf{Trust}(T)$ expresses quantitatively the belief in the reliability of the plan for the task T. This paper, however, does not comment the issue of trust in elaborated and maintained plans in any greater details.
- **state base** (SB) -stores in its *agent section* (AS) all information on the current load of co-operating agents. This part of the state base is updated frequently and informs the agent who is busy and who is available for collaboration. In the *task section* (TS) there is stored information on the status of tasks the agent is currently solving. Formal description of the SB(A) of the agent A is thus

$$\mathsf{SB}(A) = \langle \mathsf{AS}(A), \mathsf{TS}(A) \rangle,$$

$$\mathsf{AS}(A) = \{\langle B, \mathsf{Cap}(B), \mathsf{Load}(B), \mathsf{Trust}(B) \rangle\}_{B \in \epsilon^t(A)},$$

provided that agent's B capability has the form of

$$\mathsf{Cap}(B) = \{\langle T, \mathsf{Cost}(T) \rangle\}_{T \in \beta(B)},$$

the overall agent load is Load(B), and trust in this information is $\mathsf{Trust}(B)$. TS(A) contains relevant information on all the tasks the agent A agreed to supervise recently. This set is denoted by $\tau^t(A)$. Formally

$$\mathsf{TS}(A) = \{\langle T, \mathsf{Dec}(T), \mathsf{State}(T), \mathsf{Trust}(T) \rangle\}_{T \in \tau^t(A)},$$

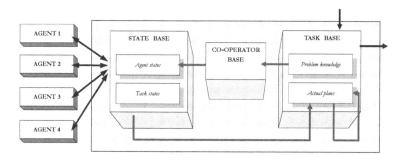

Fig. 2. Tri-base model planning

where the decomposition $\mathsf{Dec}(T)$ is taken from the $\mathsf{PIS}_1^t(A)$ at the moment of the contract (time t_1). $\mathsf{State}(T)$ partitions subtasks from $\mathsf{Dec}(T)$ into three parts: subtasks finished, actually under coordination, and the rest. The record is complemented with the trust value $\mathsf{Trust}(T)$ denoting the trust in the plan of the task T.

The agent is supposed to select an optimal plan from the $\mathsf{PIS}^t(A)$, where an appropriate number of plans prepared in advance is stored. By this it does not need to contract peer agents in order to find out the most appropriate (optimal) offers for further problem delegation. Knowledge stored in the PIS will help the agent to decide by itself. It is obvious that limiting the communication among agents will in its own way decrease the computational complexity of the entire problem. The price we have to pay for this is an increased communication traffic among agents when updating the SB.

The model maintenance algorithms are based on a simple subscribe/advertise mechanism. After parsing the PrS knowledge, each agent identifies possible collaborators and subscribes these for reporting on their statuses. The subscribed agent advertises its load, capabilities and task completion times and costs estimates either periodically or when either of these changes. This mechanism facilitates the agent to make the best decision with no further communication in the critical moment of the agent's decision making.

There are two issues to be addressed here: (i) how many peer agents to subscribe and (ii) how many plans to keep pre-prepared. *Cooperation neighbourhood* $\epsilon^t(A)$ denotes a collection of such agents B who belong to the agent's A scope of collaboration. All agents $B \in \epsilon^t(A)$ are subscribed by the agent A. The maximum neighbourhood $\epsilon^t(A)$ is specified when the agent parses its problem solving knowledge-base (PrS) and detects who will be needed for further collaboration. $\epsilon^t(A)$ is fixed here for the entire course of agent's decision making. In this way, the agent is collecting lots of redundant data, which slows the community down substantially. The possible role of the meta-agent can be in analysing inter-agent communication and optimising the $\epsilon^t(A)$ neighbourhood.

On the other hand, $\pi^t(A)$ neighbourhood, agent's A *scope of reasoning*, specifies how many of plans from PrS will be kept instantiated and on-line evaluated in PLS of the TB. We distinguish among two marginal cases. If $\pi(A) = \emptyset$, there is no plan pre-prepared and planning in the critical time requires substantially more of computational time for constructing the PIS plans. If $\pi(A)$ is maximal, there is no time needed for constructing the PIS plans, but each minor change within the community results in massive re-computation and re-evaluation of the PIS plans. Designers of the system rely on meta-agent machine learning capabilities in setting $\pi(A)$ agent's scope of reasoning.

3 Reducing Complexity of Distributed Planning

If the knowledge stored in the tri-base model is carefully organised and appropriate mechanisms for setting models parameters $\epsilon^t(A)$ and $\pi^t(A)$ are well designed this methodology is expected to provide substantial communication savings. In the following we will show how this fact contributes to reducing complexity of distributed problem solving.

The reason why we may use an agent-based paradigm for complex software system implementation is twofold. Firstly, and most frequently, means for **integration** of heterogeneous (often pre-existing) pieces of software within the framework of multi-agent system is provided. Secondly, more interestingly however, substituting the process of problem solving with the problem of negotiation and job delegation among agents may **decrease** an overall **computational complexity** of the system and increase its tractability.

Usually, what reduces the computational complexity requirements in knowledge based systems is knowledge. The problem knowledge organises the space of possible problem solving primitives (say states) so that the course of automated problem solving is carried out in an intelligent/optimal way. In the problem of production planning this can be:

- problem specification knowledge in terms of precedence constraints - $t_i \prec t_j$ (we say that task t_i precedes task t_j)
- knowledge of responsibility for the task - $t_i \in \mathcal{T}_m$ (we say that task t_i can be assigned to machine m)
- knowledge of task decomposition - $t_i \rightarrow \langle t_j, t_k \rangle$ (we say that task t_i is decomposable into task t_j and t_k

These pieces of knowledge specifying the state space structure define the architecture of the multi-agent system. Parsing such a state space corresponds to collaborative problem solving where requirements (job delegation) are broadcast among all the concerned agents that may be involved in problem solving within specific sub-community. If such a system would run on a single processor computer, the complexity of problem solving is obviously just the same. Using a multi-agent system with no social knowledge reduces thus problem complexity only through distributing a computational workload among more processing units.

Agent's mutual awareness would eliminate searching non-optimal branches of the state space (if the problem is viewed as a state-space parsing problem) or contracting agents that would not bring an efficient benefit to the problem solving (in terms of distributed problem solving). The truth is that an agent cannot avoid seeking information it requires for making its decision. Instead of communicating this pieces of information in the agents' critical problem solving time, agents can maintain approximate models of their collaborating environment and update it in their idle times. The *tri-base acquaintance model* provides knowledge structures and algorithms for implementing the concept of agents dynamic mutual awareness.

3.1   Experiments

Utilisation of the tri-based acquaintance model has been tested on the ProPlanT multi-agent system. We have experimented with a hierarchical community of 16 agents (see Fig 3) simulating the process of TV-transmitter manufacturing. Utilisation of an acquaintance model depends very much on (i) frequency of requests on the system and (2) agent's degree of freedom to make a decision who to cooperate with.

Frequency: The communication savings offered by this approach may be seen as a specific communication load shift. The communication load is minimised in the agent's *critical time* (i.e.: moment when the agents are required to fulfill, through delegation, a request) while a new advertising activity appears in the agent's *idle times*. Moreover each request is answered quickly but it brings substantial communication flows following the request fulfilment. The truth is that successful operation of such a multi-agent system depends on the community lifecycle. In order to utilise this acquaintance model

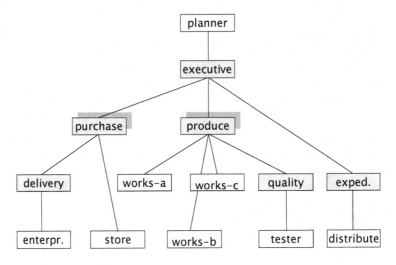

Fig. 3. Testing Community

based mechanism and to guarantee its communication savings for the frequency f of requirements to plan the following condition should be met

$$\frac{1}{f} \geq t_c + t_i,$$

where t_c is maximum amount of time spent in the *critical time* planning and t_i is maximum amount of time needed for processing the subscription/advertise mechanism in agents' *idle time*.

Degree of Freedom: For the sake of the experiment explanation, let us specify the term *degree of cooperating freedom* $\phi(\Theta)$ of the community. An agent is *free* to decide about its collaborators if its knowledge base provides several alternatives how to decompose at least one requirement and how to delegate responsibility. In such a case an agent either broadcasts a request and waits for offers from possible candidates or uses some of social knowledge to make the decision. On the other hand, if an agent's knowledge provides only fixed decomposition assignments, the agent does not have any freedom to select its collaborators. It is obvious that in the latter case the communication complexity is substantially smaller. The *degree of cooperating freedom* of the community is thus equivalent to number of agents free to form the team collaborators for a specific project.

The higher is the degree of cooperating freedom of the community, the more communication traffic is required and consequently more significant impact has got an acquaintance model on communication savings. In the marginal case with fixed task decomposition and job delegation ($\phi(\Theta) = 0$), the acquaintance model has no utilisation while substantial communication needed for the model is required.

In the mentioned example, reflecting the real organisational structure in the plant, there are only two agents (production, purchase) making their own choices in terms of optimal allocation of collaborating agents workload. Thus the community is rather fixed. We have measured communication requirements of the community when broadcasting and with acquaintance models for the real-life case ($\phi(\Theta) = 2$) and for both marginal cases (no cooperating freedom - ($\phi(\Theta) = 0$)and full cooperating freedom ($\phi(\Theta) = 7$)).

$\phi(\Theta)$	m(tri-base)	m(broadcast)	m(maintenance)
0	21	21	12
2	21	32	12
7	21	47	12

Table 1: *Utilisation of an acquaintance model (number of messages)*

Table 1 indicates that utilisation of the acquaintance model limits the amount of needed communication (number of communicated messages - m(tri-base)) in the critical time to communication needed for directly addressed problem decomposition ($\phi(\Theta) = 0$), i.e. minimal required communication. The number of messages needed for model maintenance (m(maintenance)) in the community idle time is constant and would pay off if separated from the critical time communication. An interesting observation is that even with a very fixed agent's community (our real example - $\phi(\Theta) = 2$) we have managed to achieve 30% of communication savings in the community critical times.

3.2   MetaAgent

Another, quite different way of assuring system's optimal operation is involvement of a meta-agent, a special agent observing the overall community behaviour and providing efficiency improvements suggestions.

In our understanding a meta-agent is an agent who is capable of some sort of meta-level reasoning about the multi-agent community. Unlike facilitators or brokers in classical agent based systems [7] it is not central to the rest of agents. It neither controls the community nor serves as a communication centre in the physical and symbolic sense. Instead, the meta-agent observes the communication traffic of the community and tries to draw corresponding conclusions regarding the agents' behaviour with intention to improve performance of the whole system. If the meta-agent ceases to operate the community has no difficulty to survive and it lives its ordinary (possibly inefficient) life.

The meta-agent [4] can for example predict approaching critical overload of an agent. In such a case the meta-agent announces to all the agents in the community that attempts to contract such an agent will result in excessive waiting time. The meta-agent may identify a specific problem-solving pattern involving the critical agent. All agents involved in this problem solving-pattern other than those directly collaborating with the critical agent will benefit from this information. If there is time enough the meta-agent can carry out more sophisticated reasoning resulting in detection of e.g. heuristics that help the planning processes within particular agents (e.g. by introducing new precedence constraints used in decomposition of the considered tasks). Such heuristics correspond to the problem solving *'shortcuts'*, e.g. frequently used solutions of the considered problems of task planning. As another example of heuristics, we may see formulae describing the frame/ramification problem of planning to appear in conditions of decomposition. From the point of view of the meta-agent's impact on the community we distinguish two principal roles:

– *Passive role* - The meta-agent does not influence the community lifecycle. Here it provides the user with the information on how the community evolves in time. The meta-agent playing a passive role does not have any direct vehicles how to modify directly the multi-agent community. It allows the user interactively step into and affect multi-agent system course of planning.

– *Active role* - The meta-agent affects directly some other agents within the community. Here the meta-agent uses deduced knowledge for revision of the agents' tri-base acquaintance model (via direct communication). While agent's state base is maintained by already described *subscribe/advertise* mechanism, semi-permanent knowledge stored in the cooperator base (parameter $\epsilon^t(A)$ maintenance) and problem section of the task base are revised according to meta-agent suggestions. If the meta-agent detects communication anomaly, it provides revisions regarding an agent's termination, agent's loss of its capability, agent's acquiring new capability, new agent creation or an agent changing its properties [4].

Setting and maintenance of $\pi^t(A)$ can be implemented in a number of ways. Static, manual specification has shown its usefulness in the practical industrial problems. The entire planning activity was viewed in terms of three subsequent stages: *pre-planning* (specification of $\pi^t(A)$), *re-planning* (on-line re-evaluation of plans with respect to changing values in the state base), and *planning* (fixing an optimal plan). However, more intelligent way of dynamic maintenance of $\pi^t(A)$ can be implemented through machine learning. An agent itself would start with a very inefficient behaviour having either $\pi^t(A)$ too large or empty and expanding or restricting the scope as it solves community requirement. Similarly meta-agent can deduce revisions not only about agents performance but also some sort of meta-knowledge about the domain agents solve. By this it can provide agent with suggestions about which plans it is worthwhile to keep pre-prepared. Meta-agent can thus maintain $\pi^t(A)$.

4 Conclusions

Keeping reasonable extent of communication and coordination complexity seems to be the crucial problem when designing an agent based software system. The role of knowledge available to the agents is essential. The bigger is the volume of knowledge administered by individual agents, the lesser complexity of the inter-agents' activities should be expected.

The approach presented in this paper illustrates the role of acquaintance models incorporated into the wrappers of autonomous agents. A specific model, the tri-base acquaintance model, is collection of dynamic knowledge-based structures organizing and maintaining relevant knowledge in a flexible and transparent way. Together with specific knowledge maintenance algorithms (subscribe/advertise mechanism), meta-level information processing and administration formalisms represent the core of the methodology. The meta-agents are aimed at influencing the multi-agent community workflow by providing valuable feedback and thus significantly enhancing the workflow efficiency.

The tri-base acquaintance model and the concept of the meta-agent have been implemented within the architecture of the ProPlanT production planning system. Several types of agents, differing in their functionalities, have been implemented. The tri-base models have been proven to be an efficient formalism for organizing the processes of communication/coordination within the community as well as for agentification processes, e.g. processes which convert the legacy systems into agents. The current formalization of the tri-base model strongly simplifies formulation of the re-planning problems [3]. The ProPlanT system prototype for production planning tasks was tested in the industrial environment with a success.

The innovative ideas behind the ProPlanT system, specifically the tri-base acquaintance model proved to be general enough to be re-used in solving problems of different types. This approach has been successfully applied for e.g. the workflow simulation problems and proposed for intruder detection in the communication networks [4].

5   Acknowledgement

The research has been carried out under the support of the project contract no.: F61775-99-WE099 of the U.S. Air Force EAORD, further by the support from the EC funded project EUREKA No.1439 and the Czech Ministry of Education grants No. VS 96047 and J04/98:212300013.

References

1. Cao W., Bian C.-G., Hartvigsen G.: Cooperator-Base and Task-Base for Agent Modeling: The Virtual Secretary Approach. In: Proc. of AAAI-96 Workshop on Agent Modeling, AAAI Press, 1996, pp. 105-111.
2. Lamb N., Preece A.: Verification of Multi-Agent Knowledge-Based Systems. In: Proc ECAI-96 Workshop on Validation, Verification and Refinement of KBS, August 1996.
3. Mařík V., Pĕchouček M., Lažanský J., Roche, C.: PVS'98 Agents: Structures, Models and Production Planning Application. In: Robotics and Autonomous Systems, vol. 27, No. 1-2, Elsevier, 1999, pp.29-44. ISSN 0921-8890
4. Pĕchouček M. , Štĕpánková O, Mařík V..: Potential Roles of Acquaintance Models and Meta-Agents in Communication Safety/Efficiency Improvements. In: Multi-Agent Systems in Communications, US AirForce Research Project Report, published also as a Gerstner Laboratory research Report GL-94-2000, CTU-Prague, 2000
5. Singh M.P., Rao A., Wooldridge M.J. (eds.): Intelligent Agents IV, LNAI No. 1365, Springer Verlag, Heidelberg, 1998
6. Sycara K.: Intelligent Agents and Information Retrieval. Unicom Seminar on Intelligent Agents and their Business Applications, 8-9 November, London, 1995, pp. 143-159
7. Toomey C., Mark W.: Satellite Image Dissemination via Software Agents. IEEE Expert, Vol. 10 (1996), No. 5, pp. 44-50
8. Weiss G. (ed.): Multi-Agent Systems: A Modern Approach to Distributed Artificial Intelligence, MIT Press, Cambridge MA, 1999
9. Wittig T. (Ed.): ARCHON: An Architecture for Multi-agent System. Ellis Horwood, Chichester, 1992
10. Wooldridge M., Jennings N.: Intelligent Agents: Theory and Practice. The Knowledge Engineering Review, 10 (1995), No.2, pp. 115-152
11. Zhong N., Kakemoto Y., Ohsuga S.: An Organised Society of Autonomous Discovery Agents. In: Cooperative Information Agents (Kandzia P., Klusch M. eds.), LNAI 1202, Springer-Verlag, Heidelberg, 1997, pp.183-194

Agent Communication and Cooperative Information Agents

Frank Dignum

Faculty of Mathematics & Computer Science,
Eindhoven University of Technology
The Netherlands
e-mail: dignum@win.tue.nl

Abstract. In any multi-agent system the coordination between the agents is an important element that determines to a large extent the effectiveness of the system. One way to facilitate the coordination between the agents are agent communication languages. In this paper we will present a short introduction to agent communication languages in general and will indicate the main topics of interest in agent communication research. We will relate these developments to the characteristics of cooperative information agents in particular. This leads to a number of short term goals for the development of agent communication between cooperative information agents, which are for some part very practical and also deviate in emphasis from agent communication in general.

1 Introduction

Agent technology is an exciting and important new way to create complex software systems. Agents blend many of the classical properties of AI programs - autonomy, adaptivity, pro-activeness, goal-directedness, and so forth - with insights gained from distributed computing, negotiation and teamwork theory, and the social sciences. This blend promises programs that continuously adjust their behavior to balance changes in their environment, collaborating with other agents to satisfy both their internal goals and the external demands generated by virtue of their participation in agent society. And, although it is possible to design agent programs that are completely unaware of each other, much of the power of the agent approach derives from the principle that agents (like humans) can function more effectively in societies characterized by division of labor and cooperation in service of shared goals. In this paper we will study the communication that has to take place in order for agents to cooperate. First we will look at agent communication in general. Then we will indicate which parts are particularly relevant for cooperative information agents and what extra requirements might hold for this situation.

Agents typically employ specialized *Agent Communication Languages (ACLs)* in order to support the types of multiagent interaction alluded to above.[1] Formally, ACLs

---

[1] Agents can also communicate with actions other than classically linguistic productions, simply by making observable changes in the environment that have semantic force. For example, an agent that locks a resource for itself might be assumed to communicating to an observer its

M. Klusch and L. Kerschberg (Eds.): CIA '2000, LNAI 1860, pp. 191-207, 2000.

are high-level languages whose primitives and structures are expressly tailored to support the kinds of collaboration, negotiation, and information transfer required in multiagent interaction.

Although the above gives some indication about the requirements for ACLs, a term like "high-level" can be interpreted in many ways. The way it is meant here can be made most clear by refering to the ISO layers that can be distinguished in communication. On the lowest levels one talks about the hardware and the routing software. In top of that there are message transport protocols such as TCP/IP, HTTP, or IIOP. They deal with communication protocols at the level of message transport. In top of these protocols one can use standards like CORBA that regulates the exchange of data between programs by providing standard formats. ACLs are situated on the level above the data exchange level. ACL's are dealing with communication on the mental and social level. This means that a message in an ACL indicates the purpose for which it is send. E.g. whether it is a request for information or a request to perform a task. Typical ACLs also have a characteristic semantics (see below) that is far more complex than standard distributed object protocols. The formal elements of an ACL must be carefully structured to balance the communicative needs of the agent with the ability of receivers to derive (ideally in tractable time) the intended meaning of the message. Further, it is important that the syntax, semantics, and pragmatics of the ACL be as precise and explicit as possible, so that the resultant agent systems can be as open and accessible to developers beyond the original group.

This last point bears some emphasis. Historically, many multiagent systems have been built using somewhat *ad-hoc* and developer-private communication mechanisms. Although these systems often contain many independent agents and can exhibit impressive accomplishments, the agents involved often rely on a large number of communicative assumptions that are not generally true of arbitrary agent collections. These range from the general assumption of a shared ontology and problem domain to specific nonstandard meanings for messages (or the absence of a message) in particular contexts. Often domain specific solutions are implemented for reasons of efficiency. However, knowledge of these often-undocumented assumptions is critical to properly interpret the agent message traffic in these systems. So, while such purpose-built agent collections are important to test and validate different hypotheses and approaches to agent problems, they are extremely difficult to generalize and extend without extensive interaction with the original developers. The locus of this problem can be traced to these implicit assumptions in the agent interaction design. We will come back to this point later on when discussing ACLs in the context of cooperative information agents.

Although most ACL's described in the literature are very generic, they all make some assumptions about the agents and/or the environment. It is important to note that it is hardly possible to device an ACL without any assumption at all about the agents, but it is equally important to make those assumptions explicit! The combination of explicitness and generality leads to extremely expressive languages with well-defined

---

need for the resource at that time. However, without a general semantic and pragmatic theory of action, it is impossible for other agents to precisely characterize the meaning of such actions, or to understand them as communicative. And, the provision of such a theory simply turns the applicable actions into a *de facto* communication system, albeit one with an unorthodox syntax.

semantics that are grounded in powerful logics. These ACLs demand a great deal from the agents that must interpret them: computing the meaning of an arbitrary message may require extensive deductive machinery, and can even be formally intractable. However, using a strong ACL with a semantics that can be precisely known in advance is a great advantage when creating heterogeneous agent systems that are designed to be easily extendible and broadly useful. One of the challenges for ACL research at this time is to find the right balance between richness and generality of the language and computational efficiency of the communication.

In the next section we will introduce some of the current available ACLs and some of the current research topics. In section 3 we discuss the characteristics of CIA systems in the light of their communication requirements. In section 4 we will indicate some consequences for the development of ACLs for this domain. In section 5 we discuss some future developments and expectations. We conclude the paper in section 6.

2 Agent communication

A first attempt to produce an ACL that was both standard and general came out of the DARPA knowledge sharing initiative. The Knowledge Query and Manipulation Language (KQML)[8] was originally devised as a means for exchanging information between heterogeneous knowledge systems. However, because of the generality of its high level primitives and its message orientated structure, KQML also functions well as language for agent communication. KQML is the most widely implemented and used ACL in the agents community. The messages are based on the theory of Speech Acts [1, 11]. The main innovation of this theory was to take communication not just as an exchange of information, but to see the utterance of a sentence as an action in itself. These actions (the communication) thus also have a purpose and an (intended) effect, etc. just like other actions. This viewpoint relates very closely to the way communication between agents is viewed. At this level it is not just the exchange of messages that counts, but the purpose for which they are exchanged. For instance, whether a message is a request or an inform or an order. These elements are needed if an agent has to initiate a conversation. In that case it has to determine how the communication is going to fulfil some goal of its own. This is only possible if the agent can reason about the expected effects of the communication. E.g. if the agent wants to have certain information and it expects that another agent has the information, than it can request the other agent to send the information. Note that the main novelty here over more traditional information exchanges is that the agent reasons about the information that it needs and the way that it can get it. There is no standard in-built procedure that forces the agents to exchange all their information periodically or on the cue of some external user.

Basically speech acts consist of three elements: the illocution of the message, the context of the message and the content of the message. The illocution determines the purpose of the message. E.g. a request, an inform, an order, a commitment, etc. The context of the message determines who are the sender and receiver of the message, whether the message is a reply to another message, the conversation that the message is part of, the language that is used to describe the content, the time of the sending of the message, etc. Finally, the content of the message describes what the message is about.

These elements are all incorporated in most ACLs as well. The following is a typical message in KQML format:

```
(tell :sender        CDagent
      :receiver      Dignumagent
      :in-reply-to   id9100.145
      :ontology      EC.CD
      :language      Prolog
      :content       "price(cd263956,20)")
```

It states that the CDagent replies to a message from Dignumagent telling the price of a particular CD. It uses Prolog to describe the content and a particular ontology (EC.CD) that clarifies what "cd263956" stands for and also what the currency of the "20" is taken to be.

The separation of the content of the message from the other elements of the message makes it easy to exchange messages without being tied to a specific formalism to describe the contents. Agents only have to agree upon the illocutions that can be used and know which fields can be present in the message (i.e. which elements of the context are specified) to process the messages. What an agent does with the content of a message that it receives does not have to be known by the sending agent. It can be different for every agent. However, the message handling mechanism can be uniform for all agents. See [9] for a more thorough overview of KQML.

More recently, the Foundation for Intelligent Physical Agents (FIPA) has proposed its own ACL, FIPA-ACL, to remedy some perceived weaknesses of KQML. The FIPA-ACL is also based on speech act theory and the syntax of the messages does not differ widely from that of KQML. Although this is not the place to make an extensive comparison between KQML and FIPA-ACL, we would like to point out a few of the main differences that indicate why FIPA decided to use a new ACL of its own.

The first difference is that FIPA-ACL is heavily based on a multi-modal logical semantics for communication. The advantage is that it facilitates a precise formal description of the communication and its effects. The disadvantage is that agents are usually not equiped with the logical abilities that would be needed to actually act according to this multi-modal logics. In [10] some more concerns on the semantics of the FIPA-ACL are given. One of their main points is that the semantics is based for a large part on believes of agents, which in one hand are unknown for other agents and in the other hand can change quickly and easily. This makes many of the preconditions on communication either difficult to check or easy to fulfil, which was not the intended purpose of these pre-conditions. One famous example is the sincerity condition, which states that agents only tell what they believe in themselves. Of course, it is usually impossible for another agent to check what an agent believes in. Also when an agent really wants to tell something it does not believe in it can add the belief temporarily and retract it again after the message is sent.

KQML does have a formal specification, but this one is much simpler and puts less burden on the agents. The disadvantage being that some messages still have an ambiguous meaning.

Another big difference is that KQML has a number of special administrative and networking messages. E.g. to "register" an agent in a kind of yellow-guide. These messages facilitate finding other agnts that an agent wants to communicate with. In FIPA-ACL they have to be performed using the "normal" messages. Although this makes the ACL appear cleaner, it also moves a number of problems to a lower level, where they have to be solved and of which little can be seen (and changed!) on the top level.

A last difference worth mentioning is the way new message types can be defined. In FIPA-ACL this can only be done by combining existing messages using a few well-defined operators. This has the advantage that all messages have a well-defined semantics. In KQML it is possible to define new message types at will. This makes it easy to define some message types that are useful for a specific domain and can be implemented efficiently. The disadvantage is that the new messages do not necessarily have a well-defined semantics and also many "dialects" might arise.

It is worthwhile to point out an important area of agent communication and ACL use that is usually not mentioned. Successfully using an ACL to communicate between two agent programs is dependent on the proper functioning of a great deal of non-ACL communications infrastructure. This infrastructure involves message ordering and delivery, formatting and addressing, directory services, gateway-style translation, and other standard distributed communications issues. In practice, implemented agent systems have used both centralized strategies that handle all aspects of messaging between agents (implemented in KQML through the introduction of a "facilitator" agent), as well as more decentralized systems that devolve this functionality to the communication handlers of the agents themselves (as is done in the FIPA-ACL). Agent systems exhibit little standardization in this area. Further, implementations of ACLs often expose more of the details of this infrastructure than one might strictly like. However, the problems of designing a general agent communications infrastructure that is efficient and reliable for different communication topologies and networking systems are deep and difficult.

In the following subsection we will introduce a set of issues that have been important in the development of ACLs and agent communication theory generally.

2.1   Issues in Agent Communication

Although in this section we often use KQML and FIPA-ACL as examples and point out a number of potential problems with them, we do not intend to criticize the effort put into the design of these languages. Much of our knowledge of these problems came from the practical experience of researchers applying KQML or FIPA-ACL in their systems. The topics that are presented in this section are taken from [3] which discusses current issues in agent communication in more detail.

semantics of ACL messages

One of the core research issues in the agent communication community involves the linkage between the semantic underpinnings of the ACL and the theory of agency that regulates and defines the agent's behavior. In order for the messages of an ACL to be formally coherent, these two theories must be aligned.

A theory of agency is a general formal model that specifies what actions an agent can or should perform in various situations. These theories are usually based on logics of mental attitudes such as beliefs, goals and intentions. A complete theory of agency also includes things like the agent's general reasoning strategy and (perhaps resource-aware) deductive model, its theory of action and causality, its account of planning and goal satisfaction, its system of belief dynamics and revision, and so forth. An agent need not directly implement its theory of agency, but it must behave as if it did. Examples of the elements which compose a theory of agency include Moore's accounts of knowledge and action, Rao and Georgeff's BDI architectures, Linder's KARO system including abilities and opportunities, Cohen and Levesque's intention theories, and so forth. Different agent systems will combine different elements to comprise their own theory of agency.

An agent's communicative behavior is among the behaviors regulated by a theory of agency. Because of this, the semantic theories that define the meaning of an ACL message must ultimately be linked to the entities provided by the agent's baseline theory of agency. Current versions of both KQML and FIPA-ACL handle the linkage between the semantic theory and the theory of agency by appealing to speech act theory as developed in Searle [1, 11] and Grice [4]. Communicative acts are performed in service of intentions in the same way as any other act. Unlike physical acts, however, the primary effect of a communicative act is to change the mental attitudes of the parties involved in the communication.[2]

The current semantic theory of FIPA-ACL requires that the theory of agency supply a set of BDI-style primitives. The semantics of FIPA-ACL is based on mentalistic notions such as belief and intention, and (because of the speech-act theory component) takes messaging to be a type of action. This approach has, in turn, led to the requirement that FIPA-ACL's semantics be expressed in an extremely powerful quantified multimodal logic involving both belief and intention operators, as well as a simple theory of action. As a result, agents that aspire to use FIPA-ACL in a semantically coherent way are required to adhere to (but not necessarily implement) a BDI-style theory of agency. They also face the somewhat daunting task of acting as if they implemented a reasoning engine for the semantic account.

In contrast to the FIPA-ACL, KQML did not originally assume a full BDI architecture of the agents. Rather, the original KQML semantics were defined in terms of a very simple theory of agency centered on adding and deleting assertions from a virtual knowledge base. The assumptions made about the required behavior of KQML agents were very weak, and the resultant semantics of KQML messages were fairly permissive. As is now well know, this permissiveness allowed wide latitude in KQML implementations, and the proliferation of different and incompatible KQML dialects. Labrou's second-generation semantics for KQML ([8]) struck a clever compromise between KQML's original virtual knowledge base theory of agency and a BDI-style theory, but at the cost of introducing modal operators back in the semantic theory, with the associated computability issues.

---

[2] Certain special classes of acts, parallel to the *explicit performatives* of natural language, can also in some circumstances directly change the properties of objects in the world. For example, a priest can marry a couple by simply pronouncing them husband and wife. In the agent world, there are examples of this when agents register themselves with a yellow-guide or when they give other agents some access rights on a database they manage.

Mismatches between the theory of agency and the semantic theory can occur when the theory of agency licenses communicative actions that are not accounted for by the semantics. The *sincerity* condition on agent communicative behavior is one such example. Sophisticated theories of agency often allow agents to act with the intent to deceive if it furthers the agent's goals. This is often cited as a requirement for electronic commerce applications and adversarial negotiations generally; for example, the locally optimal behavior of an agent might involve deceiving another agent about its true valuation of a good. However, in order to make the message semantics as useful as possible, most ACL semantic theories (such as the KQML and FIPA-ACL theories) require that agents never assert something that they do not themselves believe. This is a strengthening of the analogous principle for humans: we do not typically assume that our interlocutors are lying to us. However, because the semantic and pragmatic foundations of human communication allow for the possibility of deception, our natural language semantics allows for this as well.

The sincerity condition thus serves as a simplifying assumption for agent communication. Another such assumption involves the ability of an agent to reliably observe the effects of another agent's actions. Applied to agent communication, this is often taken to mean that the interagent communication channels are error-free. Agent systems routinely assume that all messages eventually arrive to their intended recipients and are not distorted by the environment (or malicious actors) in transit. Often, it is further assumed that the order of the messages that are sent to the same destination does not change during the transportation. Depending on the agent's execution context, these assumptions may not be appropriate.

Ontologies

Both FIPA-ACL and KQML include a field in the message structure in which an ontology identifier can be given. The ontology identifier is typically a string which can be used to identify the source of the vocabulary used in the message. This is designed to make these languages independent of particular application vocabularies. However, merely supplying an ontology tag does not solve the problem of how agents acquire and use the common ontological knowledge base that is a prerequisite for successful communication. This is a particularly acute problem in open systems which include agents based in different organizations. The problems associated with learning meanings and reasoning with a new set of terminology are the same as have been addressed in the area of database integration and cooperative information systems for several years as well.

Somehow the ontologies that the different organizations use have to be "integrated." Of course, it does not mean that ontologies have to be actually unified, but at least translation rules should be defined to convert relevant terms from one ontology into the other. Although a human working with representatives of each terminological community can often hash out a satisfactory set of rules, it is almost impossible to design these rules fully automatically. Consequently, agents can only really communicate if they already have a common ontology, or if a set of preexisting translation rules are provided. Although this seems very restrictive, it is not so disastrous in reality. E.g., in (international) trade it is very common to have standards for product descriptions. In the same way, in many open systems the agents communicate initially through some third party that initiates the contact between the agents. This third party may impose an ontology on all agents. This is for instance the case in electronic auctions, where selling agents have to specify their product using predefined forms.

Finally, although the use of ontology tags makes an ACL much more flexible, specifying the ontology and content completely separate from other message components, like the performative used, also makes it impossible to specify any constraints that involve both performatives and contents. E.g., an agent might request for an action to be performed before a time that has already passed when the message arrives. One could say that the message is thus not complying to the general rules for requests for actions. However, this can only be detected after the contents of the message are parsed and the ontology used to determine its meaning.

Another point is related to a problem mentioned by Cohen and Levesque in [2]. It is casued by the nesting of KQML messages in the content of other KQML messages. In general this nesting is allowed in KQML except for the "deny" message. A nesting within the deny message of for instance a tell message would lead to the question whether the content of the tell message is now denied or whether the action of telling it is denied. However, the problem does not disappear by just prohibiting KQML as language for the deny message. The content of the message can be expressed in Prolog or first order logic or something else, but still express a tell action. Then the problem of the exact meaning of the deny remains.

These are only two examples that show that it is sometimes difficult to give a precise meaning of message types without knowing anything about the possible content of the message. Also it is often difficult or impossible to check the preconditions that should hold for a message to be sent if the content cannot be checked against the precondition. So, the above leads to the fact that some rules range over both content of the message as well as over the performative (or other message components). It shows that it is not possible to determine the meaning (and correctness) of some message types completely independent of the message content. Therefore, using explicit ontologies and ontology tags in a message can help to abstract away a bit from the actual contents, but not completely (as some people would like to believe).

Standard set of message types

An issue that also comes up in many other communication standards is whether it is possible to come up with a basic set of message types (usually equated with performatives) that can be used to express all types of communication. With the intuitive idea that this set is "minimal" and "disjunct". I.e. the set should not contain redundant messages that could be expressed by other messages already and the meaning of messages should not overlap (too much). An interesting example in this respect is the X.12 EDI standard. It started with a limited set of messages (which worked in most cases), but has been repeatedly extended over the years every time some situation occurred that could not be easily captured with the existing message types. The main point was that there was a lot of attention for a precise and complete syntax description, but there was only a very informal semantics for the messages. Also they started with the message types that seemed to occur most in practice, without checking whether these message types had overlapping meanings, etc. This practical but unprincipled approach makes it very difficult at the moment, even for humans, to choose which message type to use in a particular case.

A similar case can be made for KQML. Although there is a basic set of performatives that seem to cover most aspects of communication, there is no justification of this basic set. Also, a more close inspection of the performatives shows that all performatives are either directives or assertions (in the classification used by Searle [11]). There are no performatives to express an agent's commitment (promise or something like that). This type of performatives also is absent in the FIPA ACL specification!

KQML is explicitly designed in a way that users can easily extend the basic set of performatives with their own performatives. Although this is very practical, it also leads to many situations where the designers of a multi-agent system define their own set of performatives. Although agents from this system might be able to communicate with agents of a different system using KQML, they cannot "understand" each other anymore, because they use completely different performatives.

There is one more point to be made on the syntax of the messages in ACLs. We already remarked that existing ACLs seem to have an ad-hoc set of performatives. Also the possible values of other arguments in the messages do not seem to be determined in a very principled way. One example that came up recently is the use of message identifiers. There is a simple way to refer to the message and conversation for which the present message is a reaction. In both KQML and FIPA ACL this can be done using an identifier (characterstring or number). However, it is not very well possible to parameterize this field or to refer to a message from another conversation. These kinds of references are quite common in multi-party conversations. So, also on the level of the syntax of the individual arguments of messages some improvements should be made and some more research is needed to find out which are the real needs for each argument for each type of application.

Semantics and Conversation Policies

The final issue we will address involves the theoretical framework necessary to chain individual messages together into semantically coherent agent conversations. The issues here are complex, involving binding together the semantics and pragmatics of messages.

A common way of specifying the semantics of actions involves defining the action's preconditions and postconditions. For example, the semantics of $x = 2.1$ might be expressed by the precondition that x should be the name of a location able to store a value of type real. The postcondition of this action is that the value stored in the location denoted by x is 2.1. For communicative acts, the preconditions and postconditions are typically expressed in terms of mental attitudes of the involved agents. For example, the precondition of KQML's TELL message states that the sender should believe what it tells and that it knows that the receiver wants to know that the sender believes it. The postcondition of sending the TELL message is that the receiver can conclude that the sender believes the content of the message. The FIPA-ACL semantics specifies similar preconditions and postconditions for its INFORM message type.

Although the above descriptions give a fair approximation of the intended meaning of these message types, it is impossible to specify a complete semantics. One of the problems is the distinction between the actual effect and the intended effect of a speech act. Whenever an agent tells some information to another agent it does that with the intention that the other agent will at least believe that the sending agent believes that information. However, an agent can never directly change the beliefs of another agent. Therefore the agent does not have complete control over the actual effect of the speech act.

Another point is that an agent will perform a certain communicative act with a certain expectation of getting a reaction of the receiving agent. For instance, a request for information is send with the expectation that the other agent will give that information or tell that it does not have that information (or does not want to give that information). This presupposes some (subtle) social relations between the agents. Just as any other action, the communicative acts also have to be planned by an agent. The only reason for an agent to plan a request is if it has a reasonable expectation that it will get some (valuable) reaction. Otherwise the performance of the request would be useless. However, this precondition is usually not expressed in the speech acts. Also the fact that after the speech act the sending agent is having some expectation is not easily expressed. In the same way there arises some kind of obligation for the receiving agent to react, which is difficult to express.

The above shows the social aspect of communication. It is an aspect that has hardly been addressed until now. One of the arguments is that agent societies do not have to have the same aspects as human societies. Therefore these social aspects are not important. However, it usually means that the designers of multi-agent systems take some social attitudes of agents for granted and built them into the agent architecture, while designers of other systems might not share the same values and capture different social conventions. Again this can lead to big misunderstandings between agents in open systems, because conventions are different and it is not clear that they differ.

In my opinion more research is needed into the fundamental concepts that play a role in communication. This includes concepts such as "commitment", "obligation", "convention", "power" (in the sense of hierarchical relations), etc. If there is a clear idea about which concepts are involved it becomes possible to define the semantics of communication in terms of these concepts.

In the above sections we have discussed research issues related to single messages. A last (big) issue that we want to point out is how to get from individual messages to conversations. As already mentioned in the previous section, messages hardly ever are send in isolation. For the description of communication protocols several techniques have been used. For agent communication often Finite State Diagrams have been used, but lately the use of (colored) Petri-Nets has been advocated. The most important use of these techniques is to describe the possible sequences of messages. The use of Petri-Nets gives the additional possibility to check e.g. for deadlocks and other properties of the protocol.

Although these techniques work fine for simple protocols, the figures they produce for real-life protocols are hardly readable. One of the main problems is that at any point in the protocol many exceptions can arise. Each of these exceptions has to be modeled. This causes one to loose track of the main flow of the protocol very easily.

Another disadvantage of these techniques is that they do not fix any relation between the semantics of the individual messages and the order in which they might appear in the protocols. E.g. if an agent asks information about a product it will never expect to get as answer the identical question. Although it is possible to describe all these types of restrictions they are not inherent in the techniques with which the protocols are described (as one would like).

Of course we also have to decide what kind of properties we would like to prove for conversations and how these properties can be expressed in the description formalism. It seems that the properties and semantics we use for conversations are quite different from the properties of the protocols for which most of the existing formalisms have been developed. Therefore none of these formalisms is a natural "best candidate".

Another important point (first raised in [12]) is how one can verify compliance to a protocol. Suppose an agent has to use the Contract net protocol in order to delegate its tasks. It uses some mechanism to manage its communication. Is it possible to proof that this mechanism will lead to compliance of the Contract net protocol. Even if the mechanism and the Contract net protocol are both described using e.g. Petri-Nets it is not trivial to proof that the agent's protocol is equal to (part of) the Contract net protocol.

There are also more practical issues. Is it possible to define a basic library of conversation protocols that can be used for all types of communications? I.e. can we define a kind of conversation language? If this cannot be done, agents first have to find out which conversation protocol their partners use, before they can start a conversation. A similar discussion as for the use of ontologies also applies for conversation protocols. I.e., how to integrate different protocols, how to learn protocols, etc.

Of course, the issues mentioned in all the previous sections are not the only issues to be answered. We merely tried to shed some light on the state of the ACL research and highlight the most important categories and give a general impression of which topics deserve our attention in agent communication research. In the following section we will briefly describe our view on Cooperative Information Agents with an emphasis on their communication.

3   Cooperative Information Agents

Since 1997 a sequence of workshops have been held on the topic of cooperative information agents (see [5–7]). However, just like happened with software agents in general, no single definition of cooperative information agents has been adopted yet. There seem to be two basic approaches towards CIAs. The first one starts from the users and employs agents to get the right information to the user. In this perspective usually one finds a number of different types of agents (or agents with different roles). There are user-interface agents that learn about the needs of the user and present the information in a personalized way. There are information fusion agents that integrate the data from heterogeneous sources. And there are information gathering agents that try to find the most relevant data for the user and sometimes also play a role in maintaining that data.

The second perspective sees CIAs as a further development of cooperative information systems. In this perspective each agent is related with a certain (type of) data source and the agents can communicate to keep their data consistent and to integrate the information from different sources. Usually it is assumed that a user will approach one of the CIAs with an information request. This agent will then try to provide the answer by checking its own sources and requesting the information from the other agents.

Although the two perspectives are by no means exclusive they emphasize different topics. The first perspective emphasizes the different roles of the agents and looks more at information filtering and data mining (in order to find regularities in user groups) issues. Because the emphasis is on getting information for the user, there is often little attention for information management (updating and maintaining consistency of information). Sometimes this is forced by the fact that the information sources are not under the control of the system (like the WWW) and are by definition not manageable. The agents that play different roles usually also have different architectures geared to the role they play. (Often one can even question whether all the components are really agents or just complex objects.)
The second perspective emphasizes the data integration issues and discusses common ontologies for the heterogeneous data sources and agents. In this perspective one assumes that the data sources might be autonomous but can still be analyzed and e.g. a meta-data model can be defined for (at least some of) them.

As we said earlier it is hardly possible to give a general definition of CIAs let alone a general architecture. However, the fact that the agents are CIAs does have some consequences for their components. A first point is that the planning module that manages the tasks of the agent is usually not very complicated. The domain is relatively simple with respect to the number of possible types of tasks that can be performed and the way a goal is achieved is often quite straightforward. For instance, if the goal is to find information about a topic then the agent has to perform a query on a private information source or request the information from one or more other agents. Once the answers come back it might still have to perform an integration step, but the number of steps leading to the result is usually not more than 3 or 4. This is quite different from e.g. robots that have to move and react to a physical environment.
A second point that becomes obvious very quick is that most actions that are performed are communications with other agents or users. So, the communication component is important for this type of agents (which is not the same as saying that it has to be very complex!). We will come back to this component in the next section.
In most multi-agent systems the agents must have knowledge about the other agents in the system. This is also true for CIAs. In some systems it is important to have a thorough knowledge of all the capabilities of the agents, because they might differ widely. However, in CIA systems there are only a few possible roles and related capabilities. Therefore it is relatively easy to keep track of the capabilities of the agents. For CIAs the knowledge that they must have of other agents is concerned with the type of information that they can provide. This often leads to some kind of module that describes per agent which sources it can access and possibly some meta-data about these resources. For instance agent "167" has access to the personnel data which contains names, addresses, ages and functions of all employees. As said before, a common ontology or rules to translate information are also an important factor in this respect.
A last component that we consider important for CIAs is a component that contains "social" information on other agents. It can contain for instance information about which agent provides the best information on certain topics. But can also contain information

about contracts with other CIAs representing e.g. subscriptions to information. E.g. a company might consult reports of Forrester, but has to pay a certain amount for each report it consults. Also this component might contain obligations that the agent has towards other agents to supply information (both on request and pro-actively, as in subscriptions).

In the next section we will discuss in more detail what are the communication requirements for CIAs and which of the developments sketched on ACLs are (also) important for CIAs.

4   CIAs and communication

As with all multi-agent systems the complexity of the communication between the agents depends to a large extend on the autonomy of the agents. If the agents are designed to cooperate and thus many social conventions are fixed in all agents then the communication becomes less complex, because many things are already determined by the context. If the agents are operating in an open environment where they interact with agents of other organizations and agents can appear and disappear at will the ACL has to determine more elements of the context and thus is more complex c.q. rich.

For CIAs operating within one organization often the first situation arises. That is, the agents might be autonomous, but the social conventions are actually completely determined by the organizational structure and programmed in the agents. As a consequence there is e.g. no real difference between orders and requests. Also there is usually no need for an agent to commit itself to an action. Requests are always handled and agents are by default committed to requests from other agents. This leads in general to a need for much less performatives than e.g. provided in KQML.

Another aspect that is usually handled centrally is a common ontology for the agents. This can e.g. be arranged by the use of a thesaurus that is often already present in larger companies.

Taking the above into consideration makes it doubtful whether in many situations where the CIAs operate within one organization they have need for a general ACL which brings a lot of overhead and from which they only use a small part.

This situation changes radically when the CIAs operate across organizational boundaries. Even though the agents might still be cooperative in principle they will operate in a much more autonomous way. One can easily imagine situations where a request for information is send to multiple other agents from different organizations (e.g. to give information about the annual growth of e-commerce in Asia). Each of the agents might respond with a bid on how much it would cost to provide that information and how long it might take. Then one of the agents is selected and a commitment between the agents is established to get the information before a certain deadline and to pay for it.

These types of scenarios require a much richer communication language than the ones that play within one organization. It also brings up the question of a common ontology right away. In the above example the question is what is understood as being "e-commerce"? The definition of this term may have a large influence on the outcome of the request. Also one might question what is meant by Asia. Is it the geographical Asia or are actually the countries in the Pacific rim meant by the term?

It is clear that a general ACL is more appropriate in these situations than in the one where all agents operate within the same organization.

Which are the things that most CIAs do need in their communication? First of all they usually have a number of ways to ask and send information. They can ask for information once, or they can subscribe to changes in that information. They can ask for one instance of a certain type of information or all possible information at once. The agents can always send information on request or send it periodically when they perceive a need, etc.

In all cases the agents also have to keep track of the task to which a message is related. E.g. if an agent is subscribed to information about the stock exchange and also to general news bulletins. It should know where a certain message belongs when it informs about the crash on Wall Street, because this might determine what action it will take. So, although conversations in general have a very simple structure, they can continue over long periods of time and it is not always clear when they are finished!

Another point that is important for CIAs are the messages related to registration of agents and administration of the agents. Whether these messages should be incorporated as explicit message in the ACL or just in the content of standard messages is under debate. However, it is clear that it should be possible to easily add new agents that maintain new resources, have agents going off-line and coming back again, agents changing addresses, etc. Because some task related conversations (like subscriptions) are very long lived, these messages might happen in between the "normal" conversational messages. They should not only be processed properly at the right time, but also their effect should be calculated on existing conversations. E.g. if an agent that has a subscription goes off-line it is no use to send it more messages or there should be some mailbox for that agent to which the messages are subsequently send.

Of the topics that were mentioned in the previous section as being important for ACLs the one that seems most important for communication between CIAs is that of ontologies. In every setting CIAs are used to connect heterogeneous information sources. When the sources are all under control of one organization it is often possible to define a common ontology that can be used to exchange information. This will get harder when external sources (like the WWW or newsfeeds) are also connected to the system.

The second topic that was mentioned concerned the relationship between the semantics of the messages and the models of agency of the agents. In situations where the social conventions are already fixed and sometimes a common ontology can be used, this topic is of little interest. In fact the semantics of the messages is determined by the way the system is set up and the conventions are programmed into the agents. E.g. it is predetermined what the reaction will be to a request for information (nl. a telling of the information if it is known).

However, the more sophisticated the systems become and the more open they are the more important the precise semantics of the messages becomes. E.g. precondition of giving another agent some information is that an agent believes that that other agent does not know that information yet. Now, in case an agent repeats the same query after a short period it might be that it only wants to know the latest updates (i.e. the differences with the last answer to the query) and is not interested to get all information again. Also when the system is open it becomes more important to know exactly what an agent expresses with certain messages. E.g. when it denies certain information (doesn't it have the information or does it believe the information to be false?).

Even within the limited domain of information systems we doubt whether there will appear a standard set of performatives for the messages before a more thorough theory has been developed to describe the semantics of the communication. Only such a theory will give a basis on which a standard set of performatives can be developed and against which it can be tested on completeness and disjunctiveness. At the moment performatives will arise from the needs in practice. The performatives that are needed depend for a large part on the type of application. In case the application is geared towards information retrieval it will develop many standard ways to query data. When the system is also used to maintain data it probably needs some performatives to control the data, to give authorities to agents to change data, etc. Just like in natural languages the consequence will be that there will be many overlapping performatives each suited for particular situations.

Finally, we have discussed agent conversations. As said before, for CIAs the conversations usually have a very simple structure. Therefore there is little need to prove that a conversation does not have deadlock or that it is guaranteed to end. These properties are checked easily by hand.

What is more interesting is how to interleave several conversations and how administrative messages can be interleaved with the conversations on information. Little or no research about these points has been conducted.

5   Future developments in communication between CIAs

In the previous section we have already listed a number of topics that will be of interest for communication between CIAs. In this section we will look at the prospects for the near and longer future.

As has been remarked by many people already, there is a discrepancy between agent theory and practice. The theory of agents is often concerned with logics that are developed to formally describe the (internal and external) behavior of agents and that try to give a semantics to it. In practice one is interested in systems that work (efficiently). This also holds for the communication part of agents.

In order for a standard ACL to be useful for communicating CIAs the following points should be addressed. First of all there should be a standard set of performatives that support the communication. Preferably this set should be as small as possible in order to facilitate efficient implementation. However, it should be possible to express all types of information requests easily with these performatives. Preferably the set of performatives would be constructed by surveying the performatives used in practical projects and finding some common denominators. (Note that we are not claiming this to be an ideal set theoretically, but deem it a necessary step towards this ideal set).

Secondly, the communication tools should support the administration of the agents. I.e. their addresses, their capabilities, their availability, etc. In this respect it is particularly important to pay attention to the fact that the agents often have interactions over long periods of time. This point becomes more important when the systems are large (contain many agents that can register and deregister at any time) and open (contain agents with different (and unknown) architecture and behavior).

Thirdly, a good support should be developed to describe the content of the messages. Although it is (probably) not possible to develop a standard content language, it should be easy to describe a content language. This facilitates the translation of the same message to different formats suited for different types of information sources. E.g. a query can be translated into SQL for a relation database and translated to a WWW query for the search engine on the WWW. In this respect XML might play an important role as a standard language to describe the content languages.

All of the above points are important for the short term development of the communication between CIAs. For the long term development the research on data integration and ontologies is of prime importance. This research should give some fundamental answers to the question how agents that do not share the same data models and ontologies can communicate.

Of course the general topics mentioned in section 3 are also of interest for CIA communication, but do not play a major role there.

6   Conclusions

In this paper we have tried to sketch an overview of Agent Communication Languages in general. We have given some arguments to the need for general ACLs and some current developments.

In section 3 we have tried to give an overview of the most important topics of research on ACLs at this moment. Although this overview can never be complete it gives a reasonable idea of the area. Whether all these topics are also of interest for communication between Cooperative Information Agents is discussed in section 5. Because of the type of setting it appears that e.g. conversation structures are usually very simple and thus research in this area is not of prime interest for CIA communication. In the other hand, interactions between CIAs are often spanning long periods of time and many different types of conversations can be interleaved (and even interact) with each other.

Finally we have tried to given some indications as to what type of developments we believe to be important for CIA communication in the future.

References

1. Austin, J.L. *How to do things with words* Oxford: Clarendon Press, 1962.
2. Cohen, P.R. and H.J. Levesque. Communicative actions for artificial agents In proceedings of the international conference on multi-agent systems (ICMAS-95), 1995, pp. 65-72.
3. Dignum, F. and Greaves, M. (eds) *Issues in Agent Communication*, Springer Verlag, (forthcoming).
4. Grice, P.H. Logic and conversation. In P. Cole and J. Morgan (eds.) *Syntax and semantics, vol.3, Speech acts*, Academic Press, New York, pp. 41-58.
5. Kandzia, P. and Klusch, M. (eds.)*Cooperative Information Agents* (LNAI 1202), Springer-Verlag, Berlin, 1997.
6. Klusch, M. and Weiss, G. (eds.)*Cooperative Information Agents II* (LNAI 1435), Springer-Verlag, Berlin, 1998.

7. Klusch, M., Shehory, O. and Weiss, G. (eds.)*Cooperative Information Agents III* (LNAI 1652), Springer-Verlag, Berlin, 1999.
8. Labrou, Y. *Semantics for an agent communication language*, Ph.D. thesis, University of Maryland, USA, 1997.
9. Labrou, Y. and Finin, T. Semantics and conversations for an agent communication language. In M.Huhns and M. Singh (eds.) *Readings in Agents*, Morgan Kaufmann, Los Altos, 1998, pp. 235-242.
10. Pitt, J. and Mamdani, A. Remarks on the semantics of FIPA's agent communication language. In *Autonomous Agents and Multi-Agent Systems*, vol. 2, nr. 4, 1999, pp. 333-356.
11. Searle, J.R. *Speech Acts*, Cambridge University Press, Cambridge, 1969.
12. Wooldridge, M. Verifiable semantics for agent communication languages. In Y. Demazeau (ed.) *Proceedings ICMAS'98*, IEEE Press, New York, 1998, pp. 349-356.

Towards Information Agent Interoperability

Stefan Haustein and Sascha Lüdecke

University of Dortmund, Computer Science VIII, D-44221 Dortmund, Germany
{haustein, luedecke}@ls8.cs.uni-dortmund.de

Abstract. Currently, many kinds of information agents for different purposes exist. However, agents from different systems are still unable to cooperate, even if they accurately follow a common standard like FIPA, KIF or KQML. Being able to plug agents together with little effort and exchange information easily, would be of a great use for several reasons. Among others, the agents could profit from each others' services. In addition, certain aspects of multi-agent systems could be evaluated without needing to build a complete system. Testing agent systems with standard components would allow simpler comparison. Furthermore, building different agent-based applications would be simplified by combining new software with "off the shelf"-components. In this paper, we explore the feasibility of practical software development and integration of existing systems, without developing "yet another abstract agent architecture".

1 Motivation

The demand for multi-agent systems has initiated an increasing amount of research in this area. Many different architectures, proposed interfaces, and surely good ideas are implemented in a broad range of systems. All existing multi-agent systems depend on information exchange. Building a population of information agents and building a corresponding population of consumers – let us call them application agents – are different tasks, performed by different people. It would be of a great use, if the agents could be plugged together with little effort and could exchange information easily, thus profiting from each other.

Information agent interoperability is important for research in information agent systems themselves, especially when building heterogeneous systems. For example, research on cooperative information agents often focuses on an isolated aspect of multi agent systems like mediation or brokering. Many information agent systems are build on top of very basic information agents, just wrapping a source into a format suitable for the more intelligent supervising entity. It should be possible to reuse at least these simple entities.

Furthermore, systems can be used as a testbed for each other to increase the overall quality and to prove or disprove certain theories and concepts. But this is not the situation one finds: looking at the current state, it reveals being rather babylonical. Except for the speech act level, each system speaks its own language, uses its own protocol and has its own ontology, despite some existing standards, which spread slowly.

In order to build intelligent components and to provide easy integrateable building blocks, the gap between the systems has to be closed. In this paper we will examine the areas, where the gap can be seen and propose a possible way out.

In the first section we give a short overview about the different places where the gap can be seen. The second section goes into detail an concentrates on the conversational level, which seems most problematic. In the third section we propose a FIPA-based interface, specialized for the needs of information agents. Related work will be presented in section four, whereas section five draws some conclusion and gives an outlook to future work.

M. Klusch and L. Kerschberg (Eds.): CIA 2000, LNAI 1860, pp. 208–218, 2000.

2   Levels of Misunderstanding

To make agents interoperable, they obviously have to communicate with each other in order to exchange data, normally using messages transmitted between them. Since there are several standards involved in agent to agent communication at different levels, there is a great chance of incompatibility. This can happen both on the message exchange and on the conversational level. In this section, we give a rough overview of the different layers involved in the communication. We split our overview into two parts. Message exchange covers the range from basic transport layers up to speech acts. Conversations are based on the message exchange and follow mostly semantic and pragmatic conventions. The possible choices an agent designer has, are discussed more detailed in the next section. Let's start with the different levels of message exchange:

ISO/OSI Transport Layers: For agent communication, we can use the abstraction of these levels provided by application level protocols. Nevertheless, exceptions like agents at the physical level controlling a certain device are imaginable. But this normally doesn't touch agent to agent communication as we investigate here.

Application Level Protocol: The application level protocol, like HTTP, IIOP and SMTP, normally is the lowest relevant level for agent communication. It provides a mechanism for platform independent message exchange, but agents obviously cannot even "hear" each other if they use different protocols at this level.

Speech Acts: In many multi-agent systems a communication subsystem uses the application level protocol to provide a more abstract message exchanging interface to the software agents. The messages exchanged, like INFORM, QUERY, REQUEST etc., are based on the speech act theory. At this level, two relevant standards, namely KQML [7] and FIPA [8] exist. Even though two agents or systems are using the same application level protocol, they cannot know the others intention without using the same standard.

Besides the different options for simply composing and exchanging messages, the conversational dimension allows misunderstanding between several agents. Whereas the aforementioned distinction is of a rather syntactic nature, communication can further fail on a semantical and a pragmatic level, too. These are the content and the query language and the model of information access.

Content Language and Query Language: The content language is the language used by the information agent to encode the gathered information, the query language is used by the application agent to inform the information agent about what kind of information it is looking for.
The content and query languages are often related to each other, and in the case of expressive languages like KIF[9] or SL[18] they are normally identical.
The problem with content languages is that even if two agents are using the same content language, they still may not be able to understand each other due to different vocabularies or different ontologies. This can be seen as semantic misunderstanding.

Access Model: In multi agent information systems, the access to the information agents is often directed through mediator, matchmaker, or broker agents. They group agents together and provide a unique simple access model to the requested information.
Furthermore, the information agents and can roughly be grouped into two general access models: information push and information pull. In the pull model, the client "pulls" information from the agent by sending an explicit query. The

agent sends back information corresponding to the concrete request. In the push model, the information agents know what they need to do, and gathered information is "pushed" to the client whenever available. This level is addressed by the majority of information agent papers, though usually only one model is provided.

System Application	Communication Language	Content / Query Language	Ontology / Structure
SIMS-based network of agents for logistics planning, including information gathering [14].	KQML	Loom	Proprietary
WARREN: A multi-agent financial portfolio management system [4]	KQML[1]	unspecified	unspecified
Information gathering based on low level retrieval agents accessing HTML, supervised by planning, coordination and scheduling agents. [3].	KQML	unspecified	unspecified
Infomaster: information Integration [6].	unspecified	KIF[2]	unspecified
Agents for Hypermedia Information Discovery [16].	KQML	XML / Prolog	unspecified
Multi-agent Systems in Information-Rich Environments [13].	KQML	SQL	KIF-ontologies[3]
COMRIS [11, 17].	FIPA ACL (XML)	XML	Proprietary

Table 1. Communication properties of some information agent or related system implementations. Although most systems are using KQML for communication, they are not interoperable due to mismatches in lower or higher communication layers.

3   How can Information Agents "Plug and Play" be achieved?

After describing the several levels where misunderstanding can take place, we will now investigate some levels in more detail and point out, how interoperability can be achieved there. First of all, a possible solution for making information agents more interoperable is to provide $O(n^2)$ wrappers between all the incompatible standards available. Another possibility could be to agree on a suitable standard for each level.

---

[1] Using ASK, ASK-ALL, STREAM-ALL instead of RECRUIT, BROKER, RECOM-MEND

[2] For describing information sources

[3] Created with the JAVA ontology editor JOE

But since standards have their specific benefits and disadvantages, it is difficult for the community to achieve an agreement on a certain one.

The following subsections provide a view on the conversational communication levels. The lower levels will not be visited again, since we think that they don't differ much in their properties and thus could be chosen easily. We try to include an imaginable way out of the dilemma of misunderstanding.

3.1 Speech Act and Communication Protocols

The two relevant protocols for the speech act protocol are KQML and FIPA. KQML was introduced 1992 by [7], and table 1 shows that KQML is currently used in the majority of existing information agent systems. FIPA ACL is a newer protocol introduced in 1997 by the Foundation of Physical Agents that is mainly based on [19]. In contrast to KQML, FIPA ACL does not attempt to cover categories like agent management, but provides separate entities for the corresponding purposes.

However, if we look at the question "which standard covers most levels", FIPA is the clear winner: in contrast to KQML it does not cover the speech act level solely, but includes all lower levels of communication. Additionally, the FIPA framework includes an agent management platform. FIPA provides simple services for administrating agent populations, without assuming a concrete agent model limiting possible implementations. Also, several more or less free FIPA platforms are available[4] and there is a noticeable trend of moving towards a FIPA compliant system. This weakens the argument from Huhns and Singh, that KQML has the broader support [12]. So misunderstanding at the speech act level and below will probably vanish in the near future.

3.2 Access Models

Even if we agree on FIPA as "lingua franca" for information agents, and the message exchange problem would be solved completely, problems concerning the protocols of information exchange or ways of collaboration still remain open.

The question, how information agents are able to collaborate is probably the question where most research effort in collaborative information system has gone. Several types of middle agents, namely mediators, matchmakers and brokers have been built. Each type of those middle agents abstracts from the concrete information agents or provides a search mechanism for concrete information agent meeting a certain purpose. In the following paragraphs, we summarize the approaches including their shortcomings for the purpose of general interoperability.

Mediators: Very often, a system needs access to information distributed over several, heterogeneous and even instable data sources like the world wide web, local and online (remote) databases. Mediators like Infomaster[6] typically aim to integrate these sources and to provide a single, consistent interface to all data. They act as intelligent proxies or filters. Mediators typically consist of a set of wrappers around several data-sources and an integrating component, which provides an interface to information requesting agents. Communication normally takes place bidirectionally. Both agents answer requests and update information in the data.

Mediators are mostly passive components. That means that no information gathering is initiated automatically and all requests are answered "online". Even the accessed information systems are forced to stay passive and cannot provide information in advance. However, some might gather information depending

---

[4] see http://www.fipa.org/fipa9706.pdf

on their own internal state and therefore cannot be made accessible through a mediator. Because information gathering and information requesting takes place synchronously, both parts, providers and consumers, are tightly coupled. This often implies a shared interface, which hinders the interoperability and exchangeability of agents. The information is provided by a pull mechanism.

General Matchmaking Agents: Matchmaking agents are agents that are able to bring service providing and service requesting agents together. To get this done, specifying each service agent and each request in a meta-language is necessary. The matchmaking agent then evaluates them against each other by certain heuristics to produce a list of service agents that fulfill a request. The requesting agent must now choose from this list and contact the service agent directly. This approach is used by [22]: services and requests must be specified by context, input/output, and, optionally, further in-/out-constraints and a description of used concepts. Five different methods for match-making are provided, which can be combined by the user. The representation language and semantic matchmaking process is roughly based on KL-ONE [21].

The general matchmaking approach does a good job on mediating between information services and requesters. Providing even plug-and-play functionality, it doesn't decouple requesting agents from information agents, since they have to communicate directly. Thus all communication modalities like the interfaces, the communication language, together with a common ontology, still need to be defined.

Broker Systems: The difference between a matchmaker and a broker is that the matchmaker only introduces matching agents to each other, whereas a broker also remains active when the matching agents are found: all communication between the matched agents goes through the broker, the agents perform indirect communication only. Thus, a broker service necessarily needs to care about possible language and protocol problems.

In contrast to mediators, existing broker systems like Ontobroker [5] are able to collect information from different providers similar to data warehouses. Unfortunately, they are not able to forward queries to external databases like mediators do. Thus, information agents that gather information on demand only, cannot be integrated into systems like Ontobroker and no information pull will be possible.

A general problem with the existing systems is that they do not overcome the gap between push and pull access to information. Each of the systems is fixed to one access model or has either gaps in the interfaces for accessing information or in the conversation definition such as a missing ontology. Because of the typically different natures of information needs in practical multi-agent system, both types of access to information are applicable, especially in heterogeneous populations. For example, an agent controlling a satellite on a fixed orbit sending weather forecast images would probably be an information pushing agent, whereas the corresponding proxy on the ground station could forward the pictures to different clients on demand, thus provide a pull mechanism.

By caching data from a "push"-source, a combination of a mediator and a broker could solve the access mismatch problem, providing both access modes. Systems like Ontobroker [5] or the COMRIS information layer [11] could be extended to such an entity.

3.3   Content and Query Language

For content languages, there is even a broader range of choices which can lead to misunderstandings. The following list gives a rough overview only. Several other content and query languages are used in agent systems, as shown in table 1.

Knowledge Interchange Format (KIF): KIF was introduced 1992 by Gene-sereth, Fikes and others[9]. It provides a prefix notation for predicate calculus with functional terms and equality, developed at the Stanford Knowledge System Laboratory in the ARPA Knowledge Sharing Effort.

Semantic Language (SL): SL is a content language used by the directory faciliatior, agent management system, and agent communication channel of the FIPA agent platform. Similar to KIF, SL provides full first order logic (see [18] for details) and three different levels of less expressive subsets. SL is one of the content languages proposed for FIPA ACL messages.

Extensible Markup Language (XML): XML[1] is becoming popular as a simplified successor of SGML with the potential to replace HTML in many application. XML is a simple generic markup language, XML-Document Type Definitions are used to create concrete languages for different purposes. A disadvantage of (plain) XML is that the data model is limited to simple trees. The great advantage of XML is that several XML-based schemas for information interchange are under development or are already available.

Resource Description Format (RDF): RDF[15] was introduced by the World Wide Web consortium as a generic meta language for inclusion in HTML and XML. It provides a more powerful data model (conceptual graphs) than XML. Similar to the DTD in XML, RDF provides a mechanism for schema definition, RDF-Schema (RDFS). RDF-Schema itself is specified in RDF, and a RDF Schema for RDF schema exists. Like SL, RDF is one of the content languages proposed for FIPA messages [2]. A disadvantage of RDF is that it uses a more complicated syntax that allows RDF to be embedded in XML. However, there are approaches to use a simplified RDF syntax[5].

A "General" language, fitting all possible needs, currently seems as far away as a general problem solver. SL and KIF have the advantage of using the same language for content and queries. But their expressiveness has the corresponding tradeoff, too.

A major problem for information agent plug-and-play is ontology mismatch, which is still an unsolved problem. Thus, the availability of commonly used and accepted data structures is of major importance for choosing the "right" content language.

An advantage of XML and RDF is that a growing range of concrete schemas is developed for these languages. Also, XML and RDF are already designed for use on the WEB, a major "hunting ground" for information agents. Since XML and RDF are used not only in research but have a broad acceptance in industry, it is likely that more and more information will be available in these formats.

4   An Interface for Information Agents

If we assume that FIPA standards are used for agent communication, and XML or RDF with the corresponding schema definitions and query languages are used for content, the only gap that needs to be filled exists at an intermediate level: What does the concrete registration at the FIPA Directory Faciliator (DF) look like, and which performatives is an information agent required to supported. The FIPA Directory Facilator is a component of the FIPA infrastructure providing a kind of "yellow pages" for software agents.

If we choose simplicity as main goal, the interface between a client and a basic low level information agent should be similar to the abstraction of a complete multi

---

[5] see http://www.w3.org/DesignIssues/Syntax and
http://WWW-DB.Stanford.EDU/~melnik/rdf/syntax.html

information agent system. On the other hand, strategies and features of intelligent cooperative information agent systems should not be limited in any way by imposing a complete agent system structure. If the system internally makes use of simple basic information gathering agents, the interface may also be useful for advanced middle agents to control the information agents. For other information agent systems, using proprietary communication internally may be a more suitable approach.

Figure 1 shows an example, how agents could be plugged together using unique interfaces. Basic information agents "push" discovered knowledge to an intelligent broker. The broker provides an information service that abstracts from the information sources. Since the application requires pull access to the gathered information, a pull/push converter stores the gathering results and forwards them on demand only. Like the pull/push converter, other intermediate agents like DTD translators are imaginable. Filtering agents can just republish the properties of the covered information providers with their additional or changed features at the DF.

The minimum requirements for an information agent interface are

- a unique definition of how information providers register themselves at the FIPA Directory Facilitator, and
- a concrete description of the performatives the information providers and clients need to implement.

4.1   Registration at the Directory Facilitator

While it is more or less clear, which properties the information agents needs to publish using the Directory Facilitator, there are several ways to map them into the structure the DF provides. For example, basic information agents could put all information into the FIPA `agent description`, while large information agent systems may require the `df-service-description` structure in order to provide all meta-information a client may be interested in. Tables 4 and 3 show an allocation of the corresponding FIPA DF structures suitable for both kinds of agents.

4.2   Client and Provider interfaces

Table 2 shows the minimum set of FIPA performatives that need to be supported by the corresponding types of agents.

A client requesting information or subscribing to information providers just needs to be able to understand the corresponding ACL `inform` messages. In order to receive information, it should also be able to generate `query-ref` or `subscribe` messages.

The minimum requirement for an information agent or information agent system is that it is able to send inform messages to the client. If the information agent is able to perform queries, should also be able to respond to corresponding query messages with an inform message.

The following paragraphs show a short description of the corresponding FIPA performatives.

	Client	Provider
Pull	query-ref	inform
Push	subscribe and cancel	inform

Table 2. Performatives used in pull and push based communication

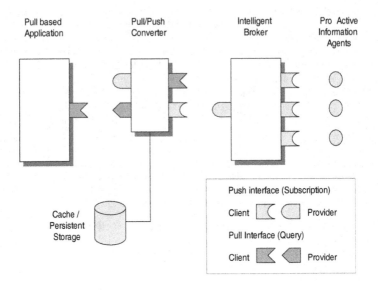

Fig. 1. Architecture Example

Attribute	Content
:agent-name	name of the agent (see FIPA specification)
:services	see table 4
:type	type of the agent: information-agent
:interaction-protocols	supported access models: pull, push
:ontology	not filled, because defined in service description
:address	address of the agent (see FIPA specification)
:ownership	ownership of the agent (see FIPA specification)
:df-state	state of the agent (see FIPA specification)

Table 3. Content of the FIPA-DF-Description structure

Attribute	Content
:service-name	name of the service, chosen freely
:service-type	type of the service: information-provider
:service-ontology	reference to a certain XML-DTD or RDF-schema
:fixed-properties	(content-language rdf), (content-language xml) (query-language XPATH), ...

Table 4. Content of the FIPA-Service-Desc structure

Subscription

Fipa-Performative	subscribe
Content	Query expression

Subscribes an agent to a kind of information defined by a query expression. The provider returns a confirmation including a handle the agent can use to unsubscribe.

Cancel

Fipa-Performative	cancel
Content	Subscription handle obtained from the broker when subscribing

Unsubscribes an agent from a subscription previously sent to the broker.

Query-Ref

Fipa-Performative	query-ref
Content	Query expression

The information broker performs a query. The query is possibly forwarded to other agents. The querying agent may get multiple responses. The broker is allowed to instruct the query processing agents to send the results directly to the originator of the query.

Inform

Fipa-Performative	inform
Content	Query or gathering results from information agents

An information agent informs the broker about newly discovered knowledge or the result of a query. The broker determines from the `in-reply-to` parameter if the content is the answer to a previously sent query or newly discovered information from an autonomous information agent. It distributes the information to the subscribers of the corresponding category or to the query originator.

5 Related Work

This work was inspired by other interoperability and agent communication papers like [20, 10], but we address a more concrete level: While the previous work concentrates on higher levels like semantic brokering and general communication structures, we are addressing more basic issues. These basic issues need to be solved first in our opinion. However, we are keeping the higher levels in mind in order to avoid misdesigning the lower communication levels we address, possibly blocking some higher level features.

The REusable Task Structure-based Intelligent Network Agents System model (RETSINA) [4] tries to provide an abstract framework for the implementation of information agents. This framework related to the interfaces provided here. However, the RETSINA framework does not limit itself to a simple set of interfaces. In this respect, RETSINA is more powerful, but the tradeoff is that it limits the implementation to a certain agent model (i.e. the RETSINA agent model).

6   Conclusions and Outlook

In this paper we have demonstrated the different areas where misunderstanding can take place when exchanging information components between multi-agent systems. We further presented a novel approach to enable interoperability of information agents by specifying a corresponding, simple FIPA compliant interface. In contrast to complete abstract multi agent systems like RETSINA, the described approach does not limit information agent implementation to a certain agent model.

The interface definition will hopefully help integrating information agents of different vendors. Development of large agent systems and new approaches to mediation, can profit from the synergy effects obtained when basic information agents or agent systems for different purposes are available "off-the-shelf". Our next step is to make our own agent system completely compliant to the proposed interfaces, making a set of open source information agents for bibliography search available for the community.

Furthermore, the proposed interfaces provide a base for new intermediate agent concepts like a combined mediator and broker with a local cache, translating between pull and push access. Generally, fixed interfaces are an important precondition for developing intermediate or translating agents that are independent from a concrete agent system or application.

Acknowledgements

The research reported in this paper is supported by the ESPRIT LTR 25500 COM-RIS project.

References

1. BRAY, T., AND SPERBERG-MCQUEEN, C. M.   Extensible Markup Language (XML): Part I. syntax.   Tech. rep., World Wide Web Consortium, 1997. http://www.w3.org/pub/WWW/TR/WD-xml-lang-970331.html.
2. BRICKLEY, D., AND GUHA, R., Eds. *Resource Description Framework (RDF) Schema Specification*. World Wide Web Consortium, 1999. http://www.w3.org/TR/1999/PR-rdf-schema-19990303.
3. DECKER, K., LESSER, V., NAGENDRA PRASAD, M. V., AND WAGNER, T. An architecture for multi-agent cooperative information gathering. In *CIKM Conference, Workshop on Intelligent Information Agents* (1995).
4. DECKER, K. S., AND SYCARA, K. Intelligent adaptive information agents. *Journal of Intelligent Information Systems*, 9 (1997), 239–260.
5. DECKER, S., ERDMANN, M., FENSEL, D., AND STUDER, R. Ontobroker: Ontology based access to distributed and semi-structured information. In *Semantic Issues in Multimedia Systems, Kluwer Academic Publisher, Boston, 1999*, R. Meersman and other, Eds. Kluwer Academic Publisher, Boston, 1999.
6. DUSCHKA, O. M., AND GENESERETH, M. R. Infomaster - An Information Integration Tool. In *Proceedings of the International Workshop "Intelligent InformationIntegration"* (1997), vol. 1303 of *LNAI*, Springer.
7. FININ, T., WEBER, J., WIEDERHOLD, G., GENESERETH, M., FRITZSON, R., MCKAY, D., MCGUIRE, J., PELAVIN, P., SHAPIRO, S., AND BECK, C. Specification of the KQMLagent-communication language. Tech. rep., Enterprise Integration Technologies, Palo Alto, CA, 1992.
8. FIPA. Agent communication language. Tech. rep., FIPA, 1999. FIPA Specification 2 1999.
9. GENESERETH, M. R., AND FIKES, R. E. Knowledge interchange format, version 3.0 – reference manual. Tech. rep., Computer Science Department, Stanford University, Stanford, California 94305, 1992.

10. GOMAA, H. Inter-agent communication in cooperative information agent-based systes. In *Cooperative Information Agents III* (1999), vol. 1652 of *LNAI*, Springer.

11. HAUSTEIN, S. Information environments for software agents. In *KI-99: Advances in Artificial Intelligence* (Bonn, Germany, September 1999), W. Burgard, T. Christaller, and A. B. Cremers, Eds., vol. 1701 of *LNAI*, Springer Verlag, pp. 295 – 298.

12. HUHNS, M. N., AND SINGH, M. P. Conversational agents. *IEEE Internet Computing 2* (1997), 73 – 75.

13. HUHNS, M. N., AND SINGH, M. P. *Readings in Agents*. Morgan Kaufmann, San Francisco, Calif., 1998.

14. KNOBLOCK, C. A., AND JOSÉ. Agents for information gathering. In *Software Agents*, J. M. Bradshaw, Ed. AAAI Press, Menlo Park, Calif., 1997, pp. 347 – 374.

15. LASSILA, O., AND SWICK, R. R., Eds. *Resource Description Framework (RDF) Model and Syntax Specification*. World Wide Web Consortium, 1999. http://www.w3.org/TR/1999/REC-rdf-syntax-19990222.

16. LAZAROU, V. S., AND CLARK, K. L. Agents for hypermedia information discovery. In *Cooperative Information Agents II* (1998), no. 1435 in Lecture Notes in Artificial Intellignce.

17. PLAZA, E., ARCOS, J. L., NORIEGA, P., AND SIERRA, C. Competing agents in agent-mediated institutions. *Personal Technologies Journal 2*, 3 (1998), 1–9.

18. SADEK, M. *Attitudes mentales et interaction rationelle: ver une theéorie formelle de la communication*. PhD thesis, Université de Rennes I, France, 1991.

19. SADEK, M. D., BRETIER, P., CARODET, V., COZANNET, A., DUPONT, P., FERRIEUX, A., AND PANAGET, F. A cooperative spoken dialogue system based on a rational agent model: A first implementation an the ags application. In *Proceedings of the ESCA/ETR Workshop on Spoken Dialogue Systems: Theories and Applications* (Vigso, Denmark, 1995).

20. SHETH, A., KASHYAP, V., AND LIMA, T. Semantic information brokering – how can a multi-agent approach help? In *Cooperative Information Agents III* (1999), vol. 1652 of *LNAI*, Springer.

21. SYCARA, K., LU, J., AND KLUSCH, M. Interoperability among Heterogeneous Software Agents on the Internet. Tech. Rep. CMU-RI-TR-98-22, CMU Pittsburgh, USA, 1998.

22. SYCARA, K., LU, J., KLUSCH, M., AND WIDOFF, S. Dynamic Service Matchmaking among Agents in Open Information Environments. *ACM SIGMOD Record* (1999). Special Issue on Semantic Interoperability in Global Information Systems.

Exploiting the Ontological Qualities of Web Resources: Task-Driven Agents Structure Knowledge for Problem Solving

Louise Crow[1] and Nigel Shadbolt[2]

[1]Artificial Intelligence Group
School of Psychology, University of Nottingham
University Park, Nottingham, NG7 2RD, U.K.
+44 (0)115 951 5280
lrc@psychology.nottingham.ac.uk
[2]Department of Electronics and Computer Science
University of Southampton
Highfield, Southampton, SO17 1BJ
+44 (0)23 8059 7682
nrs@ecs.soton.ac.uk

Abstract. There are structured and semi-structured sources of knowledge on the Web that present implicit or explicit ontologies of domains. Knowledge level models have a role to play in structuring and extracting useful and focused problem solving knowledge from these Web sources. The IMPS (Internet-based Multi-agent Problem Solving) architecture described here is an agent-based architecture driven by knowledge level models. It is designed to facilitate the retrieval, restructuring, integration and formalization of problem solving knowledge from the Web. This research draws on models of agency particularly suited to supporting the functionality required of a system like IMPS.

1 Introduction

This paper presents the IMPS (Internet-based Multi-agent Problem Solving) architecture. IMPS is an agent-based architecture driven by knowledge level models. It is designed to facilitate the retrieval and restructuring of information from the Web. Our aim is to use the resulting knowledge for problem solving knowledge in a knowledge-based system although the results could be used in any knowledge intensive activity. IMPS uses an approach that extracts and transforms information based on two criteria. The approach considers firstly the domain or subject (e.g. geology, respiratory medicine, electronic engineering), and secondly the kind of task in which the information is to be used (e.g. classification, diagnosis, scheduling). It exploits the implicit and explicit ontological properties of heterogeneous Web resources.

M. Klusch and L. Kerschberg (Eds.): CIA 2000, LNAI 1860, pp. 220-231, 2000.
© Springer-Verlag Berlin Heidelberg 2000

The structure of the rest of this paper will be as follows: We will describe how knowledge level models such as task models may be useful in structuring domain knowledge. Next we will discuss the motivations for extracting domain knowledge structures or ontologies from the Web and where such knowledge may be found. We will describe the functionality of IMPS and the way in which this functionality is supported by a multi-agent architecture. After a description of the implementation of the architecture, we will end with some conclusions and thoughts about future directions.

2   Knowledge Level Models

Knowledge engineering is concerned with the development of knowledge-based (expert) systems to perform tasks within a domain. Knowledge engineers acquire knowledge from various sources and represent it in a form that can be used to solve problems in a knowledge-based system. The prevailing view of knowledge within the field of knowledge engineering is that it is the body of information applied to a task in order to create new information and to reach a goal (e.g. [1]). Knowledge level models are relatively stable structures used to partition the knowledge used in tasks in order to facilitate use and reuse of that knowledge. They generally apply to a class of problem situations [2]. A model could describe features common to problem situations that are all in the same domain. In this case, the model imposed is a domain model that could be useful in various tasks within the domain. Alternatively, the common feature of the class of problem situations might be that they share a common task structure, although they appear in different domains. In this case, the knowledge level model is a task model. A third class of models, reusable problem-solving methods, focus on the idea that certain kinds of common task can be tackled by using the same problem-solving behaviour (e.g. generate and test a set of hypotheses), regardless of the domain in which they appear. An abstract model of this behavior is a problem solving method, which comprises a set of inferences and the control structure that organizes them. There may be more than one way to solve problems that share a task model. For instance, there are many problem solving methods for carrying out classification tasks.

The separation of knowledge into different models allows the use of domain independent models (task models and problem solving methods) to guide the acquisition of domain knowledge. In the latest version of the CommonKADS methodology for knowledge engineering [1], the authors present a range of task templates for knowledge-intensive tasks. These templates include descriptions of default problem solving methods that can be applied to the task and specifications for the kinds domain knowledge that will be required to tackle the task.

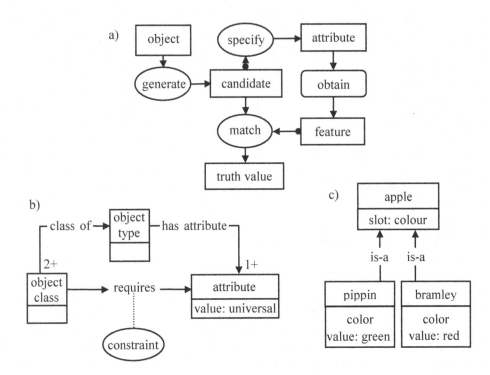

Fig. 1a) Inference structure for the pruning classification method [1] **b)** Typical domain knowledge schema for classification tasks [1] **c)** An example of domain knowledge structured according to the requirements of the domain knowledge schema

In Fig. 1 we show how the nature of the task and method applied to it can shape the domain knowledge required for problem solving. Fig 1a) shows pruning classification, a simple default problem solving method for classification. Each oval represents an inference step taken in the pruning classification method. The input to the method is the *object* to be classified. A *candidate* class that the object might belong to is generated and an *attribute* determined that will be required for membership of that class. The value of this attribute for the object – the *feature* - is determined. The output of the method is a *truth value* indicating whether the object and the class are matched on that attribute. In Fig. 1b), this method's domain knowledge requirements are expressed. The object type being classified must have two or more subclasses into which objects may be grouped. It must also posses at least one attribute, the value of which can determine class membership. Fig. 1c) shows an example of the minimal domain knowledge needed to fulfill these requirements.

Domain knowledge models are often built around ontologies. These are structured descriptions of a conceptualization of the domain, usually consisting of domain terms, their definitions and axioms relating to them. A primary use for ontologies is to define shared and agreed concepts between agents and thus allow them to share knowledge.

3   A Climate of Reuse

In knowledge engineering, the 'knowledge acquisition bottleneck' refers to the time- and resource- intensive process of getting the knowledge about a domain that is necessary to perform the required task. It is particularly difficult to get access to human domain experts who are, by definition, rare and often very busy. This problem has lead to a great interest in technologies and techniques that can promote the reuse of existing knowledge, particularly domain knowledge.

The great benefit derived from Task Models and Problem Solving Methods is that they are domain independent. Their power is in wide applicability and reuse – a knowledge engineer can call upon libraries of such models to construct a knowledge-based system. However, significant obstacles would need to be overcome in the creation of a comprehensive library of domain ontologies [3]. In order to provide usable ontologies for a significant range of domain areas, the library itself would have to be huge. In order to make a system useful in areas not covered by the library, some method for supplying ontologies to 'cover the gaps' would be required. The final problem is that like full domain models, the representational choices in encoding ontologies depend on the task model and problem solving method being used. Thus a classification model that relies on feature discrimination is likely to aggregate and differentiate concepts differently than one that is using an underlying model of the processes at work within a concept.

Although obsolescence is more of a problem with instantiated knowledge bases, domain conceptualizations also change as disciplines advance, and ontologies will need updating. Stable, relatively task-independent ontologies do occur in some fields through standardization efforts and/or years of conceptual development (e.g. the Periodic Table in the physical sciences). Very often the ontologies are volatile and take time to stabilize. These problems with ontology reuse are made more significant by the fact that it is the precious domain knowledge that presents real problems in reuse. There has been real effort to overcome or mitigate the problems in ontology research. A recent review of the field identified the three main goals as 1) to make ontologies sharable by developing common formalisms and tools; 2) to develop the content of ontologies; and 3) to compare, gather, translate and compose different ontologies [4].

It seems that what is required are tools for editing ontologies that can import and integrate existing ontologies in a task driven way, while allowing the user, a knowledge engineer, to add new concepts and relationships. A system that can integrate and use knowledge from different sources to construct a domain-specific, task-specific ontology could be used both to create new ontologies for domains, and also to update existing ontologies, or adapt ontologies created for different tasks.

4   The Ontological Qualities of Web Resources

The integration of ontologies is a thorny problem requiring close attention to both the syntactic and semantic level of abstraction. However, due to the rise of the Internet, the integration of information from heterogeneous sources is a rapidly developing field, from which ideas may be profitably used. The Web has facilitated ontology integration in another respect – well-formed A.I. ontologies, such as those that reside on ontology servers like Ontolingua [5], are now available worldwide.

However, we believe there is another much broader category of resources on the Web that can be exploited for ontological content. These are knowledge sources that have ontological qualities i.e. they define concepts and relationships used in a domain, but are not formal AI ontologies. There are many resources on the Web that contain high quality knowledge about domains. The creation of components of inference is an abstract task that requires careful analysis and is not frequently considered by those solving a problem in a domain. However, components of domain knowledge - concepts and relationships – are common currency. This is the level at which normal task-based discourse occurs amongst domain experts. In the following sections, we describe Web resources that are particularly rich from an ontology construction perspective.

4.1   Upper Level Ontologies

High-level or Upper-level ontologies are knowledge structures that provide a general knowledge description framework that could organize many of the concepts we use to describe the world. Some are domain independent and aim to cover every possible subject area with at least a low level of detail. High level ontological information is that which is most useful across a range of domains as it represents the shared assumptions of a large community. For example, a huge range of applications may require basic concepts such as mass and velocity.

The idea of generating domain ontologies automatically from high-level ontologies was explored in the SENSUS project [6]. This involved the use of a broad coverage general ontology to develop a specialized, domain specific ontology semi-automatically. While high-quality high-level knowledge engineering ontologies within a domain can be used in this way if they are available, they may well not exist.

In contrast, the availability of high level, very broad coverage ontologies on the Internet is increasing. Some of these ontologies, such as the 'upper CYC® ontology' [7] are explicitly aimed at supporting reasoning. Others, such as WordNet [8], which we use as a knowledge source for IMPS, are high-level linguistic ontologies. We believe that these could be particularly useful in bridging the gap between "common sense" knowledge and domain specific knowledge that can be obtained from specialist sources by providing a general high-level structure in which to situate domain specific knowledge. WordNet is a semantically organized lexical database [9]. It is one of the most well-developed lexical ontologies [4] and contains approx. 57,000 noun word forms organized into around 48,800 word meanings.

4.2   Semantic Markup

The Extensible Markup Language [10] XML has emerged as a representation standard for semi-structured knowledge and is being used to markup documents on the Web for a wide variety of domains and tasks. An XML document primarily consists of a strictly nested hierarchy of elements with a single root. Elements can contain character data, child elements, or a mixture of both. In addition, elements can have attributes. XML differs from HTML in three main ways. It is extensible – users can create their own domain-specific tags or attributes to semantically qualify their data. It also allows for the specification of deep structures. Finally, XML has something called a document type definition (DTD) that allows users to define the tags they have created. This forms a description of the XML grammar for use by applications that need to perform validate a document as being of a certain sort.

In effect, this DTD expresses an agreed set of terms and relationships that anyone writing an XML document which uses the same DTD must comply with. It is easy to recognize that a DTD is, in effect, a simple domain ontology. Efforts have been made to use ontologies to *create* XML DTDs [11], increasing the semantic sophistication of XML documents. However, this is a centralized approach, which relies on XML content being tailored to the requirements of the ontology that is being used. We use the existing DTD structure that has been generated by those working in the domain to extract knowledge about the terms and relationships in the domain.

4.3   Implicit Structural Ontologies

Our approach can exploit such ontological annotation by information providers, but it also uses heuristics to exploit the more implicit ontologies contained in the structure of sources.

The use of simple heuristics to extract implicit domain structure can be seen in the example of a database table. We can identify 'instance' columns in a database in which each row has a different value, and 'class' columns, in which values are repeated. A simple heuristic rule might be that the unique values from the first columns may be hyponyms (sub-classes) of the items in the 'class' columns (see Fig. 2).

Rock name	Rock type
tachylite	volcanic
basalt	volcanic
gabbro	plutonic
obsidian	volcanic
granite	plutonic

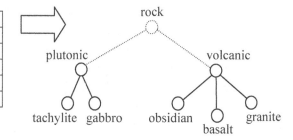

Fig. 2. An ontological fragment in the domain of geology is generated from the structure of a database table

5   The IMPS System

The IMPS (Internet Multi-Agent Problem Solving) architecture is designed to facilitate the retrieval and restructuring of information from the Web according to (a) the domain and (b) the kind of task in which the information is to be used. In the following sections we will discuss what the system does in more detail and how the architecture supports this functionality.

5.1   Functionality

The prototype IMPS system extracts domain concepts and relationships from heterogeneous and possibly dynamic Web sources that contain explicit or implicit ontological statements. It does this in a task-driven way by composing hierarchies of concepts and appropriate relationships around domain keywords that the user has matched to knowledge roles in a CommonKADS task model. So, referring back to the classification task shown in Fig. 1, if a domain keyword "rock" was nominated by the user to match the role of "object type", this would indicate that the types of knowledge required for the task would be sub-classes of the concept "rock" and the features that differentiate between those sub-classes.

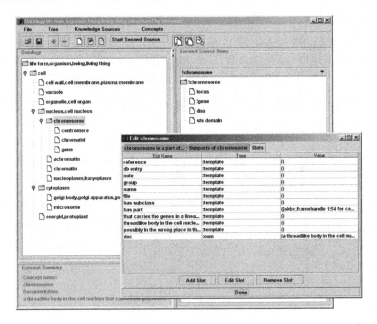

Fig. 3. An ontology being built in IMPS for a fault diagnosis task in the domain of molecular biology

IMPS performs clean syntactic merging of these ontological fragments into a frame-based knowledge representation that is expressive enough to support reasoning and assists the user in constructing a domain ontology by merging ontological fragments from these sources.

It acts as a "concept multiplier" [6] speeding up ontology construction by coupling user-supplied knowledge with large information resources and simple heuristics to perform rapid ontology formation. IMPS takes a "conservative" approach to the reuse of existing large-scale resources by allowing the user to refine the data from these sources so that the advanced representation requirements imposed by a more expressive knowledge representation can be met (as advocated in [12]). This is occurring in Fig. 3, where the semantics of the knowledge extracted from an XML DTD in the domain of molecular biology (on the right hand side of the picture) are rather ambiguous. The concept 'chromosome' has subparts that are physical parts – e.g. 'gene' and 'locus', and subparts which are not physical parts e.g. 'db_entry' and 'reference'. In the concept editing interface, the user is changing these incorrect subparts to attribute slots on the concept chromosome before merging it into the upper-level ontology shown on the left. IMPS uses an OKBC-compliant [13] frame system with slots and inheritance to represent domain knowledge in order to support reasoning.

Generally, IMPS uses two knowledge sources. A skeletal domain ontology is constructed using a general high-level source. This is based on a taxonomy or partonomy hierarchy of concepts depending on the requirements of the task model. It is edited by the user and then supplemented with ontological information extracted from a more detailed domain-specific source (see Figs. 3 and 4).

The ontology provides a conceptual framework for the organization of domain knowledge. The border between ontology construction and knowledge acquisition can be a fuzzy one - as the ontology becomes instantiated with further structured acquisition, it produces a domain knowledge base which could in turn underpin problem solving guided by the same task model structure.

5.2   Architecture

In this section, we will describe the way in which the IMPS architecture supports the functionality we have described. IMPS is a multi-agent architecture, in which two specialist agents work together with the user, using a knowledge library which contains task model descriptions and knowledge extraction heuristics.

There are several motivations for using an agent architecture. In terms of the specific task of constructing an ontology using the Web sources, one of the great advantages of the agent metaphor is that agents possess intentionality - the ability to express 'attitudes' towards information. This property becomes more significant in a multi-agent architecture where the agents express their intentionality in knowledge-level communication. This is particularly important because information on the Web may be contradictory or simply incorrect. An intentional system has some capacity to reason about conflicting information.

Whilst this property of intentionality suggests a deliberative symbol-manipulation system, the agents also need to deal appropriately and in a timely way with the requirements of dynamic knowledge sources and actions by the user and by other agents. The IMPS agents combine reasoning with some response to the changing environment in a hybrid layered architecture. The more reactive, low level behaviour is driven by external events, such as instructions from the user and messages from other agents and is encapsulated in a generic agent shell. The more deliberative behaviour stems from an inference engine powered by rules unique to the agents and is prompted by changes in the internal state of the agent's knowledge.

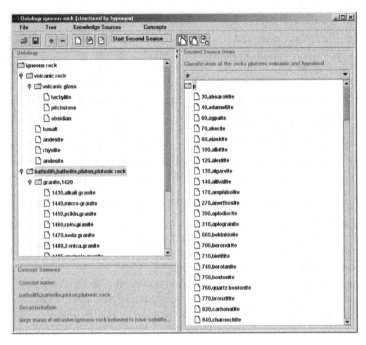

Fig. 4. An ontology is constructed in IMPS for a classification task in the geology

We have suggested that IMPS needs to perform large-scale extraction and translation of concepts while allowing the user to manage some aspects of the semantic integration. This is congruent with the principle that agents should be designed as semiformal systems, not computational agents that try to solve complex problems all alone [14]. The boundary between what software agents do and what humans do must be a flexible one. The benefits of this approach can be seen in Fig. 4. This shows a user merging ontological concepts extracted from different sources. It would be very difficult for the IMPS agent to make the semantic connection between the concept named "batholith, pluton, plutonic rock" extracted from WordNet and the concept "p" from a domain specific database in the field of geology. However, IMPS is showing the user that the title of the database "A classification of the rocks plutonic, volcanic and hypabisal", and that the concept "p" has many subclasses. It is a trivial task for the user to make the match. Similarly, it would be a very laborious task for the user to extract and re-represent the information contained in the database. With the user and an agent acting in a complementary way, a small amount of effort can be used to greatest effect, generating a larger, richer ontology.

In order to achieve this semiformality, the agents must be *transparent*. They should not try to figure out for themselves things that humans could easily tell them, but it should be as easy as possible for humans to see and modify the same information and reasoning processes that their agents are using [14]. This property of transparency is particularly important for agents that assist the user in manipulating information.

Individual IMPS agents achieve this transparency by keeping the functions of the reactive layer of the architecture relatively hidden, whilst allowing the user to view both the ontology representation and the facts and rules used to construct it. At the multi-agent level, the functional decomposition of tasks between the agents is clear to both the system designer and the user, and additionally, the communication between agents occurs at a high, human-readable level.

The agents in the architecture are:

- The Knowledge Extraction Agent (KExA), acting as an Agent Name Server (ANS) and the interface through which the user interacts with IMPS during initialization. The KExA helps the user fill task templates with domain terms that can then be used by the OCA for ontology structuring.
- The Ontology Construction Agent (OCA), which is able to use modules from the knowledge library to extract information from networked knowledge sources and re-represent it so that it can be integrated into a coherent whole.

The knowledge library component of IMPS is as essential to its operation as the agent component. The extraction classes used to obtain particular kinds of knowledge from knowledge sources are all based around common interfaces for general and specific sources, with standard inputs and outputs. The actual mechanisms by which the class extracts information from a source and parses it into a form comprehensible to the inference engine are completely hidden from the agent loading the class. New classes can be added to the library as appropriate, in a 'plug-and-play' manner, without any change to the rest of the architecture. Within the library, the knowledge sources are indexed by type - e.g. database, XML DTD or WordNet etc., so new instances of a particular type of source just need to be identified as such to be used by the system. This is also true of the task model components, which are based around a (different) common interface. The system has four task models at present - classification, diagnosis, configuration design and assessment.

5.3   Implementation

Having outlined the functionality and general structure of the IMPS architecture, this section will trace the ideas introduced earlier to their software implementations.

IMPS is coded in Java, making use of the robust and easy networking functionality and object orientation. The basic structure on which all the IMPS agents are based is supplied by the Java Agent Template (JAT) 0.3 [15]. The template provides Java classes to support a multi-agent architecture composed of agents with individual knowledge bases. These classes support the low-level reactive functions like agent registration, messaging and class-loading.

In IMPS, the JAT is supplemented with Jess. Jess is a version of the popular expert system shell CLIPS, rewritten entirely in Java [16]. It provides the agents with internal representation and inference mechanisms. In effect, the addition of Jess means that whilst the agents share a common architecture, each agent reasons and acts like a small knowledge-based system following its own set of rules. Jess can be used to manipulate external Java objects so there is a tight coupling between the inference engine, and the agent shell. The agents uses the Knowledge Query and Manipulation Language (KQML) [17] to communicate, as specified and supported by the JAT, with KIF[18] as the content language.

6   Conclusions and Future Directions

In this paper, we have described an agent-based model-driven approach to the problem of getting useful knowledge from distributed and implicit information sources. The IMPS architecture features the clean syntactic integration of information presented originally in different formats, and supports the user in semantic information integration. It does this through the use of standardized modular components to filter information while maintaining a lightweight multi-agent architecture. The modular design means that IMPS is open to the use of new technologies and standards.

In the future, we see IMPS as an architecture in which the specialist information agents we have described provide knowledge to Inference Agents on demand. The Inference Agents will represent CommonKADS primitive inference types [1] embodied in agent shells to produce agents that specialize in performing a particular kind of inference. For a classification task, agents might specialize in generation of classes, specification of attributes, or matching features.

To this end, it would be useful to support the extraction of a wider range of relationships from WordNet. Our exploitation of WordNet is not exhaustive at this time. IMPS uses only the noun portion of the database -- WordNet also contains some 19,500 adjectives [22], and 21,000 verbs [23]. It also has some unused semantic structure based in causality.

At the moment, IMPS constructs ontologies based around the role a domain term plays in a specific task (e.g. a candidate class in our simple classifier in Fig 1.). We would also like to support the integration of several of these structures to form larger heterogeneous ontologies. Although this introduces the vexed question of whether task specific ontologies can be easily generalised and integrated.

Having successfully created a full ontology using knowledge extracted from XML DTDs, it would be interesting to attempt to exploit this to facilitate the automatic extraction of domain knowledge from XML documents that comply to those DTDs in order to instantiate ontologies into knowledge bases and knowledge repositories.

Acknowledgements

This research was carried out as part Louise Crow's Ph.D., which was supported by a University of Nottingham Research Scholarship.

References

1.   Schreiber, A. Th., Akkermans, M., Anjewierden, A. A., de Hoog, R., Shadbolt, N. R., Van de Velde, W. and Wielinga, B. J.: Knowledge Engineering and Management: The CommonKADS Methodology. MIT Press, Cambridge, MA (2000)
2.   Van de Velde, W.: Issues in Knowledge Level Modelling. In David, J. M., and Krivine, J. P, and Simmons, R. (eds.) Second Generation Expert Systems. Springer Verlag, Berlin (1993)
3.   van Heijst, G., Schreiber, A. Th., and Wielinga, B. J.: Using Explicit Ontologies for KBS Development. Int. J. Human-Computer Studies/Knowledge Acquisition 2(3) (1997) 183-292

4. Fridman Noy, N. and Hafner, C.: The State of the Art in Ontology Design: A Survey and Comparative Review. A.I. Magazine (1997) 53-74
5. Gruber, T. R.: A Translation Approach to Portable Ontology Specifications. Knowledge Acquisition 5(2) (1993) 199-220.
6. Swartout, B., Patil, R., Knight, K., and Russ, T.: Toward Distributed Use of Large-Scale Ontologies. In Proc. of the Tenth KA for KBSs Workshop. SRDG Publications, Banff, Canada (1996)
7. Cycorp, Inc.: The Cycorp homepage. http://www.cyc.com (1996)
8. Miller, G. 1990. WordNet: An on-line lexical database. Int. J. Lexicography 3(4) 235-302
9. Beckwith, R., and Miller, G. A. Implementing a lexical network. Int. J. Lexicography 3(4) (1990) 302 - 312
10. Bray, T. Paoli, J. and Sperberg-McQueen, C. M. (eds.): Extensible Markup Language (XML) 1.0. W3C Recommendation, Feb. 10 (1998) http://www.w3c.org/TR/1998/REC-xml-19980210
11. Erdmann, M. and Studer, R.: Ontologies as Conceptual Models for XML Documents. In Proc. 12th Workshop on K.A for KBS. SRDG Publications, Banff, Canada (1999)
12. Schulz, S., Romacker, M., Faggioli, G. and Hahn, U.: From Knowledge Import to Knowledge Finishing: Automatic Acquisition and Semi-Automatic Refinement of Medical Knowledge. Proc. 12th Workshop on K.A. for KBS. SRDG Publications, Banff, Canada (1999)
13. Chaudri, V. K., Farquhar, A., Fikes, R., Karp, P. D., and Rice, J. P.: Open Knowledge Base Connectivity 2.0.2, Knowledge Systems Laboratory (1998)
14. Malone, T. W., Lai, K.-Y. and Grant, K. R.: Agents for information sharing and coordination: A history and some reflections. In J. Bradshaw (ed.) Software agents. AAAI/MIT Press, Cambridge MA (1997) 109-143
15. Frost, H. R.: Documentation for the Java Agent Template, Version 0.3. Center for Design   Research,   Stanford   University. http://cdr.stanford.edu/ABE/documentation/index.html (1996)
16. Friedman-Hill, E. J.: Jess, The Java Expert System Shell, Technical Report, SAND98-8206   Sandia   National   Laboratories,   Livermore. http://herzberg.ca.sandia.gov/jess (1998)
17. Finin, T., Labrou, Y., and Mayfield, J.: KQML as an Agent Communication Language. In J. Bradshaw (ed.) Software agents. AAAI/MIT Press, Cambridge MA (1997)
18. Genesereth, M. R., and Fikes, R. E.: Knowledge Interchange Format Version 3.0 Reference Manual, Technical Report, Logic-92-1, Computer Science Department, Stanford University. (1992)
19. Crow, L. R., and Shadbolt, N. R.: Internet Agents for Knowledge Engineering. In Proc. of the Eleventh Banff KA for KBSs Workshop. SRDG Publications, Banff, Canada (1998)
20. Fellbaum, C., Gross, D., and Miller, K.: Adjectives in WordNet. (1993) Unpublished report.
21. Fellbaum, C.: English Verbs as a Semantic Net. Int. J. Lexicography 3(4) (1990) 278 - 301

Automatic Ontology Construction for a Multiagent-based Software Gathering Service*

E. Mena[1], A. Illarramendi[2], and A. Goñi[2]

[1] IIS depart., Univ. de Zaragoza. Spain. http://www.cps.unizar.es/~mena/
[2] LSI depart., UPV. San Sebastián. Spain. http://siul02.si.ehu.es/~jirgbdat/

Abstract. Ontologies and agents are two topics that raise a particular attention those days from the theoretical as well as from the application point of view. In this paper we present a software gathering service that is mainly supported by an ontology, SoftOnt, and several agents. The main goal of the paper is to show how the SoftOnt ontology is built from distributed and heterogeneous software repositories. In the particular domain considered, software repositories, we advocate for an automatic creation of a global unique ontology versus a manual creation and the use of multiple ontologies.
Keywords: ontologies as metadata, agent technology, distributed software retrieval

1 Introduction

Currently, there is a great deal of interest in the development of ontologies to facilitate knowledge sharing in general, and data repositories integration in particular. In this paper we advocate using an ontology to describe *semantically* the content of a set of data sources containing pieces of software. So, instead of users have to deal directly with different software repositories, the goal is that a system uses an ontology to help users to retrieve software. Furthermore, user requests will be mapped automatically to queries on that ontology and the proposed system takes the responsibility of retrieving and installing the appropriate software in an efficient way using for that specialized agents.

One of the most frequent tasks of computer users is to obtain new software, in order to improve the capabilities of their computers. For that, a common procedure is to visit some of the several websites that contain freeware, shareware and demos (such as Tucows [24] and CNET Download.com [4]), games (such as Games Domain [2] and CNET Gamescenter.com[5]), java-related software (like Gamelan [6]) or many others. Different kinds of users need different kinds of software. For example, naive users could be interested in entertainment programs like computer games and CD players. On the contrary, some other users could be interested in DBMS's, word processors, spreadsheets, or backup utilities, among

---

* This work has been supported by *CICYT (Comisión Interministerial de Ciencia y Tecnología*, Spain [TIC97-0962]), MoviStar (a spanish cellular phone company) and the University of the Basque Country.

M. Klusch and L. Kerschberg (Eds.): CIA 2000, LNAI 1860, pp. 232-243, 2000.

many others. Other kind of software could be interesting for most of users, like antivirus, Web browsers, etc.

We summarize in the following the three main problems that users must face when they want to obtain a new piece of software:

1. **To know the different programs that fulfil their needs.** Not only their names but also where to find them in the vast Web space. This task is complex enough to discourage naive users from installing new software by themselves.
2. **To know the features of their computers,** in order to select the most appropriate version. This task implies having technical knowledge about her/his system (CPU, OS and version, free disk space available, RAM memory, etc.) and the software installed previously (for requesting a full version or just an update).
3. **To be aware of new software and/or new releases of software of interest.** Although few commercial programs currently alert about new releases, users need to keep an eye on the Web, or on other repositories, if they want to be informed about new software that could be of their interest.

With the goal of alleviating the previous problems we have developed a Software Retrieval Service to provide users with a transparent access to local or remote software sites [16]. We present in this paper the technique used to encapsulate software sites which is based on the use of an ontology and the agent technology.

Ontologies and agents are two topics that raise a particular attention nowadays [10, 1, 11]. Several works can be found in the literature that consider each topic separately and even jointly as in our case [12]. However, we have not found, so far, any significant one that also treats the main focus of this paper: how to build an ontology automatically from distributed and heterogeneous websites that contain software repositories. Among those that can be related somehow, we mention some of them. In [9] they use Yahoo! [25] categories to describe documents. In [13] they propose to extend HTML in order to annotate pages with terms from a concrete ontology. Finally, in [14] they use an ontology managed by an agent to resolve knowledge disparities that may occur when heterogeneous information sources must interact.

In the rest of the paper, we first explain the reasons for which we propose to build one ontology in an automatic way (Section 2). In Section 3 we provide a brief description of the agents used in the Software Retrieval Service. The translation step that permits obtaining ontologies from software repositories and the integration step that generates a global ontology by integrating the previously obtained ones are explained in Sections 4 and 5, respectively. Finally, some conclusions appear in Section 6.

2   SoftOnt: a Software Ontology Built in an Automatic Way

Ontologies are very interesting specification tools for the task of describing a set of terms of interest in the particular domain of software repositories. The terms of the ontology are linked with the corresponding software repositories through the mapping information, which is managed by the proposed system. So, the users only have to express their software needs by using terms in the ontology, and do not have to care about the distribution and heterogeneity of the (web or local) repositories that contain software.

2.1   One Ontology vs. Multiple Ontologies

When ontologies are selected to describe data sources contents of a particular domain, we must decide on dealing with one global integrated ontology or dealing with multiple ontologies linked by interontology relationships. In general, the relevant features that must be taken into consideration before choosing between a global ontology or several ontologies linked by semantic relationships are the following:

- The number of data sources involved. A huge number will lead to very complex mappings in the case of a global ontology.
- The number of categories that we will need to extract from the data sources. A huge number will lead to many terms and relationships between them, in the case of a global ontology.
- The vocabulary problem existing across data sources. The integration of data sources designed under different points of view will lead to a global ontology with many terms due to the existence of many specializations, generalizations but not synonyms between those data sources.

Taking the above features into account, we propose to deal with only one ontology in the considered software domain for the reasons that we enumerate in the following:

1. **The number of data sources is low.** Just by integrating a few software repositories we would offer access to most of the (freeware/shareware) software available on the Web. Notice that the most popular software websites have a good set of categories and pieces of software. In fact, we usually find what we look for just visiting one website.
2. **The number of categories is not very high.** Although different organizations could develop different categorizations of kinds of software, the biggest websites keep that number below one thousand (around 270 in Download.com and around 900[1] in Tucows). Only in the case of several hundreds or thousands of kinds of software (a huge ontology) we would need a different approach.
3. **The vocabulary heterogeneity problem is limited.** The restricted domain of kinds of software does not allow a big heterogeneity with respect to names used to describe different categories.

---

[1] After removing inner synonyms among different OS.

2.2   Automatic vs. Manual Ontology Construction

Another decision that must be taken when dealing with ontologies is the automatic versus manual ontology building process. It is widely accepted that the automation of the process of federating different data sources is difficult due to the need of managing semantic information that cannot be extracted automatically [22]. However, we explain in the following the features of our context, mostly concerning to the kind of data sources involved, that allow an automatic federation:

- Low syntactic heterogeneity. For the public websites that contain software (like Tucows, Download.com, etc.), we need to develop specialized wrappers that extract information from HTML or XML pages. It is important to stress that most of the public websites are already categorized (games, networking, entertainment, by OS, etc.) and we can take profit of it: the hierarchical categorization of a website can be used to create an ontology where subcategories in the website are transformed into subterms (specializations) in the ontology (see Figure 1). Concerning to the access to local software repositories, we would have control on them so the development of a wrapper is not a difficult task.

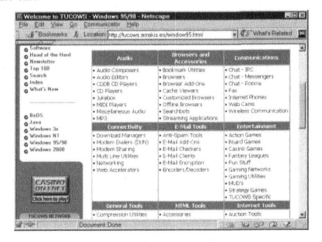

Fig. 1. Windows95 categories in Tucows

- Low semantic heterogeneity. In similar contexts, very different categorizations can be done by different organizations, for instance, bibliographic data [15]. That leads to the establishment of complex mapping relationships between the data elements in the data sources and the terms in the semantic descriptions (ontologies). These semantic relationships must be asserted by persons, although semi-automatic approaches can be taken in order to suggest some probable properties by considering the syntactic relationships [23]. However, in the scenery of software repositories the problem is minor. This can be seen by visiting different software websites: most of them have many categories in common, or use synonyms to denote the same category. For example, kinds of games in Download.com (Figure 2) are quite similar to categories of Entertainment in Tucows (Figure 1).

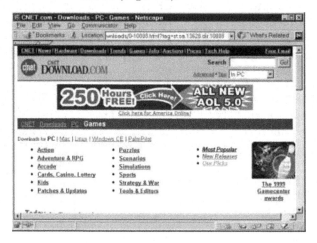

Fig. 2. Games categories in Download.com

Therefore, we believe that an automatic integration is possible and is a good solution for the construction of a software catalog. By avoiding human intervention our system can update, with a certain time granularity, the software offered, which definitely increases the quality of the proposed service. For the integration process, the two classical steps defined in the specialized literature of federating data sources, translation and integration, will be followed.

3   Agents involved in the system

In this section we present briefly all the agents that take part of the Software Retrieval Service. This service, situated in a concrete server that we call GSN[2], offers to the users the possibility to select, retrieve and install software in an easy and efficient way. The Software Retrieval Service uses the SoftOnt ontology mentioned in the previous section.

Agents are executed in contexts denominated *places* [20]. Mobile agents can travel from one place to another. The proposed service incorporates four places (see Figure 3):

1. **The User place**, located on the user computer. It includes an agent that belongs to the user, *Alfred*. Alfred is an efficient majordomo that serves the

---

[2] The *Gateway Support Node (GSN)* is the proxy that provides services to computer users.

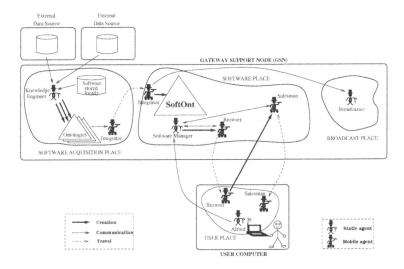

Fig. 3. Main architecture for the Software Retrieval Service

user and is in charge of storing as much information about the user computer, and the user himself, as possible. Alfred is the mediator between the user and the rest of the system.

2. **The Software Acquisition place**, located on the GSN. It groups those agents related to the *SoftOnt* ontology creation process (the main goal of this paper): 1) *The Knowledge Engineer* whose goal is to mine (local or remote) software repositories, with the help of specialized wrappers, in order to obtain a semantic description (an ontology) for each repository; and 2) *The Integrator*, which performs the integration of all the ontologies obtained by the Knowledge Engineer, with the goal of obtaining the ontology Soft-Ont. During the integration process it uses a thesaurus for the automatic vocabulary problem resolution.

3. **The Software place**, located on the GSN. It groups those agents related to the SoftOnt ontology exploitation process: 1) *The Software Manager* whose main goal is to provide the Browser agent with a catalog of the available software, after consulting and pruning the SoftOnt ontology according to the needs expressed by Alfred (on behalf of the user); 2) *The Browser*, whose goal is to interact with the user in order to refine a catalog of software until the user finally chooses a concrete piece of software; and 3) *The Salesman* which is in charge of finally carrying the program selected by the user to her/his computer, and performing any e-commerce interaction needed (which depends on the concrete piece of software).

4. **The Broadcast place**, located on the GSN. It includes *The Broadcaster*, whose goal is to inform users about new software releases.

A more detailed description of the role and interaction of these agents in the Software Retrieval Service can be found in [16].

4   The Translation Step: Obtaining a Description of Data Sources

In our context, most of the underlying repositories are remote websites containing software, which are classified as semistructured repositories, i.e., there does not exist a data schema of the information stored. Fortunately, HTML pages in websites containing software classify the different pieces of software in several categories, and we can take advantage of this. The solution for the translation step is the construction of specialized *wrappers* [7, 15, 21, 8] that access the HTML pages that compound the website and extract from them the different categories of software that can be found in such a website.

The design of such wrappers must consider that HTML pages can change. Some works have developed techniques to easily construct or adapt wrappers to semistructured data repositories [7, 15]. These works suggest the use of free-context grammars to define the structure of the data sources (HTML pages, in our case). Thus, wrappers extract certain information from the pages (software categories, in our context), taking a grammar as basis. If a change in the structure of some HTML page happens, the grammar can be adapted to the new syntactic structure of the page, but that would not have a great impact from the point of view of implementation. Following the suggestion, we have built wrappers based on grammars in order to extract the software categories from remote websites of public software.

```
<TD VALIGN="TOP" BGCOLOR="#ffffff">
<FONT FACE="Tahoma" SIZE=2><P>
  <a href="action95.html">Action Games</a><br>
  <a href="board95.html">Board Games</a><br>
  <a href="casino95.html">Casino Games</a><br>
  <a href="fanleague95.html">Fantasy Leagues</a><br>
  <a href="fun95.html">Fun Stuff</a><br>
  <a href="gnetwork95.html">Gaming Networks</a><br>
  <a href="gameutils95.html">Gaming Utilities</a><br>
  <a href="mud95.html">MUD's</a><br>
  <a href="strat95.html">Strategy Games</a><br>
  <a href="tucows95.html">TUCOWS Specific</a><br>
</FONT></TD>

              (1)
```

```
<start> ::= <begin> <list-of-categories> <end>

<begin> ::= '<TD VALIGN="TOP" BGCOLOR="#ffffff">'
            '<FONT FACE="Tahoma" SIZE=2><P>'

<list-of-categories> ::= <category>
                       | <category> <list-of-categories>

<category> ::= '<a href="'
               link  {store URL with subcategories or software}
               '">'
               category-name {store name of category analyzed}

<end> ::= '</FONT></TD>'

              (2)
```

Fig. 4. Tucows Entertainment categories in HTML (1) and grammar-based category extractor (2)

We can observe in Figure 4, on the left, that the information related to the categories and links to other pages containing sub-categories or software are included in the HTML description, but mixed with HTML tags. In Figure 4, on the right, we show a grammar that, taking the previous HTML page as entry, extracts the different Tucows Entertainment categories. We would like to stress that the category extraction mechanism also extracts all the information needed to download the pieces of software under each category.

In this manner, a wrapper constructed with this technique can 1) access a remote website, 2) mine its web pages and 3) obtain as result of that process a set of categories and the features of the programs belonging to them. With that information, an ontology can be easily built using some KBMS. In Figure 5 we show the concept hierarchy corresponding to an ontology obtained using this technique: it is the semantic description of Tucows that we looked for. Due to space limitations we have only detailed the branch Entertainment.

Fig. 5. Extract of ontology for Tucows

When an ontology describes a set of data sources it is necessary to define some kind of mapping information between terms in the ontology and data elements in the data sources, where the information is stored. In our context, during the process of mining software repositories to build an ontology, all the mapping information needed is also recollected.

Thus, the above process of translation is repeated for other websites, using different wrappers as they have different HTML pages and structure. See Figure 6 where the ontology corresponding to Download.com is shown. Due to space limitations we have only detailed the branch Games.We can observe that the obtained ontologies present a certain similarity.

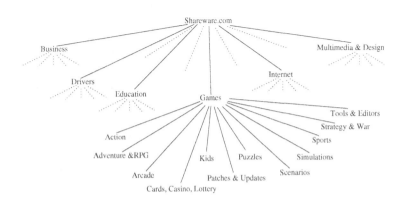

Fig. 6. Extract of ontology for Download.com

Finally, remember that the task corresponding to the translation step is developed by the Knowledge Engineer agent.

5   The Integration Step: Creation of SoftOnt

The ontologies obtained from the different software repositories must be integrated into only one ontology[3], SoftOnt. As different repositories can have classified their software in different ways, the main problem to perform an automatic integration is the *vocabulary problem*, i.e., the existence of synonyms, hyponyms or hypernyms among terms in different ontologies. In an open and dynamic environment, this problem is very difficult to solve although some approaches have been suggested, like the OBSERVER system [15].

5.1   The Vocabulary Problem

In our context, the vocabulary problem is not so serious due to the restricted nature of the type of information stored in the software repositories. There are many kinds of software but in most of the repositories that we have studied, the categories used are very similar: Internet tools, games, Audio, Video, etc. In a first approach we decided to use only a specialized thesaurus (well-known web tools as WordNet [19] could be used) in order to deal with synonyms, hyponyms and hypernyms. More expressive but complex mechanisms, that will require some kind of user intervention, are out of the scope of this paper (a proposal appears in [17, 18]).

As example, we present in Figure 7 the result of integrating the Tucows and Download.com ontologies, after detecting the following semantic properties using WordNet as thesaurus (terms from Tucows are in uppercase and terms from Download.com are in lowercase): 'ENTERTAINMENT' subsumes 'Games', 'ACTION GAMES' is a synonym of 'Action', 'CASINO GAMES' is subsumed by 'Cards, Casino, Lottery', and 'STRATEGY GAMES' is subsumed by 'Strategy & Wars' (only semantic properties between 'ENTERTAINMENT' and 'Games' are included). Many other properties could be found with the help of a thesaurus specialized on Computer Science.

For the task of integrating, with the help of a thesaurus for automatic vocabulary problem resolution, the different ontologies obtained by the Knowledge Engineer agent, we have designed the *Integrator* agent, which is in charge of creating SoftOnt. The Integrator is a mobile agent: after the integration is performed it moves from the Software Acquisition place to the Software place in order to update the previous version of SoftOnt. In this way, the Software Acquisition place could be on a different computer than the GSN. The Integrator is also capable to detect the changes occurred with respect to the previous version of SoftOnt. Such changes are communicated to the Broadcaster which will communicate to interested users that SoftOnt has been updated.

---

[3] The mapping information of the integrated ontology can be generated automatically by combining the mappings of the ontologies that are being integrated [3].

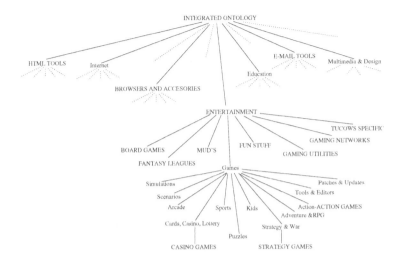

Fig. 7. Integration of Tucows and Download.com ontologies

5.2 Justification for the design of the Knowledge Engineer and Integrator agents

In order to achieve the same goal, someone could think of alternative architectures, including those that do not make use of agent technology, as well as those that advocate for mobile agents to access remote repositories. The arguments for our proposal are the following:

Concerning to the use of agents, in order to 1) translate software repositories into ontologies; and 2) integrate them into a global ontology, the system needs to manage specialized knowledge in an autonomous way. Moreover, the update strategy of the SoftOnt ontology must be independent of the rest of the system, in order to completely isolate the generation of SoftOnt from its exploitation. The previous tasks are too complex for a unique module. Therefore, we advocate for the design of two autonomous agents, the Knowledge Engineer for translation, and the Integrator for integration, which generate some information, an ontology called SoftOnt, that is used by the other agents in the system (which actually ignore when or why SoftOnt is created and updated).

The access to software repositories is one of the most appropriate scenery to use agents. The Knowledge Engineer could create different specialized *mobile agents* that would travel to remote software repositories in order to extract the information right there. This implies a very much faster execution as the HTML pages are accessed locally. This approach is also better with respect to network disconnections. Then, mobile agents could travel back to the Software Acquisition Place to return the extracted information to the Knowledge Engineer. They would be *mobile wrappers*. Unfortunately, the mechanisms needed to receive mobile agents are not very popular yet (for example, Tucows and Download.com sites do not accept incoming agents). Therefore, taking into account the current situation, we thought of local wrappers that access the remote information.

6   Conclusions

In this paper we have presented a multiagent-based application for the creation and exploitation of an ontology in the particular context of software gathering. We can conclude that:

- An ontology is an interesting specification tool to describe software repository contents. Thus, users do not need to deal with several distributed and heterogeneous software repositories.
- The ontology can be created automatically due to context features. Moreover, it can be updated easily to maintain it continuously up to date.
- Agents provide interesting features to create and exploit the ontology, such as autonomy and mobility. They also allow the management of knowledge used to solve problems and take appropriate decisions.

Finally, we can say that our proposed architecture for the Software Retrieval Service, based on agents and one ontology, offers flexibility and adaptability with a low overhead, as shown by our preliminary performance results. We believe that our proposal establishes an interesting trade-off in the use of classical distributed access techniques and new agent technology.

Acknowledgements

We would like to thank Ignacio García for his valuable help in the implementation of the prototype.

References

1. Y. Arens, C.Y. Chee, C. Hsu, and C.A. Knoblock. Retrieving and integrating data from multiple information sources. *International Journal on Intelligent and Cooperative Information Systems*, 2(2):127–158, 1993.
2. Attitude Network Ltd., 1999. http://www.gamesdomain.com.
3. J.M. Blanco, A. Goñi, and A. Illarramendi. Mapping among knowledge bases and data repositories: Precise definition of its syntax and semantics. *Information Systems*, 24(4):275–301, 1999.
4. CNET Inc., 1999. http://www.download.com.
5. CNET Inc., 1999. http://www.gamecenter.com.
6. Earthweb & Sun Microsystems, 1999. http://www.gamelan.com.
7. J. Hammer, M. Breunig, H. Garcia-Molina, S. Nestorov, V. Vassalos, and R. Y-erneni. Template-based wrappers in the tsimmis system. In *Proceedings of the Twenty-Sixth SIGMOD International Conference on Management of Data, Tucson, Arizona*, May 1997.
8. T. Kirk, A.Y. Levy, Y. Sagiv, and D. Srivastava. The information manifold. In *Proceedings of the AAAI Spring Symposium on Information Gathering in Distributed Heterogeneous Environments, Stanford, CA*, March 1995.
9. Y. Labrou and T. Finin. Yahoo! as an ontology – using yahoo! categories to describe documents. In *Proceedings of the International Conference on Information and Knowledge Management (CIKM99)*, 1999.

10. J.L. Lee, S.E. Madnick, and M.D. Siegel. Conceptualizing semantic interoperability: A perspective from the knowledge level. *International Journal on Cooperative Information Systems (IJCIS)*, 4(4), 1996.

11. A.Y. Levy, A. Rajamaran, and J.J. Ordille. Querying heterogeneous information sources using source descriptions. In *Proc. of the VLDB 96.*, 1996.

12. A.Y. Levy, A. Rajaraman, and J.J. Ordille. Query-answering algorithms for information agents. In *Proceedings of the Thirteenth National Conference on Artificial Intelligence (AAAI96), Portland, Oregon*, 1996.

13. S. Luke, L. Spector, and D. Rager. Ontology-based Web agents. In *Proceedings of the First International Conference on Autonomous Agents*, 1997.

14. Z. Maamar, B. Moulin, G. Babin, and Y. Bedard. Software Agent-Oriented Frameworks for Global Query Processing. *Journal of Intelligent Information Systems (JIIS)*, 13:235–259, 1999.

15. E. Mena. *OBSERVER: An Approach for Query Processing in Global Information Systems based on Interoperation across Pre-existing Ontologies.* PhD thesis, University of Zaragoza, November 1998. http://siul02.si.ehu.es/PUBLICATIONS/thesis98.ps.gz.

16. E. Mena, A. Illarramendi, and A. Goñi. Customizable Software Retrieval Facility for Mobile Computers using Agents. In *proceedings of the Seventh International Conference on Parallel and Distributed Systems (ICPADS'2000), workshop International Flexible Networking and Cooperative Distributed Agents (FNCDA'2000), IEEE Computer Society, Iwate (Japan)*, July 2000.

17. E. Mena, A. Illarramendi, V. Kashyap, and A. Sheth. Observer: An approach for query processing in global information systems based on interoperation across pre-existing ontologies. *International journal on Distributed And Parallel Databases (DAPD)*, 8(2), April 2000.

18. E. Mena, V. Kashyap, A. Illarramendi, and A. Sheth. Imprecise answers on highly open and distributed environments: An approach based on information loss for multi-ontology based query processing. Accepted for publication in a special issue of the International Journal of Cooperative Information Systems (IJCIS), 2000.

19. G. Miller. World Wide Web interface to WordNet 1.5, June 1995. http://www.cogsci.princeton.edu/~wn/w3wn.html.

20. D. Milojicic, M. Breugst, I. Busse, J. Campbell, S. Covaci, B. Friedman, K. Kosaka, D. Lange, K. Ono, M. Oshima, C. Tham, S. Virdhagriswaran, and J. White. MASIF, the OMG mobile agent system interoperability facility. In *Proceedings of Mobile Agents '98*, September 1998.

21. Y. Papakonstantinou, A. Gupta, H. Garcia-Molina, and J. Ullman. A query translation scheme for rapid implementation of wrappers. In *Proceedings of the International Conference on Deductive and Object-Oriented Databases*, 1995.

22. A.P. Sheth, S.K. Gala, and S.B. Navathe. On automatic reasoning for schema integration. *International Journal on Intelligent and Cooperative Information Systems*, 2(1):23–50, 1993.

23. S. Spaccapietra, C. Parent, and Y. Dupont. Model independent assertions for integration of heterogeneous schemas. *VLDB*, 1:81–126, 1992.

24. Tucows.Com Inc., 1999. http://www.tucows.com.

25. Yahoo! Inc. http://www.yahoo.com/.

Inspiration for Future Autonomous Space Systems

Dr. Richard J. Doyle

Leader, Center for Space Mission Information and Software Systems
Manager, Information Technology and Software Systems Division
Jet Propulsion Laboratory, California Institute of Technology
Pasadena, California 91109-8099 USA
rdoyle@jpl.nasa.gov
http://it.jpl.nasa.gov

1 The Future NASA Mission Challenge

NASA is embarking on a new phase of space exploration. In the solar system, an initial reconnaissance of all of the planets except Pluto has been accomplished. In the next phase of planetary exploration, the emphasis will be on direct, i.e., in-situ scientific investigation in the remote environments. In the next phase of astrophysics investigation, the emphasis is on new observing instruments, often based on principles of interferometry, to accomplish unprecedented resolution in remote observing. A theme that runs through all of these science missions is the search for life.

The development of autonomy capabilities is on the critical path to addressing a set of vastly important strategic technical challenges arising from the future NASA mission set: reduction of mission costs, increased efficiency in the return of quality science products, and the launching of a new era of solar system exploration characterized by sustained presence, in-situ science investigations and missions accomplished via multiple, coordinated space platforms. These new classes of space exploration missions, as a rule, require new capabilities and technologies.

1.1 Future Missions and Autonomy

Mars is a primary target for future exploration, and certainly has captured the interest of the general public. The set of Mars missions under development differ from previous space exploration in one important aspect: they are being conceived as a collective whole, with the establishment and evolution of infrastructure at Mars as an important sub-goal. Such proposed infrastructure includes permanent science stations on the surface, propellant production plants, and a network of communications satellites in orbit to extend internet-like capability to Mars, and to enable the coordination of an array of heterogeneous, autonomous agents as explorers: rovers, balloons, airplanes, perhaps even subsurface devices. No longer would each mission be

M. Klusch and L. Kerschberg (Eds.): CIA 2000, LNAI 1860, pp. 244-248, 2000.
© Springer-Verlag Berlin Heidelberg 2000

conceived and executed in isolation, but through a combination of in situ and constellation mission concepts humanity's presence at Mars would continually expand, culminating in the arrival and safe return of the first human explorers.

Europa is a notable focus for future exploration, second only to Mars as a target of interest within the solar system. The reason, of course, is the possibility that a liquid water ocean may exist beneath its surface, with obvious implications for the search for life. Three mission concepts for Europa exploration are at various stages of maturity: the Europa Orbiter mission, approved and set to launch in 2003, which should resolve the question of whether the subsurface ocean exists or not, followed by the Europa Lander, and perhaps by a Europa Cyrobot/Hydrobot mission. The Lander would have similar challenges of safe landing and surface operations as described above, plus the additional complication of survivability in the intense radiation environment at Europa, deeply embedded in the Jovian magnetosphere. If the Europan ocean does indeed exist, the Cryobot/Hydrobot mission concept involves melting through the ice surface of Europa, then releasing an underwater submersible to reach and explore the ocean floor, looking for signs of life. The submersible would require high degrees of autonomy, including onboard algorithms embodying knowledge of biosignatures, in order to perform its mission.

2   The Emergence of Autonomy

Intelligent, highly autonomous space platforms will evolve and deploy in major phases. The first phase involves automation of the basic engineering and mission accomplishment functions of the space platform. The relevant capabilities include mission planning and resource management, health management and fault protection, and guidance, navigation and control. Stated differently, these autonomous capabilities will make the space platform *self-commanding* and *self-preserving*. At this point, mission accomplishment is becoming largely autonomous, and cost savings is seen in the form of reduced, shared ground staffing which responds on demand to the spacecraft's beacon-based requests for interaction. Also in this phase, the first elements of *science-directed autonomy* will appear.

Work on automating the spacecraft will continue into challenging areas like greater onboard adaptability in responding to events, and operation of the multiple free-flying elements of space-based telescopes and interferometers. In addition, in the next phase of autonomy development and deployment, a portion of the scientist's awareness, i.e., an observing and discovery presence, will begin to move onboard. At this point, the space platform begins to become *self-directing*, and can respond to uncertainty within the mission context, a prerequisite for moving beyond reconnaissance to interactive, in situ exploration. Ultimately, a significant portion of the information routinely returned from platforms would not simply and strictly match features of stated prior interest, but would be deemed by the onboard software to be "interesting" and worthy of further examination by appropriate science experts on the ground.

For a survey of recent autonomy technology activities at NASA, see [1].

Beyond these initial phases, we can project a phase where space platforms become web nodes, with direction interaction enabled among space platforms, the science community, and the general public. Interested users may "register" with autonomous spacecraft to learn about just-breaking results.

The next phase may involve self-organizing constellations of space platforms consisting of heterogeneous assets performing joint, coordinated execution of mission objectives, with self-calibration and adaptation enabled at the level of the mission.

2.1   The Remote Agent

The most notable and successful effort in spacecraft autonomy development at NASA to date has been the Remote Agent, a joint technology development project by NASA Ames Research Center and the Jet Propulsion Laboratory (JPL) [2]. The Remote Agent Experiment was conducted on the New Millennium Deep Space One (DS1) spacecraft in May 1999 [3], a mission whose primary goal was to flight validate new technologies.

The demonstration objectives of the Remote Agent Experiment (RAX) on DS1 included nominal operations with goal-oriented commanding, closed-loop plan execution, onboard failure diagnosis and recovery, onboard planning following unrecoverable failures, and system-level fault protection. All of the technology validation objectives for RAX were accomplished. Additional details may be found in [4]. The Remote Agent was a co-winner of the NASA Software of the Year Award in 1999.

2.2   Some Definitions

Automation applies to the creation of functionality (typically via algorithms) which can be fully defined independent of the context in which the functionality will be deployed, or when the context (e.g., the remote environment) can be modeled with sufficient confidence that the required functionality is well understood.

Autonomy, on the other hand, applies to the creation of functionality (typically via reasoning or inference capability) which is designed to be effective when context is important, and when the ability to model context (again, e.g., the remote environment) is limited. Knowledge and importance of context is the key consideration for distinguishing the need for automation vs. autonomy.

We can conceive of a form of autonomy that takes the next step: allowing for *evolving* functionality after deployment. This evolution would take place within the resources of the remote autonomous system itself (i.e., not via uplinked software patches or new loads) and would be driven by feedback from and understanding of the remote environment. A possible term for this next-generation form of autonomy is *flexibility*.

2.3   Flexible Systems

The concept of flexible systems is meant to enable *phase change* in the functionality of deployed space systems. Unlike current conceptions of autonomous systems, flexible systems would not have their functionality fixed at deployment time. Rather, the space of possible functionalities would continue to be explored after arrival in the remote environment, and would be responsive to both internal system changes and external environmental changes. Latent functionality would be explored first in software, and when well understood, would be "compiled" or implemented in hardware changes. Flexibility may ultimately imply a merging of hardware- and software-based capabilities, and directly supports goals for long-term survivability, continuing mission accomplishment and evolvability under changing circumstances and objectives. Within the model for flexibility, space systems may undergo several phase changes over their lifetime. Evolvability is an example of a characteristic exhibited by biological systems which may one day be embodied in our designed and engineered space systems to great advantage [5].

Acknowledgements

The work described in this article was performed at the Jet Propulsion Laboratory, California Institute of Technology, under a contract with the National Aeronautics and Space Administration.

References

[1] Richard J. Doyle, "Spacecraft Autonomy and the Missions of Exploration," Guest Editor's Introduction, Special Issue on Autonomous Space Vehicles, *IEEE Intelligent Systems*, September/October 1998.

[2] Barney Pell et al, "An Autonomous Spacecraft Agent Prototype," *Autonomous Robots,* vol. 5, no. 1, March 1998.

[3] Douglas E. Bernard et al, "Autonomy and Software Technology Experiments on NASA's Deep Space One Mission," *IEEE Intelligent Systems*, May/June 1999.

[4] Pandu Nayak et al, "Validating the DS-1 Remote Agent Experiment," *5th International Symposium on Artificial Intelligence and Robotics Applications for Space,* Noorrdvijk, The Netherlands, June 1999.

[5] Ahmed K. Noor, Richard J. Doyle, and Samuel L. Venneri, "Bringing Life to Space Exploration," *Aerospace America,* November 1999.

Mobile Information Agents for Cyberspace - State of the Art and Visions

Todd Papaioannou

DALi, Inc. 1020 Mission Street, South Pasadena, CA 91030, USA,
toddp@acm.org,
http://www.luckyspin.org

Abstract. As ubiquitous computing becomes a reality, the amount of information we are confronted by is becoming overwhelming. In addition, the myriad of devices we can use to access this information is continually increasing. We require new technologies to assist us in locating and filtering this information, which are also able to deliver it at our conveniance. One technology that show potential in this area is Mobile Information Agents. In this paper, we review the current state-of-the-art in this field, and suggest key issues that must be addresssed if widespread adoption is to happen. Lastly, we look forward to the future and postulate where this new technology may take us.

1 Introduction

The last decade has seen an explosion in the growth and use of the Internet. Rapidly evolving network and computer technology, coupled with the exponential growth of services and information available on the Internet, is heralding a new era of ubiquitous computing. Hundreds of millions of people will soon have pervasive access to a huge amount of information, which they will be able to access through a plethora of diverse computational devices. These devices are no longer isolated number crunching machines; rather they are on our desks, on our wrists, in our clothes, embedded in our cars, phones and even washing machines. These computers are constantly communicating with each other via LANs, Intranets, the Internet, and through wireless networks, in which the size and topology of the network is constantly changing. And somewhere in this network, lies the piece of information that we desperately require; lost among the flotsam and jetsam of the Information Age. As our lives change, we are not only being overloaded with information, generated from a myriad of sources, but its topology can actually change from one day to the next. In this shifting sea, we require new techniques and technologies that are able to locate and filter the information on our behalf. One solution to these problems are mobile information agents.

2 Why Mobility?

In recent years the agent research field has become one of the most active and vibrant areas in information technology. For many, the question of whether this

M. Klusch and L. Kerschberg (Eds.): CIA 2000, LNAI 1860, pp. 247-261, 2000.

technology will realise its potential is not an issue, they are convinced. In certain quarters of the intelligent agent community, however, there has often been a certain degree of dismissal when the topic of agent mobility is raised. Their view has been that every system can be constructed by using static agents, which communicate with each other across the network to achieve their goals. Fortunately, this view is beginning to change, since the position is becoming untenable.

The nature of the network is changing. No longer can we view it as a core and pervasive aspect of our computing architecture. It is no longer the reliable backbone we envisage, accessible from everywhere. The harsh reality is that bandwidth has become a commodity, and a scarce one at best. A plethora of new computing devices continually arriving on the market are going to eat up even more of the precious resource. These devices are no longer isolated number crunching machines; rather they are on our desks, on our wrists, in our clothes, embedded in our cars, phones and even washing machines. Further, these new devices do not enjoy the same connection speeds as say, a corporate network. But while they may be the poorer netizens, their numbers are prolific, and rising.

To understand how to architect information system in this environment, we should stop conceptualising the network as a connection of major arteries, which allow a constant flow of information. Rather we should view it as a lung, which has many differing sizes of information conduit. There are bronchi where large volumes of information can flow freely. These represent the Internet backbone, haven for mega corporations and academic institutions. Then, there are the bronchioles, which represent corporate LANs and well off home users. But at the boundaries of the network, are the minute alveoli, the portable devices and modem users, whose transfer rate is small. Pervasive information access from these different access points requires rethinking how we architect our systems.

Many opponents of mobility point towards a future when there will be enough bandwidth for everyone, and mobility will not be an issue. This argument is flawed in two aspects. Firstly, while there may indeed be plentiful bandwidth at the bronchial level, the many devices at the fringes of the network will never enjoy the types of connection speed users will have come to accept as the norm. Secondly, it is not clear whether we will ever be able to outpace demand and provide enough bandwidth to satisfy everyone's requirements. To illustrate let us imagine our kitchen has one waste bin. Currently, when it is full, we have to empty it or find it overflowing. If we add another bin to double our waste capacity, is it likely that we will think to empty one before the other is full. Or will we simply wait until both are full before taking action? If we look to the road systems around the globe, this is similar to what occurs with traffic systems, demand usually outstrips capacity on the major roads.

In addition, users are no longer satisfied with having their connection to the wider world rooted to a single location. Ubiquitous computing is seducing people with its pervasive nature, and users are becoming accustomed to accessing their information immediately, from wherever they may be at that time. Web-based email has demonstrated that users value the ability to access their email from any computer. Soon, web terminals will be commonplace in public spaces, such as cafes, airports, taxi's and hotels. In the future, users will expect full access to any of their information from any device. Despite this, mobile devices will proliferate unchecked, since just as with public phones, Web terminals will never be available everywhere that a user might find themselves. WAP enabled cell phones are already becoming increasingly common.

2.1 What Does Mobility Offer Us?

The advantages that the mobile agent abstraction bring are extensive. They have been covered in greater detail in many other locations [6] [21] but are briefly summarised below.

Table 1. Summary of Advantages of Mobile Information Agents

Advantages	Description
Bandwidth savings	Instead of transferring lots of over the network, move the logic to be local to the data source
Limiting latency	By having the logic and data on the same machine, latency can be reduced
Disconnected operation	If a computer is going to be offline, then it is possible to move the active processes to another host
Stability	By using mobile code, software can be less dependant on the network, and therefore more stable. Mobility can be used to achieve replication for fault tolerance
Server Flexibility	A client isn't limited to the functions a server provides. Code mobility allows clients to upload new (or improved) functionality to the server
Simplicity of installed server base	Servers can become simpler, requiring less functionality pre-engineered from the outset which can help prevent legacy
Enable distributed computation	Mobile agents are inherently distributed, and as such can be a fundamental enabler for distributed computation

More importantly however, it is a software architecture that offers many abstractions to a designer. These include Client/server, Mobile Computation, Remote Evaluation and Mobile Agents and are covered extensively by in [19] and [24].

2.2 Research Status

Code mobility is not a completely new idea. There have been several widely used and successful mechanisms for moving code around a network previously employed, perhaps the best known being the PostScript language [1] that is used to control printers. Recently though, mobility has been examined from a different perspective, and has become a burgeoning topic for discussion in mainstream distributed systems research. Mobility currently boasts a flourishing research community dedicated to investigating the potential of this new paradigm [15]. In this paper we define a mobile agent as:

> "a software agent that is able to autonomously migrate from one host to another in a computer network."

The notion of a mobile agent was first established in 1994 with the release of a white paper by White [33] that described a computational environment known as "Telescript" [34]. In this environment, executing programs were able to transport themselves from one node to another in a computer network, in order to interact locally with resources at those nodes. Telescript was never a commercial success, but it did generate a lot of academic interest.

Since that time, this field has exploded in popularity, with a plethora of new frameworks and infrastructures appearing almost continually [16]. This profusion of experimental frameworks is reminiscent of the explosion of new programming languages in the early days of computing and is indicative of a new and immature research field. Many frameworks and platforms spring up, and are continually written about, but unfortunately, these papers remain qualitative and subjective in their nature. The dearth of quantitative results, however, means it has not yet been possible to fully evaluate the potential of either the technology or the paradigm. In the last year a trickle of results is beginning to validate some of the claims [23] [24], and these results are certainly important in establishing the credibility of mobile code systems. In addition, there has been work done to attempt to fully understand this new paradigm at the abstraction level [19], and develop metrics for system evaluation [22].

3   Issues Facing Mobility

Despite the increasing popularity of the concept, there are a number of key issues that the research community must face if it is to gain widespread acceptance and deployment. They remain fundamental issues that address questions such as:

- Is it safe? (Security)
- What's in it for me? (Payment)
- What good is it if I'm the only one? (Interoperation)

In the following sections we elaborate on these issues and review existing research that has been done in these areas.

3.1   Security

Security is one of the most emotive issues raised when discussing mobile agent systems. It is often quoted [12] as the major reason mobile agent systems have not taken off in the mainstream. There is currently a wealth of research being done on this particular subject [31]. The very nature and architecture of these systems enables new and interesting forms of attack on both host environments and agents in the system. Table 2 summarises the many and varied types of attack identified Lange and Oshima [14] and Jansen and Karygiannis [11]. In particular, the latters' report is extensive, and analyses security in mobile agent systems in quite some depth. The reader is referred to it for in depth coverage of the subject.

As with much in the mobile agent arena, progress in the area of security has been slow. If security has been considered in a platform at all, it is usually biased towards host protection, with much less thought given towards the integrity of an executing agent. Certainly, this approach may go some way to alleviating the fears of systems administrators considering hosting mobile agent environments. It does not however, allay the concerns of the user who has entrusted private information to their agent. Admittedly, protecting the mobile agent is a much harder task since agents are invariably interpreted within an execution environment, but there have been advances made in this area too.

Some agent protection can be gained through continual contact with the originating host. JumpingBeans [13] uses a client/server architecture where an agent returns to a secure central host before every migration where it can be checked for tampering. This approach is impractical and severely hinders, indeed breaks, the mobile agent abstraction. Aglets [2] enforces a trust based policy, whereby hosting environments will not accept or dispatch agents to remote hosts they do not trust. Both these examples are useful in controlled or closed situations, but are not practical when applied to open public networks such as the Internet.

Vigna [30] has proposed protecting agents through Action Tracing. As an agent executes at a host a log is made of any actions it performs there. These traces are non-repudiatable, and allow the agent owner to check with a high degree of confidence whether there has been any tampering with the agent's state during its execution. The drawback to this approach is of course, the size of the traces could potentially be huge.

Riordan and Schneier [26] advocate a technique they term Environmental Key Generation, in which an agent is able to decrypt a predefined section of code upon a task specific trigger. The trigger itself causes the generation of the decrypting key, and thus, a malicious host is unable to inspect an agent's internal to ascertain what it's response may be to a particular situation. The major drawback to this technique is that even trusted agent hosts are unlikely to allow an agent to execute a dynamically created piece of code.

Young and Yung [32] propose a technique known as Sliding Encryption, that enables mobile agents to perform encryption on any information it may accumulate at a host. This data is encrypted with a public key, so the host may not extract the text without access to the private key. On return to its origin, the agent is able to access the private key, and decrypt all of its stored data.

Finally, Sander and Tschudin [27] have made some progress in debunking the widely held view that because mobile agents are usually interpreted, the

Table 2. Common Security Issues identified in Mobile Agent Systems

Type	Example	Description
Agent/Host	Masquerading	Agent poses as another agent to gain access to services, information or resources at a host
	Denial of Service	An incoming agent may try to access and corrupt the host's local files, resources or even try crashing the server in a denial of service attack
	Unauthorised Access	Agent obtains access to sensitive information by violating ill implemented security mechanisms, or cached information
Host/Agent	Masquerading	Host assumes false identity in order to lure agent, so it may gain payment, or eavesdrop on the transactions of other agents
	Denial of Service	Host can completely ignore an agent's requests for resources, flood the agent with messages, etc
	Eavesdropping	Since agents are interpreted, host can inspect internal algorithms, trade secrets, c-card info, etc
	Alteration	Host can change essential internal data, or results from previous hosts, to e.g. Bias results returned to agent's owner
Agent/Agent	Masquerading	Agent assumes identify of another agent to extract sensitive data, e.g. credit card info, or extract a payment
	Denial of Service	Agent may flood another with messages, or distribute false information, or tie up an agents resources in another similar manner
	Repudiation	After agreeing to some contract, agent subsequently denies that any agreement took place
	Unauthorised Access	Agent interferes with another agent to gain access to sensitive internal data, or modify its behaviour
Other	Masquerading	Remote hosts and agents can act in concert to deceive another, to gain access to info, payment, etc
	Network D.O.S.	Agent may attempt to flood the network with messages or copies of itself, etc
	Copy and Replay	Once an agent has migrated, a host, or agent may attempt to replay the "pay agent" message or code repeatedly to steal money

hosting environment must be able to understand an agent it is hosting in its entirety. Whilst this assumption remains true for all plaintext data and programs, they have devised a mathematical technique that allows a mobile agent to safely compute cryptographic primitives in an untrusted computing environment. This process pivots around the ability to execute encrypted polynomial functions, without decrypting them in the first place. This is an extremely promising avenue of research, but to date there are few examples of functions that can be transformed in this manner. The single example described by Sander and Tschudin is of a function that enables digital signing with this technique.

3.2   Micropayments

In order for mobile information agent systems to achieve widespread adoption, there must be an incentive for hosting sites to allow these alien software programs onto their machines. This implies that hosts should be compensated for the additional load and security risks associated with supporting a mobile-agent platform. By providing a mechanism for the agents to carry limited amounts of some type of currency, they would be able to purchase computing services from public hosts. To date, most examples of mobile agent applications operate in a closed environment [20], and the variety of actual hosts the mobile agents migrate between are relatively low. Further, these applications usually feature mobile agents that are acting for a single user, or a party of mutually interested participants. Thus it is usually in the interest of the user population if their agents cooperate. In an open system, this will certainly not be the case as agents vie for limited computing resources, or compete to provide services.

The question of providing micropayment mechanisms in the information age is a concern in many fields of research. It is not even particularly new, with examples appearing in the late 1960's [28]. More recently, Huberman's [10] edited volume discusses man possibility for computational economies. Indeed, the World Wide Web Consortium have a micro payments group who are actively developing protocols [35] and strategies for web based micro payment.

The question of resource allocation in a mobile agent system however, was first tackled in Telescript, where agents were given permits whose strength diminished over time as they travelled through the network. In the Messengers project, Tschudin [29] developed a mechanism for non discriminatory open resource allocation in which agents were able to purchase key computing resources such as CPU, memory and bandwidth. Each agent was treated as an equal and there was no weighting given to the particular task, destination or origin of the agent.

More recently, Bredin et al [5] have proposed a bidding strategy that minimizes an agent's execution time for a given itinerary, while preserving a fixed budget constraint. They have constructed a resource allocation policy where hosts take bids from agents for prioritized access to computational resources (CPU time). The priority of access to a resource an agent receives is proportional to its bid relative to the sum of all current bids at the host. Hosts collect revenues from each agent at a rate equal to the agents' bids.

To date, there are few full-scale implementations of micropayment schemes in mobile agent systems. Bredin's work, which is very promising, has been realised in a simulation but is yet to be transferred to a proper system. Ultimately, we require mechanisms that support resource owners in allowing agents controlled and metered access to resources and services, so that agents can traverse the globe, searching and paying for their data, interacting with other agents, and selling their services to sites or other agents. However, if this vision is to become reality, then we most certainly require infrastructures to support platform interoperability.

3.3   Interoperability

So far, most mobile agent platforms and applications have operated in a closed environment. By that we mean that all hosts and agent types in the system are known at the outset. They are all built from the same platform and thus inter-agent communication is solely with other agents from the system. In addition, the range of sites to which an agent travels is usually extremely limited. If we are to achieve a future of pervasive mobile information agents that is non-monopolistic, then we require mechanisms and infrastructures that enable interoperability between different manufacturers' platforms.

In the mobile agent arena, the biggest drive for interoperability has come from a joint submission to the OMG known as the Mobile Agent System Interoperability Facilities (MASIF) [8], which is a joint proposal by Crystaliz, General Magic, GMD Focus, IBM and The Open Group. The aim of the MASIF standard is to standardize such things are agent management, agent transfer, agent and agent system naming conventions, agent system types, and location syntax. The aim is to achieve a certain degree of interoperability between mobile agent platforms without enforcing radical platform modifications. MASIF is not intended as a reference model from which to build a new mobile agent platform. Rather, it provides specifications that can be used as an add-on to existing systems. To date there are a handful of mobile agent platforms that support the MASIF standard, for example Grasshopper [9], MAP [25], SOMA [3] and Aglets [2]. In reality though, the standard has failed to gain widespread adoption amongst platform implementers, due mainly in part to its reliance on many other OMG specifications, for example CORBA and IDL, and its bias towards many of the standard submitters' systems. In truth, after a flurry of activity in 1998, the MASIF standard's impetus has petered out.

More recently the SAFT [4] proposal by Blixt and Öberg encompassed the design of a mobile software agent framework that was based on existing standards as much as possible. The majority of the standards were drawn from the Java(tm) 2 Enterprise Edition and HTTP. Initially, the authors had hoped to provide a reference model specification that any platform implementer could follow in creating their product. Their objective was to allow the creation of many different products that all conformed to the same standard, as is seen in the web-server market. Unfortunately, as is the case with many thought experiments, many of the problems that appear are not immediately visible from the outset. The authors have since implemented a prototype system and discovered that many of their specifications were unsuitable. However, they intend to update their specification with the experience they have gained from their work.

3.4 Commentary

From this brief review, it would seem that the state-of-the-art is relatively poor. In many respects this is true, for this is a fairly new research field that only a few years old. There are still debates as to the best methodology for actually achieving mobility in platforms, although the ubiquitous Java is rapidly becoming the language of choice. The proliferation of new mobile agent packages/platforms (currently listed at 72 by the Mobile Agent List [16]) points towards continued improvements in our understanding and experience from building infrastructures and the amount of reported implementations of real-world inspired systems is also increasingly. Indeed, the position does not fair too badly when considered in context. In the early years of programming, the number of new languages and extensions was initially prolific before common practices and techniques became widely accepted. We are currently moving through that phase in this research field. Things just take time. Remember the twenty years it took for objects to become commonplace?

We have briefly discussed some of the issues that face the mobile agent community if they are to achieve widespread adoption. There are others, for example adding intelligence to mobile agents, which have traditionally been very dumb; providing mechanisms for data description; and enabling true agent communication through the use of language. These are not solely the remit of the mobile agent community and thus, have not been covered in our discussion, but they are equally important.

4   Visions

It is our belief that in the future the network will become to be viewed as the computing environment of choice. Local computing will take place on PC's between users and static applications. The network however will be populated by thriving ecologies of agents. Mobile information agents will be able to travel from host to host, alighting where they wish to take advantage of a service or resource, before moving on to complete their goals elsewhere. These hosts are mere islands of resources in the vast expanse of the network. Upon them, languish static agents, rooted to the spot. They will act as interfaces to information sources, such as databases, file systems and web servers, and external devices, such as databases, printers and cameras. In return for providing these services, they will receive payment from the mobile agents, as will the host environments in return for providing essential resources such as CPU, memory and storage.

In the following sections we leave behind our review of the research field. Since this paper accompanies an invited talk, with a provided title, we have taken the opportunity to let our minds wander to the future, to see where mobile information agents can take us.

4.1 Mobile Agents in Space

The launch of the Deep Space One (DS1) probe heralded the beginning of a new phase for NASA, which will be embarking on a series of missions to test and deploy low cost, demonstration technologies. In an attempt to cut mission costs from billions to under 100 million, NASA is looking towards autonomous spacecraft and robots to establish a virtual presence in space. The increasing motives for space exploration, and the diversity of the environments and missions being encountered require machines that are both robust mechanically, as well as computationally. The recent paradigm shift from billion dollar missions with massive ground crews, to cheaper, targeted missions with much smaller ground crews has required the creation of spacecraft that are largely controlled by intelligent and self sufficient entities, known as Remote Agents [17].

Current research is investigating how to control the interaction between agents, their internal sub-systems and humans. Adjustable autonomy is of particular interest when dealing with systems that may have to function for several years unattended [7], or may be forced to halt their mission until they can get further instructions from human operators. However, the increasing distances and time delays involved with space exploration make remote operation of robotic probes and vehicles logistically impossible. New methods to support assuming full control of a probe, or subtle alteration of its operating constraints, are required that can overcome amongst other things, the problem of long distance interaction.

Even if the future brings the reality of unlimited bandwidth (and that is unlikely - see Section 2) we may discard it in this example since the network we are considering is extremely vast, i.e. a network of spacecraft distributed across the solar system and beyond. With a network this large, immutable factors such as the speed of light will come into effect, that can not be over come with any amount of bandwidth. Thus, local agent interaction via migration through the network rather than traditional client/server or asynchronous messaging must have a role to play in the future of our virtual presence in space. By now, it should be clear that mobile agents are inherently suited for long distance interaction.

To examine the use of mobile agents in this scenario we will place them in a hypothetical context. Their particular strengths of being able to react to situations that may have been unforeseen at the time of their dispatch makes them a viable option for interacting with deep space probes, missions into the farther reaches of the solar system, and planetary ground teams (be they human or robotic). Let us imagine that we have moved into the near future, and the solar system has been populated with a network of probes, spacecraft and robots. Circling the moon Europa is a small transport ship from which a group of hydrobots are sequentially dispatched to search for life under the ice rafts. At some point, one of the hydrobots returns to the surface with what looks like some very exciting results. On arrival at Earth, the results cause several scientists to get extremely excited and they pull an all-nighter devising a mission to further examine these results. The command sequence is dispatched to the transport ship, which receives and programs one of the remaining hydrobots with the new mission. The hydrobot is launched and carries out the new mission.

This scenario seems plausible enough, but what is the effect of new results emerging whilst the mission is in transit? Perhaps the initial hydrobot happens to run a routine diagnostic and discovers that one of its sensors was damaged and reports from it have been skewed. In the mobile code instance (the command sequence), the second hydrobot would probably still be launched and might in fact be wasting valuable resources investigating a worthless area. With a mobile agent, the agent would update its knowledge base on arrival with any reports it had missed en route and deduce that the mission it was tasked with was not required. The decision could be made to terminate itself, or perhaps continue with an alternative mission plan. In either case, a potential waste of a valuable hydrobot or other irreplaceable resources would be avoided. It can be argued that the sensor check should have been done before the report transmission, or that conditional command sequences might alleviate some of the problems with long distance interaction, but Murphy's Law may rear its head at any time. Unforeseen circumstances are a reality in space exploration. Mobile agents offer a solution to long distance interaction by providing a flexible, reactive approach to re-tasking probes and robots in-situ rather than a less flexible approach.

Ultimately, we envisage a vision of space inhabited by an ecology of robots, satellites, spacecraft, rovers, planetary bases and the like. In contrast to most visions, these entities act not only as fundamental actors in the vision, but as a network of resources. In it, each entity has some level of autonomy, which may range from very simple task specific instructions, to more complex autonomous agent architectures. Mobile agents live in the network, able to migrate, clone, sleep, wake, but in reality insert a higher layer of control and abstraction over the underlying hardware and software.

In truth, it will be some time before sufficient numbers of these entities inhabit space to make the vision reality. However, the advantages of local interaction, adjustable autonomy and interaction at a distance make mobile agents a particularly useful technology even with a single spacecraft. These ideas have been aired before [18].

4.2   Self Tuning Networks

As we have seen, the nature of the network is changing and we require new software architectures for exploiting these new frontiers. Nearly all contemporary computer networks consist of a mixture of disparate hardware, operating systems and other computing devices, the topology of which is continually changing. Current methods for resource location revolve around a centralised registry that participants in the network may query to locate required services. This type of architecture quite clearly can not work in the networks of tomorrow. In this section, we present a mobile agent based architecture for resource discovery that is completely decentralised, and further, is able to tune itself in response to changing demands placed upon it.

At each node in a network sits a static DirectoryAgent. The role of this agent is to maintain a local list of other known hosts, along with a record of the services and resources available at that host. DirectoryAgents communicate exclusively with local agents, they do not communicate across the network. In addition, the system contains Roamers, agents that travel the network, alighting at nodes. When they come to rest at a node, they briefly interact with the local DirectoryAgent before moving on to another node. Again, Roamers do not communicate across the network.

The interaction between the DirectoryAgents and the Roamers is the essential aspect of this system. At each node, the Roamers update DirectoryAgent's registry of known hosts, resources and services. In addition, it makes a note of the resources and services available at the current node, before moving on to another host. Which host they choose to go to next, is chosen at random. To avoid Roamers becoming too bloated, there is mortality in the system. Roamers die before becoming too old, or after making a certain amount of hops.

To avoid the information stored in a registry becoming out of date, the records that a Roamer carries are inspired by ant pheromones, in that they become weaker over time. As soon as the Roamer departs the current node, the newly acquired record begins to decay. If a Roamer alights at a node whose DirectoryAgent's registry contains a more recently record, it is able to update the one it carries with the new information.

The novel part of this system is that Roamers are created by the DirectoryAgents themselves. If a DirectoryAgent hasn't received a visit from a Roamer for a certain amount of time, it creates a new Roamer and dispatches it out into the network. In addition, to avoid clogging the network, DirectoryAgent's are intelligent enough to be able to respond to the time since a last visit. Eventually the network of nodes could tune itself with respect to how many Roamers exist within the system, and how frequently they must be generated. Further, each DirectoryAgent can tune itself in direct response to its situation, and is unlikely to create Roamers at exactly the same time as a near neighbour. For example, a DirectoryAgent located on the core network may never need to create any Roamers! In effect, the network becomes an emergent ecology that tunes itself self referentially.

We can further expand this vision to consider how large-scale networks and subnets can interact. If a Roamer was able to do a lookup on the node to which it was next heading, it would be able to discover if that node was on the same subnet, or LAN. Depending on what type of Roamer it was, it could determine whether to venture out of the local network, or choose another node to visit. At each join of a network, a special type of DirectoryAgent, a GateKeeper, sits whose role it is to be a local resource for knowledge of location of services outside the current catchment area (ie. Subnet or LAN). The GateKeeper could even be mobile itself, in case some of the nodes needed to shutdown. It would not matter, as the Roamers will find it in the end, and its new location will trickle through the network eventually. The last additions to the family of agents are

Trackers, whose role it is to specifically locate a particular resource, wherever it is, and return with the information.

While this vision seems far fetched, it illustrates some fundamental principles that we must adopt if we are to build software architectures of the future. Decentralisation ensures that our networks can reliably scale, without major bottlenecks occurring certain nodes. In addition, redundancy in the system ensures that failure of any single node does not compromise the integrity of the entire system.

5   Conclusions

In this new era of pervasive computing we require new paradigms for building software systems that can support users in the Information age. Users require tools that can locate and filter information for them, presenting it at their convenience, wherever they connect to the network. This paper has reviewed the state-of-the-art of Mobile Information Agents, a technology that promises to fulfil many of these requirements. We have found that the technology remains youthful and that many of the essential issues for enabling this future have yet to be truly realised, although there is much promising progress in understanding them.

In the latter sections we have presented visions of where this technology may take us. Ultimately, this paper presents a vision of the network inhabited by an ecology of agents, representing a myriad of users and devices. The ecology is vibrant and dynamic, with its topology changing frequently. In contrast to most visions, all the agents are not static, but consist of a hybrid mixture of mobile and static agents. Static agents act as brokers for resources and services, in addition to performing more traditional roles as proxies for their owners. Mobile agents live in the network, able to travel, clone, sleep, wake, and autonomously go about fulfilling their owner's requirements.

References

1. Adobe Systems Inc.: The Postscript Language Reference Manual. Addison-Wesley, 1985.
2. Aglet Software Development Kit: IBM, http://www.trl.ibm.co.jo/aglets
3. Bellavista, P., Cavallari, C.,Corradi, A., Stefanelli, C.: Mobile Agents for Internet Services: Directions of Standardization and their Implementation in SOMA, Proceedings of the 37th Conference of the Associazione Italiana per l'Informatica ed il Calcolo Automatico (AICA'99), Abano Terme, Italy, pp. 19-31, September 27-29, 1999.
4. Blixt, K-F., Oberg, R.: Software Agent Framework Technology. Master's Thesis Linköping University, 2000. Available at http://www-und.ida.liu.se/~karbl058/saft/
5. Bredin, J., Maheswaran, R.T., Imer, T.B., Kotz, D., Rus, D.: A Game-Theoretic Formulation of Multi-Agent Resource Allocation. Proceedings of Autonomous Agents 2000, Barcelona, 2000.

6. Chess, D., Harrison, C., Kershenbaum, A.: Mobile Agents: Are They a Good Idea?. In: Vitek, J., Tschudin, C.,: Mobile Object Systems, Towards a Programmable Internet. LNCS Vol 1222, Springer-Verlag, 1997.
7. Dorais et al: Adjustable Autonomy for Human Centered Autonomous Systems on Mars. Proc. of the First International Conference on Mars Society, August, 1998.
8. GMD FOKUS, IBM Corp: Mobile Agent Systems Interoperability Facilities Specification. OMG TC Document, available at ftp://ftp.omg.org/pub/docs/orbos/1997/97-10-05.pdf.
9. GMD FOKUS: Grasshopper Platform, http://www.ikv.de/products/grass hopper/overview.html
10. Huberman, B.A., (ed): The Ecology of Computation. Elsevier, 1998.
11. Jansen, W., Karygiannis, T.: NIST Special Publication 800-19 - Mobile Agent Security. National Institute of Standards and Technology, 2000.
12. Johansen, D.: Interview in: Milojicic, D.: Trend Wars: Mobile Agent Applications. IEEE Concurrency, pp 80-90, July-September, 1999.
13. JumpingBeans, Ad Astra Engineering Inc, http://www.jumpingbeans.com
14. Lange, D, Oshima, M.: Programming and Deploying Java Mobile Agents with Aglets. Addison-Wesley, 1998.
15. The Mobility Mailing List. De facto mailing for discussion of mobility. Home page at http://mobility.lboro.ac.uk
16. The Mobile Agents List, a respository of mobile agent systems, available at http://www.informatik.uni-stuttgart.de/ipvr/vs/projekte/mole/mal/
17. Muscettola, N., Nayak, P.P., Pell, B., Williams, B.C.:Remote Agent: To Boldly Go Where No AI System Has Gone Before. Artificial Intelligence 103(1/1), August 1998.
18. Papaioannou, T.: Mobile Agents: Are They Useful for Establishing a Virtual Presence in Space?. In: Agents with Adjustable Autonomy Symposium, part of the AAAI 1999 Spring Symposium Series.
19. Papaioannou, T.: On the Structuring of Distributed Systems: The Argument for Mobility. PhD thesis, Loughborough University, 2000.
20. Papaioannou, T., Edwards, J.M.: Using Mobile Agents To Improve the Alignment Between Manufacturing and its IT Support Systems. Journal of Robotics and Autonomous Systems, Vol 27, pp 45-57, 1999.
21. Papaioannou, T., Edwards, J.M.: Manufacturing System Integration and Agility: Can Mobile Agents Help?. To appear in Jan 2001 Special Issue of Integrated Computer-Aided Engineering, IOPress.
22. Papaioannou, T., Edwards, J.M.: Towards Understanding and Evaluating Mobile Code Systems. To appear in forthcoming special issue of Journal of Autonomous Agents and Multi-Agent Systems.
23. Papastavrou, S., Samaras, G., Pitoura, E.: Mobile Agents for WWW Distributed Database Access. Proceedings of IEEE International Conference on Data Engineering (ICDE99), 1999.
24. Picco, G.P., Baldi, M.: Evaluating Tradeoffs of Mobile Code Design Para digms in Network Management Applications. In: Kemmerer, R., Futatsugi, K. (eds): Proceedings of 20th International Conference on Software Engineering (ICSE'98), Kyoto (Japan), IEEE CS Press, 1998.
25. Puliafito, A., Tomarchio, O., Vita, L.: MAP: Design and Implementation of a Mobile Agents Platform. Journal of System Architecture. to be published.
26. Riordan, J., Schneier, B.: Environmental Key Generation Towards Clueless Agents. In [vigna98], 1998.

27. Sander, T., Tschudin, C.F.,: Protecting Mobile Agents Against Malicious Hosts. Appears in [vigna98], 1998.
28. Sutherland, L.E.: A futures market in computer time. CACM, Vol. 11 (6), 1968.
29. Tschudin, C.F.: Open Resource Allocation for Mobile Code. In Proceedings of The First Workshop on Mobile Agents, Berlin, 1997.
30. Vigna, G.: Protecting Mobile Agents through Tracing. Proceedings of Third ECOOP Workshop on Mobile Object Systems, Jyvälskylä, 1997.
31. Vigna, G., (ed): Mobile Agents and Security. LNCS 1419, Springer-Verlag, 1998.
32. Young, A., Yung, M.: Sliding Encryption: A Cryptographic Tool for Mobile Agents. (ed) Eli Biham, Proceedings of the 4th International Workshop on Fast Software Encryption, FSE'97, January 1997, LNCS 1267, Springer-Verlag, 1997.
33. White, J.E.: Telescript technology: the foundation for the electronic marketplace. White Paper, General Magic Inc., Moutainview, Sunnyvale CA, USA, 1994.
34. White, J.E.: Telescript TEchnology: Mobile Agents. In: Bradshaw, J. (ed): Software Agents. AAAI Press/MIT Press, 1996
35. World Wide Web Consortium, Micro Payment Transfer Protocol (MPTP) Version 0.1, Nov 1995

Design of Collaborative Information Agents

Catholijn Jonker[1], Matthias Klusch[2], and Jan Treur[1]

[1]Vrije Universiteit Amsterdam, Department of Artificial Intelligence
De Boelelaan 1081a, 1081 HV, Amsterdam, The Netherlands
{jonker,treur}@cs.vu.nl
http://www.cs.vu.nl/~{jonker,treur}
[2]German Research Center for Artificial Intelligence
Stuhlsatzenhausweg 3, 66123 Saarbrücken, Germany
klusch@dfki.de
http://www.dfki.de/~klusch

Abstract. Effective development of nontrivial systems of collaborative information agents requires that an in-depth analysis is made resulting in (1) specification of requirements at different levels of the system, (2) specification of design structures, and (3) a systematic verification. To support a widespread use of intelligent information agents for the Internet, the challenges are (1) to identify and classify a variety of instances of the different types of reusable (requirement, design and proof) patterns, (2) build libraries of them, and (3) provide corresponding easy-to-use plug-in information agent components to the common user. In a simplified example it is shown which types of reusable requirements patterns, design patterns, and proof patterns can be exploited, and how these patterns relate to each other.

1 Introduction

The domain of collaborative information agents (cf. [27]) imposes specific requirements on the functionality and behaviour of the agents and their interaction. Various applications have been developed and are being developed; e.g., [7,8,24,25,26,31,33]. Usually it is required that the information agents cooperate with each other and the users in a coordinated manner. Although, especially for the simpler applications, it is tempting to just focus on the programming of these agents, for more sophisticated information agent applications it is essential to design them on a higher conceptual level. A principled design process not only involves conceptual design specifications but also requirements specifications (e.g., [11,28,32]) and verification e.g., [30]).

In the first place, in order to develop a system with appropriate properties, such a design process includes the analysis of *requirements* on the functionality or behaviour of the overall (multi-agent) system consisting of the information agents. Moreover, requirements (to be) imposed on the individual information agents and the relationship of these requirements to dynamic properties of the overall (multi-agent) system are important. Requirements can be specified in a conceptual and precise manner. In addition or instead of direct requirement formulations, often *scenario's* are used as a means to specify required behaviour.

M. Klusch and L. Kerschberg (Eds.): CIA 2000, LNAI 1860, pp. 262-283, 2000.
© Springer-Verlag Berlin Heidelberg 2000

During further design, in relation to these requirements *design structures* are used which are specified in a conceptual and precise manner. Both requirements and design structures can take the form of reusable patterns, which are maintained in a library.

A *verification* process, after a system has been designed can demonstrate that the designed system actually will show the required behaviour. In verification formalised behavioural requirements and a formalised conceptual design play a main role. Also for verification proofs reusable patterns can be specified.

The methodological approach discussed in this paper assumes two specification languages: a language to specify (behavioural) *requirements* and *scenarios* for (systems of) information agents, and a language to specify *design descriptions.* Each of these languages fulfills its own purpose. A language to specify a (multi-agent) system architecture needs features different from a language to express properties of such a system. Therefore, in principle the two languages are different. The distinction between these specification languages follows the distinction made in the AI and Design community (cf. [20]) between the *structure* of a design object on the one hand, and *function* or *behaviour* on the other hand. For both languages informal, semi-formal and formal variants are assumed, to facilitate the step from informal to formal. Formal models specified in the two languages can be related in a formal manner: it is formally defined when a design description satisfies a requirement or scenario specification, and this formal relation is used to verify that the design description fulfills the requirements and scenarios.

Reusability can be supported for all of the above aspects. Reusable requirement and scenario patterns can be used to identify and classify the type of properties required for the overall system and for each of the information agents. Reusable design patterns can be used to identify and classify a system design description. Reusable verification proof structures can be used to establish, for example, that a design description indeed fulfills certain requirements

For reasons of presentation we will use a *simple example domain* for illustration: the design of an information agent which collaborates with multiple information providers to keep its human users informed about information available on the Web within their scope of interests, both with (pull) or without (push) explicit requests from the user. Representations of requirements and scenarios for this example domain are discussed in section 2. In section 3 design structures are discussed. Verification is the topic of section 4 while section 5 concludes with a brief discussion.

2   Specification of Requirements and Scenarios

In Requirements Engineering (cf. [11,13,14,15,22,28,29,32]) the role of scenarios, in addition to requirements, has gained more importance; e.g., see [17,34]. Traditionally, scenarios or use cases are examples of interaction patterns between the users and a system; they are often used during the requirement elicitation, being regarded as effective ways of communicating with the stakeholders (i.e., domain experts, users, system customers, managers, and developers). In the specific case of designing collaborative information agents, requirements and scenarios of the following types can be specified:

- for a *multi-agent system as a whole* with respect to users and environment, abstracting from the specific agents in the system
- for the *interaction patterns between specific (groups of) agents* within the system, and
- for *individual agents* within the system.

During a development process, starting from behavioural requirements and given scenarios for the system as a whole (with respect to users and environment) we can identify requirements for interaction patterns and behavioural properties of the agents themselves by requirement refinement. This leads to the identification of agents within the system, and their properties. Such an approach actually makes part of the heuristics of the design process explicit (e.g., the design choice for which agents to distinguish, and with which properties). One of the underlying assumptions is that such a design method will lead to designs that are more transparent, better maintainable, and can be (partially) reused more easily within other designs.

Different representations can be used to express the same requirement or scenario, varying from informal to formal. Representations can be made, for example, in a graphical representation language, or a natural language, or in combinations of these languages, as is done in UML's use cases (cf. [18], [21]). Scenarios, for instance, can be represented using a format that supports branching points in the process, or in a language that only takes linear structures into account.

Fig. 1. Overall system requirement

2.1   Requirements for the Overall System

At the most abstract level we can specify the requirements on the behaviour of a system with respect to a user abstracting from the form (architecture) the system has or will get. Because system behaviour may depend on its further environment, often also a reference to this environment is made. These overall system requirements are expressed as temporal relationships in terms of *user output and input* and *environment output and input* at certain points in time, and make no reference to system structures; see Fig. 1. As an example, the following requirement for the overall system is shown.

Example 1: *System requirement pattern*

> *if at any point in time the environment generates output ... to the system*
> *and earlier the user generated output ... to the system,*
> *then some time later the user will receive input ... from the system*

In the context of our example domain we can state the following *informal* system requirements and a related scenario for the overall system with respect to users and the environment. The first of these requirements expresses pull behaviour of the system, and the second push behaviour.

Example 2: *Informal requirement and scenario*

1. **Global system requirements**

GR1 informal:
If   the user requests information for a scope of interest and at the WWW information
within that scope is available,
then *this information is offered to the user.*

GR2 informal:
The user is kept informed of new information on the World Wide Web which is within
the user's scope of interest.

2. **Global scenario (GS1 informal):**

- *The user generates a scope of interest*
- *The user is waiting*
- *New information within the user's scope of interest becomes available on the World Wide Web*
- *The user receives results for his/her scope of interest*

Requirements and scenarios can be reformulated to more structured and precise forms. During such an analysis process the relevant concepts (*domain ontology*) can be identified and how they relate to *input* or *output*, for example of agents, or, as in this case to input and output of user and environment. For nontrivial behavioural requirements a *temporal structure* has to be reflected in the representation. This entails that terms such as 'at any point in time', 'at an earlier point in time', 'after', 'before', 'since', 'until', and 'next' are used to clarify the temporal relationships between different fragments in the requirement. An example of a *structured semi-formal* reformulation of the informally specified overall system requirement GR2 given above is as follows.

Example 3: *Structured semi-formal system requirement*

Global system requirement (GR2 semi-formal):

> *At any point in time,*
> **if**   *at an earlier point in time*
> *user output :*   *a scope of interest,* **and**
>   since then
> *not user output :*   *retraction of this scope of interest,* **and**
>   just now
> *World Wide Web output:* *new information within this scope*
> **then** just after now
> *user input:*   *new information within this scope*

The scenario GS1 can be formalized by utilizing ontological concepts (input and output) and sequence of events as a temporal trace as part of a formal temporal model. Regarding the formalization of requirement GR1 the following (sorted first order logic) formal ontology elements can be used.

Example 4: *Ontological elements and relations*

ontology element:	*explanation:*
SCOPE	a sort for the scopes of users' interests
USER	a sort for the names of different users
INFO_ELEMENT	a sort for the information delivered by the agent
result_for_scope	a binary relation on INFO_ELEMENT and SCOPE
input:	
is_interested_in	a binary relation on USER,and SCOPE
output:	
result_for_user	a ternary relation on INFO_ELEMENT, USER and SCOPE

In addition, the temporal structure has to be expressed in a formal manner. For to obtain a more sophisticated formalisation of requirements of the domain we can use different variants of temporal logic (cf. [1]) depending on the type of properties to be expressed. For example, linear or branching time temporal logic are appropriate to specify various agent (system) behavioural properties. Examples of formal requirement specification languages based on such variants of temporal logic are described in [9,10,13,14,15,16,19,30]. However, for information agents, it might be necessary to specify adaptive properties such as 'exercise improves skill' for which we have to explicitly express a comparison between different histories. This requires a form of temporal logic language which is more expressive than those allowing to model at each time point only one history. An example of such a more expressive formal language in which different histories can be compared was introduced in [23]; it is defined as follows.

Definition 1: *Temporal Requirement Language TRL*

The semantics of TRL are based on *compositional information states* which evolve over time.

1. An *information state* I of a (part of a) system S (e.g., the overall system, or an input or output interface of an agent) is an assignment of truth values {true, false, unknown} to the set of ground atoms describing the information within S.
2. The set of all possible information states of S is denoted by *IS*(S).
3. A *trace* IT of S is a sequence of information states $(I^t)_{t\in N}$ in *IS*(S). Given a trace IT of S, the information state of the input interface of an agent A at time point t is denoted by $state_S(IT, t, input(A))$. Analogously, $state_S(IT, t, output(A))$, denotes the information state of the output interface of agent A at time point t within system S.
4. The information states can be related to statements via the formally defined satisfaction relation |=, comparable to the Holds-predicate in the situation calculus. Behavioural properties can be formulated in a formal manner, using quantifiers over time and the usual logical connectives such as not, &, ⇒.

The requirement and scenario informally described above in Example 2 can formally be specified in TRL as given in the following example.

Example 5: *Formal requirement and scenario*

Global system requirements

GR1 formal:
∀ IT, t
  [$state_S($ IT, t, output(U)) |= is_interested_in(U:USER, S:SCOPE)   &
    $state_S$(IT , t, output(Web)) |= result_for_scope(I:INFO_ELEMENT, S:SCOPE)]
  ⇒ ∃t' > t:
    $state_S$(M , t', input(U)) |= result_for_user(I:INFO_ELEMENT, U:USER,S:SCOPE)

GR2 formal:
∀IT, t1, t2>t1
    $state_S$(IT, t1, output(U)) |= is_interested_in(U:USER, S:SCOPE)   &
    $state_S$(IT, t2, output(Web)) |= result_for_scope(I:INFO_ELEMENT, S:SCOPE)   &
    ∀t' [t1 < t' < t2   ⇒
    [not $state_S$(IT, t', output(Web)) |= result_for_scope(I:INFO_ELEMENT, S:SCOPE)   &
    not $state_S$(IT, t', output(U)) |= not is_interested_in(U:USER, S:SCOPE)]
  ⇒ ∃t3 > t2
    $state_S$(IT , t3, input(U)) |= result_for_user(I:INFO_ELEMENT, U:USER, S:SCOPE)]

Global scenario (GS1 formal):

state$_s$ (IT, 1, output(U))	|= is_interested_in(U:USER, S:SCOPE)
state$_s$ (IT, 3, output(Web))	|= result_for_scope(I:INFO_ELEMENT, S:SCOPE)
state$_s$ (IT, 4, input(U))	|= result_for_user(I:INFO_ELEMENT, U:USER, S:SCOPE)

GR1 addresses the case that information relating to a scope is already present (pull), whereas GR2 addresses the case that the information becomes available later (push). Note that in contrast to situation calculus, an infix notation is used for the \|=-predicate and an explicit reference is made to a trace. This allows for specification of adaptive properties by comparison of different histories.

The formal scenario representation (GS1 formal) relates to the second formal requirement representation expressed above. Note that at time point 2 nothing happens, which corresponds to the waiting of the user, of course in another (but similar) scenario the waiting could take more time.

So far the requirements and scenarios have been formulated for the system as a whole with respect to the users and the Web considered as the given environment. They express the desired behaviour from a global perspective, and only refer to input and output of users and the environment. Otherwise no assumptions were made on the design of the multi-agent system; in particular, no specific agents were assumed. However, one can identify more elementary units of behaviour by refining these requirements and scenarios (*behavioural refinement*); of course, which units of behaviour are chosen is a specific design decision.

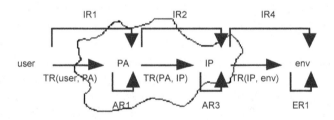

Fig. 2. Refinement of overall system requirements into interaction (IR), transfer (TR), agent (AR), and environment (ER) requirements.

In relation with the refinements for our example domain the design decision is made to identify at least two types of agents:

- *Personal Assistant agents*, that are in direct contact with users, and
- *Information Provider agents*, that only handle unpersonalized needs for information and are in contact with (parts of) the environment, i.e., the Web.

Fig. 2 summarizes the different types of requirements between the user, personal assistant agent (PA), information provider agents (IP), and the Web considered as to be the environment. Each of these types is discussed informally in subsequent sections.

2.2 Requirements for Interaction Patterns

The interaction between units of behaviour can be specified in terms of temporal relationships between their *output*. A typical example interaction pattern between two agents A and B is as follows.

Example 6: *Agent interaction pattern*
   At any point in time
      if A generates as output ....
         [and in the past *at the output of A it was generated* ...
         and in the past *at the output of B it was generated* ... *]*
      then some time later *B generates as output* ....

This example can be generalised to interaction between an arbitrary number of agents. As an illustration, in the following examples the requirements for the interactions between the different agents of our example domain are discussed (see also fig.2).

2.2.1 Interaction between User and Personal Assistant

For our example, it can be postulated that on the basis of specific user outputs concerning their interest, an unpersonalized scope of interest is identified by the Personal Assistant agent (PA): interaction requirement IR2 below. Interaction requirement IR1 describes an interaction between three agents: user, PA and IP. It expresses that if the user puts forward a request scope, and earlier an IP has generated information for the PA within this scope, then this will be generated for the user.

Example 7: *Interaction requirement between user and PA*

User-PA interaction requirements
(IR1 informal):
At any point in time
   if a user has generated on its output a personal scope of interest,
   and earlier an Information Provider generated as output for the Personal
   Assistant information within that scope which was not retracted in the meantime
   then the Personal Assistant will generate this information on its output for the
   user
(IR2 informal):
At any point in time
a. *if* a user has generated on its output a personal scope of interest,
   then the Personal Assistant will generate on its output an unpersonal scope
      based on this scope for a set of Information Providers
b. *if* a user has generated on its output a personal interest scope retraction,
      and no other users have generated the same scope without having it retracted,
   then the Personal Assistant will generate on its output an unpersonal scope
      retraction based on this scope.

Note that by IR1 & IR2 new ontology elements are created that need not to be part of the ontologies of a user or system environment input or output (and are also not meant to be part of these ontologies).

2.2.2 Interaction between Personal Assistant and Information Provider

The requirements IR1 and IR2 are imposed on the interaction between users and personal assistants whereas the following requirements are valid for any interaction between assistant and provider agents. For example, the requirement IR4 expresses that a personal assistant will receive information within a specified scope from a provider agent as soon as it is available.

Example 8: *Interaction requiremenst between assistant and provider agent*

Interaction requirement (IR3 informal)
>*At any point in time*
>***if** a Personal Assistant has generated on its output an unpersonal scope for a set*
>   *of Information Providers*
>***then** every Information Provider from this set generates a related scope for its*
>   *environment*

Interaction requirement (IR4 informal)
>*At any point in time*
>***if** an Information Provider generated on its output new information for a*
>   *Personal Assistant, **and** the new information matches an unretracted scope*
>   *that the Personal Assistant received earlier on its input from a user,*
>***then** this Personal Assistant will generate the new information on its output for*
>   *this user.*

2.2.3 Interaction between Information Provider and Environment

The following requirements specify the required interaction requirement pattern between information provider agents and the environment:

Example 9: *Interaction requirement between information provider and environment*

Interaction requirement (IR5 informal):
>*At any point in time*
>***if** an Information Provider has generated a scope on its output for its environment*
>   ***and** later information becomes newly available in its environment that matches*
>   *this scope,*
>   ***and** this scope was not retracted before the new information became*
>   *available,*
>***then** the environment will generate this information as output for the information*
>   *Provider*

Interaction requirement (IR6 informal):
At any point in time
if the environment of an Information Provider generates on its output new
information,
and the new information matches an unretracted unpersonal scope that the
Information Provider received earlier *on its input from a Personal Assistant,*
then this Information Provider will generate the new information at its output for
the Personal Assistant.

2.3 Transfer Requirements

Any successful collaboration in our domain requires a secure, reliable transfer of information between different components of the system (e.g., communication between agents). This can be specified as a temporal relationship between *output* of one agent or component and *input* of another one. The following transfer requirement pattern between components A and B expresses this.

<u>**Example 10**</u>: *Transfer requirement between system components*

Transfer requirement between components A and B (TR(A, B) informal):
At any point in time
if A generates information for B at its output,
then some time later B will receive this information on its input.

2.4 Requirements for an Individual Information Agent

Temporal relationships between an individual agent's *own input and output* define its behaviour. A typical pattern for an agent A is as follows:
if A receives as input ....
[and in the past as input A received ...
and in the past as output A generated ...]
then some time later A generates as output ....

Please note that such behaviour patterns describe requirements which are of a lower process abstraction level compared to the overall system requirements. For example, the following requirements can be imposed on individual personal assistant and information provider agents.

Example 11: *Assistant (PA) and provider (IP) agent requirements*

Personal assistant agent behaviour requirement (AR1 informal):
At any point in time
if *an incoming scope of interest of a user is received,*
then some time later *the PA will communicate an unpersonal scope based on that user scope to a set of Information Provider agents.*

Personal Assistant agent behaviour requirement (AR2 informal):
At any point in time
if *a PA receives new information on its input ,*
then some time later *for each user which communicated earlier a scope matching that information the PA will generate on its output the related scope result for that user, unless the PA received a corresponding scope retraction from this user before it received the new information.*

Information provider agent behaviour requirement (AR3 informal):
At any point in time
if *an incoming scope of interest is received by an IP,*
then some time later *the IP will generate this scope as output for its environment*

Information Provider agent behaviour requirement (AR4 informal):
At any point in time
if *an IP receives new information on its input ,*
then some time later *for each PA which communicated earlier a scope matching that information the IP will generate on its output the related scope result for that PA,* **unless** *the IP received a corresponding scope retraction from this PA before it received the new information.*

2.5 Requirements for the Environment

Assumptions on the environment can be formulated as temporal relationships between the *environment's input and output,* according to the same patterns as for agents. In our example, it is assumed that the environment of the overall system (the Web) is partitioned according to different information provider agents each of which have information about their own (part of the) environment. An example of an environment requirement is the following.

Example 11: *Environment requirements*

Environment requirement (ER1 informal):
At any point in time
if *the environment of an Information Provider has received a scope on its input*
and *now or later information is or becomes newly available in this environment that matches this scope, and this scope was not retracted before*

the new information became available,
then some time later *the environment will generate this information as output for the Information Provider*

2.6 Requirements for Components within an Information Agent

It is possible to define more elementary units of behaviour within an agent by refining some of the overall requirements imposed on the agent. Whether this is desirable or appears to be too complex to do for an agent certainly depends on whether or not its requirements are sufficiently elementary to serve as a starting point for a transparent design. For example, a possible behavioural refinement of the requirements imposed on personal assistants implies the internall use of user profiles.

<u>**Example 12**</u>: *Personal Assistant agent (PA) component requirements*

Component requirement (CR1 informal):
> *The PA maintains a profile of its users that satisfies the following:*
> *At any point in time*
> a. *if a user scope is received on PA's input,* ***then*** *it is added to the profile.*
> b. *if a scope retraction is received on PA's input,* ***then*** *the corresponding user scope is removed from the profile .*

Component requirement (CR2 informal):
> *At any point in time*
> *if the PA receives new information on its input ,*
> ***then for each*** *user profile matching that information the PA will generate on its output the related scope result for that user*

3   Specification of Agent and Multiagent System Design Structures

In accordance to the specified requirements of agent behaviour and the environment in our example domain we can create now a design structure for individual agents and the multiagent system as a whole. Figure 3 depicts such a design structure. In this example, the multiagent system consists of two users, one personal assistant, two information providers, and the Web. An example of a specification language for such kind of design descriptions is given in DESIRE (cf. [5] for the principles behind DESIRE, and [3] for a case study). A personal assistant communicates with human agents (its users) and information provider agents which in turn communicate with the assistants and interact with their environment.

Based on the requirements on the personal assistant agent as given above we can make the following design decisions in that we identify at least three sub-components of the agent:

1. a component to maintain the user profiles (called Maintenance of Agent Information),
2. a component capable of matching information with scopes (Proposal Determination, which takes place within Cooperation Management), and
3. a component that handles communication with other agents (called Agent Interaction Management).

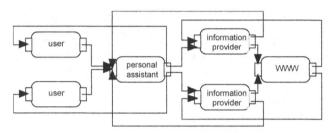

Fig. 3. Global multi-agent system design description in DESIRE.

The design description shown in Fig. 4 includes these components. Moreover components 'Own Process Control' and 'Maintenance of World Information' are part of the design for internal coordination and maintenance of a world model, respectively. The design of the agent is based on a reusable design pattern for the weak agent notion (cf. [35]), called GAM (Generic Agent Model) (cf. [6]). A more extensive description of this design pattern can be found in [6]. At the highest abstraction level within the agent, a number of processes is distinguished (see Fig. 4).

First, we model a process that manages communication with other agents by the component agent interaction management. This component is supposed to identify and extract the information from incoming messages. It determines which of the other internal processes of the agent needs this communicated information and prepares outgoing communication. Next, the agent needs to maintain (e.g., profile) information on the other agents with which it co-operates: maintenance of agent information.

The component maintenance of world information is included to store the world information (e.g., information on attributes of information). The process own process control defines different characteristics of the agent and determines foci of behaviour. The component world interaction management within GAM models interaction with the world: initiating observations, receiving observation results, and execution of actions in the world. As the PA only communicates and has itself no direct interaction with the world, this component was left out for the example here.

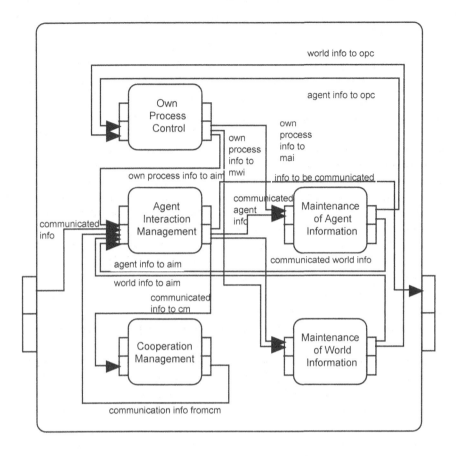

Fig. 4. Internal design description of the Personal Assistant.

The component **cooperation management** models collaboration with other agents; in this example it is meant to model the matching between information and scopes.

4   Verification

In general, verification can take place in different forms. For example:

- to verify scenarios against requirements
- to verify requirements on a system or agent against other requirements on the system or agent
- to verify requirements on a system against requirements of agents included in the system
- to verify a design structure against requirements

Each of these types of verification will be discussed briefly in subsequent sections.

4.1   Verification of Requirements against Scenarios

Having specified both, requirements and scenarios in a requirements engineering process provides the possibility of mutual comparison and verification: the requirements can be verified against the scenarios, and vice versa. By this, ambiguities and inconsistencies within and between the existing requirements or scenarios may be identified, but also missing requirements or scenarios.

Checking a temporal formula F, which formally represents a requirement, against a temporal model IT, formally representing a scenario, means that formal verification of requirements against scenarios can be done by *model checking*. A formal representation IT of a scenario SC and a formal representation F of a requirement are compatible if the temporal formula is valid for the model. As an example, scenario GS1 can be verified against requirement GR2 to find out that the scenario indeed fulfills the requirement. It is possible to reformulate and/or refine requirements at the same (system or agent) level. It can be verified whether the reformulation implies the original requirement, or that they are even logically equivalent.

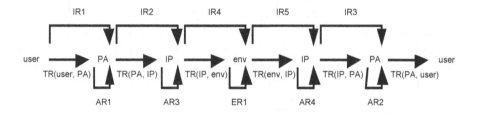

Fig. 5. Overview of different relations between requirements

4.2   Verification of System Requirements against Other System Requirements

Consider the following example.

Example 13: *Verification of system/system requirements*

Assume a given transfer requirement TR(PA, user) from PA to user is proven to be satisfied. Then, requirement GR1 on the system level is implied by the interaction requirements IR1, IR2, IR3, IR4, and IR5; this yields the following proof pattern (see Fig. 5, upper part):

(pp1) IR1 & IR2 & IR3 & IR4 & IR5 & TR(PA, user) => GR1

4.3   Verification of System Requirements against Requirements on Agents

Obviously, to prove that overall system requirements are fulfilled we need to prove the behavioural requirements of the agents involved. In particular, if it can be proven that the agent requirements are fulfilled, then also the interaction requirements hold. This requires that the appropriate transfer requirements (for agents communication) hold. In our example domain we can give the following example.

Example 13: *Verification of system/agents requirements*

Personal Assistant agent requirement AR1 (cf. ex. 11) implies the interaction requirement IR1 (cf. Example 7) under the condition that the communication successfulness requirement TR(user, PA) (cf. Example 10) holds. This is expressed by the following proof pattern:

(pp2) AR1 => [TR(user, PA) => IR1]

A similar proof pattern shows that the other interaction requirements can be derived from the agent requirements, assuming communication successfulness:

(pp3)   AR3 => [TR(PA, IP) => IR2]
                 ER1 => [TR(IP, env) => IR4]
                 AR4 => [TR(env, IP) => IR5]
                 AR2 => [TR(IP, PA) => IR3]

In terms of Fig. 3, this can be formulated as 'the upper steps are implied by the lower steps'. As a result, the combination of proof patterns (pp3) and (pp1) yields the following proof pattern:

(pp4) [TR(user, PA) & TR(PA, IP) & TR(IP, env) & TR(env, IP) & TR(IP, PA)
          & AR1 & AR2 & AR3 & AR4 & ER1]
      => GR1

□

4.4   Verification of Agent Requirements against Component Requirements

Within an agent it is possible to determine logical relationships between requirements of the agent as a whole and requirements on components within the agent. As an example, both component requirements CR1 and CR2 (cf. Example 12) together imply the individual agent requirement AR2 (cf. Example 11), assuming the appropriate transfer requirements within the agent.

4.5   Verification of Requirements Specification against Design Specification

In the case that no refined requirements for agents or agent components exist, it can be directly verified that the given requirements are implied by the design description. This requires a (standard) embedding of the information involved in a design specification in the specification language for behavioural properties.

4.6   Compositional Verification as a Verification Method

A refinement of a behavioural requirement during a design process defines requirements on more elementary units of behaviour. According to this, starting with behavioural requirements of the entire system, it can be decided about what kind of agents to use in the system, and in particular, which individual agent is meant to show which type of behaviour. In a next step, for each of the agents it can be decided whether it is desirable to further refine its requirements depending on whether or not they are elementary enough to serve as a starting point for a transparent design of the agent itself. This, in turn, can lead to the identification of requirements on more elementary units of behaviour within the agent and, in relation to this, to different components within the agent to perform this behaviour. This iterative requirements refinement process may yield an arbitrary number of high to lower process abstraction levels within the system and agents (see Fig. 6). Sets of requirements at a lower level can be chosen in such a way that they realise a higher level requirement, in the following sense:

> **given** the *process composition* relation defined in the design description,
> **if** the chosen *refinements* of a given requirement *are satisfied,*
> **then** also the original *requirement is satisfied.*

This defines the logical aspect of a behavioural refinement relation between requirements. Based on this logical relation, refinement relationships can also be used to verify requirements: e.g., if the chosen refinements of a given requirement all hold for a given system description, then this requirement can be proven to hold for that system description. Similarly, scenarios can be refined to lower process abstraction levels by adding the interactions between the sub-processes. At each level of abstraction, requirements and scenarios employ the terminology defined in the ontology for that level. The methodological approach to the creation of different process abstraction levels in relation to requirements refinement has a natural connection to the process of *compositional verification* (cf. [23]).

highest process abstraction level:
required behavioural properties of entire system

/ | \

next process abstraction level:
behavioural properties of agents

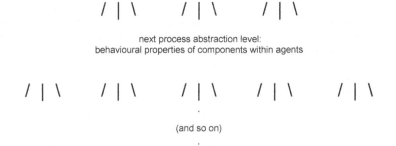

next process abstraction level:
behavioural properties of components within agents

(and so on)

Fig. 6. Behavioural properties at different process abstraction levels

The purpose of verification is to prove that, under a certain set of assumptions, a system will adhere to a certain set of properties, expressed as requirements and scenarios. In order to prove that a system is behaving as required, not only a complete specification of the system is necessary, but also the set of requirements and scenarios to verify the system against. If this set is not available, the verification process is hampered to a great extent, because formulating sufficiently precise requirements (and scenarios) for an existing system is nontrivial. For the purpose of verification it has turned out useful to exploit compositionality.

Compositional verification as described in [23] takes the compositional structure of the system into account. The requirements and scenarios are formulated formally in terms of temporal semantics. During the verification process the requirements and scenarios of the system as a whole can be derived from properties of agents (one process abstraction level lower) and these agent properties, in turn, can be derived from properties of the agent components (again one abstraction level lower), and so on (see Fig. 6).

Primitive components (those components that are not composed of others) can be verified using more traditional verification methods making use of the design description only. Verification of a (composed) component at a given process abstraction level is done using:

- *properties of the sub-components* it embeds
- a specification of the *process composition relation*
- *environmental properties* of the component (depending on the rest of the system, including the world).

This exploits the compositionality in the verification process. Given a set of environmental properties, the proof that a certain component adheres to a set of behavioural properties depends on the (assumed) properties of its sub-components, and the composition relation: properties of the interactions between those sub-components, and the manner in which they are controlled. The assumptions under which the component functions properly, are the properties to be proven for its sub-components. This implies that properties at different levels of process abstraction play their own role in the verification process. A condition to apply a compositional verification method is the availability of an explicit specification of how the system description at an abstraction level is composed from the descriptions at the adjacent lower abstraction level.

Compositionality in verification reduces the search space for the properties to be identified, and the proofs, and supports reuse of agents and components. Complexity in a compositional verification process is two-fold: both the identification of the appropriate properties at different levels of abstraction and finding proofs for these properties can be complex. If the properties already are identified as part of the requirements engineering process, this means that the complexity of part of the verification process is reduced: 'only' the complexity of finding the proofs remains. Our experience in a number of case studies is that having the right properties reduces much more than half of the work for verification: due to the compositionality, at each process abstraction level the search space for the proofs is relatively small.

If no explicit requirements engineering has been performed, finding these properties for the different process abstraction levels can be very hard indeed, as even for a given process abstraction level the search space for possible behavioural requirement formulations can be nontrivial. If as part of the design process requirements have been (formally) specified as well at different levels of process abstraction, these can be used as a useful starting point for a verification process; they provide a detailed map for the verification process and thus reduce the complexity by eliminating the search space for the requirement formulations at different process abstraction levels.

Integration of the requirements engineering process within the system design process leads to system designs that are more appropriate for verification than arbitrary architectures. Moreover, reuse is supported; for example, replacing one component by another is possible without violating the overall requirements and scenarios, as long as the new component satisfies the same requirements and scenarios as the replaced component. Note that the idea of refinement is well-known in the area of (sequential) programs, e.g., [12]. The method of compositional requirements specification proposed here exploits a similar idea in the context of behavioural requirements.

5   Discussion

Effective development of nontrivial systems of collaborative information agents requires an in-depth analysis resulting in   (1) specification of requirements at different levels of the system, (2) specification of design structures, and (3) a systematic verification. To support a widespread use of intelligent information agents for the Internet, the challenges are (1) to identify and classify a variety of instances of the different types of reusable (requirement, design and proof) patterns, (2) build libraries of them, and (3) provide corresponding easy-to-use plug-in information agent components to the common user. In this paper we have informally shown by the use of a simplified example, which types of reusable requirements patterns, design patterns, and proof patterns can be exploited, and how these patterns relate to each other.

In particular, it is proposed that two specification languages are used: a language to specify *design descriptions* such as DESIRE, and a language to specify (behavioural) *requirements* and *scenarios* such as TRL (cf. section 2.1). Each of these languages has its own chacteristics to fulfill its purpose. The distinction is similar to the one made in the AI and Design community [20], namely to distinguish between the structure of a design object on the one hand, and *function or behaviour* on the other hand. For both languages informal, semi-formal and formal variants have to be available to support the step from informal to formal, and, for example, to support a communication with stakeholders.

As said above, a formal specification language of the first type, and a semi-formal and graphical variant of this language, is already available in the compositional multi-agent system development method DESIRE, and is supported by the DESIRE software environment. A number of generic models or design patterns for agents are available; for example for weak agents [6], for cooperative agents able to work in projects [2], and BDI-agents [4]. However, this language focuses on design structures and was never meant to specify requirements or scenarios; a language to specify a (multi-agent) system architecture at a conceptual design level needs features different from a language to express properties of a system. In current research, further integration of the approach to requirements engineering is addressed.

Another main challenge in the design of (collaborative) information agents is the thoughtful design and deployment of standardized plug-in information agent components to the community. This would enable the common user of the Internet to build its own intelligent information agent thereby treating the Web as a common public good, in contrast to the current practice of searchbots and associated ranking warfare. The examples included in this paper are meant to serve only as a starting point for a more systematic exploration of this vision of composite plug-in information agents. We will continue research and development in this direction.

References

1.   Benthem, J.F.A.K. van, The Logic of Time: A Model-Theoretic Investigation into the Varieties of Temporal Ontology and Temporal Discourse, Dordrecht: Reidel, 1983.

2.   Brazier, F.M.T., Cornelissen, F., Jonker, C.M., and Treur, J., Compositional Specification of a Reusable Co-operative Agent Model International Journal of Cooperative Information Systems. In press, 2000.

3.   Brazier, F.M.T., Dunin-Keplicz, B., Jennings, N.R. and Treur, J. Formal specification of Multi-Agent Systems: a real World Case. In: Lesser, V. (ed.), Proceedings of the First International Conference on Multi-Agent Systems, ICMAS'95, MIT Press, Menlo Park, VS, 1995, pp. 25-32. Extended version in: International Journal of Cooperative Information Systems, M. Huhns, M. Singh, (eds.), special issue on Formal Methods in Cooperative Information Systems: Multi-Agent Systems, vol. 6, 1997, pp. 67-94.

4.   Brazier, F.M.T., Dunin-Keplicz, B.M., Treur, J., and Verbrugge, L.C., Modelling Internal Dynamic Behaviour of BDI agents. In: J.-J. Ch. Meyer and P.Y. Schobbes (eds.), Formal Models of Agents (Selected papers from final ModelAge Workshop). Lecture Notes in AI, vol. 1760, Springer Verlag, 1999, pp. 36-56.

5.   Brazier, F.M.T., Jonker, C.M., and Treur, J., Principles of Compositional Multi-agent System Development. In: J. Cuena (ed.), Proceedings of the 15th IFIP World Computer Congress, WCC'98, Conference on Information Technology and Knowledge Systems, IT&KNOWS'98, 1998, pp. 347-360. To be published by IOS Press, 2000.

6.   Brazier, F.M.T., Jonker, C.M., and Treur, J., Compositional Design and Reuse of a Generic Agent Model. Applied Artificial Intelligence Journal. In press, 2000.

7. Chavez, A., Maes, P., Kasbah: An Agent Marketplace for Buying and Selling goods. In: Proceedings of the First International Conference on the Practical Application of Intelligent Agents and Multi-Agent Technology, PAAM'96, The Practical Application Company Ltd, Blackpool, 1996, pp. 75-90.

8. Chavez, A., Dreilinger, D., Gutman, R., Maes, P., A Real-Life Experiment in Creating an Agent Market Place. In: Proceedings of the Second International Conference on the Practical Application of Intelligent Agents and Multi-Agent Technology, PAAM'97, The Practical Application Company Ltd, Blackpool, 1997, pp. 159-178.

9. Dardenne, A., Lamsweerde, A. van, and Fickas, S., Goal-directed Requirements Acquisition. Science in Computer Programming, vol. 20, 1993, pp. 3-50.

10. Darimont, R., and Lamsweerde, A. van, Formal Refinement Patterns for Goal-Driven Requirements Elaboration. Proc. of the Fourth ACM Symposium on the Foundation of Software Engineering (FSE4), 1996, pp. 179-190.

11. Davis, A. M., Software requirements: Objects, Functions, and States, Prentice Hall, New Jersey, 1993.

12. Dijkstra, E.W., A discipline of programming. Prentice Hall, 1976.

13. Dubois, E. (1998). ALBERT: a Formal Language and its supporting Tools for Requirements Engineering.

14. Dubois, E., Du Bois, P., and Zeippen, J.M., A Formal Requirements Engineering Method for Real-Time, Concurrent, and Distributed Systems. In: Proceedings of the Real-Time Systems Conference, RTS'95, 1995.

15. Dubois, E., Yu, E., Petit, M., From Early to Late Formal Requirements. In: Proceedings IWSSD'98. IEEE Computer Society Press, 1998.

16. Engelfriet, J., Jonker, C.M. and Treur, J., Compositional Verification of Multi-Agent Systems in Temporal Multi-Epistemic Logic. In: J.P. Mueller, M.P. Singh, A.S. Rao (eds.), Intelligent Agents V, Proc. of the Fifth International Workshop on Agent Theories, Architectures and Languages, ATAL'98. Lecture Notes in AI, vol. 1555, Springer Verlag, 1999, pp. 177-194. Extended version in Journal of Logic, Language and Information, to appear, 2000.

17. Erdmann, M. and Studer, R., Use-Cases and Scenarios for Developing Knowledge-based Systems. In: Proceedings of the 15th IFIP World Computer Congress, WCC'98, Conference on Information Technologies and Knowledge Systems, IT&KNOWS (J. Cuena, ed.), 1998, pp. 259-272.

18. Eriksson, H. E., and Penker, M., UML Toolkit. Wiley Computer Publishing, John Wiley and Sons, Inc., New York, 1998.

19. Fisher, M., Wooldridge, M., On the Formal Specification and Verification of Multi-Agent Systems. International Journal of Cooperative Information Systems, M. Huhns, M. Singh, (eds.), special issue on Formal Methods in Cooperative Information Systems: Multi-Agent Systems, vol. 6, 1997, pp. 67-94.

20. Gero, J.S., and Sudweeks, F., (eds.), Artificial Intelligence in Design '98, Kluwer Academic Publishers, Dordrecht, 1998.

21. Harmon, P., and Watson, M., Understanding UML, the Developer's Guide. Morgan Kaufmann Publishers, San Francisco, 1998.

22. Herlea, D.E., Jonker, C.M., Treur, J., and Wijngaards, N.J.E., Specification of Behavioural Requirements within Compositional Multi-Agent System Design. In: F.J. Garijo, M. Boman (eds.), Multi-Agent System Engineering, Proceedings of the 9th European Workshop on Modelling Autonomous in a Multi-Agent World, MAAMAW'99. Lecture Notes in AI, vol. 1647, Springer Verlag, Berlin, 1999, pp. 8-27.

Author Index